Macroeconomics
AN INTRODUCTION
Fourth Edition

Charles R. Nelson
University of Washington

The McGraw-Hill Companies, Inc.
Primis Custom Publishing

New York St. Louis San Francisco Auckland P
Caracas Lisbon London Madrid Mexico Milan
New Delhi Paris San Juan Singapore Sydney Toky

McGraw-Hill Higher Education

A Division of The McGraw-Hill Companies

Macroeconomics
An Introduction

Requests for permission or further information should be addressed to:
Professor Charles R. Nelson
Department of Economics
Box 353330
University of Washington
Seattle, WA 98195, USA.
E-mail: cnelson@u.washington.edu

McGraw-Hill's Primis Custom Series consists of products that are produced from camera-ready copy. Peer review, class testing, and accuracy are primarily the responsibility of the author(s).

1 2 3 4 5 6 7 8 9 0 QSR QSR 9 0 9

ISBN 07-240132-X

Editor: Julie Kehrwald
Designer: Kyle A. Zimmerman
Printer/Binder: Quebecor Printing Dubuque, Inc.

Preface

Macroeconomics deals with events and issues that affect everyone: unemployment, recession, economic growth, inflation, the value of the dollar, the federal deficit, and international trade. *Macro* means big, and *macro*economics is the big picture of the economy.

An understanding of macroeconomics is essential to making informed business and personal decisions. What are the implications of the Fed's latest actions? What are the risks of inflation? A grasp of basic macroeconomics is essential to being an informed voter. Candidate Clinton's mantra in the 1992 campaign was: "It's the economy, stupid!"

Because an understanding of macroeconomics is so important, it should be taught in a way that makes its insights accessible to students with a range of interests and math abilities. A text should demonstrate the power of macroeconomics to help the student understand and respond to the economic environment we live in. Most of the students using this book will go on to careers in business rather than economics. The relationship of macroeconomics to Wall Street becomes clear in Chapter 3 where we examine the linkage between savings and investment through financial intermediaries and the stock and bond markets. I will consider this book successful if it equips the student to read *The Wall Street Journal, The New York Times*, or *Business Week* with a fluency in macroeconomics that makes the latest indicators of inflation or recession, the likely reaction of the Fed, and the response of the bond market into exciting reading instead of opaque jargon.

Reflecting my belief that empirical evidence is more persuasive than theory, the book relies heavily on data presented in charts to help the student see relationships. For example, the Fisher relation between interest rates and inflation is instantly clear from a chart. The reader also gains a sense of the magnitude of events such as the inflation of the 1970s, the leads and lags among cyclical variables, and a long term perspective on current macroeconomic issues. An emphasis on visual presentation is also more reflective of how information is presented in the business world today.

This book is *an* introduction to macroeconomics. It tells a story that has a beginning and an end. Certain key concepts are stressed and reinforced as the story develops: the distinction between real and nominal, the equivalence of output and income, the role of the interest rate in connecting the real economy and the monetary economy, and the linkage between the federal budget deficit and the trade deficit. This is not intended to be an encyclopedia or compendium of the field. My objective is to provide the reader with a framework in which the key relationships become comprehensible within the time frame of one academic term. It is ideal if the student has already had an introduction to principles of microeconomics, but those principles are reviewed here in a supplement following Chapter 1. My experience is that students without a prior course in microeconomics do not have a serious handicap in reading this book.

The emphasis given to monetary policy in this book recognizes the emergence of the Federal Reserve as the primary macroeconomic policy-maker in the U.S. today. This represents a shift away from traditional texts which have placed Keynesian discretionary fiscal policy at the center of the story. Indeed, the 1993 tax increase was aimed not at cooling down the economy, as it would in the Keynesian paradigm, but at reducing the deficit in hopes of making more private savings available to finance long term growth.

I am grateful to my students and teaching assistants at the University of Washington for their patience during the development of this text. I am particularly grateful to colleagues Alan Bellas, Thom Cook, Natan Epstein, Paul Heyne, James Hubert, David Layton, Chris Murray, David O'Hara, Haideh Salehi-Esfahani, and Eva Tanlapco for moral support and helpful insights. Responsibility for shortcomings is entirely mine.

Charles R. Nelson
cnelson@u.washington.edu

Table of Contents

Chapter 1

An Overview of Economics

Outline

Preview

1.1 What are "the Economy" and "Economics"?
The Standard of Living
The Productivity of Labor
Economic Growth

1.2 The Four Sectors of the Economy
Business
Households
Government
The Rest-of-the-World

1.3 What is Microeconomics?

1.4 What is Macroeconomics?
The Twin Deficits: International Trade and the Federal Budget.
The Challenge of Globalization
Social Security and Medicare; Will They Impoverish the Young?
Will We Have Inflation, Recession, or Both?

Index

Supplement: Review of the Principles of Microeconomics

Preview

Economics is one of the oldest and influential of intellectual disciplines. Most all the great thinkers, from Aristotle to Einstein, have taken a try at it, and the great economists of history like Adam Smith, Thomas Malthus, David Ricardo, and John Maynard Keynes rank among the most influential thinkers. The economic paradigm permeates our thinking about practically every area of human activity. Military analysts talk in terms of "assets" and "trade-offs" while theologians quote economic statistics. Adam Smith's ideas about competition had a strong influence on Charles Darwin's study of biology. Insect colonies are said to "invest" in nest building. Our thinking about politics and social behavior draws heavily on ideas about incentives, trading, and maximization under constraints that come from economics.

The word economics comes from ancient Greece (like so many words and important ideas) and then an economist was the manager of an estate. That very practical economist grappled with all the basic problems of economic decision-making that modern executive do today. What is the optimal mix of crops? How much to invest in new equipment? Should you sell your grain now, or wait until prices improve? Modern economics returns the compliment by providing the foundations of business administration today. Successful executives have often told this writer that the principles they draw on every day in making decisions are those that they learned in their first courses in economics. Good reason to "invest" in learning the foundations of economic analysis!

1.1 What are "the Economy" and "Economics"?

Every society must provide goods and services for the welfare of its citizens. The economy consists of all of the activities involved in the production and distribution of these goods and services.

Economics, as the study of the economy, seeks to address three basic questions:

- **Are there fundamental principles that help us understand how the economy works?**

- **How well does the economy perform in achieving social objectives?**

- **How would changes in laws or political institutions affect the performance of the economy?**

The production and distribution of goods and services requires the use of factors of production. These are economic resources which are the inputs to economic activity. These factors of production are usually thought of as falling into one of four categories:

- **Land**
This includes not only territory but all of the natural resources, such as minerals and fossil fuels, which the economy is endowed with.

- **Labor**
This refers to the services of human beings who bring not only their time and effort to the economy but also their skills.

- **Capital**
This consists of the human-made tools used in the economy: machinery, computers, buildings, vehicles, and transportation systems. These tools of production are called capital goods.

- **Entrepreneurship**
This is the bringing together of land, labor, and capital into productive units. For example, when Henry Ford organized the mass production of automobiles early in this century, he brought labor and capital together in a new way on an assembly line, bringing the cost of an automobile down to within the reach of the average American.

The Standard of Living

We measure the success of an economic system by the standard of living it provides to its participants. By this we mean not only the quantity and quality of goods and services consumed, but also leisure and environmental quality. Clearly, the standard of living depends crucially on the productivity of labor, defined as the amount of goods and services produced per hour of labor input. Higher productivity makes possible a higher standard of living because it allows society to increase the consumption of goods and services, or leisure, or environmental quality, or all three.

In measuring the standard of living we are concerned both with the average level of consumption in the population, and its distribution among households. Few people consider consumption per capita a sufficient measure of the standard of living for a country; we are also interested in how it is distributed across households. An economy with extremely unequal household consumption levels cannot be considered completely successful, but we do not expect a successful economy to produce exact equality.

The Productivity of Labor

The productivity of labor is determined by the amount of land and capital available per worker, the level of technology embodied in that capital, the skills of the workers who use it, and the creativity of its entrepreneurs. Productivity can be increased by producing more capital goods, advancing technology through research and development, and improving skills through education and training. Affluent societies are notable for the quantity, quality, and technological advancement of their capital goods and for the high level of skills and education of their citizens. In contrast, poor societies are marked by the paucity of both capital and skills.

Economic Growth

The process of economic growth, which is a continuing increase in the standard of living that persists over decades, can only come from growth in the productivity of labor. An increase in the standard of living requires, in turn, that a society devote a portion of its economic output to research and development of new technologies, to education and training of workers, and to the production of capital goods. This can only happen if society is willing to forgo some immediate consumption of goods and services, freeing a portion of the output of the economy for investment in future growth.

Exercises 1.1

A. Discuss the extent to which society can change each of the four factors of production. Give some examples.

B. Education is sometimes referred to as "human capital." In what sense is education like capital goods?

C. Compare briefly the standard of living in Switzerland and India. Trace the difference to the productivity of labor, and hence to differences in the quantity and quality of the factors of production present in the two countries.

D. What are some options that a country has if it wishes to raise its standard of living? Can we say that people are happier in the country with the higher standard of living?

1.2 *The Four Sectors of the Economy*

Modern complex economies involve the interactions of large numbers of people and organizations. These "agents" in the economy fall into one of three categories: *business*, *households*, and *government*. Economists find it useful to think of these groupings as *sectors* of the economy. Let's look at each of these sectors in turn:

Business

The business sector is where production takes place in the economy. The individual agents making up the business sector are called firms. These are the organizations within which entrepreneurship brings together land, labor and capital for the production of goods or services. Economies in which firms are generally owned by private individuals rather than by governments are called capitalist or private enterprise economies. These include almost all the countries in the world today.

A firm may be as small as one individual. An example is a plumber with a truck and tools whose income is whatever is left over from sales after paying expenses. These one-owner firms are called individual proprietorships. A large firm is typically a corporation which is a legal entity in itself, having many of the same rights and privileges under law as does a person. The corporation purchases factors of production and receives payment from buyers of its output. The difference between its sales revenue and its costs of production is its profit or <u>earnings</u>. A corporation purchases capital goods, plant and equipment, from earning profits, borrowing from lenders, and selling shares in the ownership of the corporation. The latter is called stock.

The owners of a corporation are called shareholders. A large firm typically has many shareholders, some of which are other firms. Firms which primarily invest in other firms are called financial intermediaries. Shareholders play no direct role in the running of the firm, rather they are represented by a board of directors who are elected by shareholders on a one vote per share basis. Shareholders are not liable, in general, for the debts of the corporation. The term "Ltd." used in the names of corporations in Britain refers to the limited liability of the shareholders.

The entrepreneurial input to the corporation is often provided by salaried managers who may not even be shareholders. These managers are appointed by the directors as officers of the corporation who are then legally empowered to conduct its business. A primary responsibility of the directors of a corporation is the hiring and oversight of the officers.

Households

These are us, the people, the family units that make up society. They consume the goods and services produced by the economy. It is for their benefit that the economy exists.

The household sector provides the labor used in production, receiving payment of wages and salaries in return. Households also provides financial capital to the business sector which includes loans to firms, direct ownership, or the purchase of shares. Households may invest directly in firms by purchasing their stock or bonds, but more typically households invest indirectly through financial intermediaries such as pension funds, insurance companies, banks, and mutual funds.

Households own the firms and have claim to all the income produced by the business sector, including wages, interest, and profits.

Government

We can think of government as having four basic functions in the economy:

First, it establishes the legal framework within which the economy operates. Economists sometimes refer to this framework as the rules of the game. A complex body of commercial law clarifies relations between buyers and sellers, employers and employees, and parties involved in private contracts.

The corporation, an essential building block of modern economies, is a creation of the law. It was the development of the limited liability corporation in Britain during the industrial revolution that made possible the formation of very large firms owned by many individuals. Such enterprises could not exist without the assurance that individual shareholders are not personally liable for the actions of the corporation.

Property rights are not unconditional but rather are defined by laws which establish the privileges, obligations, and limitations of ownership. For example, city government decides what the owner of a city lot can and cannot do with it. The owner of a residence is entitled to live in it, rent it to someone else to live in, or sell it, but usually is prevented by zoning laws from tearing down the house and putting in a fast food restaurant or a rifle range. Regulations enacted by legislation and enforced by government control entry into certain economic activities such as banking or medicine, restrict what firms can say in their ads, and even prohibit sale of goods deemed not in the public interest.

Second, taxes are collected by government from households and firms. The federal government collects most of its revenue from individual income taxes. It also taxes corporate profits and estates, levies excise taxes on the value of certain goods and tariffs on imports from abroad, and it collects payroll taxes. State governments collect sales taxes on retail purchases and often income taxes on both individuals and corporations. County and municipal governments levy a tax on the value of real estate property, and often also participate in sales tax or income tax revenues.

The structure of these tax systems, including what activities are taxed and how heavily, gives government many levers with which to encourage or discourage specific economic activities. The tax on gasoline is cents per gallon in the U.S. and dollars per gallon in Europe and Japan. The gas tax is one factor affecting the individual's choice between different sizes of car and between auto and public transportation. Cars in Europe and Japan are typically much less powerful than even the same models sold in the U.S., and public transportation is much less popular in the U.S. The gas tax is a major factor in shaping the transportation system and has far reaching effects on the environment and the configuration of cities.

Third, government spends some of these tax revenues to provide goods and services through agencies that operate much like firms, for example the National Park Service which produces recreation and the US Navy which produces national defense. The types of firms operated by government in largely private enterprise economies are usually engaged in the production of public goods, those which we consume as a society rather than as individuals. The prime example is national defense which cannot be provided to one individual without providing it to others. Profit incentives that encourage firms to engage in the production of private goods like refrigerators do not work effectively to encourage the production of public goods like defense. Many goods have both private and public dimensions. For example, education benefits not only the individual who is educated but society as a whole, and so is generally considered to be an appropriate activity of government.

In socialist economies government operates a much wider range of firms, including those producing primarily private goods. In the former Soviet Union and its satellites, all firms were under government ownership and now these countries are struggling to establish private enterprise economies. Advocates of socialism contended (past tense, since advocates of socialism seem to be an extinct species these days) that government ownership of firms leads to the greater good of society because government-run firms will be more productive, more responsive to the needs of society, and kinder to employees. These ideas were very popular in Europe following World War II, and large sectors of those economies were "nationalized" under government ownership or control. The abandonment of socialism in Eastern Europe and the wave of "privatization" of industry in Europe and elsewhere in the decade since the fall of the Berlin Wall reflect the realization that socialism failed to deliver on those rosy promises. What remains of socialist ideas is the very large role that governments play in most developed countries today in providing basic health care and a "safety net" in the form of welfare programs.

The allocation of government spending among alternatives also influences how firms and households allocate their private resources. For example, police protection is a public good, but the level of police protection will affect whether the Jones family will install a burglar alarm or even move out of the community. Whether government builds freeways or subways affects private choices among alternative forms of transportation. But providing goods and services is not the only kind of government spending.

Fourth, government also makes cash payments called transfer payments to firms and individuals. These are not payments for services rendered or goods, but rather are made to those who qualify to receive them under various programs enacted by legislatures. For example, households qualify to receive Social Security benefits on the basis of age or disability. Farm subsidies are paid by the U.S. government to firms which qualify by engaging in certain farming activities.

Transfer payments redistribute income among groups in society, and are a larger part of the total expenditures of the federal government than is the purchase of goods and services including defense. The distribution of income between the young and the old in the U.S. has been substantially altered by the growth in Social Security benefits received primarily by the elderly and the corresponding increase in Social Security taxes paid primarily by the young. Transfer payments also affect private decisions. For example, the increase in the number of people choosing earlier retirement is surely related to the increase in the level of Social Security benefits as well as the penalties which the rules put on continued work by those qualifying for old age benefits.

We tend to focus on the federal government in thinking about the role of government in the economy, but state and local governments also play important roles in all four functions of government. Economists refer to governments at all levels as the public sector.

The Rest-of-the-World

We naturally focus on the economy of our nation because government plays an important role in economic life and because economic interactions are usually concentrated within political borders. However, the movement of goods and services as well as factors of productions across national borders is also an important aspect of economic activity. U.S. households consume stereos made in Asia and US firms purchase machine tools produced in Europe. Foreign airlines fly airplanes made in the U.S. and serve their passengers food exported from the U.S. International trade now comprises about 11% of our national economy and is growing rapidly. Growth in trade has been accelerated by the removal of barriers under the North American Free Trade Agreement

(NAFTA), and the 1994 round of the General Agreement on Trade and Tariffs (GATT) lowers barriers to trade around the world.

We think of the Rest-of-the-World, or ROW, as a fourth sector of the economy. In addition to trading with the ROW, American firms, government, and households also borrow from the ROW and lend to it. In recent years, Japanese investors have been substantial lenders to both firms and government in the US American firms and households also have large investments in Europe and Asia.

Exercises 1.2

A. Indicate which of the four factors of production each of the following is an example of: 1) a Macintosh computer. 2) an electronics engineer. 3) a Boeing 767. 4) crude petroleum. 5) the Empire State Building. 6) the lot it sits on. 7) Henry Ford. 8) college graduates.

B. Name one or more prominent entrepreneur of today and explain briefly what this person has done.

C. Categorize the following by economic sector: 1) the Hernandez family. 2) the Ford Motor Company. 3) the State of California. 4) the University of California. 5) Durn-Good Grocery. 6) Toyota Motors, Ltd.

D. Which of the functions of government in the economy is represented by the following: 1) Aid to Families of Dependent Children. 2) the Federal Aviation Administration. 3) truth-in-advertising laws. 4) the state sales tax. 5) the Washington State Ferry System. 6) Small Claims Court.

E. Russia has attempted to convert from a centrally planned, socialist economy under Communism to a largely private enterprise economy. What basic function of government in a private enterprise economy has been lacking in Russia and now needs to be developed there before a private enterprise economy can function?

1.3 What is Microeconomics?

It is already apparent from this brief overview that the subject of economics is a very broad one. Just as the study of the physical world is divided into fields such as physics and chemistry, economics is likewise divided into fields comprised of closely related topics. The two major fields of economics are *micro* economics and *macro* economics. Since the second is the subject of this book, let's take a minute to review what microeconomics is about.

Microeconomics is the study of how markets function. For example, how do the prices of airline tickets and the frequency of service to various airports get determined in the US economy? An airline decides whether to raise or lower fares, whether to add a flights between LA and Chicago, and whether to put a new 747 in service on the San Francisco to Honolulu route. Travelers respond by buying more or fewer trips. The airline's objective is to maximize profits, constrained by the rules of the game established and enforced by government. Travelers, in turn, hope to buy transportation at the lowest possible price with the best possible convenience and comfort.

The diffuse but very real arena in which such firms and their customers interact is called the marketplace. Physically, the marketplace for airline tickets is all the ticket counters and travel agencies where transactions take place. Conceptually, the market encompasses all the interactions between the economic agents that produce and consume air travel.

Prior to the late 1970's the prices of airline tickets, as well as the routes and airline could fly, were set by the federal government as a part of the regulation of air travel. Largely due to the urging of economists, the airline ticket market was deregulated so that airlines are now free to raise or lower fares and alter service to airports as they see it to be to their advantage to do so. Advocates of deregulation contended that freeing the air travel market would result in a more efficient allocation of resources within the airline industry, making society as a whole better off. The term "resources" here means the factors of production, not just natural resources. The analysis of airline deregulation, the arguments for and against it, as well appraising its success or failure to date, are interesting and important problems in microeconomics.

In private enterprise economies it is primarily in the marketplace that the three fundamental economic decisions are made:

1. **What will be produced?**
2. **How will it be produced?**
3. **Who will consume it?**

For example, it is in the marketplace that society decides how many tennis rackets will be produced, whether they will be made in Ohio or in Taiwan, and which consumers will buy them.

It was the remarkable insight of Adam Smith, pondering the workings of the British economy two centuries ago, that products and services are provided for the benefit of society mainly as a result of the pursuit of self interest by producers and consumers interacting in the marketplace rather than because of their good intentions. Producers who supply what consumers demand are rewarded with higher profits, while those who do not are punished for wasting society's valuable land, labor and capital resources by suffering losses. In a famous passage in his book *The Wealth of Nations*, Smith wrote:

> *"It is not from the benevolence of the butcher, the brewer, or the baker that we expect our dinner, but from their regard to their own interest."*

Adam Smith realized that the market provides incentives for agents to behave in ways that generally improve economic welfare.

Microeconomists are also interested in studying ways in which markets fail to provide the proper incentives to allocate resources. This happens when an economic activity produces consequences for agents that are not a party to that activity. An example of such an externality is the air pollution caused by combustion. Unless there is a way to make agents pay for producing pollutants, they will tend to produce more of it than is good for society. The design of taxes, regulations, and pricing schemes to deal with externalities is an important issue in microeconomics. Evaluating the cost-effectiveness of a proposed or existing program for reducing externalities is an important area of microeconomics.

This chapter contains a supplement entitled *Review of the Principles of Microeconomics* which is intended to provide a basic understanding of microeconomics to students who have not encountered it before. It will also be helpful for those who have taken a prior course but wish to get a firmer grasp of basic microeconomic principles, particularly those that will be used in this book.

Exercises 1.3

A. What are the three fundamental decisions that have to be made in any economic system? Discuss what those decisions are in the context of trips between San Francisco and Hong Kong. How has technology changed the outcomes of those decisions during the last half century?

B. Express in your own words Adam Smith's idea of what makes a private enterprise economy work.

C. Federal law requires that electric generating stations install scrubbers on their exhaust stacks to reduce emissions of certain compounds. Discuss why utilities might not install these scrubbers on their own, and how you might approach the question of whether such scrubbers should be required by law.

1.4 What is Macroeconomics?

Macroeconomics focuses on trying to understand events that affect the whole economy. Beginning in the fall of 1990, and continuing through the winter of 1991, there occurred a decline in output and employment that affected not just a few firms or industries but almost all firms in the US. The total output all of the firms in the US economy and the total number of workers employed by them fell sharply. That kind of pervasive decline in economic activity when it lasts for more than six months is called a recession.

Since recessions are felt throughout the economy, it seems unlikely that the explanation for a recession will be found in the microeconomics of individual markets. The causes of recession must involve forces that have widespread influence on economic activity. While the U.S. was experiencing a very slow recovery from its recession during 1992, other major industrial nations in Europe and Asia were slipping into recessions of their own. It would seem that economic fluctuations are now international in scope.

What caused this latest recession? Should the government do something about it? If so, what? What forces will bring it to an end, allowing resumption of normal levels of employment and production? How will the actions of foreign governments affect our economy? These are problems in macroeconomics.

Here is another example of a problem in macroeconomics. In the late 1970s the price of practically every good and service in the US economy rose at double digit rates. A pervasive and persistent rise in prices is called inflation. Since inflation is so widespread across so many different kinds of industries it seems clear that the explanation for inflation must lie with factors affecting the entire economy. In 1989 inflation again became a serious concern for the U.S. economy, and continues to be a source of worry in the 1990s.

The division of economics between microeconomics and macroeconomics is not a precise one, and the analytic tools of each are important in understanding the other. For example, the computer industry is of growing importance to the economy, but the study of the economics of that industry belongs in the domain of microeconomics. On the other hand, although banking is also an industry, its influence on the economy is so pervasive that the study of banking is usually considered part of macroeconomics. Nevertheless, the macroeconomist studying banking will make use of the analytical tools of microeconomics, and the microeconomist studying the computer industry will be concerned with the impact on the industry of macroeconomic events such as recession and inflation.

The topics which economists usually group under the heading of macroeconomics include the following:

- **The Measurement of National Income**

- **The Relationship Between Savings and Investment**

- **The Cost of Living and Inflation**

- **Interest Rates and What Influences Them**

- **Recession, Unemployment, and Economic Growth**

- **Money and Banks**

- **The Federal Reserve System and Monetary Policy**

- **Government Taxation, Spending, and Fiscal Policy**

- **International Trade and Exchange Rates**

Macroeconomic issues are always the subject of major news coverage by the media because they affect all of us. Macroeconomic issues were the most hotly debated issues of the 1992 Presidential campaign ("It's the economy, stupid!") and they are again in 1996. Here are some of the major macroeconomic issues that will continue to receive a lot of attention:

The Twin Deficits: International Trade and the Federal Budget.
In 1980 the value of goods exported by the US was $25 billion less than the value of the goods we imported. When the amount we earn from exports falls short of the amount we spend on imports then there is a trade deficit. By 1987 the US trade deficit had swollen to $159 billion. After narrowing somewhat it has ballooned again and for 1999 is about $250 billion! This seemingly relentless widening of the trade gap is a source of continuing concern to many.

In 1980 the federal government spent $74 billion more than it collected in taxes. The amount by which federal spending exceeds tax revenues is called the federal deficit. By 1992 the federal deficit had widened to $290 billion, and motivated a major tax increase by the Clinton administration in 1993. That, combined with a long and vigorous economic expansion has eliminated the budget deficit at the end of the 1990s, but many expect that the deficit will again be a problem when baby-boomers begin to retire on Social Security.

The trade deficit and the federal budget deficit have become known as the twin deficits. Both grew alarmingly in the 1980s. Is the similarity in the timing and size of the twin deficits coincidental? Are they harmful to the economy? What caused them, and are their causes related? What should we do about them, if anything?

The Challenge of Globalization

After World War II, US business faced little competition from abroad. Germany and Japan were struggling to rebuild and Great Britain was in the process of losing its empire. The only imported car of note in the 1950s was the VW beetle, admired for its simplicity and eccentricity, but of no real threat to US competitors. General Motors was the largest industrial corporation and it could claim with some authority that its Cadillac was "The Standard of the World." How things have changed!

By the late 1980s US industry faced strong competition from Europe and Japan in many fields. Japan particularly had become an economic powerhouse. In 1989 the biggest selling car in America was for the first time not made by an American company. It was the Honda Accord. Nippon Telephone and Telegraph was larger (in market value) than all US corporations except Exxon. The seven largest banks in the world were all Japanese! The five largest securities firms (dealing in stocks and bonds) were also all Japanese. In 1987 Japan became the world's richest nation with assets worth $44 trillion. The US was spending about $50 billion more on imports from Japan each year than it earned from sales to Japan. Japan invested these trade surplus dollars in the U.S., much in the form of direct investment in the U.S. based subsidiaries of Japanese corporations. Japanese investors also became a major owners of real estate and stocks and bonds in the U.S.

Then in the 1990s, Japan's stock market took a severe tumble and its economy entered a decade of stagnation. Meanwhile, U.S. economic growth was strong, and American firms emerged as the leaders in the new technologies of personal computers and telecommunications. In part because of technological advance, competition is now on a global scale. Nokia, the Finnish maker of mobile phones came out of nowhere to become a leader in its field and among the 30 most valuable corporations in the world. Nor is competition limited to manufacturing. Of the ten largest banks in the world, only one is American. The largest is Deutsche Bank (with assets equivalent to $700 *billion*) followed by a Swiss and a Japanese bank in the next two positions. All of these banks have global reach, offer a full range of financial services, and make use of the latest telecommunications to knit their world-wide operations together.

What should be our response to globalization? Do we have any choice but to participate? Or should we try to limit our exposure to international competition and foreign ownership in the U.S.? Public sentiment was once strong for Congress to take action to protect US industry from Japanese competition, but that competition proved to be the stimulus for a new era of change. Now our officials scold Japan that it is doing too little to encourage growth! Some observers worry about the impact of globalization on third-world countries where economic development is happening at a dizzying pace, and on the labor market in the U.S. which now is thrown open to world competition. In this debate, economists are almost always a voice for free trade and open world markets. The issues are complex and will play an important role in debate on public policy in the decades ahead.

Social Security and Medicare; Will They Impoverish the Young?

Benefits for the aged account for 27% of federal spending but the elderly constitute only 12% of the population. Today there are about 3 and a half workers per Social Security recipient, by the turn of the century there will be only 2. Medicare benefits for the elderly have proved to be about ten times as costly as was projected when the program started in 1965; the actual expenditure now is about $200 billion per year. Taxes to fund Social Security and Medicare are now the major tax burden of many lower income young families.

The Social Security trust fund is now in surplus because the baby-boomers are in their peak earning years. Also, that is a much larger age cohort than the retired age cohort. This favorable balance will be reversed in the new century.

Should Social Security taxes be cut now to reduce the tax burden on young wage earners, or should the surplus be allowed to accumulate to cover the anticipated deficit ahead? Is the Social Security system, as it is now designed, fair to both young and old? Should Medicare benefits be broadened? Should they be subject to a minimum income requirement? These and other vexing questions will figure in public debate for coming decades.

Will We Have Inflation, Recession, or Both?

The 1990s turned out to be a decade of sustained growth and low inflation, to say nothing of a soaring stock market. But that success is only apparent in hindsight. The road along the way was marked by risks and false alarms. The growth rate of the US economy had slowed markedly in early 1990 in response to efforts by the Federal Reserve to restrain inflation. Then in August, Iraq invaded Kuwait and oil prices soared. By the fall of 1990 inflation had accelerated and the economy had slipped into recession.

The resolution of the Gulf War in early 1991 led many observers to anticipate a quick rebound in the economy. The economy did show modest growth in mid 1991, but by the fall the expectation of a strong recovery had been replaced by fear of a "double dip" recession. While a second dip not occur, growth in the economy remained very sluggish during 1992. Meanwhile, inflation remained stubbornly persistent during the recession, but it did finally slow down during 1992.

Did the Federal Reserve cause the recession of 1990-91? And what is the Federal Reserve anyway? Why did it take the economy so long to recover? When will we have another recession?

By 1994 attention had shifted again to the danger of renewed inflation. The Federal Reserve raised interest rates (how do they do that?) in several steps, hoping to dampen the economy and cool down inflation. Inflation remained under control in 1995 and 1996, but concern lingered that it would rebound rapidly if the economy continued to expand. It turned out that the "Fed" was able to perform a delicate balancing act between inflation and recession and keep the economy on track through the end of the decade.

But what about the future? Are recession and inflation banished on the eve of the Millennium, or will they visit us again? Can the Fed protect us, even after its legendary leader, Chairman Alan Greenspan, has passed from the scene?

As you can see, there is no lack of macroeconomic issues to concern us; they occupy the news media every day. People are interested in macroeconomic issues precisely because they touch the lives of every one of us. Politicians understand that their chances for reelection hinge to a great extent on peoples' perception of the health of the macroeconomy. As citizens we all need to understand as much as we can about its workings, and that understanding may well be the key factor in our coping with the uncertainties and opportunities that the economy presents to each of us.

A. Indicate whether each of the following topics falls under the umbrella of microeconomics or macroeconomics.

1) the effect of protecting the spotted owl on the price of lumber,

2) causes of the decline in inflation during the 1990's,

3) the persistent deficit in our trade with Japan,

4) effect of a proposed increase in the gas tax on demand,

5) the impact of a change in the exchange rate between the German Mark and the US dollar on employment in the US and Germany,

6) a cost-benefit analysis of federal exhaust emission standards.

B. Give brief and perhaps tentative responses to some of the macroeconomic issues discussed in this section. What are some other issues that feature prominently in the news currently? Which of these issues is of greatest importance to you? Briefly, why?

Index to Chapter 1

Supplement to Chapter 1

Review of the Principles of Microeconomics

S.1 What is Microeconomics All About?

Microeconomics is the study of how decisions are made by consumers and suppliers, how these decisions determine the allocation of scarce resources in the marketplace, and how public policy can influence market outcomes for better or worse. A basic understanding of microeconomics is essential to the study of macroeconomics because "micro" provides the foundations upon which "macro" is built. It is pointless to try to explain, for example, the demand for money and how it affects interest rates in the economy without a grasp of how suppliers and buyers interact in a market. The objective of this supplement to *MACROECONOMICS: An Introduction, Third Edition* is to provide a relatively compact overview of microeconomics for use in a course where micro is not a prerequisite for macro, and for students who want to brush up on their micro.

Economists think of there being two sides to a market, the demand side and the supply side. The demand side consists of economic agents, households and sometimes firms, who come to the market to buy a specific good or service. The supply side consists of the suppliers of the good or service, generally firms that produce the item.

In markets for final goods, which are ready for consumption, the demanders are usually the consumers in the household sector; for example, someone buying a croissant. However, in the case of capital goods, it is a firm that is the buyer of the final good; for example, a bakery buying a new automated oven. There are also markets for intermediate goods where the buyers are firms purchasing a good or service used in the production of another good or service, for example bakeries purchasing flour from millers, or millers purchasing wheat from farmers.

We study the demand and supply sides of a markets separately, because each involves a different groups of agents. Within each group there is a common goal but the two groups have very distinct goals. Buyers all come to the market with the same goal of getting as much satisfaction, or what economists call utility, as they can from their limited budget. Suppliers are maximizing profit by using the factors of production - land, labor, capital, and entrepreneurship, - as effectively as possible, given the costs of those factors and the price at which they can sell their product.

Let us start by studying the behavior of consumers in a market familiar to most of us, the market for audio compact discs (CDs).

S.2 The Law of Demand

Think for a moment about your plans to buy audio CDs over the next year. Do you expect to buy about 1 per month? or 2? or 5? What would cause you to change the number you plan to buy? Certainly, a change in the price of CDs or a change in your income would cause you to reconsider the number you buy. Think first about your response to price.

Suppose that CDs sell for $12 each, and you currently buy about 2 per month, on average. How many would you buy if the price were $20 instead? Certainly fewer, perhaps only 1. On the other hand, if the price fell to $4 each, you would surely buy more, maybe as many as 3 per month. In each case we assume that your income has not changed. We can summarize this information in a table as follows:

One Person's Demand for CDs

Price of a CD	Number of CDs you would buy per month at that price
$4	3
$12	2
$20	1

We have taken a one person marketing survey here to see how the quantity of the CDs you would buy, which economists call the quantity demanded, varies as a function of price, holding income and all other variables that might affect your decision constant. If we could ask this question of all CD buyers we could add up the quantity demanded by each and get the quantity demanded in the CD market by all consumers. The results might look like this:

All Consumers' Demand for CDs

Price of a CD	Quantity Demanded per Month
$4	150 million
$12	100 million
$20	50 million

Economists call this the demand schedule. We can capture the same information in a graph such as Figure S.1.

Notice that price is measured on the "y axis" and quantity demanded on the "x axis." The prices and quantities in the above table are only three points on a line that tells us what the quantity demanded would be at any price in the range of $4 through $20. This line is called the demand curve. In practice, we would have data only at specific prices where we have made an observation of the quantity demanded, and the demand curve is based on interpolating between those points of observation.

25

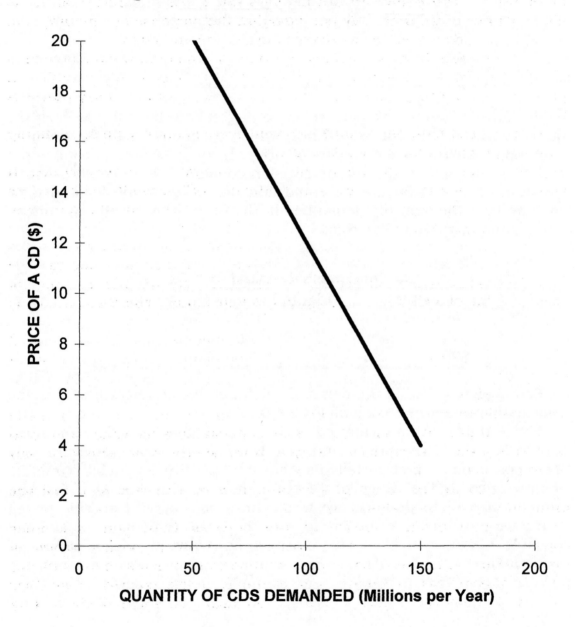

Figure S.1: The Demand Curve For CDs

Notice too that the demand curve slopes downward, meaning that people will buy less of the good at a higher price, and more of it at a lower price. The points on the demand curve tell us what quantity is demanded at each price. We can visualize the response of consumers to a change in price, then, as a move along the demand curve.

This inverse relationship between price and the quantity demanded is called the Law of Demand. It is one of the most firmly established principles in the social sciences and it is no exaggeration to say that it is the keystone of economics.

Why are economists so convinced that there is an inverse relationship between price and quantity demanded?

First of all, we all see the law of demand at work in every day life. If Ford has too many trucks left over at the end of the model year it offers discounts to stimulate demand. What we call a "sale" is just the use of the law of demand to increase the quantity sold by cutting price. We saw that when personal computers became cheaper, the number of homes owning one increased rapidly. Traveling around the country one can see that in states where electricity is relatively cheap, the amount of electricity used per home is higher than in states where electricity is expensive.

Secondly, the way that price affects consumer choice is easily and well understood, and that analysis is compelling in its support of the law of demand. Here is a summary of the theory of how a consumer reacts to a change in price.

Suppose that you are a buyer of CDs and you find one day that the price has jumped up from the $12 to which you have been accustomed to $20. There are two very clear reasons to reduce the number of CDs you purchase.

One reason is that CDs have become more expensive *relative to* other forms of music or entertainment.

If there were an increase in the price of CDs, you and other consumers would surely think about buying other goods or services instead, those that yield some of the same kind of satisfaction but are now *relatively* less expensive. For example, a live concert is another source of music entertainment that you might be more likely to buy instead. At a price of $100 for a CD you might well give up buying them altogether and only attend concerts. The tendency to shift your demand away from a good or service when the price rises and toward other goods or services is called the substitution effect. The goods or services consumers tend to shift towards in a particular case are called substitutes. For example, live concerts, tapes, records and video tapes are all substitutes for CDs. The demand for jeans will probably not change a lot in reaction to a change in the price of CDs because jeans are not a good substitute for CDs.

Of course, we assume for the moment that the prices of everything else, including concert tickets, and your income, stay the same. Why do we make this assumption? You might think that it is unrealistic to assume that everything else except the price of a CD is the same, when in real life all prices and incomes are often changing at the same time. It is not that we assume that all other prices and your income *do* in fact remain constant, but rather we can isolate the effect of one variable, the price of CDs, on your behavior only by *temporarily* considering the effect of a change in that one price alone. We can only hope to understand the combined effect of several variables on behavior by understanding first the effect of each, one variable at a time. This is the reason for the "others things held constant" or "ceteris paribus" assumption of economic analysis that students often find puzzling at first.

The *second* reason why a consumer will purchase less of a good when the price rises is that the consumer can no longer buy all of the same goods and services as before with the same amount of income. If CDs now cost $20 instead of $12, and your income hasn't changed, then you have to reduce your demand for *something* because you simply do not have enough dollars of income now to buy all the same quantities of everything you bought before. You can buy fewer CDs, fewer jeans, fewer espressos, or fewer things in the future by reducing your savings, but something has to give. This effect is just like what would happen if your income fell, so it is called the income effect. We use this term even though your dollar income has not changed. The higher price of CDs has made you poorer, and you must make the same kinds of adjustments to your budget that you would if your income had fallen.

To sum up, the law of demand says that the quantity of a good or service that is demanded varies inversely with changes in the price, holding other factors constant. This effect has two components, the substitution effect and the income effect. Both work in the direction of making the quantity demanded change in the opposite direction to a change in price.

S.3 What Happens to the Demand Curve When Consumers' Incomes Change?

Suppose that your main source of income as a college student is a part time job that has been paying $7 per hour but your boss is so impressed by the grade you got in Economics that now you get a raise to $9. What happens to your demand for CDs? Obviously you can now afford more of any of the goods and services you purchase, and it seems likely that you will use part of your increase in income to buy more CDs. Your demand schedule might change something like this:

How One Person's Demand for CDs Depends on Their Income

Price of a CD	Number of CDs you demand when you earn $7 per hour	Number of CDs you demand when you earn $9 per hour
$4	3	4
$12	2	3
$20	1	2

At any given price you will now buy an additional CD per month as compared with your previous demand schedule. The income change has changed your demand schedule, the quantities demanded moving in the same direction as income.

Similarly, if many consumers experience a rise in income due to a booming economy, the demand schedule for all consumers will also shift. We would observe this if we compared the demand schedule for CDs during the recession of 1990-91 with the demand schedule during the boom in 1993:

The Demand Schedules for CDs at Low and High Incomes

Price of a CD	Quantity Demanded During Recession	Quantity Demanded During Boom
$4	150	200
$12	100	150
$20	50	100

Notice, again, that an increase in income, this time as the economy recovers from a recession and households experience rising income, increases the quantity of CDs demanded at any given price. The entire demand schedule has changed, and we can see this clearly in a graph of the two corresponding demand curves in Figure S.2. At any price, the boom-time demand curve lies to the right of the recession-time demand curve. We think of this as a shift in the demand curve to the right as the economy makes the transition from recession to boom. If the economy were to fall again into recession, then the demand curve for CDs would shift back to the left and then consumers would demand fewer CDs at any given price.

To sum up, economists visualize the demand for a good or service as a curve that shows the quantity demanded at various prices, holding income and other variables (such as consumers' "tastes") constant. A change in price is seen as a move along the demand curve as discussed in the previous section. For example, a change in the price of a CD from $12 to $20 during the 1990-91 recession would have resulted in a move along the demand curve from a quantity demanded of 100 million per month to only 50 million. A change in income on the other hand, is visualized as a shift in the demand curve. On this new demand curve, the quantity of CDs demanded at any given price has changed.

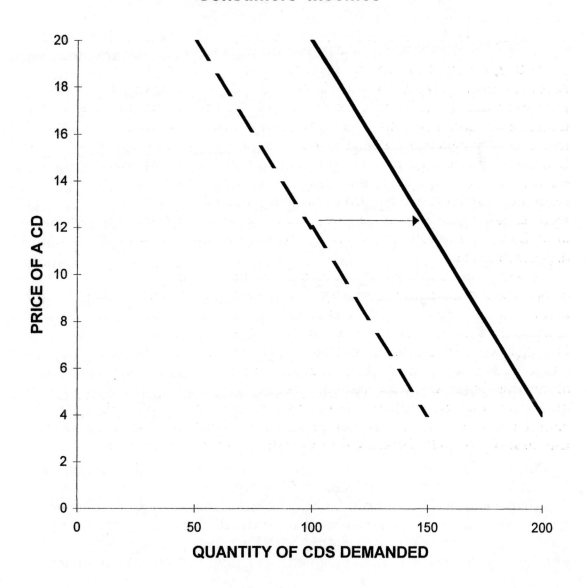

Figure S.2: The Demand Curve For CDs Before (Dash) And After (Solid) An Increase In Consumers' Incomes

S.4 How Other Variables Affect Demand

We have just seen that a change in consumers' incomes will shift the demand curve; to the right in the case of an increase in income and to the left in the case of a decrease in income. Many other variables will also shift the demand curve, and the most important of these are tastes and prices of substitute goods.

What economists mean by tastes is the set of preferences that people have for the various goods and services that they choose among. Tastes for specific goods are often derived from more basic motivations. The taste for CDs is derived from a taste for music, which, in turn, depends on past experience, education, and the stimulation we receive from advertising, conversation, and listening to music. Tastes can change and when that happens the demand for goods changes. Experiencing the clarity of a CD will induce many people to demand more CDs than before, without any change in price or income. We depict the impact of an increased taste for CDs by a shift in the demand curve to the right, just as in Figure S.2 for a change in income. Again, the ceteris paribus statement that demand increases, holding incomes and prices constant, does not mean that incomes and prices *are* constant, but rather it isolates the effect of a change in tastes on the demand.

Prices of substitutes, goods and services that provide similar satisfactions, will also affect the demand for CDs. An increase in the price of concert tickets will induce us to shift from consuming music live to consuming it electronically. That would cause a shift in the demand curve to the right, just as in the case of in increase in income or an increased taste for music. On the other hand, a fall in the cost of digital tapes, another substitute for CDs, would cause the demand curve to shift to the left, because people would be more inclined to buy digital tapes rather than CDs than they had been before.

Finally, the growth of population will, over time, tend to increase the demand for goods and services, shifting the demand curve to the right. The demographics of the population, the distribution of people across age groups, is also very important in shifting the demand for particular goods over time. For example, as the baby boomers, those born between roughly 1945 and 1965, have aged, the demand for sporty cars has diminished while the demand for cruise ship vacations has grown dramatically. Demographic trends are among the most important factors for marketing researchers to study.

S.5 *The Law of Supply*

The supply side of the market for CDs includes all of the firms that produce and market CDs. Each firm decides how many CDs it will produce and how many employees it hires. Over a longer time horizon, the firm must also decide how much plantto build, where by "plant" we mean not only factories for manufacturing CDs but also warehouses, marketing programs, and contracts with performers. At the same time, each firm takes as given the price it can charge for a CD in any particular category. For example, today the price for a CD from a recognized band is, say, $12, although a new release hit might command $16. We will abstract from such gradations and talk about a standard CD selling for $12. That price is not something that the individual firm has any control over.

The decision facing Murky Music Corp. today is this: how many CDs do we crank out of the factory and distribute to stores next month? This is the firm's "short run" supply decision. Murky also has to decide whether to expand over the next several years by investing in new manufacturing facilities and warehouses, seeking new contracts with performers, and launching new advertising campaigns. These are "long run" decisions, meaning that they take effect over a long enough time horizon for the firm to alter its size by investing in new capacity. In this section we focus on the short run supply for a good, how much the firm will want to supply for the market over a short enough time horizon that we can take its capacity or plant size as fixed.

How do Murky and other firms decide what quantity to supply to the marketplace? Microeconomics assumes that the primary motive of firms is to maximize profit. What rate of output, then, will maximize Murky's profits?

Suppose that Murky is now producing CDs at a rate of 10 million per year and is considering raising output to 10.1 million per year. Profit will go up if the additional cost or marginal cost of producing that extra 0.1 million CDs is less than the additional revenue or marginal revenue of $1.2 million Murky that will receive by selling them. If Murky's management sees that marginal revenue exceeds marginal cost, the Murky will boost its production rate to 10.1 million CDs. If marginal cost is just balanced by marginal revenue, then there is no profit to be gained by raising production to 10.1 million units. In that case, we can also be quite certain that there is no point in considering production levels above 10.1 million units. That is because marginal cost would only increase more as Murky contemplates production levels above 10.1.

The general principle here is that *marginal cost increases as a function of output.* How can we be so sure that is true? Because the firm will always use its lowest cost resources first. For example, suppose Murky can produce 10 million CDs per year at its factory in California under normal conditions. If it wants to produce more than that it must either produce the additional units at its plant in Amsterdam and air ship them at considerable cost to markets in the U.S., or pay its workers in California overtime to work evenings and weekends. It would never make sense to use higher cost facilities first and leave lower cost facilities idle. Similarly, in agriculture the land that is best suited to growing wheat is already growing wheat. The land that would be put into production to produce more wheat is land that requires more fertilizer, more tilling, or is farther from market.

Suppose, then, that Murky would produce 10 million CDs per year when the price is $12, because that is the production level that maximizes profit. Similarly, suppose that the industry in total would produce 100 million CDs per year. The way economists put it is that at a price of $12 the quantity supplied is 100 million units. What would happen to the quantity supplied if the price were $20 instead? Clearly, Murky and other producers would then bring higher cost facilities into production, air shipping CDs from Amsterdam and, say, Singapore. Perhaps Murky would supply as many as 15 million and the entire industry 150 million CDs to the U. S. market per year.

On the other hand, if the price were only $4 per CD, how many would be supplied? At such a low price, only the facilities with the lowest cost would be used. Certainly firms would not use expensive air shipment from abroad, they would not pay overtime, and some employees would be laid off as less efficient facilities were shut down. Murky might reduce output to, say, a 5 million rate and the industry in total to 50 million. We can summarize this supply schedule for Murky and the industry in the following table:

The Supply Schedules for Murky Music and the Industry

Price of a CD	Supplied by Murky	Supplied by the Industry
$4	5 million	50 million
$12	10 million	100 million
$20	15 million	150 million

The important attribute of a supply schedule is that *the quantity of the good supplied increases as the price increases*. This is called the Law of Supply. The positive relationship between price and quantity supplied is captured graphically in Figure S.3 where the curve represents the supply schedule for the CD industry.

We should think of this as the short run supply schedule for the industry because it takes as given the present size of the industry. In a later section we will think about what the supply schedule and supply curve look like over a long enough time period for the industry to alter its size, but first we need to consider the impact on the supply schedule of a change in cost structure.

Figure S.3: The Supply Curve For CDs

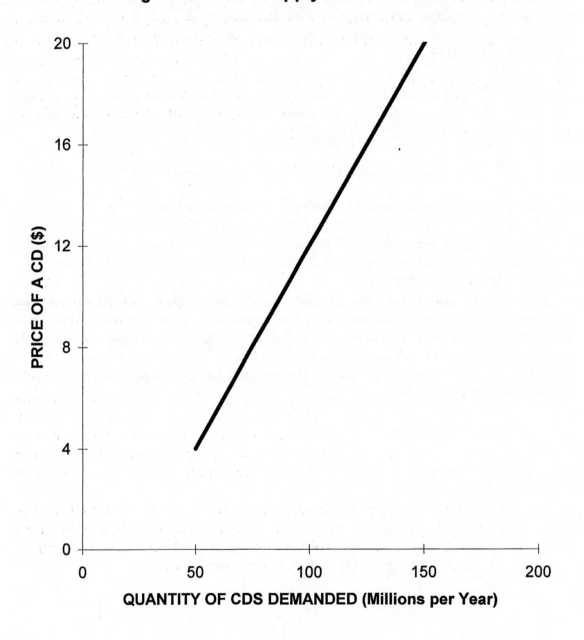

S.6 The Supply Curve Shifts When Costs Change

Suppose that the wages and salaries of employees in the CD industry take an upward jump due to competition from other high tech industries for talented people with training in using computers. The immediate effect of higher labor costs is to raise the marginal cost of producing another CD. Thus, the price at which the industry would be willing to supply, say, 100 million CDs might be $14 instead of $12. Similarly, it might take a price of $22 to elicit a supply of 150 million CDs per year, and the industry might require a price $6 instead of $4 to supply 50 million per year. The new supply schedule would be:

Industry Supply Schedule After a Wage Increase

Price of a CD	Quantity of CDs Supplied
$5	50 million
$13	100 million
$21	150 million

The old and new supply schedules are plotted in Figure S.4. Notice that the new schedule lies above the old one; the supply curve has shifted upward. What we see is that an increase in the marginal cost of production means that a correspondingly higher price is required to elicit the same supply as before.

What would happen in response to a cost decrease? For example, suppose that new technology makes it cheaper to manufacture CDs by reducing the amount of lamination required. That implies a fall in marginal cost at every level of output and, therefore, a shift downward in the supply curve of the industry. After the cost reduction, it would not take as a high a price as before to elicit the same quantity of CDs to be supplied by the industry.

In general, technological change tends to reduce marginal cost and to shift supply curves downward. We might imagine that this new technology offsets the recent rise in labor costs, so that the supply curve in Figure S.4 shifts back down to its original position.

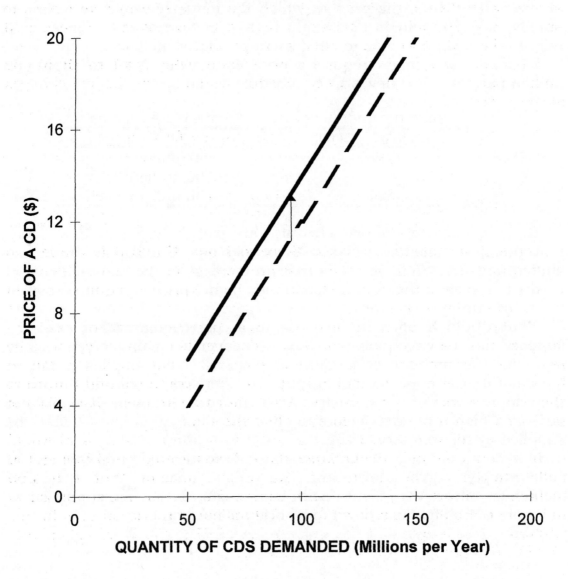

Figure S.4: The Supply Curve For CDs Before (Dash) And After (Solid) An Increase In The Marginal Cost Of Production

S7. *How Supply and Demand Determine Price*

It is a cliché that when someone expresses consternation at the high price of something, someone else says "hey, its all a matter of supply and demand." Unfortunately, many people who use that phrase do not have a very clear understanding of what it means. In this section we see how the supply schedule interacts with the demand schedule to determine the price, how changes in supply and demand cause the price to change, and how markets are affected by government policies.

When we combine the supply and demand schedules for CDs in one table (the original quantities, before we considered hypothetical changes affecting supply or demand) we have:

The Supply and Demand Schedules for CDs

Price	Quantity Demanded	Quantity Supplied	Excess Demand
$4	150 million	50 million	100 million
$12	100 million	100 million	zero
$20	50 million	150 million	-50 million

The fourth column is labeled "Excess Demand" and it is the key to understanding how price is determined in a market. The excess demand is the difference between the quantity demanded at any given price and the quantity supplied at that price. In this example, at a price of $4 the quantity demanded is 150 million while the quantity supplied is only 50 million; thus the excess demand at $4 is 100 million CDs per year. If the price were $4 per CD, the quantity demand by consumers would exceed the quantity supplied by the industry, and retailers would find that their shelves were bare and customers were clambering for more CDs. That is not a situation that we would expect to continue.

If the price were $20, then according to the table consumers would wish to buy only 50 million while the industry would be shipping 150 million to the stores. The excess demand at a price of $20 is minus 50 million. Another term for negative excess demand is excess supply; in this case there is an excess supply of 50 million at a price of $20. In this situation, retailers would see inventories of CDs pile ever higher, and that clearly could not continue indefinitely.

But if the price were $12 we see that the quantity demanded is equal to the quantity supplied, so that excess demand is zero. At that price, retailers would find that shipments from the industry would be just adequate to meet demand from customers, allowing them to keep their inventories in control.

The demand curve and supply curve are both depicted in Figure S.5. Note that they intersect where price is $12 and quantity is 100 million. Excess demand is the horizontal distance between the demand and supply curves, and it is zero only where they intersect.

We know that demand and supply are in balance when price is $12, but is there any reason to believe that the price in the CD market will actually be $12? How does it get there, and why would it stay there?

The price in this market will move to $12 and stay there because the actions of suppliers and consumers, in pursuit of their own best interests, will push it there. At any price below $12, suppliers will find that they can sell more CDs than they are producing. They will find that they can raise their price because consumers will be willing to pay more since there is excess demand at any price below $12. Suppliers are happy to produce more CDs as prices rise because a higher price will offset the rising marginal cost of production. Thus, should the price be below $12 at any time, forces are set into motion that push it upwards to $12.

If the price at some time is above $12, suppliers will not be able to sell their output. They have no choice but to cut prices, since otherwise their inventories will grow. As the price settles down closer to $12, firms produce fewer CDs since they will use only those facilities that have a lower cost of production. Thus, at a price above $12, forces are set into motion that push the price downward to $12.

At a price of $12, then, the market is in equilibrium, meaning there is no further tendency for either price or quantity to change.

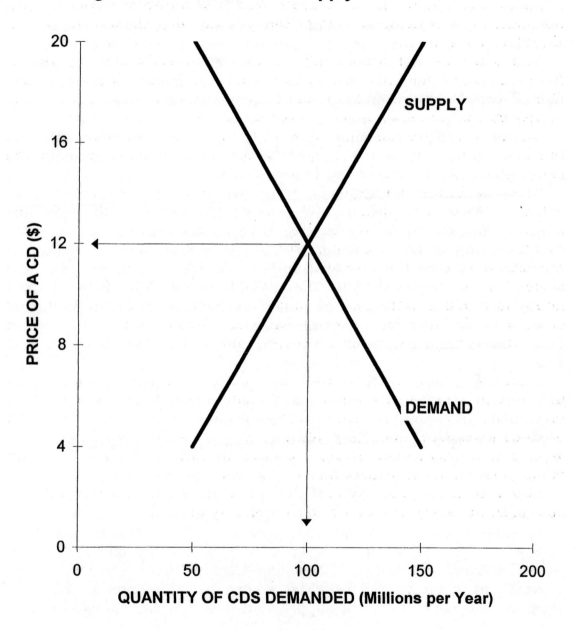

Figure S.5: Demand And Supply Curves For CDs

Suppose now that the government passed a law, in response to pressure from consumer groups concerned about the high cost of CDs, requiring the price to be no higher than $4. What we would observe in the market is a severe shortage of CDs; demand would far exceed supply, and lines would form at the retail stores as consumers waited to buy the limited supply offered at that price. While consumers would pay less for the CDs they do buy, they would buy and enjoy far few of them, in fact half as many in our example.

The fact that *government price controls have always resulted in shortages*, based on observations from the time of the Roman Emperor Diocletian to U.S. President Jimmy Carter, is a striking confirmation of the validity of our theory of how markets work.

Suppose instead that CD firms succeeded in getting Congress to pass a law requiring a *minimum* price level of $20 · per CD. To make this happen, the government would have to be prepared to buy all the extra CDs that would be produced at that price but not purchased by consumers. In fact, it would have to buy 100 million CDs per year, the excess supply at a price of $20. The wastefulness of such a policy is clear in the fact that the industry responds to the high price by producing another 50 million CDs per year, while consumers buy and enjoy 50 million fewer than they would if the market were setting the price and output. Nevertheless, it is precisely a price support program of this kind that has dominated U. S. agricultural policy for decades, resulting in higher prices to consumers while surpluses purchased by the U.S. Department of Agriculture rotted in storage bins.

What happens to price and quantity if consumers' incomes or tastes change, or prices of substitutes changes, or producers' costs change? These changes are of course constantly occurring in real markets, and they can be understood as shifts in the curves causing the point of intersection to move. Figure S.6 depicts the response of the CD market to an increase in consumers' incomes, causing them to demand more CDs at any given price. The intersection of supply and demand shifts to a price of $16 and a quantity of 125 million CDs per year.

Note that this is accomplished by *a move along the supply curve*. It is demand that has shifted, not supply, and it is only the change in price that brings about a change in the quantity supplied as producers bring higher cost facilities into production to meet the greater demand.

S.8 Supply in the Long Run

Recall that the "long run" is a period of time sufficient for a firm to adjust its size by changing its capital stock, the factories, equipment, and long term contracts that cannot be altered over the "short run." According to our hypothetical supply schedule, Murky Music will supply a quantity of 10 million CDs per year to the market *this year* when the price is $12, but it may well not *continue* to supply one million CDs if the price stays at $12.

If the price of a CD is expected to remain at $12, Murky's management must consider whether the firm should make the investments required to expand its CD business, or just try to maintain its current position in the industry, or even go out of business as its plant wears out and contracts with performers expire. Although the output of one million CDs gives Murky the highest profit it can possibly earn today, that does not necessarily mean that this profit level is perceived to be attractive over the long run. Murky may be able to do better by expanding or contracting its CD operations.

For example, suppose that Murky's profit represents only a 1% return on the financial capital that the shareholders have invested. They might well decide that they are better off selling some or all of Murky's assets to other firms and reinvesting their capital in another business, or just purchase U.S. Treasury bills that yield 5%. In that case, Murky would not continue to supply 10 million CDs to the market at $12. It would supply fewer than that over the long run and perhaps none at all if Murky goes out of business.

Figure S.6: Response To A Shift In The Demand Curve For CDs

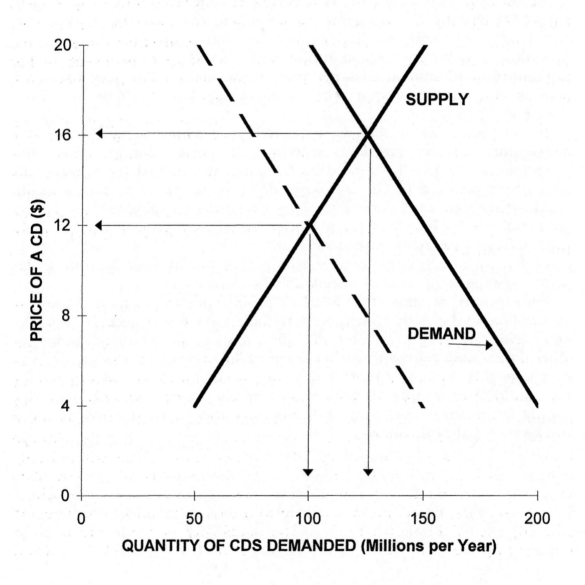

Short run profit maximization does not even imply that Murky is making a positive profit. It could be that Murky cannot make a profit at $12 per CD and is only able to minimize its losses in the short run by producing 10 million CDs. In that case its management and shareholders must consider seriously whether to continue in the CD business at all. Perhaps the firm would become profitable if additional capital expenditures were made, say a new warehouse in the midwest that would cut costs. Perhaps they would conclude that there are too many firms in the CD business and that they should not invest further but rather sell the warehouses, factories, and equipment that they have, exit the industry, and deploy their capital elsewhere.

On the other hand, it may be that Murky is not only maximizing profits but actually making a very large profit. Murky's management may also see that by expanding the firm it can increase profits further. For example, investment in a new warehouse in the midwest might be estimated to earn a return of 50% per year, so Murky's management borrows from its bank, paying only 13% interest on the loan, to build the warehouse. In the long run, Murky would then be supplying many more than 10 million CDs to the market.

The conclusion from these thought experiments is that *firms will expand and supply more if they see that expansion will add to their profits over the long run, and they will contract or even exit the industry if they see that such a course of action will be more profitable over the long run.*

Clearly, at higher prices firms will tend to increase their long run supply more than at lower prices. For example, if the CD is expected to be $20 instead of $12, there are many more expansion opportunities that become profitable. In fact, new firms will see the CD industry as a very attractive one to be in, so new firms will enter the industry. The effect of the entry of new firms is to expand long run supply even further. On the other hand, if the price is expected to stay at $4, then firms will not only contract their operations over time but exit the industry altogether. This suggests that the quantity supplied in the long run is not only positively related to price, but is more sensitive to a change in price than is short run supply. Economists refer to the sensitivity of supply to a given change in price as the elasticity of supply, What we can call the Second

Law of Supply states that *the elasticity of supply is greater in the long run than in the short run.*

We might imagine that the long run supply schedule for the CD industry would compare with the short run supply schedule shown below.

In this example, at a price of $12 the industry would continue to supply what it does today, but at a lower price the industry would "downsize" drastically. Indeed, at a price of $4 the industry would disappear in the long run. A higher price would bring about an expansion of the industry. The corresponding short and long run supply curves are depicted in Figure S.7. Note that the long run supply curve is flatter than the short run curve, reflecting the greater elasticity of supply in the long run.

A very important implication of the second law of supply is that the response to a shift in demand is greater in the short run than in the long run. If consumers suddenly develop a taste for CDs, the price will rise sharply in the short run with little increase in production. Over the next several years the CD industry will add new capacity, moving along its long run supply curve, so that in the long run there will be less change in price but a larger increase in production.

Quantity of CDs Supplied Per Year by the Industry		
Price of a CD	In the Short Run	In the Long Run
$4	50 million	zero
$12	100 million	100 million
$20	120 million	200 million

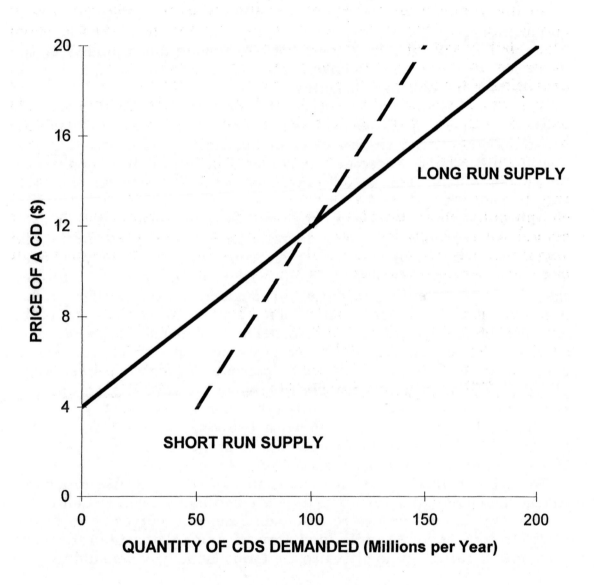

Figure S.7: The Supply Curve For CDs In The Short And Lng Run

LONG RUN SUPPLY

SHORT RUN SUPPLY

PRICE OF A CD ($)

QUANTITY OF CDS DEMANDED (Millions per Year)

S.9 Long Run Demand

Think about a change in the price of CDs from $12 to $20 and what your response as a consumer might be after one month, after one year, and after several years, assuming that the new, higher price is maintained. It seems clear that the longer the price increase remains in effect the more will you reduce your purchase of CDs. After one month you might simply substitute a movie or concert, after one year you would probably find that you have gone back to buying tapes, and after two years you would very likely have made the investment in equipment to play digital tapes or music diskettes.

This thought experiment suggests that demand is more responsive or elastic to price changes over periods long enough for people to alter their consumption patterns, in part by changing the "capital goods" that they use in consumption. These are consumer durables such as appliances, housing, and cars. Here, again, is the distinction between the short run and the long run.

An example from American experience is the change in the demand for gasoline that followed a large increase in the price of gas in the mid 1970s. At first, people reduced their consumption by only a small amount since they were largely stuck with their gas guzzling cars and their existing commuting patterns. But smaller, more fuel efficient cars began to sell well, and over a period of a few years the composition of the auto fleet shifted toward cars with better fuel economy. People also had adjusted their commuting to reduce gas consumption, for example by using car pools. Thus, the long run response to higher gas prices, over a period long enough for consumers to change the capital good used for transportation, was much greater than the short run response.

We can imagine that the difference between a short run, say one month, and a long run, say two years, demand schedule for CDs might look something like the one shown below.

These two demand schedules illustrate how the response to a price change increases if it is maintained for a long time. We can visualize this contrast by plotting the two corresponding demand curves as in Figure S.8. Note that the long run demand curve is much flatter than the short run demand curve. Economists use the term elasticity of demand to refer to the percentage change in the quantity demanded relative to a given percentage change in price. It is clear from the table and the figure that *demand is more elastic in the long run than it is in the short run.*

This phenomenon is so pervasive in economic behavior that it is sometimes referred to as the Second Law of Demand.

The Demand for CDs in the U. S. Per Year

Price of a CD	Quantity Demanded in the Short Run	Quantity Demanded in the Long Run
$4	150 million	200 million
$12	100 million	100 million
$20	50 million	zero

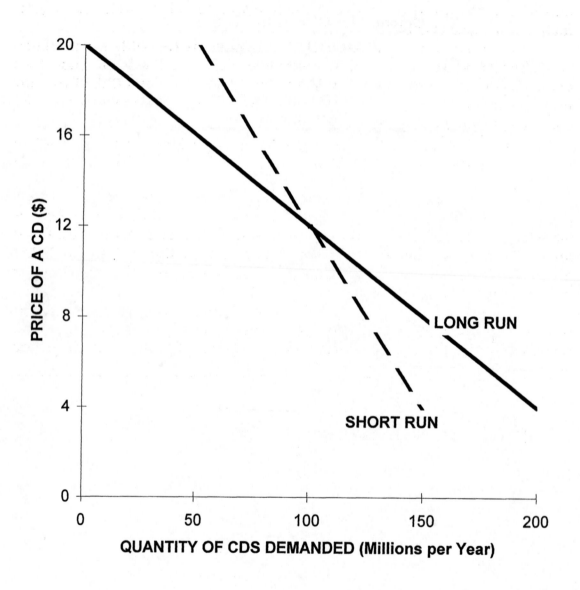

Figure S.8: The Demand Curve For CDs In The Short And Long Run

Exercises for Microeconomics

A. Pick a consumer good or service that you normally buy and make a table of the quantity you would buy over a range of prices that includes the actual price today and hypothetical prices both lower and higher. Express in your own words what information this table contains. Now add another column of quantities that estimate your purchases if your income increased by 50%.

B. Now estimate the number of consumers in the U.S. for the good you chose and make a table of your estimates of the total quantities demanded over the same range of prices. Graph the result. Add to your table and graph the demand schedule under the assumption that all consumers enjoy a 50% increase in income.

C. What would be a substitute for the good you chose? What will happen to the demand schedule if the price of that substitute were to fall by 50%?

D. Use your imagination to sketch a short run supply curve for your good and a long run supply curve. Why do they differ in shape? Re-sketch your short run demand curve under the assumption that the largest factory in the industry was destroyed by fire last night. What effect will that event have on the price and how is this reflected in your graph of supply and demand?

E. Suppose that the supply of this good were permanently restricted for some reason. Compare the short run response in the price to the response over, say two years. What aspect of consumer behavior accounts for the difference?

Chapter 2

National Income

Outline

Preview

We all have a pretty good understanding of the concept of income on an individual level and what our own income is. But how should we measure the income of a whole society? Why is our national income what it is instead of some other amount? How do we add up the incomes of the household, business, government, and rest-of-the-world without counting something twice? What does the nation spend its income on, and what does it save? How does savings relate to investment?

These are all questions that we will answer in this chapter, starting with the simplest kind of society, one person. By understanding that case we can readily grasp the national income concepts for a complex economy like that of the U.S. Finally, we will review what magnitude of national income is for the U.S. and what are its component parts.

2.1 Robinson Crusoe's National Income

In Daniel Defoe's great adventure novel, Robinson Crusoe finds himself shipwrecked and alone on a tropical island. He sets about gathering food and making things that he needs using the few tools and materials that he is able to salvage from the shipwreck. Robinson Crusoe is a one person economy. His income is what he produces. It is not money but the coconuts he gathers, the fish he catches, and the objects that he makes.

Crusoe spends part of his time producing things for immediate use: fish caught in the lagoon, coconuts gathered nearby, and furniture to make his life more comfortable. Crusoe also puts part of his effort into making tools which will enhance his productivity in the future, for example a raft that takes him out to better fishing spots. Finding evidence that cannibals visit his island, Crusoe also builds a stockade to protect himself. We see that his time is divided between producing consumption goods for his immediate use, capital goods that are an investment in an improved standard of living in the future, and goods that would be purchased by government in a more complex society.

Crusoe is obliged to decide how much of his income, the things he produces, will be allocated to consumption now, how much to investment so he can consume more in the future, and how much to defense. His opportunities to consume, invest, and defend are limited by his ability to produce. The portion of his income that is not consumed or expended on defense is his savings, and that is invested in capital goods which will increase his income in the future.

Even though Crusoe's economy is just a one person economy (until he finds a native he calls Friday who has just narrowly escaped being a consumption good for the cannibals) and uses no money, it teaches us some fundamental rules that apply even to the most complex modern economies. These are:

- **The income of a society is the value of what it produces.**

- **Income is divided between three alternative uses: consumption, investment, and government.**

- **To increase any one of these uses, society must either increase its income or reduce one or both of the others.**

- **Savings, the amount of income that is not consumed by households or government, is equal to the investment in new capital goods.**

- **An increase in income requires investment in capital goods that make the economy more productive.**

The choices facing any society are basically the same that Crusoe faced, and they are reflected in the issues that occupy public debate today: Are we investing enough in modern factories and equipment to produce the growth in income that we would like? Are Americans on a consumption binge that is reducing economic growth? Does Japan grow faster than we do because it saves a larger part of its national income? Should something be done to encourage Americans to save more? What effect did the build-up in defense spending in the 1980s have on our economy? What will be the economic fall-out from the defense build-down of the 1990s?

Crusoe alone decided how to allocate his income between consumption, investment, and defense, but in our economy these decisions are made separately by the four sectors of the economy. The household sector makes consumption decisions while firms decide how much to invest in capital goods. Households do not receive the goods they produce directly, but rather they receive money which they can spend or save. Similarly, government through legislative bodies makes spending decisions and levies taxes to pay for them. While these decisions are made by different agents in different sectors of the economy, they must always obey the rule that in any economy the amount consumed by households, plus government purchases, plus investment in capital goods is equal to total income. Income, in turn, cannot exceed the productive capacity of the economy.

Let's see how a simple model of the economy can help us understand how the sectors of a complex economy interact. A model in economics is much like a model in architecture or car design: it is a representation of the real thing which is useful for exploring some of the properties of the real thing but is vastly less complex. From a scale model of a proposed office building we can learn a lot about how the building will function for the people who will work in it, even though the model leaves out much of the complex structural detail of the real building. Models of the economy can help us see important aspects of an economy that is far too complex for humans to understand in all its details. A good strategy in using models is to start with the simplest version we can think of and then make the model progressively more realistic and complex as we need to.

Exercises 2.1

A. Classify each of the following goods produced by Robinson Crusoe as consumption, investment, or "government:" a fishing net, a fish, a chair, a spear, a look-out tower, a cleared garden plot. Similarly, classify a theater ticket, a car, a taxi, a Boeing 747, a stealth fighter.

2.2 An Economy Producing Consumption Goods: Model I

Figure 2.1 depicts Model I. Here, we imagine an economy that produces only consumption goods. To keep Model I as simple as possible we further suppose that the only consumption good is cars. These cars are produced by firms which are staffed by the households and owned by the households. There is no role for government or for the rest-of-the-world in Model I, so these sectors are omitted.

The two sectors of this economy are represented by icons. Even though Model I is clearly not realistic as a description of an actual economy, it will allow us to see some basic relationships that are present in the most complex economies.

The cars that are produced by the firms flow from the firms to the households in Model I and labor services flow from the households to the firms. Suppose that the output of cars is one per worker per year. There are 100 workers so the output of the firms is 100 cars per year. All 100 cars produced are delivered to the households.

The market for cars sets the price that households pay for a car, and let's suppose that turns out to be $10,000 per car. This implies that the annual consumption expenditure of households in Model I is $1,000,000 (= 100 cars • $10,000), where "•" means multiplication. .

That spending by households is income to the auto firms which distribute it to the factors of production. Suppose that in the labor market the wage has been established at $8,000 per year, so wages paid by the firms to households total $800,000 per year. Notice that firms are receiving more money from car sales than they pay out in wages. The difference is profit, in this case $200,000. The factor incomes that result from the production of autos are therefore $800,000 for labor and $200,000 for capital.

Notice also that dollars flow clockwise in Figure 2.1, representing payments for the goods and services which flow counterclockwise. We see from this simple model that there are two sides to any economy: the expenditure side and the income side. We also see that they must be equal in dollar terms because every dollar spent on a good or service generates a dollar of income to the factors of production.

Figure 2.1: Product and Income Flows in Model I

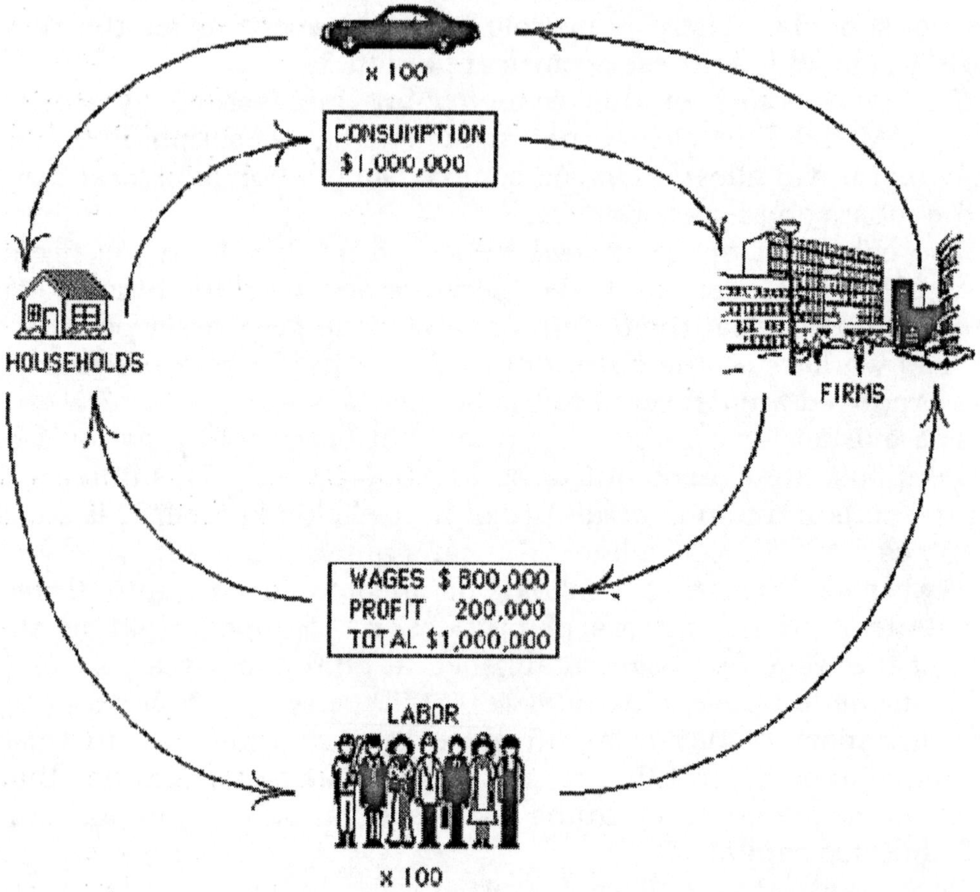

The market value of all the goods and services produced by an economy is called the National Product. It is $1,000,000 per year for Model I since that is the total expenditure for the cars that are produced.

The total of all factor incomes is called National Income. Since factor incomes account for all of the market value of the goods produced, it must be that National Income and National Product are equal. In other words, the total income of a society is the value of what it produces. This is a basic equality that holds even in the most complex economies.

Putting the value of what is produced in one column and the factor incomes arising from production in another column, we see the equivalence of these two sides of the Model I economy in the table below.

The left hand column shows that total expenditures in the economy are equal to National Product; the right hand column shows that the incomes of the two factors of production add up to National Income. Comparing the two totals, we see that National Product equals National Income as it always must.

Table 2.1: National Product and Income in Model I

Value of Goods Produced		Factor Income	
Consumption goods	$1,000,000	Wages	$800,000
		Profits	200,000
National Product	$1,000,000	National Income	$1,000,000

Exercises 2.2

A. Imagine that the price of cars jumps to $20,000 and the wage to $16,000 per year. Rework the model. What has changed and what has not? Has the income of the society changed?

B. Now suppose that an improvement in production technology makes it possible for factory output to reach 1.2 cars per worker. Has the income of the society changed? What do you imagine would happen to wages? Suppose that the new level of wages is $9,000 per year; show what the flows of goods and incomes look like now.

2.3 An Economy That Also Produces Capital Goods: Model II

Now let's make our model more realistic by recognizing that factories require capital goods, the equipment used in production. For example, car makers need trucks to deliver the new cars to consumers. These trucks are made by other firms in the business sector which sell their output to the car firms rather than to households. Figure 2.2 depicts Model II.

Notice that there are still only 100 workers, but now they can be employed making either cars or trucks. Recall that one worker can make one car per year, and we now suppose that it takes two workers to produce one truck per year. How many of each good will be produced and what will they sell for? This will be determined in the markets for cars and trucks, as firms seek to maximize their profit. *What we do know as economists is that the economy is constrained in its choices because resources are limited.* Since there are 100 workers and their efforts will be divided between producing the two goods, it must be that the numbers of car workers plus the number of truck workers = 100 workers.

Now it takes one worker to make one car per year and two to make a truck so we also know that

(cars per year • 1) + (trucks per year • 2) = 100 workers.

This simple relationship describes what is called the production possibilities frontier of this economy. Any combination of car and production and truck production which satisfies this equation is possible. For example the economy can produce 98 cars and 1 truck, or 96 cars and 2 trucks, but not 100 cars and 2 trucks. It is a frontier because the economy cannot go beyond it, although it may fall short of it. It is possible, for example, for the economy to produce only 98 cars and zero trucks, but then two workers will be unemployed. But we will assume that the economy is using its resources efficiently.

We see from the production possibilities frontier that in order to produce one more truck society must sacrifice the consumption of two cars. The opportunity cost of a truck, what society has to give up to get another one, is two cars. The idea of opportunity cost, that society must give up something to get more of something else, is one that many economists regard as the single most important concept in economics. This is why the economist's mantra is:

There is no such thing as a free lunch!

To complete our model, we assume that supply and demand in both the car and truck markets determine that a car sells for $10,000 and a truck for $20,000, and that the economy produces 90 cars and 5 trucks. This implies that 90 workers are employed by car firms and the remaining 10 by truck producers. Notice in Figure 2.2 the flow of trucks from truck producers to car producers, of cars from car producers to households, and labor from households to firms. Dollars flow in the opposite direction, from households to firms to pay for cars, from auto firms to truck firms to pay for trucks, and from firms to households to pay for the factors of production.

To see what National Product and National Income are in Model II we look at the two groups of firms successively. Let's take the auto firms first. Sales of cars totals $900,000 per year (90 cars times $10,000 per car) and this is the value of the goods produced by these firms. Incomes to the factors of production include wages for 90 workers at $8,000 per worker, which comes to $720,000.

This leaves a profit of $180,000 which is the factor income going to capital. This profit belongs to the households that are shareholders of the car-producing firms. However, not all of the profit will be paid out to the households because the auto firms have to pay for the 5 trucks they bought at $20,000 each, a total of $100,000. The car firms can pay out the remaining $80,000 as a dividend to their owners.

Figure 2.2: PRODUCT AND INCOME FLOWS IN MODEL II

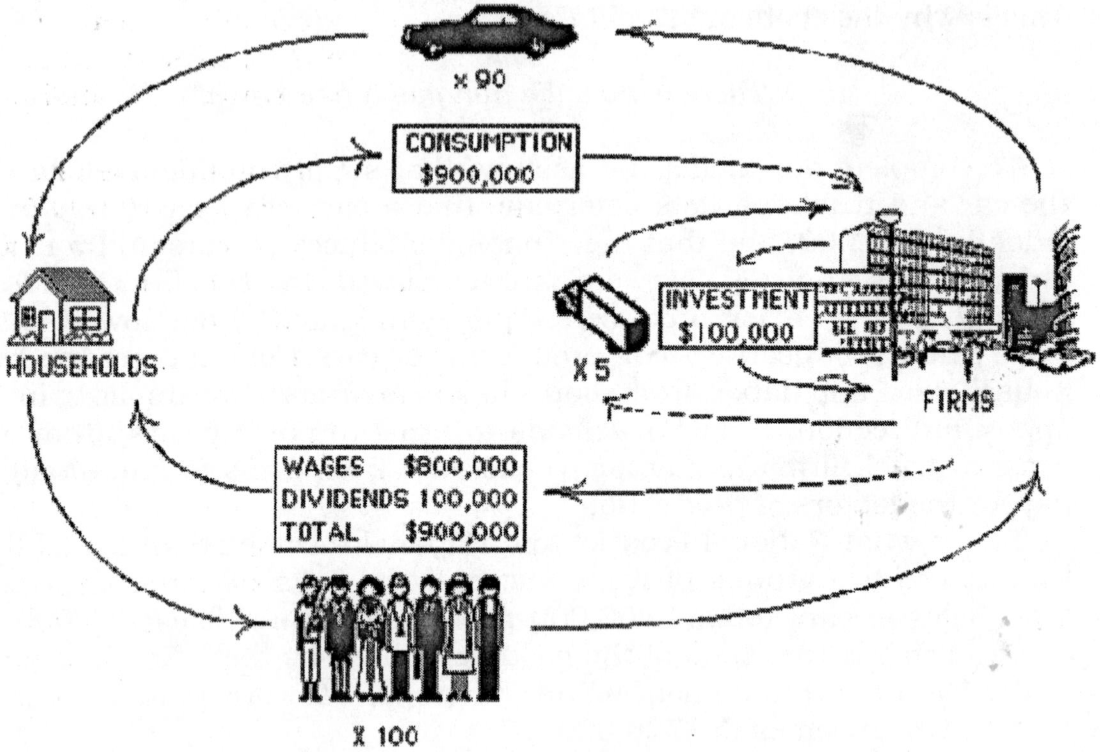

The distinction between profit and dividends is that profit is the amount left over after deducting the costs of running the firm, while dividends are the amount actually paid out to the firm's owners. The dividend payment is usually less than the amount of profit because firms generally want to retain some of their profit to pay for capital goods. The portion of profits not paid out in dividends is called undistributed profit or retained earnings.

But isn't the cost of those five trucks a cost of running the firm that should be subtracted from profit? Isn't the profit really only $80,000? It would be if those trucks were used up during the year they were purchased. At the time they are bought the trucks are a capital investment by the firm, an addition to its existing fleet of trucks. To the extent that trucks wear out during the year the firm would incur an expense, and we will introduce that concept in the next model. For the moment, let's pretend that trucks don't wear out, so those five new trucks are an addition to the assets of the firm and thus to the property owned by the shareholders.

To summarize the role of the auto firms in the economy we construct a table much like the table of National Product and National Income introduced in the Model I, listing the value of product in the left column and the distribution of factor incomes in the right column:

Table 2.2: Auto Firms' Product and Factor Income in Model II

Value of Goods Produced		Factor Incomes	
Sales to Households:		Wages:	
90 cars @ $10,000 =	$900,000	90 workers @ $8,000 =	$720,000
		Profit of $180,000	
		allocated to -	
		Capital investment:	
		5 trucks @ $20,000	100,000
		Dividend payment	80,000
		to shareholders	
Value of Product	$900,000	Total Factor Income	$900,000

For the auto firms, the value of what they produce is their sales of cars to the households. Factor incomes resulting from this activity are wages of $720,000 and profit of $180,000. Profit is not all paid out to shareholders, rather $100,000 is retained to pay for capital investment and the remaining $80,000 is paid to shareholders as a dividend. Of course, the totals in the two columns are equal because the sales of cars become income to the factors of production.

Now we can readily do the same analysis for the truck firms which are not making any capital investments of their own in Model II:

Table 2.3: Truck Firms' Product and Factor Income in Model II

Value of Goods Produced		Factor Income	
Sales:		Wages:	
5 trucks @ $20,000 =	$100,000	10 workers @ $8000 =	$80,000
		Profit of $20,000	
		allocated to -	
		Dividend payment	
		to shareholders:	20,000
Value of Product	$100,000	Total Factor Income	$100,000

The sales of each industry and the total wage and dividend payments to the household sector are shown in Figure 2.2. Now let's summarize the whole economy of Model II with a statement of National Product and Income.

Table 2.4: National Product and Income in Model II

Value of Goods Produced		Factor Income	
Consumption goods	$900,000	Wages	$800,000
Investment goods	100,000	Profits	200,000
National Product	$1,000,000	National Income	$1,000,000

In the left hand column we add up the expenditures in the economy for consumption and investment goods. The total of these expenditures is the value of the goods produced, or National Product. In the right hand column we add up the factor incomes that result from the sales of the goods produced, namely wages and profits. The total of factor incomes is National Income. Since National Product and National Income are just two ways of accounting for the value of the goods produced in the economy they must be the same amount, $1 million in this case.

Model II reminds us that society has to choose between consumption goods and capital goods. Only by giving up some of one can it have more of the other. But why bother giving up consumption goods in order to invest in capital goods, that is, why would the economic agents of Model II choose to give up 10 cars so that car firms can have 5 trucks?

The pay-off to society from capital investment is higher productivity in the future. Imagine that before buying those 5 trucks, cars were individually driven to their new owners, but now one worker can deliver a whole truck load at once. This means that the same number of workers will be able to produce more cars next year. Next year the productivity of labor in producing cars will rise, say to 1.1 cars per worker. When that happens the production possibilities frontier will be:

(cars/1.1) + (trucks•2) = 100 workers

Since the number of workers needed now to produce a car is not one but 1/1.1 or about .9. This new production possibilities frontier means that the society of Model II can now have more cars, or more trucks, or more of both than before.

We can also see from the table of National Product and Income that *Savings equals Investment* in the economy. Savings is what society has left after paying for consumption. In this case it is:

National Income:	$1,000,000
less Consumption:	-900,000
equals Savings:	$ 100,000

Notice that Savings is exactly the value of the investment in trucks, $100,000. It is not coincidental that savings equals investment in Model II. What we have here is a fundamental equality in macroeconomics that holds in any economy. How does it work? National Product consists of consumption goods and Investment goods, but National Product is equivalent to National Income. We can write this equality as:

Consumption + Investment = National Income

then subtracting consumption from both sides we get

National Income - Consumption = Investment

or, in other words,

Savings = Investment.

This fundamental result tells us that if society is to invest in new capital goods to achieve higher productivity in the future, it must give up an equivalent amount of consumption now.

Exercises 2.3

A. Suppose that the car producers had bought 6 trucks this year instead of 5. Assume that prices and wages are as before and rework the model and the figure. Verify that income equals expenditure.

B. Suppose that the car makers did buy 5 trucks and that it resulted in a rise in worker productivity next year to 1.1 cars produced per year. (1) What is the new production possibilities frontier, and what is the maximum number of cars that the economy can produce? (2) How many cars are produced if the economy still produces 5 trucks? (3) Work out the Product and Factor Income table for car firms and for truck firms, assuming that the yearly wage rises to $8,800. (4) Verify the equality of income and expenditure and the equality of savings and investment.

C. The fraction of national income that is saved by US households has been unusually low during the last decade and much lower than in other major industrial economies such as Japan. Many observers are concerned that the US will lose its competitiveness in the world economy and experience slower economic growth as a result of the low savings rate. Can you explain how these concerns are motivated?

D. Imagine an economy that produces only pizzas and ovens. One worker can produce 1000 pizzas or 2 ovens per year, and there are 50 workers in all. Suppose also that workers earn $9,000 per year, pizzas go for $10 each, and the purchase price of a new oven is $5,000. (1) Write out the production possibilities frontier equation for this economy and graph it. (2) What is the opportunity cost to society of producing an oven? (3) Write out the accounts for this economy when it produces 6 ovens per year, verifying the relationships we established for Model II.

2.4 Gross National Product and Net National Product: Model III

In reality, capital goods like trucks wear out over time from use. Depreciation, the decline in the value of capital goods due to usage, is a cost to society which we need to account for in computing National Income.

To illustrate, suppose that the auto firms in Model II start the year with a fleet of 20 trucks that are used to deliver new cars to consumers and that during the year two trucks wear out and are scrapped. This loss of two trucks is depreciation and it is a cost of production to the auto firms and to society. Two new trucks are needed just to keep the auto firms' truck fleet intact. Therefore two of the five trucks produced during the year are not an investment in new capital goods but are just replacements for ones that wore out. Only the other three actually expand the truck fleet and are therefore investment in additional capital.

Summarizing the changes in the truck fleet during the year:

Fleet at beginning of year	20
Trucks produced	+5
Trucks scrapped	-2
Fleet at end of year	23

Let's call this economy with depreciation Model III. Clearly there is a distinction in this economy between the value of all goods produced during the year and the value net of the capital goods that have to be replaced.

The former is called, Gross National Product or GNP. It is the value of all goods and services produced by the economy. The latter is Net National Product, or NNP. It is GNP minus, or "net of," depreciation. The *net* output of the economy in Model III is three trucks and 90 cars after deducting depreciation of two trucks from the *gross* output of 5 trucks and 90 cars. Recognizing that the dollar value of the depreciation of two trucks is $40,000 we can calculate the dollar values of GNP and NNP for Model III:

Gross National Product	$1,000,000
less Depreciation	-40,000
= Net National Product	$ 960,000

It is natural to apply the same concept to distinguish between gross investment and net investment. In Model III we have:

Gross Investment	$100,000
less Depreciation	-40,000
= Net Investment	$ 60,000

Now let's take a look at the product and income flows in Model III and see where they differ from Model II. First, the auto firms' profits are reduced by the $40,000 in depreciation expense as seen in Table 2.5. The product and factor incomes for the auto firms, shown in Table 2.6, also need to be revised to recognize that these firms now have a depreciation expense of $40,000 to replace the two trucks that have worn out.

Table 2.5: Auto Firms' Profits in Model III

Sales: 90 cars @ $10,000	$900,000
less Wages: 90 workers @ $8,000	-720,000
less Depreciation: 2 trucks @ $20,000 =	-40,000
equals Profit	$140,000

Table 2.6: Auto Firms' Product and Factor Income in Model III

Value of Goods Produced		Factor Incomes	
Sales to Households:90 cars @ $10,000 =	$900,000	Wages:90 workers @ $8,000 =	$720,000
Gross value of product	900,000	Profit of $140,000 allocated to -	
		Net investment:3 trucks @ $20,000 =	60,000
less Depreciation:2 trucks @ $20,000 =	-40,000	Dividend payment to shareholders	80,000
Net Value of Product	$860,000	Total Factor Income	$860,000

It may be helpful to compare Table 2.6 with Table 2.2 from Model II. On the "Value of Goods Produced" side we have subtracted $40,000 from the gross value of product to obtain the net value of product. This is the contribution that the auto firms make to NNP. Correspondingly, on the "Factor Incomes" side we have subtracted $40,000 from profit, recognizing that net investment is also $40,000 less than in Model II. The dividend of $80,000 is not affected.

Since we have assumed in this model that only the auto firms have depreciation costs, no revision is necessary for the truck firms. In reality, all firms have depreciation expense that is subtracted in calculating profit. The flows of products and income in Model III can still be represented by Figure 2.2 since by recognizing depreciation we do not change production or payments. Bringing together the product and income statements for both truck firms and auto firms we have the table of National Income for the economy of Model III shown below.

This table looks only a little different from the table for Model II. Notice that National Income is smaller by the amount of $40,000 than it was in Model II because of depreciation. Also notice that it is Net National Product, the value of goods produced by the economy net of depreciation, that is equal to National Income. It makes sense that depreciation reduces the income of society. It is easy to verify that savings is again equal to investment, but now we understand that to mean net investment. This basic equivalence must hold because the portion of the output of the economy that is not consumed or used to replace worn out capital goods is a net addition to the capital goods available for use in the future.

Table 2.7: National Product and Income in Model III

Value of Goods Produced		Factor Income	
Consumption goods	$900,000	Wages	$800,000
Gross Investment	100,000	Profits	160,000
Gross Nat'l Product	1,000,000		
less Depreciation	-40,000		
Net National Product	$960,000	National Income	$960,000

Exercises 2.4

A. Confirm that savings equals investment in Model III.

B. Could this economy produce 100 cars as did the economy of Model I? Could this economy continue to produce one hundred cars per year, year after year?

C. Rework the model under the assumption that three trucks wear out and need to be replaced during the year.

D. Recall question D of Exercises 2.3 above. Suppose that the number of ovens in that economy at the beginning of the year is 40 and that during each year 10% of the ovens burn out and have to be discarded. Work out the accounts for that economy as we have for Model III.

2.5 Government Spending and Taxation: Model IV

Now we take another step in making our model more realistic by introducing the government sector as a purchaser of some of the output of the business sector and a collector of taxes to pay for it. In Model IV we suppose that government also uses trucks, and that Congress has decided to buy 6 per year. Obviously the economy cannot continue to supply 5 trucks to the business sector and 90 cars to the households sector while, in addition, producing 6 trucks for the government. Clearly, something has to give.

Since it takes one worker to build a car, and two workers to produce a truck regardless of who buys it, the production possibilities frontier for the economy of Model IV is

$$\text{cars} \cdot 1 \ + \ \text{business trucks} \cdot 2 \ + \ \text{gov't trucks} \cdot 2$$
$$= 100 \text{ workers.}$$

We see that if Congress is going to buy 6 trucks, then the economy must choose one of the following: 1) reduce the level of investment in new trucks for the auto producers, or 2) produce fewer cars for the households so that labor and capital can be shifted to the production of more trucks, or 3) do some of both. Let's assume that the workings of market forces are such that the economy does some of both, in particular it reduces car production by 10 and the production of business trucks by one. The capacity freed up by these reductions is sufficient to make room in the economy for the production of 6 trucks for government, since 5 trucks can be produced in place of 10 cars and one less business truck allows for production of another truck for government.

Where will government get the money to pay for 6 trucks? Congress decides to impose an income tax of 10% on the profits of firms and the income received by households. If this is not enough to cover the full cost then the government will be running a deficit and the Department of the Treasury will borrow what it needs from the households.

We start our analysis of this economy by taking a look at the situation for the auto producers in Model IV. Their profits and tax owed to the Treasury are as follows:

Table 2.8: Auto Firms' Profits in Model IV	
Sales (80 cars x $10,000)	$800,000
less Wages (80 workers x $8,000)	-640,000
less depreciation (2 trucks x $20,000)	-40,000
equals Profit Before Tax:	120,000
less Income Tax of 10%:	-12,000
equals Profit After Tax:	$108,000

Auto sales are lower than in Model III by $100,000 because the economy has made room for the production of more trucks by producing 10 less cars. The auto firms have fewer workers as well, the others now being employed making more trucks. The income tax is 10% of profit, leaving "profit after tax" of $108,000 available for purchase of additional trucks and for payment of dividends.

Capital Investment by the auto firms is also lower in Model IV because one of the trucks formerly available to the auto firms in Model III will now go to the government. Net investment is now 2 trucks costing $40,000 in total. The amount of the dividend paid to shareholders is decided by the directors of a corporation. Here we will assume that the dividend payment is $70,000. Although this is a smaller dividend payment than the auto firms made in Model III, the firms do not have enough money to pay the dividend and also buy the new trucks since these amounts add up to $110,000 and undistributed profit is only $108,000. Clearly, the auto firms will have to borrow $2,000 from somebody to make up the difference. The table of product and factor incomes for the auto firms now looks like this:

Table 2.9: Auto Firms' Product and Factor Income in Model IV

Value of Goods Produced		Factor Income	
Sales to Households:80 cars @ $10,000 =	$800,000	Wages:80 workers @ $8,000 =	$640,000
Gross value of product	800,000	Profit of $120,000 allocated to -	
		Net investment:2 trucks @ $20,000 =	40,000
		Dividend payment to shareholders	70,000
		Income Tax paid	12,000
less Depreciation:2 trucks @ $20,000 =	-40,000	- amount borrowed	-2,000
Net Value of Product	$760,000	Total Factor Income	$760,000

Notice that the result of making room in the economy for the production of trucks for the government is that fewer cars are produced for households and fewer trucks are added to the fleet used by auto producers. We can summarize changes in the business truck fleet during the year as:

Truck fleet beginning of year	20
Trucks produced during year	+4
Trucks scrapped during year	-2
Truck fleet at end of year	22

The consequence of adding only two new trucks to the fleet instead of three as in Model III will be slower gains in productivity in the future.

The truck firms have higher sales and profits in Model IV than they did in Model III. With production up to 10 trucks per year the profits of the truck firms will be:

Table 2.10: Truck Firms' Profits in Model IV

Sales: 10 trucks @ $20,000 =	$200,000
less Wages: 20 workers @ $8,000 =	-160,000
equals Profit Before Tax	40,000
less Tax of 10%	-4,000
Equals Profit After Tax	$ 36,000

Notice that truck firms now employ more workers and produce more trucks than they did in Model III; factors of production have been shifted away from the consumer goods industry to increase production of goods for government use. For simplicity we assume now that truck firms pay a dividend just equal to their profit after tax so they have no need to borrow. Here is how the table of product and factor incomes looks for the truck producers in Model IV:

Table 2.11: Truck Firms' Product and Factor Income in Model IV

Value of Goods Produced		Factor Incomes	
Sales:10 trucks @ $20,000 =	$200,000	Wages:20 workers @ $8,000 =	$160,000
		Profit of $40,000 allocated to -	
		Dividend payment to shareholders	36,000
		Income Tax paid	4,000
Value of Product	$200,000	Total Factor Income	$200,000

The situation for households will also be somewhat different in Model IV as we can see by constructing a table showing the income and expenses of the Household sector in Model IV.

Table 2.12: Households' Income and Expenses in Model IV

Wages: 100 @ $8,000 =	$800,000
plus Dividends	106,000
equals Personal Income	$906,000
less Income Tax of 10%	-90,600
equals Disposable Income	$815,400
less Consumption Spending	-800,000
equals Personal Savings	$15,400

This table introduces some terminology used by economists to describe the household sector. Starting with the first line, note that wage income has not changed from earlier models: 100 workers are still employed at $8,000 per year each. Adding to wages the dividends received from auto and truck firms we have the total income received by the households, which is called personal income. It does not include undistributed profits, the portion of profits not paid out as dividends, even though the firms are owned by the households. Income tax is collected from households on the portion of profits received by the households as dividends. Under the US tax system dividends are taxed twice: once as part of profits at the firm level and again as part of personal income at the household level. After subtracting the income tax from personal income the remaining amount is called disposable income. This is the income that households have available for spending. After paying for the 80 cars they purchased during the year, households have $15,400 left, which is personal savings. What will the household sector do with its savings? We have already seen that the auto firms need a loan, and we will soon see that the government does too.

One sector remains to be accounted for in Model IV, the Government sector. Recall that the 10 % income tax was introduced by Congress to pay for the 6 trucks. Let's see if it is sufficient to pay for them. The Income Statement of the Government looks like this:

Table 2.13: Government's Income and Expenses
in Model IV

Income Tax Revenue from -	
Business Sector	$16,000
Household Sector	90,600
equals Total Tax Revenue	$106,600
less Government Spending	-120,000
equals Government Surplus or Deficit	-$13,400

We see that the Government Sector has a budget deficit of $13,400 because the 6 trucks it bought cost that much more than it is receiving in taxes. A persistent and large budget deficit has plagued our federal government since the early 1980's and has become a major political issue. The fundamental reasons for the deficit are the same that we have in our model: the government spends a lot more than it collects in taxes, but the amount has averaged about $150 billion per year. In both the model and in reality the government comes up with the money to pay its bills by borrowing.

Having calculated the income flows for all three sectors of the economy in Model IV, we are now ready to summarize the economy in the usual table of National Product and Income:

Table 2.14: National Product and Income in Model IV

Value of Goods Produced		Factor Income	
Consumption Goods	$800,000	Wages	$800,000
Gross Investment	80,000	Profits	160,000
Gov't Purchases	120,000		
Gross Nat'l Product	1,000,00		
less Depreciation	-40,000		
Net National Product	$960,000	National Income	$960,000

The left-hand column adds up the values of goods produced for consumption, gross investment, and government to get GNP, and then subtracts depreciation to get NNP. That is equal to National Income, the sum of factor incomes in the right hand column.

Another way to look at National Income is as the sum of payments made to each of the three sectors as shown in Table 2.15. The Household sector receives wages and dividends which is Personal Income, then we subtract the income tax to get Disposable Income. Next, the profit recorded by the Business sector is reduced by the dividends paid to the households and the income tax paid to the Government sector. Finally, the income of the Government sector is the sum of the taxes collected from the other two sectors.

Table 2.15: Sector Income in Model IV

Households		
Wages	$800,000	
+ Dividends	106,000	
= Personal Income	$906,000	
- Income tax	-90,600	
= **D**isposable **I**ncome		$815,400
Business		
Profits	160,000	
- Income Tax	-16,000	
= Profits after tax	144,000	
- Dividends paid	-106,000	
= **U**ndistributed **P**rofit		38,000
Government		
Tax revenues		106,600
National Income		$960,000

The combined incomes of the three sectors are National Income which is equal to NNP. Adding up the three components of NNP and setting them equal to the sum of the incomes of the three sectors we have the simple equation

Consumption +

Net **I**nvestment +

Government Purchases

=

Disposable **I**ncome +

Undistributed **P**rofit +

Tax Revenues

Using the bold letters in each of these components as abbreviations, we can rewrite the equation as

$$C + I + G = DI + UP + T$$

which we can easily rearrange as follows:

$$(DI-C) + UP + (T-G) = I$$

The terms on the left hand side are the savings of each of the three sectors: (DI-C) is personal savings, UP is the savings of the business sector, and (T-G) is the savings of government. This equation shows us that total savings in the economy must be equal to net investment.

This fundamental relationship is expressed in words as:

Personal Savings +

Undistributed Profits +

Government Savings

= Net Investment

The values of the components of the "savings = investment" equation for Model IV are:

(DI-C)	+	UP	+	(T-G)	=	I
$15,400	+	$38,000	+	(-$13,400)	=	$40,000
Household Savings	+	Business Savings	+	Government Savings	=	Net Investment

We see now that it was no coincidence that the households in Model IV were saving just enough ($15,400) to cover the government budget deficit (-$13,400) and also lend the auto firms the extra money ($2,000) they needed to pay for new trucks. It will always be true that savings equals investment.

The continuing federal government budget deficit is one of the most hotly debated subjects in Washington these days, and this analysis helps us see why. Many observers fear that the deficit uses up personal savings that otherwise would be available to the Business sector to expand investment in modern capital goods that would make our economy more productive. If one sector saves less, the government sector in this case, then investment must fall unless another sector compensates by saving more. Some economists feel that this concern is exaggerated because they believe that the household and business sectors will increase their savings in response to government deficits since they understand that a deficit now means they will have to pay

79

higher taxes later. Most economists, however, see no evidence that the household sector has increased its saving in response to government deficits. Those who advocate a tax increase to reduce or eliminate the deficit believe that the resulting cut in disposable income would cause households to cut back their consumption spending, making room in the economy for more production of investment goods.

Exercises 2.5

A. Although the economy of Model IV is producing goods for the government sector that were not produced in Model III, GNP is the same in the two models. Explain why the increase in the production of trucks did not result in an increase in GNP.

B. It has been said that "Europe and Japan won the cold war." After explaining briefly what is meant by the production possibilities frontier, discuss how relatively low military expenditures in those countries could have helped them to grow more rapidly than the US or the USSR in recent decades.

C. Suppose Congress acts in Model IV to reduce the deficit by imposing a tax increase of $20,000 (a fixed amount, not a percentage of income) on the household sector. Show how the savings = investment equation would look if households did not alter their spending behavior in response to the additional tax. Did deficit reduction increase investment? Suppose now that households do reduce their consumption spending by $20,000 in response to having $20,000 less disposable income. How much can this economy now increase capital investment? How does this change the "savings = investment" equation?

D. Imagine that Congress enacts a citizen's benefit program in Model IV under which the Government sector sends each worker a transfer payment of $10 which is not subject to income tax. If this does not cause households to alter their spending habits, which tables in the model change and what do they look like now?

E. It has been said that the real burden of government on society is not the amount of tax it collects but the amount it spends. Comment on this statement in light of our analysis of Model IV.

F. The income tax rate in Model IV is 10%, yet the amount of tax collected is more than 10% of National Income. How does this happen?

2.6 International Trade: Model V

There is one more channel of expenditure that we need to include in our model of the economy: international trade. Some of the goods that we produce are exported and sold abroad. The US is a major exporter of grain, airplanes, and computers. Exports account for about 10% of US GNP. Likewise some of the goods we buy are produced abroad and imported into the US. The US imports large amounts of petroleum, autos, and food products. Recall from Chapter 1 that we can think of other countries as a fourth economic sector called the rest-of-the-world, or ROW. By selling us the goods that we import, the ROW earns dollars which it can use to buy goods made here. During the 1980s, foreign countries earned far more dollars than they spent on goods produced in the US. The excess of U.S. imports over exports is called the trade deficit and it averaged about $100 billion annually during most of the 1980s. Recently the trade deficit has narrowed; in 1990 it was $69 billion.

What has the ROW been doing with all those hundreds of billions of dollars it has been earning through our trade deficit? It has been lending those dollars back to us. For example, Japan, which accounts for about half of our trade deficit, has become a major lender to the US Treasury. By the end of the 1980s the U.S. had become a debtor nation, meaning that we owe more to foreigners by some estimates than they owe to us.

Why do we have a trade deficit? Is the trade deficit harmful or helpful to our economy? Will it have adverse consequences in the future? What, if anything, should we try to do about it? These are important questions and by extending our simple model of the economy we can gain some understanding of them.

To incorporate imports and exports in our model we suppose that cars are traded internationally. Recall that in Model IV the economy produces 80 cars and 10 trucks. Now we assume that this economy exports 10 cars while it imports 11, all at a price of $10,000. The dollar amount of Exports is therefore $100,000 and Imports $110,000. Consumption is

81

higher by one car or $10,000 because the imported cars are purchased by households. Gross Investment and Government Purchases however are unchanged from Model IV. Has GNP changed? Not at all. GNP is the value of goods produced by the economy, and that is still $1 million.

Adding up the expenditures made by the four sectors we have Consumption ($810,000) plus Gross Investment ($80,000) plus Government Purchases ($120,000) plus Exports ($100,000), a total of $1,110,000. Obviously, GNP is no longer just the sum of expenditures by the four sectors. This total differs from GNP by exactly the amount of Imports. Why? Because the value of Imports, eleven cars worth $110,000 which are not produced by the Model V economy, is already included in Consumption. If we now subtract Imports from expenditures then we are counting only the goods produced in the Model V economy and that will be equal to GNP. Equivalently, we can subtract Imports from Exports to get Net Exports and add this to the purchases of goods by the other three sectors. The National Product and Income table for Model V therefore looks like this:

Table 2.16: National Product and Income in Model V

Value of Goods Produced		Factor Income	
Consumption	$810,000	Wages	$800,000
Gross Investment	80,000	Profits	160,000
Gov't Purchases	120,000		
Exports 100,000			
less Imports 110,000			
equals Net Exports	-10,000		
Gross National Product	1,000,000		
less Depreciation	-40,000		
Net National Product	$960,000	National Income	$960,000

Notice that GNP, NNP, and the components of National Income are all the same as in Model IV. This is because the output of the economy has not changed. Introducing international trade has had no net effect on auto firms because they are still producing 80 cars, it is just that 10 of them are delivered to foreigners instead of to domestic buyers. The truck producers are unaffected by this change. Therefore the value of production as well as the flows of income to the Household and Government sectors are unaffected.

What has changed is that households have increased their consumption by $10,000. They are purchasing the 70 domestically produced cars that are not exported as well as the 11 imported cars, a net increase in consumption of one car and $10,000. Here is what the Income Statement of the Household sector now looks like:

Table 2.17: Households' Income and Expenses

Wages (100 @ $8,000)	$800,000
plus Dividends	106,000
equals Personal Income	$906,000
less Income Tax of 10%	-90,600
equals Disposable Income	$815,400
less Consumption spending	-810,000
equals Personal Savings	$5,400

The changes here are the $10,000 increase in Consumption spending and a corresponding $10,000 reduction in Personal Savings. Obviously, households will no longer be able to lend the Treasury $15,400 to cover the government's budget deficit since they have saved only $5,400. Recall too that the business sector needs to borrow $2,000 to finance its investment in new trucks. Where will the additional $10,000 come from? Notice that foreigners have earned $10,000 more in sales of autos in the US than they spent on US cars, so they have $10,000 to lend. The ROW has thus become another source of savings in the economy and it lends that savings to other sectors.

To see how the four sectors interact as savers and borrowers we again express the "expenditures = income" relationship as a simple equation relating the sum of expenditures to the sum of sector incomes as in Model IV. However, now we have another expenditure component, net exports which is exports minus imports. Putting the equivalence into words we have:

Consumption +

Net **I**nvestment +

Gov't purchases +

(**EX**ports-**IM**ports)

=

Disposable Income +

Undistributed **P**rofit +

Tax revenues

Using EX to stand for Exports and IM for Imports, we write the equation symbolically as

$$C + I + G + (EX-IM) =$$
$$DI + UP + T.$$

We can again rearrange the terms in the equation so that the savings of all the sectors are on the left and net investment on the right:

$$(DI-C) + UP + (T-G) + (IM-EX) = I$$

The first three terms are again the savings of the household, business, and government sectors respectively, and the new term (IM-EX) is the amount of dollars saved by the ROW since IM is the amount of dollars earned by the ROW and EX is the amount spent by the ROW. Putting the "savings = investment" equation in words:

Personal Savings +

Business Savings +

Government Savings +

Rest-Of-World Savings

= Net Investment

In Model V, ROW savings is $10,000, the excess of imports over exports. The specific numbers in the savings = investment equation for Model V are

(DI-C)	+	UP	+	(T-G)	+	(IM-EX)	=	I
$5,400	+	$38,000	+	(-$13,400)	+	$10,000	=	$40,000
Household Savings	+	Business Savings	+	Gov't Savings	+	ROW Savings	=	Net Investment

What does the ROW do with its savings of $10,000? It lends those dollars to the Government sector which needs to borrow $13,400 or it may lend some of them to the Business sector which needs to borrow $2,000 (Business Savings is $38,000 but Net Investment is $40,000). Why would the ROW want to lend those dollars rather than spend them on goods to take home? Borrowers pay lenders interest for the use of their money (the subject of the next chapter). It must be that foreigners find the interest rates offered in this economy attractive enough so that they would rather lend here than at home or somewhere else.

Why, then, does this economy have a trade deficit? Because the ROW finds that it would rather use part of its dollars earnings to buy loans than to buy cars for export. It is often suggested that the U.S. has a trade deficit because we are not sufficiently competitive. Model V shows us that there is no necessary connection between competitiveness and a trade deficit. If our goods are not attractive to foreigners then our exports will be meager, but that does not imply that we will have a trade deficit. A trade deficit implies that foreigners are interested in selling us goods in order to obtain dollars to lend in the U.S.

Are the inhabitants of Model V harmed by the fact that their economy has a trade deficit? Compare their situation with that in Model IV. The difference is that consumers in Model V enjoy a higher level of consumption (one extra car) than they would in Model IV. However, the loans from the ROW will have to be repaid at some time in the future. Model V has traded more consumption now for less consumption, or less of something, in the future. The mercantilist school of thought in 18th century France held that the welfare of a nation can be measured by its trade position, a deficit being a loss to the society and a surplus being a gain. What we see in Model V is that a trade deficit is not a gain or loss but indicates an exchange of goods for loans, and it not clear that the borrowing nation is worse off by having a trade deficit.

All we can say for sure is that we have a higher level of consumption now at the cost of incurring loans that will be repaid later.

The U.S. has an economy that resembles Model V in having a large government deficit and a large trade deficit. In both economies, the trade deficit, being a source of saving for the economy, allowed consumers to maintain a high level of consumption because households did not have to provide the saving to finance the government deficit. As one wag put it "In the 1980's we Americans held a party and Japan lent us the money to pay for it." The way that Japanese and other ROW savers obtained the dollars to lend to our government was by selling us more imports than they spent on exports from the US. Why was the ROW willing to lend us back the dollars they earned here? Because US interest rates were higher than in Japan and Europe, so lending in the U.S. was attractive to ROW savers.

What if the ROW had not been interested in making loans to us in the 1980s and we had still insisted on having a government that spends much more than it receives in taxes. What would have happened? The savings = investment equation makes the possibilities very clear. They are 1) increase household savings by reducing consumption, or 2) have a lower level of net investment in new plant and equipment and therefore sacrifice some long term growth in the economy. (Note that business savings could be increased by reducing dividend payments, but that just reduces household income and savings) It is not possible to change any one component of the equation and leave all the others unchanged.

Exercises 2.6

A. Japan is a country with a high rate of personal savings and a large trade surplus. If we were to redo Model V to depict Japan's situation, what might the quantities in the "savings = investment" equation look like?

B. Some observers expect the savings rate in the U.S. to rise over the next decade as the "Baby Boomers" born in the 1950s reach middle age. That is when people typically boost their savings in anticipation of college expenses for children and for retirement. If Personal Savings does increase substantially in the future, how might the components in the "savings = investment" equation change?

C. Japan's government is committed to making markets there more open to goods from abroad. If conditions change so that Japan begins importing more goods, what might that do to alter consumption and investment within the US?

D. The Clinton administration has suggested that the tax increases aimed at reducing the federal deficit that were enacted in 1993 will also reduce our trade deficit. Explain how reducing the federal budget deficit could lead to a fall in the trade deficit.

2.7 The National Income of the U.S.

Now we take a look at the actual National Income and Product accounts for the U.S. They can be found in the *Survey of Current Business*, a monthly publication of the U.S. Department of Commerce which is available in any college library or by subscription through the U.S. Government Printing Office. The actual tables look very similar to those we have constructed for Model V but of course contain much more detail.

Here is a simplified version of the National Income table for the year 1990.

Table 2.18: National Income of the US for 1990

	Billions of Dollars		% of NI
Wages & Salaries	2743		61
+ Fringe benefits	548		12
= Employee Compensation		3291	74
Farm Income	42		1
+ Non-farm proprietors	325		7
= Proprietors' Income		367	8
Corporate Profits		362	8
Rental Income		-12	-0
Net Interest		461	10
National Income		4468	100
+ Indirect Business Taxes		472	
Net National Product		4940	

Source: Tables 1.9 and 1.14, *Survey of Current Business*, September 1992. Totals may not agree exactly because of rounding and statistical discrepancy.

Notice that we are talking about some real money here. A billion dollars is one thousand million. NNP is about $5,000 billion, or five trillion dollars. That is about $20 billion per working day!

We see that the largest share of National Income is employee compensation which accounts for nearly three quarters of the total. It is perhaps surprising that fringe benefits have grown to constitute about one fifth of employee compensation. Business firms are divided into proprietorships, generally small businesses that are not incorporated, and corporations. It is remarkable that farm income, once a major part of the economy, has shrunk to the point where it is only about 1% of National Income. Small business as a whole represent as large a share of National Income as do corporations. Profits are income to the owners of firms, but firms also pay interest on loans they have received from the household sector. Interest paid by corporations, net of interest they receive, is larger than profits. Both profits and net interest are factor payments to capital.

You will notice next that National Income differs from Net National Product by an item called "indirect business taxes." Indirect business taxes include sales taxes, excise taxes, and customs duties which the national income accountants think of as being added to the price of a product and therefore do not treat it as income to any factor of production. These taxes were not present in our models, so this technical distinction did not arise. These taxes are added to National Income to get Net National Product.

When we look at Table 2.19 we see both Gross National Product and something called Gross Domestic Product, or GDP. The distinction arises because US-owned factors of production do not reside entirely within the US. There are both US-owned factories and US workers abroad. Similarly, some factors of production within the US are not U.S.-owned. The GNP is the output of US-owned factors of production while the GDP is the output of all factors of production within the US.

Table 2.19: Gross Domestic Product, Gross National Product, and Net National Product of the US for 1990

Consumer Expenditures	Billions of $		% of GDP
Durable goods	464		8
+ Non-durable goods	1224		22
+ Services	2060		37
= Total Consumption		3748	68
Capital Investment			
Plant and Equipment	578		10
+ New Residential housing	216		4
+ Change in Inventories	6		0
= Gross Investment		800	14
Exports and Imports			
Exports	557		10
- Imports	-626		-11
= Net Exports		-69	-1
Government Expenditures			
Federal Government	426		8
+ State and Local	617		11
= Government Purchases		1043	19
Gross Domestic Product		5522	100
+ receipts of factor income			
- payments of factor income to			
Gross National Product		5543	100
- Depreciation		-603	-11
Net National Product		4940	89

Source: Tables 1.1 and 1.9, *Survey of Current Business*, Sept. 1992.
Totals not exactly because of rounding and statistical discrepancy.

In practice the difference between GDP and GNP is small for the U.S., but it may not be small for some countries that have large investments abroad. The US has followed other countries in adopting GDP as the standard statistical measure of the output of the economy. The news media refer to GDP rather than the GNP in their reporting. In our simple models there was no difference between ownership and location, so the distinction did not arise.

Several points are worth noting about the information in Table 2.19. Consumption is broken down into expenditures on durable goods such as cars, non-durables such as breakfast cereal, and services such as medical care. Services are by far the largest category and accounts for 37% of GDP. Capital investment includes not only purchase of new plant and equipment such as trucks, but also construction of new housing and additions to inventories held by firms. The national income accountants treat homeowners and landlords alike as being in the business of renting homes to themselves or others. An implicit rental rate is estimated for owner-occupied housing, and that is included as part of Consumption spending and National Income. Newly constructed houses are therefore treated as new capital goods for these "firms."

Additions to inventories held by firms for later sale are a kind of capital investment. Inventories may fall as well as rise, so this component of investment can be negative.

About 10% of the GDP was exported in 1990, but imports amounted to even more, about 11% of GDP.

We often forget that state and local governments together are a very large sector of the economy, their expenditures substantially exceeding those of the federal government. Keep in mind that these are expenditures for goods and services such as park rangers and firetrucks, and do not include "transfer payments" such as social security benefits which are not payment for a good or service but simply a redistribution of income. Nor do government expenditures on goods and services include interest payments on the national debt.

Adding up all the uses of the GDP we are ready to make the adjustments necessary to get GNP. We add receipts of factor income from abroad which represent the value of the product of US-owned factors of production not located in the US. For example, dividends received from IBM Japan represent part of the product of US-owned factors of production which is not counted in our GDP. Then we subtract payments to foreign-owned factors of production located in the US Thus, dividend payments to Honda Motor Corp. are part of US GDP which is not part of our GNP but rather part of Japan's. After making these adjustments we come to GNP.

Note that depreciation amounts to 11% of GDP. This is the replacement of capital goods that wore out during 1990. Depreciation is subtracted from GNP to give NNP, completing the linkage between the income and product sides of the economy represented in these two tables.

The reader is probably aware from the regular announcements in the media that GDP is measured not just for the whole calendar year but each calendar quarter. The number that is announced is GDP for the quarter at an annual rate. For example, GDP for the fourth quarter (October through December) of 1990 was $5,598 which means that if the economy kept up the same pace for a full year, that would be the GDP for that year. Likewise, the growth rate of GDP for the quarter is expressed at an annual rate.

The media usually announce only the "real " growth in GDP, meaning that GDP has been adjusted for price changes to reveal the change in the volume of goods and services produced. The GDP is also adjusted for seasonal variation because people are interested in seeing whether economic activity has accelerated or slowed down apart from the usual seasonal pattern.

Finally, let's look at how the savings of the four sectors add up to equal net investment in the US in 1990. The equivalence is only approximate because of "statistical discrepancies," meaning that the components of the national income accounts are not measured precisely so they do not add up exactly.

(D-C)	+	UP	+	(T-G)	+	(IM-EX)	=	I
$176	+	$76	+	(-$136)	+	$69	☐	$197
Household	+	Business	+	Gov't	+	ROW	=	Net
Savings		Savings		Savings		Savings		Investment

Based on Table 5.1, *Survey of Current Business*, Sept. 1992. Totals do not agree exactly because of technical and statistical discrepancies.

What we see here is a situation similar the one we saw in Model V: a government budget deficit that is being financed in part by foreigners who earn the dollars they lend to the US Treasury by selling more to us than they buy from us. Government "Savings" in 1990 was actually a $136 billion deficit (the federal deficit of $166 billion plus a state and local surplus of $30 billion) which had to be financed by the savings of other sectors. The Business sector saved $76 billion but spent $197 on new capital goods, so it didn't finance the Government deficit. Clearly, both the Government and Business Sectors must have been tapping the savings of the Household and ROW sectors.

Given the fact that savings must equal net investment, it is not surprising that the trade deficit and the government budget deficit emerged together as the twin deficits of the 1980s. When the federal government began to run a large deficit in the early 1980s it had to be accompanied by a corresponding increase in savings by another sector or by reduced net investment. In succeeding chapters we will see that high interest rates in the US, caused in part by heavy borrowing by the US Treasury, made it attractive for foreigners to "save" some of the dollars earned from their exports to the US. Those dollars were lent to the US Treasury rather than spent on imports from the US.

The twin deficits is certainly one of the key economic and political issues of the 1990s. What are the long term consequences of continuing trade and federal budget deficits?

Fast growing economies like that of Mexico typically have large trade deficits because they are investing heavily in new plant and equipment. Figuratively speaking, Mexico imports bulldozers and exports loans to be paid later.

The U.S., in contrast, imports consumer goods and exports loans to be paid later. Leading economists have expressed concern that the U.S. may not continue to attract foreign savings as conditions in Japan and Europe change. If the federal budget deficit remains large, and if US households do not boost their savings by curbing consumption, then investment in new plant and equipment will have to decline. That would inevitably mean slower growth for the U.S. economy in the years ahead.

Exercises 2.7

A. Check the library for the latest edition of the *Survey of Current Business* and locate the tables for National Income, GDP, and their components. Can you verify that savings equals investment? What are the sources of savings currently in the economy?

Index to Chapter 2

Chapter 3

Savings and Investment

Outline

Preview

3.1 The Role of Financial Intermediaries
Services That Banks Provide to Savers and Borrowers
Major Types of Financial Intermediaries

3.2 The Stock Market
Wall Street
Investment Banking
What Does the Shareholder Get?
Mutual Funds

3.3 The Anatomy of a Bond
What is a Bond?
What if the Issuer Fails to Pay?
How is the Coupon Determined?

3.4 Interest Rates and Bond Yields
The Benchmark for All Interest Rates
How to Find Out What the Interest Rate Is Today
The Yield to Maturity
The Coupon on a New Bond

Preview

We learned in Chapter 2 that the total of all investment expenditures in the economy must equal total savings. But how do dollars saved become dollars invested in new plant and equipment? How do firms that want to build new buildings or buy new equipment get together with savers so that a portion of the output of the economy is diverted from the production of consumption goods to capital goods? We find there is a whole industry, financial intermediaries, that specialize in bringing together savers and investors. They assist in the conversion of savings to claims on the firms that use the savings for investment. Those take the form of stocks and bonds. The interest rate emerges as the key price in the markets for these financial instruments. Let's starts by seeing what happens when an airline wants to buy a new Boeing 777.

3.1 The Role of Financial Intermediaries

Imagine that you are the president of Blue Skies Airlines, Inc. and you have decided that Blue Skies should buy a new Boeing 777. The plane will cost $125 million and change. There is one small problem though. Blue Skies only has a few million dollars in its bank account, and those funds are needed to pay fuel bills and the salaries of its employees. How can Blue Skies get enough money to buy this new airplane? It can by tapping into the savings flows of the economy, and this chapter explains how that actually happens.

Suppose that Blue Skies approaches the First National Bank and requests a loan of $125 million. If First National agrees to make the loan, it will require Blue Skies to sign a contract agreeing to certain conditions. These would include, of course, repayment of the $125 million, called the principal, according to a specified time schedule. In addition, the bank would receive periodic interest payments. The interest to be paid is expressed as a percentage of the unpaid principal, and that percentage is called the interest rate on the loan.

Blue Skies would also be required to pledge the 777 as collateral, giving the bank the right to take possession of the plane if Blue Skies fails to make interest and principal payments on time. If that happens, Blue Skies is said to default on the loan, and the bank can go to court to enforce its contractual rights, repossessing the aircraft if necessary.

Suppose now that the interest rate on this loan is 10% per year. That means that Blue Skies will pay the bank $12,500,000 in interest the first year (assuming it does not repay any principal during the first year). Why would Blue Skies be willing to pay the bank that much money just so that it can own a new 777? Blue Skies expects to make back the interest cost and more through lower operating costs and more ticket sales. Before making the loan, the First National Bank will study Blue Skies' estimates of cost savings and ticket sales and it will not approve the loan unless it is convinced that the new plane will more than pay for itself. Banks make money by collecting interest on loans, not by owning repossessed airplanes.

But how did the bank get the $125 million to lend to Blue Skies? It borrowed it in much smaller amounts from households in the form of bank deposits. When a household deposits money in a bank account, it is making a loan to the bank. The depositor receives in return a combination of banking services, such as check cashing and access to automatic teller machines, and interest payments. The bank is willing to incur these costs because it lends the money to Blue Skies at a sufficiently high rate of interest to cover its interest payments to depositors and its administrative expenses and still make a profit.

Services That Banks Provide to Savers and Borrowers

Why don't Blue Skies and the households get together and cut the bank out of the deal, sharing the difference between the interest rate that the bank charges Blue Skies and the much lower interest rate that it pays its depositors? They don't because there are valuable services that the bank renders to both borrowers and savers. What are these services?

First, the borrower, Blue Skies, avoids dealing with thousands of different parties and having to negotiate separate loan contracts with each of them. Thus, Blue Skies' transactions costs are reduced by borrowing through the bank. Household savers also enjoy lower transactions costs by using their local bank branch where deposits can be made and withdrawn very quickly without negotiation. The bank performs a retailing function for savings just as the neighborhood supermarket does for food. The bank also offers the household saver three other services: lower information costs, liquidity, and diversification. Let's look at these in turn.

Information about Blue Skies is costly for an individual saver to acquire. Has Blue Skies met its financial obligations in the past? Does the decision to buy another 777 appear to be a sound one? Banks specialize in collecting and analyzing information about borrowers, and certain banks will specialize further is making loans to airlines. It makes sense for savers to let specialists worry about evaluating the risk that Blue Skies might not pay its debts. On the other hand, it is easy for the saver to obtain information about the bank; for example, is it covered by deposit insurance? By dealing with the bank instead of Blue Skies the saver enjoys lower information costs.

Liquidity is the degree to which something of value can be turned into money on short notice and at low cost. A checking account is very liquid because it can be turned into money by simply writing a check or visiting a cash machine. Other deposits, such as certificates of deposit, are less liquid but pay a higher rate of interest. In contrast, the loan to Blue Skies is very *illiquid* since the airline has no obligation to make payments earlier than specified by the contract. But the bank has many such loans on which it is collecting payments, so it can offer liquidity to each of its depositors while making illiquid loans. Banks convert illiquid assets, such a the loan to Blue Skies, into liquid assets for their depositors. Providing this service has some risks, as we see below when we discuss the history of Savings and Loans, but depositors are willing to pay the bank for this valuable service.

Diversification comes from the participation of each depositor in all of the loans that the bank holds, so that failure of any one lender to repay has only a fractional impact on individual depositors. In addition, deposits in US banks are insured by the Federal Deposit Insurance Corporation (FDIC), and banks are subject to regulatory oversight by government agencies. By accepting ultimate responsibility for the obligations of banks to their depositors, the government sector diversifies these risks across the economy.

Major Types of Financial Intermediaries

Instead of borrowing from a bank, Blue Skies might borrow instead from an insurance company or a pension fund. Banks, savings and loans, insurance companies, pension funds, and mutual funds are all examples of financial intermediaries, firms which pool the savings of households and lend them to other firms. While all financial intermediaries provide the four fundamental services to households in some degree, each type offers a particular mix of these. Each also combines them with other services which distinguish it. Let's take a brief look at the major types of financial intermediary, in addition to banks, which are important in the U.S. economy today.

Savings and loans traditionally specialized in mortgage lending to home buyers but today are much like banks. Indeed, the distinction is rapidly disappearing. "S&Ls" were much in the news in the 1980s because many of them failed and were either merged into more healthy ones or were taken over by government regulators and closed. When interest rates increased sharply in the late 1970s, the S&Ls were obliged to pay higher interest rates to depositors or else depositors would withdraw their savings and invest it elsewhere. At the same time, the mortgages that the S&Ls owned paid them a much lower interest rate that was fixed for as long as 30 years until the mortgage was paid off. Caught in this squeeze between the rising interest cost for funds and the fixed low interest rate earned on mortgages, many S&Ls were doomed to fail.

This was a case where financial intermediaries were not able to cope with a very large mismatch between highly liquid obligations to savers and highly illiquid assets. When many S&Ls did fail in the 1980s, depositors were protected by a government-backed insurance plan which absorbed much of the S&Ls' losses. When that fund was depleted, the burden shifted to the U.S. Treasury and so to the taxpayer, you and me.

Life insurance companies offer savings plans which protect against the possibility that the saver may not live long enough to meet an objective such as putting their children through college. Because life insurance policies are not highly liquid, insurance companies are able to make long-term loans, such as mortgages to finance large office buildings. The expertise of insurance companies in this type of lending could not be duplicated by an individual; they are able to hold a diversified portfolio of such loans, and no individual would be willing make a loan that remains illiquid for decades. Life insurance policies also enjoy tax benefits; current income is not subject to federal income tax.

Pension funds accumulate the contributions employers and employees make to retirement plans. Generally, the contributions to such plans are not subject to federal income tax until they are withdrawn in retirement, and the income from these savings accumulate tax free as well. Their size, professional management, and long time horizon make it possible for pension funds to engage in highly sophisticated investment strategies that would not be available to the individual employee. The volume assets in pension funds have grown rapidly in recent decades with the popularity of "defined contribution plans" in which the employee has ownership of funds accumulated in their name. In contrast, the older "defined benefit plans" promised only to pay a specified benefit, usually a fraction of salary at retirement based on years of service. The growth of pension funds has also been fueled by the aging of the "baby boomers" who have moved into the age group that saves most heavily for retirement, those in their 40's and 50's.

Mutual funds pool together the savings of many individuals and invest in stocks and bonds. Mutual funds offer low transaction costs, because the saver is making one investment instead of many, and low information costs, because it is easier for savers to get information on one mutual fund than on hundreds of individual stocks and bonds. Mutual fund shares are also extremely liquid. Most mutual funds are "open-end" funds that stand ready to redeem existing shares and sell new ones every day at net asset value, the market value of the fund's portfolio divided by the number of shares. This is possible because mutual funds are permitted to invest only in marketable securities, stocks and bonds for which a market price can readily be determined from recent transactions. Mutual funds also provide a high degree of diversification because they invest in a large number of different securities, often hundreds. However, mutual funds can be still be risky since it is often the case that most stocks fall or rise together. Likewise, bonds tend to all rise or fall in value at the same time, for reasons we will discuss later in this chapter. Thus, a mutual fund cannot eliminate the common "market factor" by diversification.

A mutual fund is owned by its shareholders and represented by elected trustees who contract with an investment advisory firm to manage the fund. Nevertheless, a mutual fund is usually known by the name of the advisor that manages its portfolio. All the dividends and interest that the fund collects, and any capital gains realized from sales of investments, are required to be distributed to its shareholders as taxable income, but the fund itself is not taxed.

Mutual funds developed in the 1930s as a way for the individual investor to own part of a large, diversified, and professionally managed portfolio of stocks and bonds. Over time, the mutual fund industry has developed a staggering array of different types of mutual funds. Some funds invest in a mix of bonds and stocks, others only in stocks of small firms, or stocks of firms in only one industry, or stocks of foreign firms, or only in tax-exempt bonds issued by local governments in one state! To get a sense of the variety of these offerings, thumb through *Morningstar Mutual Funds* at the library. The variety of choices available to investors today is simply astonishing.

One of the newest and fastest growing products in the financial intermediary arena combines features of life insurance, a pension fund, and a mutual fund. It is called the variable annuity. A variable annuity is sold by an insurance company to a customer who may purchase it for a lump-sum or pay the premium in small amounts over time. The premium goes in part to pay for insurance and in part is invested in a mutual fund. The customer chooses from among alternative types of mutual funds offered by the insurer, and the investment earnings are untaxed as long as they remain in the plan. At some date in the future, the accumulated sum is used to purchase an annuity, a stream of payments that continue for life, and this time would generally coincide with retirement. The size of the annuity will depend on the investment results of the mutual fund, so there is risk just as there is in any mutual fund investment. A feature of many plans is a minimum guaranteed payment, regardless of investment results, and that insurance is part of what the customer pays for. There is typically also a death benefit, another insurance feature. Details vary greatly from one plan to another, indeed the ability to customize these plans to suit the needs of the individual is part of their appeal.

Though the idea of stocks and bonds will be familiar to most readers, we now move on to discuss just what is meant by a stock and a bond, how we can locate and interpret information about them, and what determines their market value.

Exercises 3.1

A. Explain briefly the role of financial intermediaries in the economy. What are the four fundamental services provided by financial intermediaries that make using them attractive to household savers? Give specific examples of these services in the case of mutual funds.

B. Give several examples of firms in your area that are financial intermediaries. What are the services they offer to savers and borrowers?

C. Find the mutual funds table in the Friday issue of the Wall Street Journal or similar source. What are some of the types of securities that funds invest in? Identify some of the largest "families" of funds. Which types of funds have had the highest and lowest return over the past year?

D. Why would the way that open-end mutual funds operate make it infeasible for them to invest in office buildings and hotels?

E. What features of life insurance, a pensions fund, and a mutual fund are combined in a variable annuity?

3.2 The Stock Market

When you mention the word "investment" most people think of Wall Street and the stock market, not capital investment in new plant and equipment by firms. These are two distinct uses of the same word. When someone buys 100 shares of Nike Corporation they are making a financial investment. When Nike Corp. builds a new factory or warehouse, it is making a capital investment. We need to be careful not to confuse financial investment by savers with capital investment by firms, although the two kinds of investment are closely related. Both of these "investments" are part of the process of turning household savings into the production and purchase of new capital goods. Both involve taking a risk now in the hopes of earning a larger return later. To develop the concepts of financial investment, let's continue our example of Blue Skies' purchase of a new Boeing 777.

Wall Street

Instead of borrowing from a financial intermediary, Blue Skies could instead raise the money to buy that 777 by selling additional shares in the company. The ownership of a corporation is divided up into equal parts called shares, rather like pieces of a pie. Each share has one vote in the election of the directors who govern the corporation and hire its management. The collective term for shares is "stock." The value of a corporation's shares is established in the stock market which has its center on Wall Street in New York City.

The New York Stock Exchange (NYSE) is located in a very large room, known as the floor of the stock exchange, where the shares of major corporations are traded. The purchase or sale of stock is handled through brokerage firms which act as agents for buyers and sellers. When Jane Johnson places an order with her stock broker to buy 100 shares of Blue Skies, it is transmitted to the broker's representative on the floor of the NYSE. That person takes it to the "specialist" whose responsibility is to make an orderly market in that stock. The specialist tries to match her buy order with a corresponding sell order. The price is where the supply of shares just equals the demand. Each trade is recorded and displayed on the "ticker tape" which is displayed on the wall and on computer monitors and television sets around the world. This "transparency" of the exchange give investors confidence in the integrity of the trading process and the validity of prices. Tourists can watch the action on the floor from the visitors' gallery. Watching broker's representatives and clerks dashing around the floor in seeming chaos is an experience few will forget. In spite of the apparent disorder, many billions of dollars worth of stock change ownership every day.

Shares of smaller corporations are traded "over the counter" in an informal market among brokers called NASDAQ. Today, this is an electronic market in which offers to buy or sell are displayed on monitors on brokers' desks, with trades being relayed at light speed around the network. Prices are collected and trades are displayed in ticket tape fashion on screens around the world. Some very large corporations do not elect to be listed on the NYSE and their shares are also traded on the NSDAQ; examples include Intel, Microsoft, and Apple Computer. With the rapid development of electronic communication, the trading in this market has become highly efficient and transparent. Indeed, some speculate that electronic trading may some day replace the face-to-face trading of the NYSE.

Financial markets in the U.S. are regulated by the Securities and Exchange Commission ("SEC") which is an agency of the federal government. It was established to curb abuses that many felt contributed to the stock market crash of 1929, practices such as trading by insiders on the basis of priviledged information. The Securities Act of 1933 requires that any corporation planning to issue stocks or bonds in interstate commerce file detailed statements with the SEC which become a matter of public record and publish a prospectus. Issuers of securities are then required to furnish periodic reports to the SEC and their shareholders disclosing financial results. The guiding principal of SEC regulation is "full disclosure." It is not up to the SEC to guarantee that investments will turn out well, only to insure that investors receive full and accurate information that enables them to assess risks and opportunities.

To get a feeling for the intensity of activity in the stock market, tune in any of the financial news networks offered by CNN, Fox, or CNBC, and visit some of the web sites that carry market news such as

http://www.cnnfn.com/

Investment Banking

If shares in Blue Skies are trading at $10 per share on the New York Stock Exchange, then Blue Skies could expect to raise $125 million by selling another 12,500,000 shares. The new shares would be sold through an investment bank which will contract with Blue Skies to purchase all of the new shares at a negotiated price. The investment bank, which is sometimes called an underwriter, will in turn sell those shares to perhaps thousands of different investors, some of whom will be individual households and some of whom will be financial intermediaries. Not surprisingly, the investment bank is often also a brokerage firm since brokers have an established relationships with potential buyers of stock. Under the Glass-Steagall Act of 1933 commercial banks, those that take in deposits and make loans, have been prohibited from engaging in investment banking in the U.S. The separation of underwriting from ordinary banking was intended to insulate banks, many of which failed during the Depression that followed the stock market crash of 1929, from riskier investment activities. In recent years, banks have been allowed to enter areas of the investment business previously closed to them, as regulators have made increasingly loose interpretations of Glass-Steagall, and there is currently a strong movement to repeal the law all together. With large brokerage firms offering checking to their clients, and banks selling mutual funds in their lobbies, it seems sure that the gulf between banks and investment banking and brokerage will continue to narrow if not disappear.

What Does the Shareholder Get?

What does the buyer of Blue Skies stock get for that $10 per share? The investor gets the legal right to cast one vote per share in the election of directors, and each share participates equally in the future profits of the firm. Stocks offer savers a way of participating in both the rewards and risks of the ownership of firms. If Blue Skies prospers with the help of its new more efficient aircraft, then its profits will soar and the directors will declare a higher dividend payment to shareholders. But if Blue Skies does not prosper for whatever reason, the shareholders may receive smaller dividends, or none at all.

Stocks are quite liquid, since you can sell your shares in Blue Skies at any time for the market price and get your cash in a several days. However, they are risky because the market price can fluctuate. The market price is determined in the stock market and will reflect what investors, as a group, think the future of the firm is worth. When new information is disclosed that affects the firm, the market will react by adjusting the share price up or down accordingly. For example, if you buy Blue Skies stock today and next week the price of jet fuel doubles because of political upheaval in the Middle East, those shares will fall in value because investors fear that higher fuel costs mean smaller profits and therefore smaller dividends in the future.

By owning shares in many types of companies across different industries an investor can mitigate risk through diversification. For example, an oil company would benefit from higher fuel prices, so an investor in Blue Skies can hedge the risk of higher fuel prices by also holding shares of an oil producer. However, the cost of getting information on many different stocks and the broker's fees on small amounts of stock mean that diversification is costly for small investors.

Mutual Funds

As explained in our discussion of financial intermediaries, a mutual fund is a firm, but one which owns shares in other firms. Each of its shares owns a small fraction of all the stocks that the fund has invested in, thus providing diversification.

Mutual funds are an excellent way for investors to get started in the stock market. Indeed, many new investors in mutual funds are participating in the stock market for the first time, previously having only deposited their savings in a bank. There is an important difference, however, between these two types of intermediaries that they need to understand. A deposit in a bank is an obligation of the bank to repay the original investment plus the promised interest. The assets of the bank, as well as federal deposit insurance, stand behind that promise. In contrast, a mutual fund makes no promise of a specific interest payment or of gains from trading stocks or bonds. As the market value of the stocks or bonds it holds fluctuates from day to day, any gains or losses are immediately reflected in the net asset value of the fund on the same day. Thus, shareholders in a mutual fund are fully exposed to all the risk of stock market fluctuations.

The growth of the mutual fund industry has been nothing short of phenomenal in the last decade. The combined assets of mutual funds now exceed those of all banks in the U.S., and there are more than twice as many mutual funds specializing in investing in stocks as there are stocks listed on the New York Stock Exchange! Why are there so many mutual funds is a real puzzle. The portfolio managers of top performing mutual funds have become super-stars, with super-salaries to match. Their pictures are on the covers of the many magazines catering to investors and their views are eagerly sought on national news shows. Peter Lynch, legendary manager of Fidelity Magellan Fund when it grew to be the largest fund, is so well known that he is featured in TV ads. It is clear that many small investors cherish the belief that these market gurus can protect them from the risks they would face if they bought individual stocks. Unfortunately, there is no evidence that mutual funds are any less risky, or any more profitable, than investing in an average of stocks selected mechanically. Indeed, one can do this through "index funds" that invest in the stocks in one of the popular market indices, usually the Standard and Poor's Index of the 500 largest companies.

Exercises 3.2

A. Economics.com, an internet company providing forecasts of the economy, has just invested in a new server computer, and you have just invested in 100 shares of the company. Discuss how these two investments are different and how they are related.

B. What do we mean by transparency in financial markets? How has the development of the internet made stock trading more transparent?

C. What prevents your bank from selling you 100 shares of Apple Computer? Why does this restriction exist?

D. At the time of this writing Microsoft Corp. has never paid any dividends ever to its shareholders, yet the total market value of its stock is greater than that of any other corporation on earth. What motivation do people have for buying this stock if it pays no dividend?

E. Identify a story in the news about a major corporation and then check the stock market table to see how the price of the stock reacted to the news. Discuss briefly whether the response of the stock market to this news makes sense. In thinking about your answer, try to determine whether this piece of news had been widely anticipated or came as a surprise.

F. Why is it a puzzle that there are far more mutual funds than individual stocks in those funds? Can you guess at why this is the case? Given your answer, do you expect the number of mutual funds to continue to grow faster than the number of individual stocks?

3.3 The Anatomy of a Bond

We have already mentioned bonds, and that they are marketable securities that are purchased by financial intermediaries like mutual funds and pension funds as well as by individuals. We are all aware of U.S. Government bonds, but we also know that you cannot buy stock in Uncle Sam! Clearly, bonds must be different from stocks, though both are investments. Now let's be specific about what a bond is and how the bond market works.

What is a Bond?

A bond is a contract between the issuer of the bond and the owner of the bond. The issuer promises to pay the stated face value of the bond at a specified date in the future called the maturity date. The issuer also promises to make periodic coupon payments until maturity. Upon payment of the face value at maturity, a bond ceases to exist. Thus, a bond is fully described by its issuer, coupon, and maturity date. It is unnecessary to specify the face value of a bond because, by tradition, the price of a bond is always quoted per $100 of face value.

For example, if someone says that they bought the "Safeway 10s of '01 at 109" they mean that they bought the bond issued by the Safeway Corp. that pays a coupon of $10 per year and matures in 2001, and they paid $109 per $100 of face value for it. That bond may actually be available only in units of $1,000 face value, so one bond would cost the buyer $1,090. Some bonds are "callable" at the discretion of issuer at an earlier date than the maturity date. It is important when buying bonds to find out if the bond is callable or has special features that may affect its value (for example, "convertible" bonds may be exchanged for stock under certain conditions).

Notice that the market price of the Safeway bond in this example is more than its face value, $109 vs. $100. What determines the price of a bond? Supply and demand, of course! Bonds are supplied both by issuers such as the Safeway Corp. and by investors who already own bonds but wish to sell. Bonds are in demand from investors including both individuals and financial intermediaries. Buyers and sellers interact in the market place, bidding prices up or down until the quantity of bonds supplied equals the quantity demanded. The Safeway bond trades at $109 because investors are willing to pay that much for Safeway's promise to pay $10 each year until 2001 and then repay the principal or face value of $100. Note that there is no necessary equality between face value and market price.

A bond combines some of the characteristics of a loan with some of those of a stock. Like a loan, a bond is a promise by the borrower to make payments at specified dates in the future. However, the issuer promises to pay whomever owns the bond rather than a specific lender. Bonds, like stocks, are bought and sold at prices determined in the marketplace. As mentioned in the previous section, stocks and bonds together make up the class of marketable securities. When a bond is sold by one investor to another, the new owner then is entitled to all payments promised under the terms of the bond.

What if the Issuer Fails to Pay?

If the issuer fails to pay the coupon or principal on time, then the bonds are declared in default and the bondholders may take legal action against the issuer through a trustee who is appointed to represent them. A firm that goes into default may be liquidated (disbanded and its assets sold) under bankruptcy law, and the rights of the bondholders to receive a share of the proceeds will be considered by the court along with the rights of other creditors. While bondholders are entitled to be paid before stockholders, both are vulnerable if the firm fails. The possibility of default is referred to as credit risk. There is never an absolute guarantee that the bondholders will receive what they were promised when the bonds were issued. It is therefor important for investors to consider credit risk before purchasing a bond.

Since it is costly for investors to evaluate credit risk, it is not surprising that issuers of bonds are typically governments and very large corporations that are relatively well known and perceived to be good credit risks. Smaller borrowers who are less well-known usually borrow directly from financial intermediaries, particularly from commercial banks, which specialize in evaluating credit risk. In the 1980s it became briefly fashionable for poorer credit risks to issue bonds and these were dubbed "junk bonds". Some of these bond issues turned out to deserve their nickname and went into default, usually resulting in losses to the bondholders. But many junk bonds paid off handsomely for those who held on to them. Today, this sector of the bond market is more frequently referred to as the "high yield bonds", reflecting the premium interest rate paid to compensate for higher credit risk, and the buyers are generally financial intermediaries who specialize in evaluating these securities.

How is the Coupon Determined?

Returning to our favorite airline, Blue Skies could raise the $125 million it needs if it could issue 1,250,000 bonds with face value of $100 each at a price of $100. But will investors be willing to pay $100 for these bonds? That depends on the size of the coupon and their confidence that Blue Skies will be able and willing to make the promised payments. It is customary to set the coupon on a newly issued bond so that the bond will sell at par, which means that the market value of the bond *on the date of issue* is equal to its face value.

The less confidence investors have in the borrower, the higher is the coupon required to induce investors to pay $100 for the new bond. Blue Skies is competing for the investor's dollar with other borrowers and it will have to be prepared to pay a higher coupon than borrowers who are perceived to be better credit risks with a lower risk of default. For example, if firms having the highest credit ratings, such as General Electric and IBM, are paying a coupon of $8, Blue Skies may find that it needs to offer a substantially larger coupon, perhaps $10, to sell its bonds at par.

Interest is payment for the use of money, so the coupon on a bond is interest. When Blue Skies issues a $100 bond at par with a coupon of $10 it is paying $10 in interest to the bondholders or, equivalently, an interest rate of 10% per year. That interest rate is not set by Blue Skies Airlines but by the marketplace where Blue Skies must compete with other borrowers for investors' dollars.

If all goes well at Blue Skies, bondholders will receive a coupon payment of $10 each year during the life of the bond and then the face value payment of $100 on the maturity date. Of course, unexpected events such as a jump in fuel costs or a decline in airline travel could force Blue Skies to default on its bonds. In that case, bondholders may not receive all the payments promised them. On the other hand, the bondholders will *never receive more* than the promised coupons and face value, even if Blue Skies prospers well beyond the most optimistic expectations. Rather, it is the shareholders who reap all the gain from a good business climate. Thus, the bondholder gives up participation in the risks and rewards of ownership for the right to receive specified payments.

Exercises 3.3

A. Locate the table called "NEW YORK EXCHANGE BONDS" in the *Wall Street Journal* or other business newspaper. Each bond is identified by the name of the company that issued it, the coupon rate in percent, and maturity year, in that order. Find the AT&T bond with the maturity furthest in the future. What are the coupon, maturity year, and price (under the column heading "close") of that bond? What is AT&T promising to pay a purchaser of this bond? Now locate bonds with substantially larger coupons than that paid by AT&T. Are these corporations as well known as AT&T?

B. Some bonds are denoted "cv" meaning they are convertible into stock, and they frequently carry a lower coupon. Why would that make sense?

C. Locate a bond with an "f" after the year. This denotes a bond that has defaulted on coupon payments. What is the bond market lingo for such bonds (see notes to the bond table), and how does a bond having this designation seem to relate to the price quoted on that bond?

3.4 Interest Rates and Bond Yields

The interest rates paid on a loan or bond is a key variable in macroeconomics because interest is an important part of the cost of new capital goods, like airplanes, and new durable consumer goods, like cars and houses. If the interest rate facing Blue Skies were 15% instead of 10%, its management might decide not to buy that Boeing 777 since the profit the plane produces may no longer be sufficient to cover a higher interest cost. Clearly, a sharp rise in the interest rate would reduce the demand for many kinds of products and therefore affect the economy very significantly. On the other hand, a droop in interest rates would stimulate demand and give the economy a boost. This is the reason why economists and business managers pay close attention to interest rates and look for any indications of a change in interest rates.

The Benchmark for All Interest Rates

What is the interest rate today? First of all, there isn't just one interest rate in the economy. Blue Skies will pay a higher interest rate than a borrower that is perceived to be a better credit risk, such as General Motors. The interest rate paid by the borrower with the very lowest credit risk will be the lowest, and thus can serve as a benchmark for all interest rates. That borrower is the U.S. government.

The federal government is the largest borrower in the U.S. economy. Through the U.S. Department of Treasury, the federal government has sold about $200 billion in *additional* bonds to investors each year during the past decade. It already owes well over $5 trillion in the form of bonds outstanding, measured at face value. In spite of being so heavily in debt, the U.S. government is still considered to be the best possible credit risk, with the chance of default being effectively zero. Why? Because unlike any other borrower, the federal government has the power to raise taxes if necessary to make good on its promises. Treasury bonds are also the most liquid of all marketable securities because they trade in huge volumes every day and almost continuously around the clock somewhere in the world. All interest rates paid by private borrowers on loans and bonds of the same maturity are higher than that paid by the Treasury,

113

the difference depending on credit quality, and they all move with the rate on Treasuries.

The interest rate on "Treasuries" or "T bonds" is therefore the benchmark interest rate for the whole economy and is often referred to as *the* interest rate. There is one exception to the rule that the U.S. Treasury pays the lowest interest rate. Bonds issued by state and local governments, referred to as municipal bonds, are generally exempt from federal income tax and state income tax in the state where they were issued. For that reason municipal bonds pay an even lower interest rate than Treasuries, but they are a good investment only for people in the highest income tax brackets. The interest rate on Treasuries is nevertheless the benchmark rate which municipals follow.

How to Find Out What the Interest Rate Is Today

How can we find out what the benchmark interest rate on Treasury bonds is today? It is easy to get that information from the financial pages of major newspapers. Look for a table with the heading "TREASURY BONDS, NOTES AND BILLS." Treasury notes are simply bonds with ten or fewer years to maturity when issued, and Treasury bills mature in less than one year from issue. Each line of the table consists of six pieces of information describing one bond.

To illustrate, on December 31, 1998 the two Treasury notes maturing in one year were quoted in *The Wall Street Journal* as follows:

GOV'T BONDS & NOTES

Rate	Maturity	Bid	Ask	Chg	Ask Yld.
5 5/8	Dec 99n	100:30	101:00	....	4.59
7 3/4	Dec 99n	102:31	103:01	-1	4.60

The "Rate" is the coupon as a percent of face value, so 7 3/4 means the note pays a coupon of $7.75 per year per $100 of face value. Even though T bonds and notes generally have a face value of $1000, it is traditional to quote them as if they came in $100 amounts (think of a $1000 bond as a bundle of ten $100 bonds). "Maturity" is the month and year of payment of the face value, while "n" means that the security is a note as defined above. "Bid" and "Asked" are respectively the price you can sell a bond for and the price you have to pay for one, in dollars and 32nds of a dollar per $100 of face value. The bid-ask spread, the difference between these, is the mark-up that a bond dealer earns trading T bonds. "Change" is the price change from yesterday in 32nds of a dollar. Finally, "Ask Yld." stands for yield to maturity, which we will now discuss.

The Yield to Maturity

To understand the concept of yield to maturity we need to look at these two notes from the perspective of an investor. Imagine that you have an extra $1,000 from summer earnings that you wish to invest for one year so you can travel next summer. How would you choose between these two notes? At first it might seem that you would want to buy the note with the higher coupon, but you want to take into account the fact that it is more expensive. What is the right way to evaluate the two notes? All you care about these notes is how much your investment will be worth next year, and you will take the bond that grows your money the fastest. How much will you have a year from now per dollar invested today? Yield to maturity answers that question.

The yield to maturity on a bond is the percentage by which the investor's money grows from the date of purchase to maturity date, expressed at an annual rate. For sake of brevity it is customary to just say "yield." Now in the case of a one year bond it is easy to calculate the yield because we need only take the amount the investor will earn during the year and divide by the price paid for the bond, then multiply times 100 to express the result as a percentage. The formula for yield is written:

$$\text{yield} = \frac{\text{amount gained}}{\text{price}} \cdot 100\%$$

What is the amount that the investor gains during the year? It is the amount received at the end of the year, the face value of $100 plus the

115

coupon, minus the price paid for the bond at the beginning of the year. The formula for the yield on a one year bond may be expressed then as:

$$\text{yield} = \frac{\text{face value} + \text{coupon} - \text{price}}{\text{price}} \bullet 100\%$$

$$= \frac{\$100 + \text{coupon} - \text{price}}{\text{price}} \bullet 100\%$$

For example, the first one year T note listed above pays a coupon of 5 5/8, or $5.625 per year, and the asked price is $101 per $100 of face value. The amount gained is therefore $100 + $5.625 - $101 which equals $4.625. So the yield is

$$\text{yield} = \frac{\$100 + \$5.625 - \$101}{\$101} \bullet 100\%$$

$$= \frac{\$4.625}{\$101} \bullet 100\%$$

$$= 4.58\%$$

For the second bond the ask price is $103:01 or $103.03125 per $100 of face value and the coupon is $7.75 per year, so the yield is

$$\text{yield} = \frac{\$100 + \$7.75 - \$103.03}{\$103.03} \bullet 100\%$$

$$= \frac{\$4.72}{\$103.03} \bullet 100\%$$

$$= 4.58\%$$

Notice that our calculated yields on both bonds disagree slightly with those quoted from the *Wall Street Journal* above. For the first bond our yield is .01%, or 1 "basis point," lower and for the second bond two basis points lower. These small discrepancies are due to technical details that arise from the fact that the annual coupon is actually paid in two installments spaced six months apart.

Notice, too, that the two notes have the same yield (differing slightly according to the *WSJ*), and it would be surprising if they didn't. Why? Two bonds maturing at the same date must have the same yield, because all that matters to investors is how rapidly their money grows. If the two bonds had different yields, nobody would buy the one with the lower yield and its price would fall relative to other bond until the yields were equalized. The fact that there is a very slight difference in the yields on these two notes is again due to technical issues which can account for a difference of a couple of basis points.

The Coupon on a New Bond

Now suppose that the Treasury had wanted to sell new one year notes on December 31, 1998. Recall that it is customary to set the coupon rate on a bond so that it sells at par ($100) when issued. What is the required coupon rate such that the new note will offer investors the same yield as do existing one-year notes? It should be pretty clear that the coupon rate must be equal to the current market yield, but let's use the formula for yield, specifying a price of $100 and then solving for the coupon, to verify this. Inserting the desired price of $100, the yield formula becomes:

$$\text{yield} = \frac{\$100 + \text{coupon} - \$100}{\$100} \bullet 100\%$$

$$= \frac{\text{coupon}}{\$100} \bullet 100\%$$

We now solve for the coupon, given a market yield of 5.61%:

$$\text{coupon} = \frac{\text{yield}}{100\%} \bullet \$100$$

$$= \frac{4.60\%}{100\%} \bullet \$100$$

$$= \$4.60$$

This result says that a bond will sell at par only if its coupon rate is equal to the yield on comparable bonds already observed in the market.

In our example, existing one year notes yield 4.60%, so the Treasury must be prepared to offer a coupon of $4.60 on the new one year note if it is to sell at par. In practice, the coupon rate is rounded to eighths, quarters, or halves. In this case, the coupon would be set at 4 5/8 or 4.625 so the new bond would sell at close to, but slightly above, par.

What does this result tell us about the history of the two one-year T notes in the table? First, neither is a newly issued note since new notes are priced at par. Keep in mind that these two notes may have been issued years ago, but on this date they are effectively one year bonds because they will mature in one year. The coupon rate tells us what the yield was on each note on the day it was issued. Evidently, the second note was issued at a time in the past when interest rates were considerably higher than in 1999, a time when yields were closer to 8% than to 5%. Note that an original buyer would have paid only $100 for a bond now worth about $103.

We have established that the U.S. Treasury would have had to pay an interest rate of about 4.60% if it had wished to borrow money for one year at the end of 1999, because that was the yield on existing one year bonds then. That rate also established a minimum for the interest rates that other borrowers had to pay on that date to borrow for one year.

Exercises 3.4

A. Why is the bid price of an individual bond lower than the asked price? What are some factors that might influence the size of the spread between the bid and asked prices?

B. Why would it be surprising if two Treasury bonds of the same maturity had different yields, say 5% on one and 6% on another?

C. Look again at the one year bonds quoted in the text above. Why do they both sell at above par? Why does one sell for a higher price than the other when they are both guaranteed by the U.S. government? What do you infer has happened to interest rates since they were issued?

D. Find the table of U.S. Treasury bond quotations in a newspaper and identify the one year bonds or notes. Then:

1. Compute the yield on each and compare the results with the "Ask Yield" quoted in the paper.

2. Explain the price differences between these bonds.

3. What would you conclude has happened to interest rates since these bonds were issued? Explain briefly.

4. If the Treasury issued a new one year bond on this date to sell at par, what coupon rate would it have to offer?

3.5 What Happens When Interest Rates Change?

Even if the U.S. Treasury may be depended on to pay its debts, owning T bills, notes, or bonds is not free of risk. This is because future interest rates are uncertain, creating what economists call interest rate risk. This risk takes on two forms.

Fluctuations in interest rates expose holders of long term bonds to "price risk," because the market value of existing bonds depends on the interest rate. Holders of short term bills and notes, on the other had, are exposed to "income risk," because they cannot be sure what interest rate will be available to them when they receive their face value payment and wish to reinvest. Income risk is also referred to as reinvestment risk or rollover risk.

Price Risk

Let's consider first price risk and see how the market value of a bond will fluctuate during its lifetime as the interest rate changes. Imagine that the Treasury did issue new one year notes on December 31, 1998 with a coupon of 4 /58 (to produce a yield of 4.6% at a price close to par). Anyone who bought that note and held it to maturity in December 1999 would indeed earn that 4.6%. But what about an investor who sells it before the maturity date?

For example, what if the one year interest rate had jumped to 5.6%, an increase of one full percentage point, the next business day? Obviously, investors would no longer be willing to pay $100 for a note with a coupon of 4 5/8 if other notes yield well over 6%. Clearly, the note will be worth *less* than the $100, the price it sold for a day earlier.

The new market price is found by solving the yield formula,

119

$$\text{yield} = \frac{\$100 + \text{coupon} - \text{price}}{\text{price}} \bullet 100\%,$$

for the price of the note, given coupon and yield, which gives us

$$\text{price} = \frac{\$100 + \text{coupon}}{1 + \text{yield}/100\%}$$

Given the coupon of 4 5/8 and a new yield of 5.6% for our example, the new market price of the note the next day is:

$$\text{price} = \frac{\$100 + \$4.625}{1 + 5.6\%/100\%}$$
$$= \frac{\$104.625}{1.056} = \$99.08$$

Our buyer has taken a loss of about $1 on the bond. This note that was worth $100 yesterday is worth only about $99 today. Let's try to see intuitively why the market price of the note drops to $99. No one will be willing to buy this note now unless they can earn 5.6% on it, because that is the yield available now on alternative one year bonds. With the price reduced to $99 a buyer would gain almost $1, or about 1% of the price, from appreciation in the value of the note from $99 now to $100 at maturity. In addition, a buyer will collect the coupon of $4.625, roughly another 4.6% on the price paid for the note. This gives a buyer paying $99 today a total return of about 5.6%, and that is the yield available on other bonds of the same maturity.

Looking again at the formula for yield, we can see how yield is always made up of two components, one due to change in the value of the bond from now to maturity, the other due to coupon income:

$$\text{yield} = \frac{\$100 - \text{price}}{\text{price}} \bullet 100\% + \frac{\text{coupon}}{\text{price}} \bullet 100\%$$

In words, yield to maturity equals price appreciation yield plus coupon yield.

By "price appreciation" we mean the increase (or decrease if negative) in value of a bond or note from today until maturity, in this case from $99 today to $100. If this note were not selling at a discount of about $1 from par, producing the additional 1% yield from price appreciation, no one would be willing to purchase it since it is paying a coupon of only $4.625 when the prevailing yield in the market is 5.6%. But the unlucky person who bought the note yesterday at par, suffers a loss of that $1.

From this example we learn that the general principal relating bond prices to interest rates is:

When the interest rate rises, the value of existing bonds falls.

When the interest rate falls, the value of existing bonds rises.

This inverse relationship between bond prices and interest rates comes from the fact that coupon payments from an existing bond are fixed. When competing yields rise, those fixed coupons are worth less. We see then that price risk arises from fluctuations in interest rates: when interest rates rise, bond holders suffer losses, but when interest rates fall, they enjoy price gains.

Income Risk

Let's suppose that instead of buying a note or bond, our investor purchased a security that carries almost no price risk at all, a Treasury bill. The reason that there is very little price risk in buying a T bill is that the bill matures in a very short time. The most popular maturity for T bills is 90 days, about a fourth of a year. Because a T bill's life it so short, it pays no coupon at all. Since the coupon yield is therefore zero, the yield on T bills must be entirely price appreciation yield. It also follows that T bills cannot sell at par, rather they must sell at a discount from par since that discount is the sole source of the investor's yield. For example, if a 90-day T bill trades at $99, then the investor will gain $1, or about 1%, over a period of about one quarter of a year. The yield on T bills is always expressed at an annual rate, so in the case of the 90 day bill we multiply by four, obtaining a yield of about 4% in our example.

We began by claiming that there is hardly any price risk for T bills because they reach maturity so quickly. We saw that if the yield on one year notes rises by 1% that the price drops by about $1. You can easily see that if the yield on 90 day bills rises by 1% then the price falls by only about 25 cents. Indeed, a one-day T bill would have no price risk at all, maturing at full face value that next day, assuming that one day is the shortest period one would wish to invest.

While the buyer of a T bill need not fear variation in price, there is no guarantee of a fixed income stream after the bill matures. Consider a college student who is investing a gift of $1,000 that will be used to pay tuition one year from now. She has no concern that she will need the money sooner. If the student buys a one year T note then she knows exactly how much she will have at the end one year because the coupon and face value payments are known with certainty. On the other hand, if she buys a 90 day T bill she will have to reinvest the face value in 90 days, and the interest rate then may be higher or lower than what it is now. Indeed, if she continues to invest in 90-day bills, she will have to reinvest three times during the year at rates that are not known until reinvestment takes place.

We see then that the buyer of a T bill faces another form of interest rate risk, namely income risk, uncertainty about the income stream that will be earned in the future as the proceeds from maturing bills are reinvested or "rolled over," at whatever interest rate prevails at that time in the future.

A. The U.S. Treasury issues T bills in maturities of 90 and 180 days weekly, and for 360 days less often. If you wanted to buy a 30 bill, are you out of luck, or will you be able to find one?

B. Suppose a one-year T bond with a coupon of $6 is quoted today at $98.

1. What are the coupon yield and the price appreciation yield on this bond?

2. Tomorrow, the one year interest rate changes to 6%. What will be the new price of the one-year T bond in the previous question, and how much has the price changed? Why?

3. What are the coupon yield and price appreciation yield?

C. Look again at the two one-year T notes whose prices and yields are quoted in Section 3.4. Calculate the coupon yield and price appreciation yield on each.

D. On January 30, 1991 the two Treasury notes maturing in one year were quoted as follows.

Rate	Maturity	Bid	Ask	Ask Yld.
11 5/8	Jan92n	104:17	104:19	6.71
8 1/8	Jan92n	101:09	101:11	6.71

1. Calculate the coupon yield and the price appreciation yield for each.

2. What would have happened to the price of each if on the next business day the prevailing yield in the market on one-year T bonds had fallen to 5%?

3.6 The Relationship Between Bond Yield and Price: Some Rules-of-Thumb

The yield to maturity on bonds with maturity greater than one year is more complicated to calculate, but a few basic relationships are easy to see. If the bond sells at par ($100), then the only component of yield is the coupon yield and that is just the coupon rate. For example: a bond maturing in 2030 bearing a coupon of $6 and selling at an asked price of 100 has a yield to maturity of 6%. The maturity date is irrelevant for calculating yield to maturity if the bond is selling at par. If the bond is selling at a discount from par, then there is a positive price appreciation component that will be averaged over the life of the bond. Conversely, a price premium over par will reduce the yield to maturity below the coupon yield since the investor will give up that premium during the remaining life of the bond. Exact computations are complex, and go beyond the scope of an introduction, but some "rules-of-thumb" allow us to make ball-park approximations and can help us understand the relation between yield and price for longer term bonds.

A Rough But Useful Approximation

In April 1996 the "6 of 26" (meaning the Treasury bond maturing in 2026 bearing a coupon of $6 per year) was quoted at $89. This means that the buyer (and any subsequent owners) of this bond were going to receive price appreciation of $11 during its thirty years of remaining life. That price appreciation was going to add roughly 0.4% per year to the yield, since the appreciation averages $.37 per year and .37/89 = .004.

An exact calculation would have to take into account compounding over 30 years, and use mathematics that goes beyond the scope of this book, so this approach is intended only as a rough approximation. The coupon yield on this bond was about 6.7% (6/89 = .067). Thus, according to these rough calculations, the yield to maturity for this bond was about 7.1%, consisting of the coupon yield of 6.7% plus the price appreciation yield of 0.4%. The exact yield to maturity, properly accounting for compound interest over the 30 years, was actually 6.9%. Not a bad error considering the simplicity of our method!

A Consol as an Approximation to a Long Term Bond

Another way to approximate the relationship between the price and yield of a long term bond makes use of the formula for the price of a bond of infinitely long maturity. Such bonds are called consols, and have existed in Britain for a long time but never the U.S. A consol pays the stated coupon forever, never reaching maturity! The price of a consol is given exactly by:

$$\text{consol price} = \frac{\text{coupon}}{\text{yield} / 100\%}$$

For example, if a consol pays a coupon of $6 and the yield is 6.9% then the price is

$$\text{consol price} = \frac{\$6}{.069} = \$89$$

Notice that this very close to the actual price of the thirty year bond with a coupon of $6 when its yield was 6.9% in April 1996. That suggests that the face value payment is far enough in the future so that from a mathematical viewpoint a thirty year bond is a virtual consol. This formula again makes clear the inverse relation between yield and price; when yield goes up, we are dividing the fixed coupon by a larger number and the result must be smaller.

Furthermore, using the formula for the price of a consol and a simple algebraic result discussed in the next chapter, we have the following useful rule-of-thumb:

For long term bonds, the percent change in price is approximately the negative of the percent change in yield, the approximation being more accurate for small changes.

To see how this works, on May 2, 1996 the price of the 30 year T bond fell a horrendous 52 32nds, or $1.625, from 88:22 the prior day to 87:02. That was a one day loss of 1.83% for owners of that bond. On the same day, the yield rose from 6.90% to 7.04%. Is the relationship between the

125

rise in yield and the fall in price consistent with the above approximation? To apply the approximation we need to calculate the percentage change in the yield. What we are after is not the difference between 6.90% and 7.04%, which is 0.14 percentage points, but rather the percentage change between 6.90 and 7.04 which is (7.04-6.90)/6.90 = .0203 or 2.03%. The percentage change in price was very nearly the percentage change in yield, but the opposite sign, as the approximation predicts.

This approximation result helps us understand why long term bonds are subject to greater price risk than are shorter term bonds, notes, or bills. A dramatic example is the 30 year T bond in the example above. That bond had been issued only three months earlier, in February 1996. During that short time, its market value had fallen from $100 (of course it had been issued at par) to only 87:02 or $87.06! The unfortunate buyers had already lost 13% of their investment in just three months! Long-term interest rates had moved sharply higher during that time, from 6% to about 7%. While that is not a large change in yield, only about 1 percentage point, it is a large *percentage* change in yield, (7-6)/6 or about 17%, and we now know that it is the *percentage change* in yield that matters in determining the price change. Note that the rule-of-thumb is not very accurate for changes this large, but does give a useful indication of magnitude. When interest rates rose by 1%, the price of this existing bond had to fall sufficiently to give potential buyers another 1% yield *per year for the next 30 years.* Although shorter term interest rates also moved higher during that three month period, shorter term bonds and notes suffered much smaller losses. Why? Recall that a one year bond need fall only $1 in price to boost the yield by 1%, while 90-day T bills were already reaching maturity at par.

In practice, long term interest rates do not change as rapidly as do short term interest rates, as we shall see in the next section. Nevertheless, actual price fluctuations are greater the longer the term to maturity; greater for bonds than for notes, and greater for notes than for bills. While subject to price risk, a long-term bond does provide safety from income risk, because the stream of income payments are fixed for the life of the bond. This is why bonds are often purchased by people who are saving for retirement, and by pension funds, since they want to be able to count on a stream of income over many years in the future.

One important caveat: the purchasing power of that income stream will depend on future inflation, which cannot be accurately foreseen. But that is another story which we will save for Chapter 4.

Exercises 3.6

A. Find one, 5, and 30 year U.S. Treasury bond quotations in the newspaper and write down coupon, price and yield to maturity for each. Show how the yield can be broken down into coupon yield and price appreciation yield components for each of the three, using the rough rule-of-thumb developed in this section. How well does the formula for the price of a consol account for the prices of the three bonds, given their quoted yields? Can you explain why the consol approximation works better for some maturities than others?

B. Now compare two days' tables of U.S. Treasury bond quotes, noting the price and yield changes from the prior day, or from several days ago. How does the yield change seem to vary with maturity? How does the price change vary with maturity? Use the consol approximation to account for the price change, given the yield change, of one year, 5 year, and 30-year T bonds? Does the success of this seem to be related to the maturity? If so, why?

C. What is the formula for the yield on a consol, given its coupon and price? Use this result to find the yield on a consol paying $5 per year and selling for $50.

3.7 The Behavior of Interest Rates in the U.S. Since 1947

Yields on U.S. Treasury bills and bonds are watched closely by economists, executives, and investors as the benchmarks for all interest rates in the economy.

As explained above, the most popular maturity for T bills is 90 days, so the yield on the "90-day bill" has become the benchmark short term interest rate. Recall that the T bill yield is expressed at an annualized rate, so it is directly comparable to other interest rates.

The T bond with the longest term to maturity is the thirty year T bond and the yield on this "long bond" serves as the benchmark for long term interest rates. The yield on the 90 day T bill and the yield on the 30 year T bond are plotted together in Figure 3.1 for the period 1947-1998.

~~~~~~

Tips on Reading a Chart

The time period covered by the chart in Figure 3.1 is indicated along the bottom, the horizontal or "x" axis. It begins in 1947 and ends with 1998. Each interest rate, expressed in percent per year, is measured on the vertical or "y" axis. Each line in the chart is one kind of interest rate, one variable that we plotting in the chart, and a line is constructed by connecting individual points, one at each calendar quarter. All we see is the line connecting the points, not the points themselves. The line showing the history of the short-term T bill rate, is dashed and light blue in color display, wile the long-term T bond rate is the solid dark blue line. Check your understanding of what the chart shows by reading off some values at different dates. For example, in late 1992 the short-term rate was about 3% and the long-term rate was about 7.5%. While the raw numerical data are quarterly, the chart presents the information in too compressed a form for us to read off individual data points accurately. The usefulness of a chart like this is that it enables us to see patterns of behavior over time, and often that leads us to draw important conclusions. One chart is worth a thousand numbers!

~~~~~~

Figure 3.1: Short Term and Long Term Interest Rates

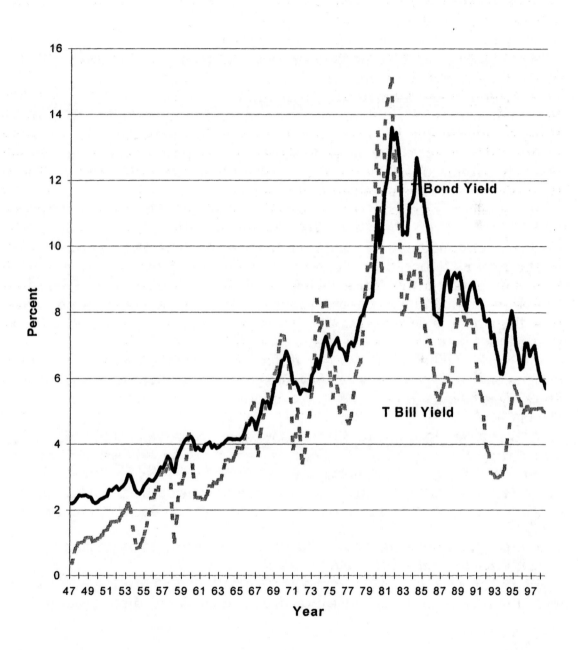

Some Observations from Fig. 3.1

Several important facts about the behavior of interest rates can be seen in Figure 3.1:

1. Long and short-term interest rates are not the same.

They often differ by a percentage point or even more, as we see in the chart. Why aren't the yields on bills and bonds just the same? After all, both promises to make future payments by the U.S. Treasury, so they have the same minimal credit risk. Most fundamentally, they differ because they differ in their time horizons. In one case, the Treasury promises to deliver a stream of dollars over a long time period, and in the other it promises to deliver one payment in the near future. Those promises have different values to investors.

An analogy with commodity futures may be helpful. The "Futures Prices" table in the Wall Street Journal or other financial section shows prices of commodities like wheat and copper for delivery on specific dates in the future. Notice that the price of wheat for delivery next month is very different from the price of wheat for delivery next year. There is a fundamental difference between those two bushels of wheat based on the time the wheat is delivered to the buyer. A bushel of wheat delivered next year cannot be made into bread next month!

Similarly, bills and bonds differ fundamentally in their time dimensions, one a promise to pay income over a short time period, the other over a long time period. We should not be surprised that their yields differ.

Another way to think about why the short term yield differs from the long term yield is that bills and bonds represent very different exposures to interest rate risk; bills being vulnerable to income risk and bonds to price risk. Depending on investors' attitudes towards these risks, we can expect systematic differences between short and long term interest rates.

2. Interest rates have varied greatly since 1947, creating large gains
and losses at different times for bond owners.

From the very low levels seen after World War II, both long and short term interest rates marched upward with occasional dips, reaching an historic peak in 1981 at "double digit" levels. From what we now know about the inverse relationship between bond yields and bond prices, it is clear that most of the period from 1947 to 1981 was one of huge price losses for owners of long term bonds. That was a period when holders of T bills were much better off than holders of bonds. Rolling over their portfolio every 90 days, the owner of bills enjoyed rising income with almost no price risk!

But the period since 1981 has seen a dramatic but not complete reversal of that experience. By 1993 the T bill yield had dropped back below 3%, a level not seen since the early 1960's and one that seasoned market observers had never expected to see again. Holders of short-term securities have been experiencing the downside of income risk during this period. Meanwhile, owners of long-term bonds enjoyed stunning price appreciation as the yield on T bonds fell almost in half. Nevertheless, the long term interest rate today remains above the low levels of the 1960's and before.

3. The long-term rate is usually higher than the short-term rate.

The difference between the long-term rate and the short-term rate is called the spread. The fact that the spread is usually positive (the long term rate is above the short term rate) has been interpreted by economists to mean that, on balance, buyers of long term bonds require additional compensation, called a risk premium or "liquidity premium," to induce them to bear price risk. The spread between T bond and T bill yields is charted below in Figure 3.2 along with the T bill yield. A risk premium is not the only reason why there is a spread, as we see below, but we can take the average spread over time as an estimate of the risk premium. It is about 1% pre year in the form of a higher yield on bonds than on bills.

4. The long-term interest rate varies less and moves more slowly than does the short-term interest rate.

The much greater volatility of short-term interest rates as compared to long-term rates is one of the best-established empirical regularities in the historical record, not only in our economy but across countries, and it is one that has long fascinated economists. It is part of a broader question:

what determines the relationship between short and long term interest rates? We have already mentioned differences in risk, and in the next section we will explore the role of investors' expectations about the future.

Exercises 3.7

A. What were short and long term interest rates at their lowest and highest points during the period covered by Figure 3.1 and when did those points occur?

B. How well did investors in long term bonds do in the decade 1972 to 1982? How well in the decade 1982 to 1992? Finally, how well since 1992? Compare these experiences with those of someone who invested in T bills during those decades.

3.8 The Term-to-Maturity Structure of Interest Rates

Why is the short-term interest rate today one number and the long-term rate another? Why do they tend to move together over time, yet the variability of the long rate is much less than that of the short rate? The key to understanding the term-to-maturity structure of interest rates is in thinking about the choice that an investor faces in the bond market.

The Expectations Theory

An investor in Treasury securities always has the choice between two strategies. The first is to buy a long-term bond with a known yield to maturity and hold it to maturity. The second strategy is to buy a 90-day bill and reinvest the face value every 90 days at the short-term rate that prevails when the old bill matures. Under the second strategy, the investor will earn the average of whatever short term rates turn out to be in the future. This suggests that investors compare the yield on long term bonds with what they *expect* short term yields to *average* over the life of the bond. The fact that an average changes more slowly than the variable being averaged helps explain the slower movement in long-term rates as compared to short-term rates that we saw in Figure 3.1. The idea that long-term interest rates reflect expectations of future short term interest rates is called the expectations theory of the term-to-maturity structure of interest rates.

Thus, the spread between long and short-term interest rates that we observe in the market reflects the decisions made by investors, given their attitudes towards interest rate risk and their expectations about the future direction of interest rates. The average level of the spread reflects a normal risk premium, but when the spread is unusually large it is reflecting the expectation by investors that short term interest rates will rise in the future. When the spread is unusually small or negative, it reflects the expectation that short-term interest rates will fall.

For example, if the T bill yield today is 5% and investors expect that it will remain at that level, then the long term interest rate will be about 6%, consisting of the expected short-term rate of 5% plus the risk premium of 1% included in long-term rates. Alternatively, if investors expect short-term interest rates to rise sharply in coming years, averaging 7%, they certainly would not buy a bond yielding only 6%, but would require a long term yield reflecting that expectation plus a risk premium, or about 8%.

Does the Theory Work?

How can we test the expectations theory? The test of any theory is to derive a prediction from the theory and then see if we find that prediction confirmed or refuted by experiment or experience. The expectations theory implies, that variation in the spread between T bond and T bill rates around its average should help to forecast the direction of the T bill yield, assuming that investors actually have some ability to forecast the direction of interest rates. If the spread is a predictor of the direction of the T bill rate, then that supports the theory. If it is not a predictor, then either the theory is wrong, or investors cannot predict the direction of T bill yields. Unlike chemistry or other laboratory sciences, we cannot do an experiment, but can only rely on historical experience in testing the theory.

In Figure 3.2 we see a chart of the T bill yield and the between the T bond and T bill yields spread (solid black line). Do we see the theory working in practice in this chart? Indeed, we see that:

A negative spread has anticipated major declines in the T bill yield, and a large positive spread has usually anticipated major rises.

The spread was at its most negative in 1981 (the T bond yield below the T bill yield) when interest rates were poised for a major decline. Evidently, investors at that time expected short-term interest rates to return to more normal levels and so were willing to accept a long term yield that was well below the short term yield. Subsequent history has shown that expectation to be correct. But the fact that long term rates have also fallen sharply since 1981 tells us that short term rates have fallen *even faster* than investors anticipated, causing them to revise downward their expectations during the 1980s. Low points in the spread in 1952, 1957, 1959, 1966, 1969, 1973-74, and 1989 also anticipated declines in short term rates.

Figure 3.2: The Yield on U.S. T Bills and the Spread

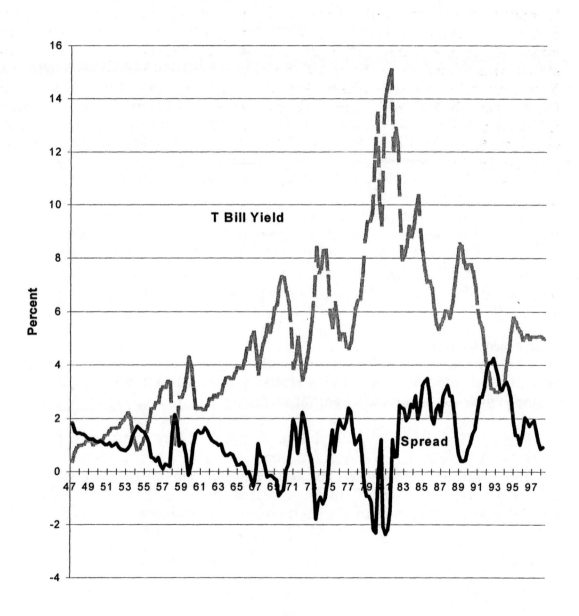

Peaks in the spread in 1954, 1958, 1961, 1967, 1972, and 1977 anticipated major upswings in the T bill yield. But notice that investors failed to predict how sharply rates would decline in the mid 1980s! The spread was positive and large from 1983 through 1987, suggesting that investors expected that interest rates, which had already fallen dramatically, would rebound upward. Rates did not rebound, but continued to fall instead. Investors did call the sharp decline in rates in the early 1990s, but by 1993 the spread was unusually large, telling us that investors did not expect that very low short term rates would persist. To be persuaded to buy a 30 year bond in 1993, investors required a yield 4 percentage points above the yield on T bills! Indeed, short term rates did rebound sharply in 1995. Recently the spread has been around its average of 1%, the normal risk premium. This suggests that in 1998 investors did not anticipate a change in interest rates in one direction or the other.

One last observation from Figure 3.2. Note that the spread has been larger more of the time since 1982 than before. This may be entirely due to continued expectations that interest rates will tend to move upward in the future, but it may also be due to a investors requiring a larger risk premium than they did before they experienced the huge price losses of the 1970s.

The Yield Curve

When we want to make a more detailed study of the term-to-maturity structure of interest rates, a very useful graphical tool is the yield curve, a plot of yield on the y-axis against maturity on the x-axis at one point in time.

Figure 3.3 shows what the yield curve looked like at the end of 1996, 1997, and 1998. The points for year-end 1996 are diamonds, 1997 squares, and 1998 triangles. The data used to construct it are the yields on the 90 day T bill and T notes or bonds of maturities 1, 2, 5, 10, 20, and 30 years. Those points are then connected to make the curve.

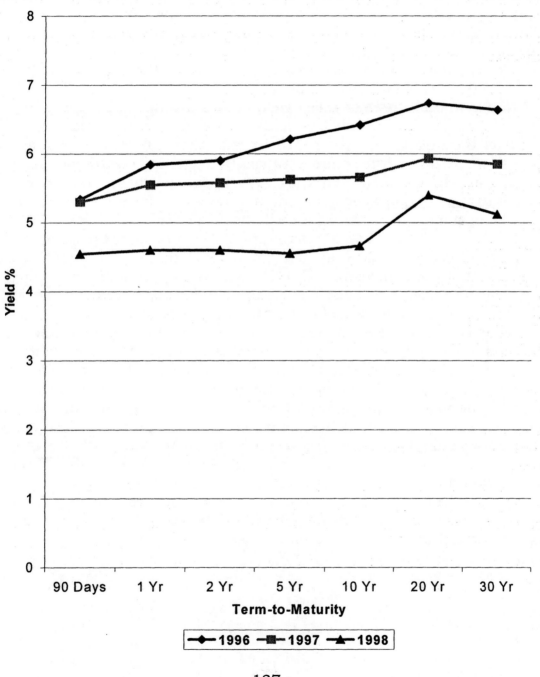

Figure 3.3: The Yield Curve at Year End

While actual bonds do not exist at every point on the curve, the relationship between yield and maturity seems to be smooth enough to give us an estimate of the yield on a bond in the range up to 30 years. Note that the time intervals between the maturities plotted in this chart are not equal.

We can make some observations from these three yield curves that hold pretty consistently over time.

Notice that all three of these yield curves are upward sloping from 90 days to 20 years to maturity. Yields curves are upward sloping during most of the history we have on them, and that reflects the positive risk premium in long-term interest rates. In fact, downward sloping yield curves are so unusual that they are called an "inverted yield curve." When that condition is observed, it is often a harbinger of a downturn in economic activity, for reasons we will discuss later in the book.

Notice too that each yield curve dips at the long end, the 30 year yield being a bit below the 20 year. We can think of that dip as resulting from the fact that those investors who do want to go very long are limited by that fact the Treasury does not issues bonds longer than 30 years, so there is some scarcity value for the very longest bonds.

What is not as clear in these curves is that usually the yield curve flattens out as we look at longer maturities. This is less apparent when the term structure of interest rates is as flat as it has been in recent years. The normal flattening of the yield curve at longer maturities reflects the fact that our expectations of future short term interest rates change less and less as we consider longer times into the future. Investors might have a reason to think interest rates will rise sharply next year, but they simply have no basis for predicting a sharp rise 20 years from now.

The yield curve seen in the bond market yesterday can usually be found in the bond section of a financial newspaper, or can easily be constructed from the data you find there.

Exercises 3.8

A. Pick out several dates from Figure 3.2 when investors apparently expected short term interest rates to fall, and several when they apparently expected them to rise. Were they right? Have there been major moves in short-term interest rates that apparently were *not* anticipated by investors?

B. Evidently, investors do not anticipate all future moves in short-term interest rates. Does that fact constitute evidence against the expectations theory? Does the theory imply that investors can forecast all future changes in short-term rates?

C. Using the bond table from the newspaper, plot the yield curve by free hand, or use graphing software. Connecting the points produces a kinked yield curve. What do you think a complete yield curve, with all maturities plotted, would look like? Sketch this complete yield curve by free hand.

Chapter 4

The Cost of Living and Living With Inflation

Outline

Preview

Jane heard the good news on the first work day of 1999: she was receiving a raise of $4,000. This brought her annual salary to $44,000, up 10% from $40,000 in 1998. Her boss congratulated her on a job well done. Now it is the end of 1999 and Jane is wondering how well she *really* did during the past year and how big that raise *really* was. Jane's salary rose by 10%, but how much did her standard of living change?

The answer depends on what happened to her cost of living during 1999. That is what it cost her to buy the market basket of goods and services that she typically purchases. If her cost of living rose by less than 10%, then the purchasing power of Jane's salary rose and her standard of living improved. But if her cost of living rose by more than 10%, then her standard of living fell in spite of that raise.

In fact, if Jane represents a typical American household her cost of living actually rose by a about 2% during 1999. So the good news is that Jane did get a raise, but the bad news it that it was less than 10%. Inflation occurs when the cost of living rises persistently. Because inflation is a fact of modern life, it is important to understand how the cost of living is measured and how to use that information to adjust salaries and other dollar values in order to see them in terms of their purchasing power. We will also learn how to adjust interest rates to reveal the real rate of interest.

4.1 The Consumer Price Index

It would be too expensive to keep track of the cost of living for every household, so the U.S. Department of Labor's Bureau of Labor Statistics estimates the cost of living for a representative American household. The result is the Consumer Price Index, usually abbreviated CPI.

The CPI is an index because the cost of living is not expressed in dollars but rather as a percentage of what the market basket cost in a base period. An index is a measure of relative magnitude rather than absolute amount and therefore is expressed as a percentage rather than in units of measure like dollars or meters or tons. It makes sense to express the cost of living as an index because what we want to know is whether the cost of living rose, and by what percentage.

The amount spent by an actual household will depend on factors such as family size, income, age, and other characteristics that vary widely from one family to another. A large and affluent family will have a larger and more expensive market basket than a small family of modest income. The mixture of items in the market basket will also vary from family to family according to individual tastes. However there is enough similarity in buying habits and in movements in prices that percentage changes in the CPI give a useful indication of percentage changes in the cost of living for most households.

How the CPI Is Constructed

Here is how the CPI is calculated. The Bureau of Labor Statistics (often abbreviated BLS) has constructed a representative market basket that includes almost all of the items purchased by a typical American family: food, energy, housing, entertainment, travel, medical services, and so forth. The amount of each item in the CPI market basket is based on a study of the actual spending patterns of urban American households during the base period 1982-84. The BLS employs sample shoppers who actually go into stores monthly in cities all over the U.S. and record the prices of items on their list: hamburger @ $2.05/lb., head of lettuce @ $1.10, and so on for thousands of items.

From this mountain of data the BLS calculates the cost of the representative market basket for that month. The CPI for a given month is the cost of the market in that month as a percentage of the cost of the market basket in the base period. It is announced a couple of weeks after the end of the month.

For example, the CPI for June 1999 was 166.2%. The BLS got that number by making the calculation:

CPI for June 1999 =

$$\frac{\text{Cost of Basket in June 1999}}{\text{Cost of Basket in 1982-84}} \cdot 100\%$$

= 166.2%

This means that the market basket of the representative consumer cost 66.2% more in June 1999 than it had in the base period 1982-84.

Economists also use the term price level to refer to the cost of living, so one might read in an article on the business page that "the price level rose more than 66% from 1983 to 1999." The BLS has also reconstructed the value of the CPI for years prior to the base period, so we can also use the CPI to compare the cost of living in 1990 with what it was in 1970.

The base period is updated occasionally to reflect the changing composition of the representative market basket. The quantities of items in the market basket change over time because of changes in tastes, because consumers will respond to changes in relative prices, and because new products are introduced. The previous base period was 1967. The 1982-84 market basket reflects not only changes in buying patterns since 1967 but also added products to the market basket that simply did not exist in 1967. Clearly, the 1982-84 market basket is now out of date; for example, compact disks were not then on the market.

Now let's get back to Jane's salary and the question: did her standard of living increase in 1999? The CPI was 166.2 in June 1999, while it had been 163.0 a year earlier. The cost of living for the typical family therefore rose in percentage terms by:

CPI Percentage Change in 1999 = (166.2-163)/163) = .02 = 2%.

We could have used averages of the CPI for both years, or year-end readings to make this comparison, but there would be little difference in the result. This is the best estimate we have of the increase in Jane's cost of living during 1999.

It is obvious now that Jane's standard of living rose in 1999, because her salary increased faster (10%) than did the cost of living (2.9%).

Biases in the CPI

It is generally acknowledged that the CPI overstates the amount by which the cost of living has risen. One source of bias is that changes in relative prices among goods will induce consumers to alter their spending decisions. For example, if the price of oranges doubles because of a freeze in California, consumers will not buy the same quantity as before, but rather will substitute other fruits like grapefruit from Florida. The ability of consumers to substitute away from goods whose prices rise the most means that their standard of living does not fall as much as the CPI , based on a fixed market basket, implies.

Second, new products are constantly being introduced which tend to be superior to the products they replace. Prices of new product tend to fall as producers realize economies of scale and because these tend to benefit the most from technological change. The market basket of 1982-84 did not include many of the electronic products, such as personal computers, that have seen the rapid price declines.

Third, the CPI does not fully capture the improvements in quality that result from technological advances. Many of these have been dramatic. While the cost of a hospital room per night has risen sharply in recent years, that change overstates the increase in the cost of hospital services. New surgical techniques are often far safer with much more rapid recovery, so the patient stays fewer nights. The BLS does make some adjustments for quality changes, but is unable to fully capture all of them.

The combination of all of these factors is an upward bias in the measured rate of inflation that economists estimate at about one percentage point on an annualized basis. Efforts are already being made to reduce the bias from the latter two sources, and we can expect a new base period to be established in the near future.

A. Construct a market basket for a typical undergraduate. What will be the main differences between it and the market basket for the Jones family of four?

B. If the BLS were to construct a new base-period market basket today, what important changes would you expect to see in it compared to the 1982-84 market basket?

C. The BLS attempts to adjust prices for changes in quality. Give an example of a product whose quality has changed significantly in the last decade. What effect has this change had on the CPI if it has not been adequately recognized by the BLS?

D. At the end of this chapter you will find a table showing supermarket prices advertised in The Seattle Times on January 29, 1948 and the prices of the same items in 1993. Choose quantities of these items to make up a family market basket. Price this basket at 1948 prices and at the 1993 prices provided or your own supermarket survey of prices today. Which items have risen the most in price? Which the least? What is the value for 1993, or now, of this "supermarket price index" using 1948 as the base year?

4.2 Jane's Real Income

To see just how much Jane's standard of living rose in 1999 we use the concept of real income which is the purchasing power of Jane's income. How much more goods and services did Jane's 1999 income buy than her 1998 income?

If the only good in Jane's market basket were coconuts then the purchasing power of Jane's income would simply be the number of coconuts that her income can buy, which is her salary divided by the price of coconuts. In a complex economy with many goods and services we can think of the purchasing power of Jane's income as how many "market baskets" it can buy. Of course we do not know what is in Jane's actual market basket or its exact cost, but we can use the CPI as an index of the cost of a representative market basket.

Calculating Real Income

This suggests that to find out what Jane's real income was in 1999 we divide her salary by the CPI. Taking the mid-year the CPI of 163% for 1998, we divide her 1998 income of $40,000 by 1.63 and we get

Jane's 1998 real income = $40,000/1.63 = $24,540

Making the same calculation for 1999, using the June CPI of 166.2%, we have

Jane's 1999 real income = $44,000/1.662 = $26,474

Notice that we express real income as a dollar amount, but what sort of dollars are they? Certainly they are not the dollars Jane received in 1998 or 1999; the amounts are far smaller. These are dollars that have the purchasing power that a dollar had in the 1982-84 base period. That is because we have *deflated* the dollars she was paid in 1998 and 1999 by the increase in the cost of the market basket since the base period. Such dollars are called constant dollars of the base period. The dollars Jane was actually paid are called current dollars. When economists wish to distinguish clearly between current dollar amounts and constant dollar amounts they refer to current dollar amounts as *nominal*. What we have done here, then, is deflate Jane's nominal income by the CPI to get her real income in constant dollars of 1982-84.

Now we calculate the change in Jane's real income from 1995 to 1996 as follows:

Percentage Change in Real Income = ($26,474-$24,540) •100% = 7.9%
$24,540

We have shown that the net result of her raise and inflation was an increase of 7.9% in real income.

A Useful Approximation

Notice that the 7.9% change in Jane's real income is roughly, but not exactly, the 10% change in her nominal income *minus* the 2% change in the CPI, since 10% - 2% = 8%. This suggests a short cut approximation to calculating rates of change in real amounts, namely

% Change in Real Income *equals*
% Change in Nominal Income *minus* % Change in the CPI

The reason why this approximation works can be seen from the relation between Jane's incomes in nominal and real terms. Her 1999 nominal income can be expressed as:

(1999 nominal income) = (1999 real income) • (1999 CPI/100)

But the 1999 amounts are just the 1998 amounts incremented by the fractional increases that occurred during 1999, so

(1999 nominal income) = (1998 nominal income) • (1.10)

and

(1999 real income) = (1998 real income) • (1.079)

and, finally,

(1999 CPI/100) = (1998 CPI/100)•(1.02).

Using the equivalent amounts to replace the 1999 amounts in the first equation we obtain the following relationship between nominal income, real income, and the CPI:

('98 nominal income)•(1.10) =
[('98 real income)•(1.079)]•[('98 CPI/100)•(1.02)]

Now, divide the left hand side of this equation by 1998 nominal income and the right had side by its equivalent, ('98 real income)•('98 CPI/100), and what we have remaining is 1.10 = (1.079) • (1.02). Notice that (1.079) • (1.02) is

$$(1+.079) • (1+.02) = 1+(.079+.02) + .0016 = 1 + sum + cross\text{-}product$$

Since the cross product of .079 times .02 is very tiny, the sum of .079 plus .02 is very close to the exact answer, .099 verses .10.

This is why the 10% change in nominal income is approximately the *sum* of the 7.9% change in real income and the 2% change in the CPI. Equivalently, the 7.9% change in real income is *approximately* the 10% change in nominal income *minus* the 2% change in the CPI.

This approximation works well only for small changes since only then is the cross-product small, being a small fraction of a small fraction. For very large changes the cross product will not be small (try a 50% change in the CPI along with a 70% change in nominal income!). But the formula is fine for calculating real changes in the low inflation environment found in most countries today if the time period is not too long. It comes in very handy because we all need to compute real changes in many economic variables in our lives besides income, for example the real change in the value of a stock, or the size of the federal budget, or that tuition bill.

Exercises 4.2

A. During summer vacation in 1995 George delivered pizzas for $5.50 an hour. When he went back to see if the job was open for the summer of 1996 his employer told George that because he had done such a great job the previous summer, his hourly wage would go up $.16 an hour if he would come back. What was the percentage change in George's real wage from 1995 to 1996? Show that there are two ways to calculate this change. Should George feel that his employer had paid him a big compliment?

B. The national minimum wage was $3.35 per hour in 1996 and had not changed for several years. Was the minimum wage constant? How much did the minimum wage change in 1996?

C. A portfolio of stocks that cost $10,000 at the beginning of 1993 was worth $11,044 at the end of the year. During that year the CPI rose from 141.9% to 145.8%. Calculate the amount by which the real value of this portfolio changed during 1993 by two methods. Why do you get slightly different answers?

D. Consider the situation where there are three variables, say y, x, and z, and they are linked by the relation y = x • z. Show that for small changes it is approximately true that

$$\text{\% change in y} = \text{\% change in x} + \text{\% change in z}$$

4.3 Inflation: the American Experience

Inflation, we have learned, is a continuing increase in the cost of living which we measure using the Consumer Price Index. When we look at the chart of the CPI since 1948 in Figure 4.1, we see that inflation has been a feature of American life for the past half century. The CPI fell slightly in 1948-49 but has increased steadily since. The CPI is 100 in 1983, the mid-point of the base period, and all changes are relative to that benchmark. Values before that date are reconstructed by the BLS for purposes of historical comparison.

From a level of 25 in 1950 the level of prices has increased almost seven fold to about 165 in 1999. A basket of goods that cost $25 in 1950 was priced at $100 by 1983 and by 1999 the cost had escalated to $165. This tells us that a salary of $16,500 in 1999 was equivalent in purchasing power to a salary of $10,000 in 1983, but it took only $2,500 to have the same purchasing power in 1950. Why has inflation been so severe during the past three decades? That is subject of Chapters 7 through 9.

The rate of inflation is the percentage change in the price index expressed at an annual rate. In Figure 4.2 we chart the inflation rate as the percent change in the CPI from the corresponding month a year earlier.

Figure 4.1: The Consumer Price Index

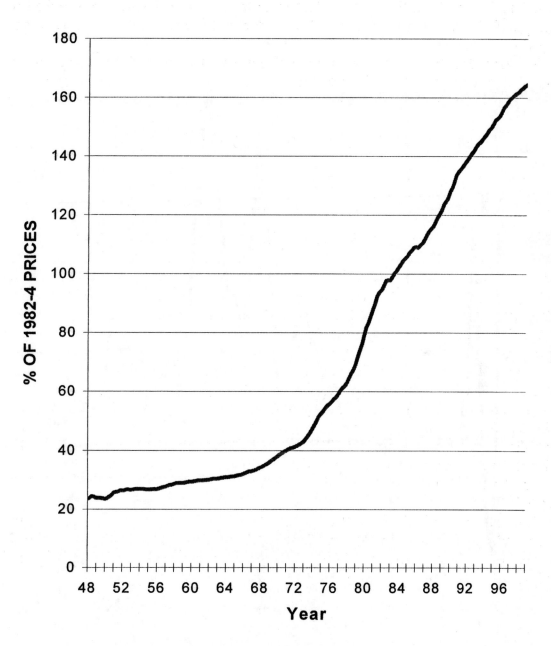

Figure 4.2: The Rate of Inflation

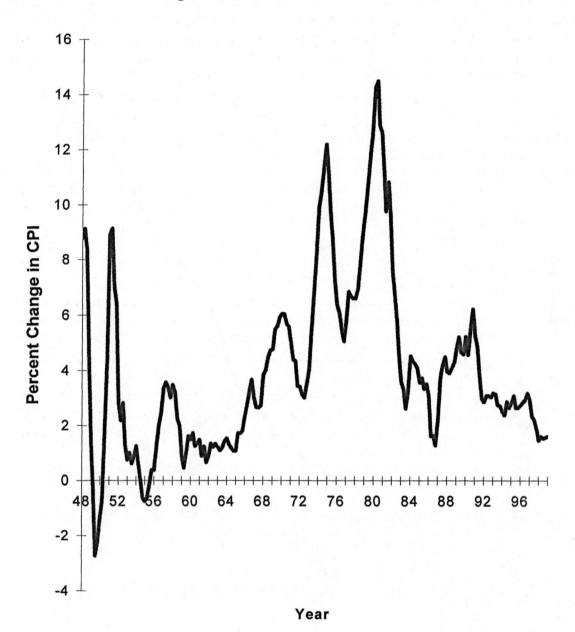

Notice the high inflation rate of 1948 that resulted from the lifting of the wage and price controls of WWII. Another burst of inflation occurs at the beginning of the Korean War when many Americans feared war related shortages. Those did not actually occur and inflation rapidly evaporated. The early 1960s was a period of low very inflation, only about 1%. But then inflation rose in successive waves to a peak of over 14% by 1980. It subsided dramatically in the 1980s and by 1999 was down to only about 2%. How this roller coaster ride occurred, and whether we need be concerned that it may continue in the future, are important questions to keep in mind as we move through the book.

Inflation and Politics

Inflation became a hot political issue during the 1980 election in which President Carter ran for reelection against Ronald Reagan. The surge in inflation during the Carter administration, along with the Iranian hostage crisis, put President Carter in a very vulnerable political position and contributed importantly to his defeat. Evidently, the American public does not like inflation.

The new Reagan administration advocated a vigorous anti-inflation policy which was executed by the Federal Reserve Board under the chairmanship of Paul Volcker. Ironically, Volcker had been appointed by President Carter. We have seen that inflation declined sharply through the mid 1980's but was rebounding by the end of the decade.

A second anti-inflation program was then put into place by Volcker's successor Alan Greenspan. By 1993 inflation had again subsided to levels not seen for three decades, and it has remained at low levels since.

The Purchasing Power of $1

As inflation pushes the cost of living upward, the purchasing power of a dollar, the amount of goods and services it buys, falls. The purchasing power of a dollar in terms of pizzas is 1 divided by the price of a pizza. If pizzas cost $5 in 1980 and $10 in 1990, then the purchasing power of $1 fell from .2 pizzas to .1 pizzas during that decade. Since we do not live by pizzas alone (though some come pretty close), a more meaningful measure of the purchasing power of the dollar would be $1 divided by the price of our whole market basket.

The CPI is not exactly the price of the market basket, but it is an index of the price of the market basket expressed relative to prices in the base period. We can therefore calculate an index of the purchasing power of the dollar as (100/CPI)•100%. This makes sense because the CPI is 100 in the base period, so our index of purchasing power will be 100% in the base period. Otherwise, it gives us the purchasing power of $1 relative to what it was in the base period.

The purchasing power of the dollar is charted in Figure 4.3. Notice that the purchasing power is 100% in 1982-84 which serves as our reference point since it is the base period for the CPI. A dollar in 1950 had over 400% of the purchasing power of a 1982-84 dollar. By 1999 a dollar retained only about 60% of the purchasing power that it had in the 1982-84, and about one seventh of its purchasing power in 1950! Our dollar has been a shrinking yardstick of value over this period, and we must keep this in mind when comparing dollar values between one year and another. For example, how have wages really changed over this period?

Figure 4.3: Purchasing Power of One Dollar

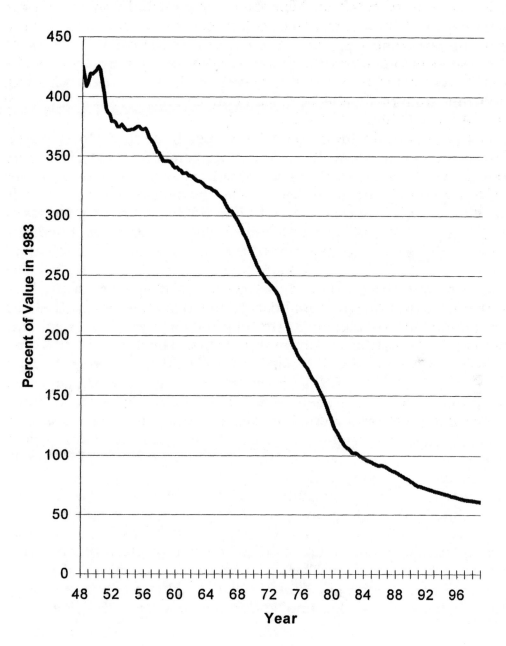

The Real Wage

We know that during the half century the growth in people's real incomes must have been much less that the growth in their nominal incomes since the inflation depicted in these charts has greatly diminished the purchasing power of the dollar being earned. But how do real and nominal incomes really compare? In Figure 4.4 we see charted the average wage of hourly production workers in U.S. manufacturing, both in current dollars (dashed line) and in constant 1982-84 dollars after deflation by the CPI.

The *nominal wage* rose from about $1.37 per hour in 1948 to nearly $14 today, a ten fold increase. While this might have seemed like a very large increase, you now know that the cost of living rose about as much over the same period. Indeed we see in the chart that the real wage is about the same today as it was in the 1960s, having reached a modestly higher level in the 1970s. Clearly, hourly factory workers have not participated in the general prosperity of the U.S. during the 1980s and 1990s.

One factor behind the erosion of the manufacturing wage in the U.S. has been the increased international competitiveness of markets that the U.S. once dominated. For example, the market for structural steel was dominated until the 1960s by large U.S. firms. The fact that they all employed workers belonging to a single unified labor union put those workers in a strong bargaining position in wage negotiations. As European economies rebuilt their steel industries and as developing countries became steel producers, the world market for structural steel became very competitive. Today, an office building in St. Louis might contain steel from any of many countries, such as Korea, Japan, Brazil, and India who are all major producers.

Another, perhaps more important, factor in the decline in the real wage is the shift in technology away from the use of manual labor and toward the use of more educated workers in manufacturing processes. The ability to work with computers is often more important on the shop floor than is physical strength. The gap between the earnings of college educated workers and hourly workers with less education has widened dramatically in recent decades and continues to widen. The flexibility that technology brings to manufacturing, with its ability to substitute microprocessors for humans in repetitive tasks, suggests that the bargaining position of organized labor will remain much weaker than it was in early years of this period.

It is important to understand that nothing about adjusting wages for inflation implies that real wages have stagnated *because* of inflation. Rather what we have learned is that only by adjusting for inflation can we see changes over time in the actual standard of living, and that is what really matters to people.

Figure 4.4: Hourly Wage in Manufacturing
Nominal and Real

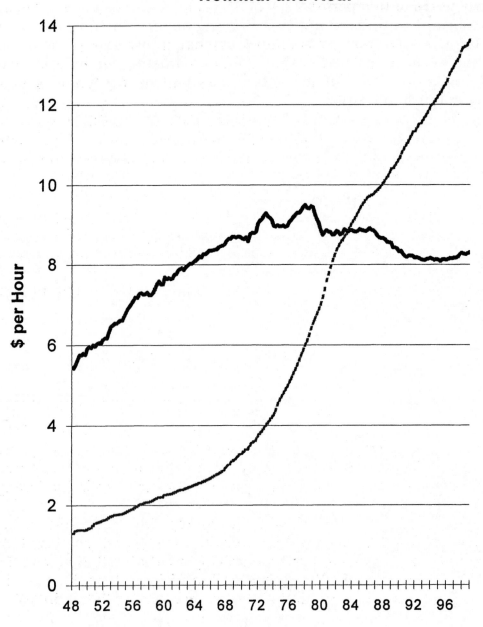

A. Using Figure 4.1 and a ruler, read off and write down the value of the CPI in 1968 and 1988. Obviously your readings from the chart will be very approximate. What was the percentage change in the cost of living over that 20 year period?

B. In 1988 the Boeing 747 was 20 years old. The first ones had cost $18.5 million in 1968, and by 1988 the latest model, which carried more passengers twice as far, was priced at $125 million. (1) What was the percentage increase in the nominal price of a 747 over the 20 years? (2) Now express the two prices in 1982-84 dollars. (3) What was the percentage increase in the real price of a 747 over the 20 years? (4) Why might this be an over estimate of the increase in the real price in view of the evolution of the 747 during its lifetime?

C. Heard at the dinner table: "I can't believe how expensive things are these days. I can remember filling up my gas tank when I was in high school in the early 1960s for 32 cents a gallon. Today I paid $1.51! On top of that, I can remember that then three hamburgers, fries, and a small cola cost $.71 at a drive in, and yesterday I paid $3.48!"

Can you set dad straight on how much the *real* cost of gas and drive-in food have changed in the last thirty years?

4.4 The Inflation Game: Who Are the Winners and Who Are the Losers?

Imagine that you belong to a union that has just negotiated a wage contract with your employer that entitles you to a 6% raise in each of the next three years. The way you will feel about this settlement three years down the road will depend very much on what the inflation rate turns out to be. You are playing the inflation game and your wage is the lottery ticket!

When the contract was signed everybody involved had some expectation of what inflation would be over the three years. Let's say that the union and the employer pretty much agree that inflation can be expected to average around 4%, so they both anticipate that the wage in real terms will be going up about 2% per year. But what if inflation speeds up to 6% unexpectedly? Then the real wage will not rise at all; the union and you are losers and the employer is the winner. If it jumps to above 6% you will actually suffer a reduction in buying power. On the other hand, if inflation slows down to 1% your wage will increase at a sprightly 5% per year in real terms and you and your fellow employees will be winners at the expense of your employer.

Inflation creates winners and losers whenever people make contractual agreements in dollars and inflation turns out to be different than what someone expected. If we knew what the inflation rate was going to be for certain over the next three years then your union and employer could simply agree on the increase in the real wage, which is what matters to both sides, and then just add on the rate of inflation that they know will happen. Unfortunately, inflation is subject to unexpected changes and it is obvious from Figure 4.2 that no one could have anticipated the extent to which it accelerated in the 1970s and how quickly it would subside in the 1980s. Inflation certainly created a lot of winners and a lot of losers in those decades.

The 1970s Inflation Game

Who were the big winners of the 1970's? They were people who had agreed to pay a certain amount of dollars in the future, for example the couple who borrowed $18,000 in 1971 to buy a $20,000 house. That probably seemed like a large mortgage in 1971, but as the rapid inflation of the 1970s eroded the value of those dollars the mortgage payments got smaller and smaller in real terms. While the homeowners' income grew along with inflation, the monthly mortgage payments remained the same for the life of the mortgage, often 30 years.

Meanwhile, the market value of the house tended to rise with inflation, so the homeowners' equity in the house, its value less the mortgage owed, grew rapidly. People who borrowed to buy real estate in the 1970s were big winners in the inflation game.

For every winner in the inflation game there is a loser. One of the losers in the 1970s was the lender of that $18,000 which was probably a savings and loan. S&Ls are much like banks, they are financial intermediaries that take in deposits from savers and make loans. Until recent years they specialized in mortgage lending. It is not surprising that many S&Ls were bankrupted by the inflation of the 1970s since the mortgage payments they received turned out to be much less valuable than they had expected.

Lenders in general were losers in the 1970s. The teenager who had received a US savings bond from her grandmother in 1970 became a lender to the US Treasury. The value of that bond was far less at maturity in 1980 than grandma ever imagined. The winner in that instance was the US Treasury which found the bond much cheaper to pay off than it had expected when it issued the bond. Owners of bonds were losers, whether the bonds were issued by the Treasury, by local government, or by private firms, because those bonds had promised only to pay a fixed amount of dollars in the future regardless of inflation.

Retirees on fixed pensions were big losers in the inflation game in the 1970s and the winner was their former employer whose burden of meeting pension obligations became ever lighter as those pension payments became cheaper in real terms. The sad plight of the elderly suffering erosion of their living standard helped to push Congress to change the Social Security system to provide for automatic adjustment of monthly benefit payments once a year by the amount of the increase in the CPI. This has greatly reduced the exposure of the elderly to the whims of the inflation game. So why not build inflation adjustments into other kinds of contracts and laws?

Protecting Yourself Against Inflation

The adjustment of Social Security benefits payments for the increase in the CPI is one example of indexation. As inflation became more rapid and more unpredictable in the last twenty years people looked for ways to isolate themselves from its effects, to find a way to avoid playing the inflation lottery.

Wage contracts more commonly today include a cost of living adjustment, or COLA for short, that is based on the CPI. Long-term leases on commercial property, for example a retail store sight, often provide for an annual adjustment of the rental based on the CPI. Mortgages increasingly carry an adjustable monthly payment with the amount changing annually according to current interest rates that, as we will see, reflect the current inflation rate.

Exercises 4.4

A: Looking again at the wage contact example at the beginning of this section, what do you think the settlement would have been if inflation were generally expected to average 10% for the next three years? How would you suggest the two parties rewrite their agreement using a COLA?

B. You are a lawyer and a client is rewriting her will. She wants to be sure that an elderly aunt will receive $10,000 per year for life in the event of your client's demise. How would you suggest that your client make this bequest so as to achieve its objective, the care of her aunt?

C. Suppose that as a result of taking this course you became convinced that inflation was going to be much more rapid in the 1990s than most people expect. How would you position yourself to benefit from your hopefully superior foresight?

D. Suppose instead that you saw that inflation was going to be very low in the 1990s, that in fact prices might be falling. How would you position yourself to benefit from a *deflation* that will come as a surprise to others?

4.5 Real and Nominal Interest Rates

You will recall that in Chapter 3 we looked at quotes on Treasury bonds, notes and bills of various terms to maturities and learned that the yield is the interest rate for that maturity. For example, if the one-year T bond has a yield of 5% today, then for every $100 you invest in one-year T bonds you will earn $5 in interest over the next year. Your $100 will grow to $105.

But how much will you *really* earn on your investment? Just as in the case of a raise in salary, it depends on how rapidly the cost of living rises during that year. If the CPI increases by 5%, then your $105 will have no more buying power when the bond matures than your $100 did a year earlier. In that case you clearly earn nothing in terms of purchasing power. But if the CPI rises by only 3%, then your investment grows faster than inflation, resulting in a gain in purchasing power.

How much of a gain? To see how much, we convert both your original investment of $100 and the $105 you will receive a year later into constant dollars, and then calculate the change in the real quantities.

Calculating the Real Rate

Suppose that the CPI today is 165 and one year from now it will be 170, so the inflation rate for that 12 month period is 3%. In terms of constant 1982-84 dollars you invest $100/1.65 or $60.61 today, and you receive $105/1.7 or $61.76 in a year, a gain of 1.9%.

Notice that this percentage gain is approximately the nominal rate of 5% minus the inflation rate of 3%. That is not a coincidence but just another application of the general formula we developed in Section 4.2: the % change in a real quantity is approximately the difference between the % change in the nominal quantity and the % change in the CPI. Using this short cut to calculating the real gain on the bond we would get 5% - 3% = 2% which is close to the exact result of 1.9%.

It is natural to call the quoted bond yield or interest rate the nominal interest rate and to call the difference between the nominal interest rate and the inflation rate the real interest rate. Putting the definition in the form of an equation we have

The Real Interest Rate *equals*
The Nominal Interest Rate *minus* The Rate of Inflation

Ex Ante & Ex Post Real Interest Rates

Of course, someone who purchases a one year bond today does not know what the inflation rate will turn out to be during the year. It is only after the fact, a year later, that we can say that the real interest rate turned out to be 2% or whatever is implied by how much the CPI grew. However, the buyer of a bond starts out with some *expectation* of what inflation will be during the period until the bond matures. If your expectation is that the CPI will rise by 2%, then your expected real interest rate is 5%-2%=3%. The expected real rate is also called the ex ante real interest rate, where *ex ante* means "from before." When the rate of inflation turns out to be 3%, more than you had expected, then the realized real interest rate is only 5%-3% = 2% which is less than you expected. The realized real rate is also called the ex post real interest rate, where ex post means "from after."

This illustrates the fact that when you own a bond or issue a bond you become a player in the inflation game. If inflation is worse than expected, bond issuers win and bond owners lose, but if inflation is lower than expected, it is the bond issuers who lose and the bond owners who win. Recall that inflation surged in the 1970s and subsided in the 1980s. Since few people anticipated these sharp swings in inflation, the 1970s were years when bond owners realized lower real interest rates than they had expected, while the 1980s were years when they realized higher real interest rates than they had expected. It will almost always be true that the ex post real interest rate will differ from its ex ante counterpart, since inflation will almost never turn out exactly as we expect.

It is easy to calculate the ex post real interest rate, a year later after the fact. But how can we tell what the ex ante real interest rate is today? We can observe the nominal interest rate today by looking at bond yields, but where do we find the expected inflation rate? Expectations of inflation vary across individuals and could only be discovered by conducting a survey of investors. Of course, each of us can determine our own expectation of inflation and our own ex ante real interest rate, but it would be interesting to measure these for the economy. One solution is to use recent inflation, say the rate of inflation over the past year, as a proxy for expected inflation on the assumption that many people will look at the recent past as a guide to the near future.

In Figure 4.5 the T bill yield minus the rate of inflation over the prior year is plotted as a measure of the expected or *ex ante* short term real interest rate.

The T bill rate minus the actual inflation rate over the three month life of the bill is the realized or *ex post* real short term interest rate and that is plotted in Figure 4.6.

Figure 4.5: The Ex Ante Real T Bill Rate

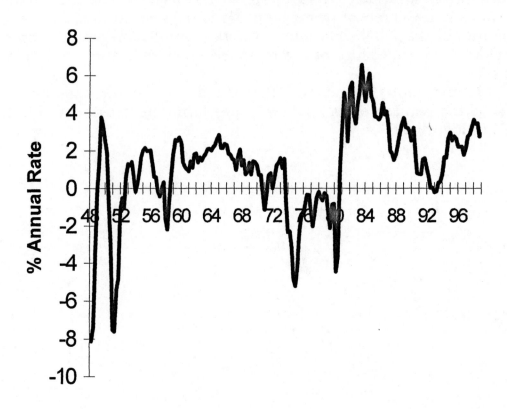

Figure 4.6: The Ex Post Real T Bill Rate

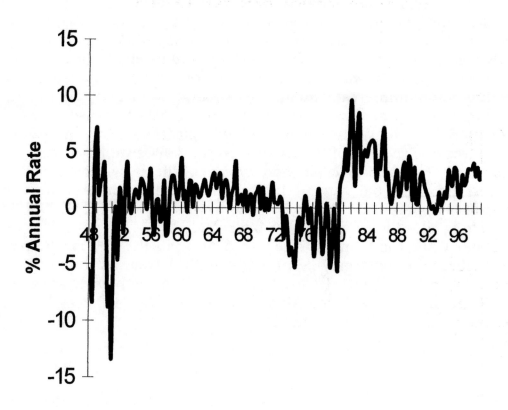

We see in comparing Figures 4.5 and 4.6 that the realized rate fluctuates more than the expected rate, but the two show a similar pattern over long periods. After the wild swings of the immediate post-WWII period, the short term real rate of interest was fairly steady during the 1960s, averaging a bit under 2% (at an annual rate). In contrast, the mid 1970s through 1980 was a period of very low and even negative real rates, so the nominal interest rate on bills was not sufficient to make up for the rapid inflation of that period. Then in the 1980s we see a third distinct period in which real rates were sharply higher but gradually diminished towards the end of the decade. In the 1990s we have seen the real interest rate rebound to levels more typical of the early period.

The fact that the real rate of interest is quite different from the nominal rate is apparent in Figure 4.7 where we see plotted the nominal T bill rate along with the ex ante real T bill rate.

Notice that while the nominal rate was soaring in the 1970s, the real rate was declining and actually becoming negative! Then as the nominal rate fell sharply in the 1980s, the real rate moved to the highest levels in recent U.S. experience. With inflation more stable the last decade, the two rates have largely moved together.

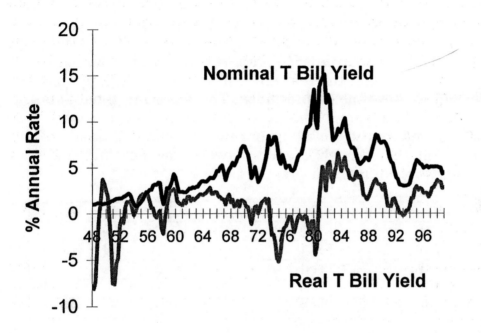

Figure 4.7: Nominal and Real T Bill Rates

Indexed Bonds – Real Interest Rates in the Marketplace

An exciting development of the last few years is the issuance of indexed bonds the U.S. Treasury. The bonds pay a coupon and face value that is adjusted fully by the change in the CPI, so these are payments in real terms, in constant dollars. The yield on these bonds is a real interest rate. Unlike the ex ante real interest rate on a nominal bond, which is only an expectation, the real interest rate on an indexed bond is known for certain at the time of purchase. The following table lists the the indexed T bonds that were available at mid-1999, their maturity year and real yield, as well as the yields on ordinary nominal T bonds of the same maturity, and then the difference between the nominal and real yield which is the implied inflation premium:

Maturity Year	Yield (real)	Nominal Bond	Expected Inflation
2002	3.7	5.2	1.5
2007	3.9	5.4	1.5
2008	3.9	5.4	1.5
2009	3.9	5.6	1.7
2028	3.9	5.8	1.9
2029	3.9	5.7	1.8

Notice that the real yield is quite high relative to the historical real yield on T bills, suggesting that real interest rates in 1999 were relatively high. When we subtract these real yields from the nominal bond yields of the same maturity we get the implied value of expected inflation, the inflation premium that is contained in the nominal rate. Finally, we get to observe expected inflation at the level of the market directly! What is surprising to many economists is how low the expected inflation rate really is, a mere one and a half percent, even when the market looks out over the next three decades. Evidently, the market expects the very low inflation rates of recent years to persist indefinitely (and supporting our assumption above that recent inflation is a reasonable proxy for expected inflation). These are not simply opinions collected in a survey, these are numbers you can bet money on! If you think inflation is likely to be much greater than the 1.5% or so that is implied by the indexed bond yield, you can act on that opinion by purchasing the real rather than the nominal bond. This is a particularly important calculation for managers of pension portfolios which are large purchasers of bonds and where the risk of inflation is an important consideration.

How is the real rate of interest determined?

The real rate is what lenders earn and what borrowers pay in real, purchasing power terms. If you think about it for a minute, it is real interest rates and not nominal interest rates that really matter to these economic agents, just as real and not nominal salaries are what really matter to both employees and employers.

It may be helpful in this discussion to think of bond buyers as suppliers of "loanable funds" to the bond market and issuers of bonds as "purchasers" of those loans. The supply of loanable funds will depend in part on the real rate. The higher the real rate the greater will be the supply of savings from U.S. households and from the rest-of-the-world (ROW) flowing into the bond market.

The demand for loanable funds by issuers of bonds - firms undertaking capital spending projects, households building houses, and governments financing deficits - will also depend on the real interest rate. The lower the real rate the greater will be their demand for loanable funds. The prevailing real interest rate will be the one that equates the supply of loanable funds in the bond market with the demand for funds.

A shift in the demand for loanable funds will cause the real interest rate to change. For example, if the federal government spends more than it receives in taxes, then the U.S. Treasury is obliged to go to the bond market as a purchaser of loanable funds. Many economists see the high level of the real interest rate through the 1980s as the result of the large and persistent federal budget deficit of that decade.

When the Treasury started borrowing about $200 billion per year in the early 1980s, the real rate had to rise to induce savers, primarily households and the ROW, to buy more bonds, that is, supply more loanable funds.

Some observers expect the aging baby boomers who were the yuppies of the 1980s to become the middle aged big savers of the 1990s as they contemplate college expenses and retirement. This would increase the supply of loanable funds to the bond market in the decade ahead, thereby tending to push real interest rates down.

Exercises 4.5

A. Based on Figures 4.5 and 4.6, make an estimate of the average real rate on T bills over the past three decades. If your crystal ball told you that the rate of inflation is going to average 4% over the next ten years, what then would be your forecast of the average T bill yield over the same period?

B. Interest income is subject to federal income tax in the US. Suppose your tax rate is 33% and T bills are yielding 6%. Further, assume that the inflation rate is 5%. Calculate the following to the nearest whole percentage point:
1) Nominal yield on T bills.
2) After-tax nominal yield.
3) Before-tax real yield.
4) After-tax real yield.
5) After-tax real yield on a $100 bill.
6) Opportunity cost of holding that $100 bill for one year.

C. Now suppose that the T bill yield increases to 9% and the inflation rate increases to 8%. Recalculate the answers to items (1) through (6) above. Why does an increase in inflation reduce the real after-tax yield on T bills even though the increase in inflation is matched by the increase in the nominal interest rate? In general, what happens to real after-tax yields as the rate of inflation rises, taking into account that nominal interest rates tend to rise with inflation? How could the tax law be changed to eliminate this effect of inflation?

D. Find the indexed bonds section of the Treasury Bonds table in the Wall Street Journal and compare those yields with the yields on the ordinary bonds of roughly corresponding maturities. What are the implied expected rates of inflation? How does expected inflation compare with recent actual inflation. Do you think this expected inflation is realistic or optimistic or pessimistic? Which type of bond would you buy for a pension fund client, and how would you justify that judgement?

4.6 The Fisher Hypothesis: Inflation and Interest Rates Go Together

Recall our observation from Figure 4.7 that the real interest rate does not fluctuate as much as the nominal interest rate. Given that the difference between the two is inflation, that observation would seem to imply that much of the fluctuation in the nominal rate corresponds to fluctuation in inflation. The fact that the nominal interest rate and inflation do move together is strikingly apparent in Figure 4.8 where the T bill yield and the CPI inflation rate are plotted together. This phenomenon is not peculiar to the U.S. or to recent experience. The strong correlation between nominal interest rates and inflation is one of the most firmly established empirical regularities in economics and one that has been documented over long periods of history and across many countries.

This relationship between interest rates and inflation was first noticed by the American economist Irving Fisher who in the early decades of this century articulated the theory of interest rates as we know it today. What Fisher discovered is that the real interest rate is relatively stable, and that large changes in the rate of inflation will be reflected primarily in corresponding changes in the nominal interest rate.

The idea that variations in nominal interest rates across time and across countries are largely due to differences in inflation is known as the Fisher Hypothesis.

Figure 4.8: The T Bill Rate and Inflation

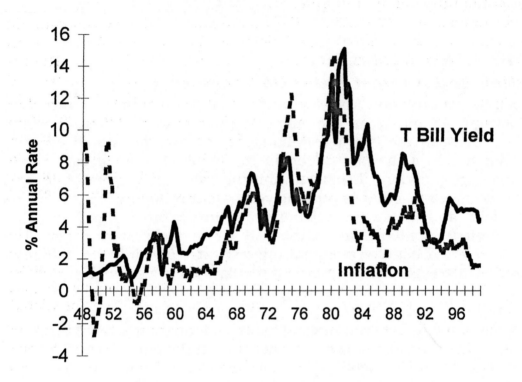

The relative stability of the real interest rate goes along with the idea, discussed above, that the real rate will be determined in the market for loanable funds where savers come together with borrowers. Recall that what matters to both lenders and borrowers is the real interest rate; they will be indifferent to a rise in the nominal rate if it only reflects a difference in inflation rates. While changes in the supply and demand for loanable funds will cause some change in the real interest rate, the main sources of savings (households saving for retirement) and borrowing (government deficits, firms building factories) are relatively stable.

174

Further, the balance between supply and demand will not be sensitive to a change in the inflation rate as long as it is reflected in a corresponding change in the nominal interest rate.

For example, suppose that with inflation at a rate of 5% and an interest rate of 7% the supply and demand for loanable funds are in balance. Evidently, a real rate of 2% is agreeable to both sides. Then it becomes apparent that inflation has sped up to 10%. Both borrowers and lenders can agree that a jump in the nominal rate to 12% leaves them in the same position they were before, since inflation has no large direct effect on either saving or borrowing. Households are still saving for retirement, the government still has a budget deficit. Doesn't it make sense that the primary effect of a change in the inflation rate will just be a corresponding change in the nominal interest rate that leaves the real rate the same?

Does the Fisher Hypothesis explain the interest rates we see in the world today? Indeed it does. Figure 4.9 is a "x-y scatter plot" of points representing the short term interest rate and the inflation rate in each of nine industrial countries. Similarly, Figure 4.10 is the same scatter plot for eight developing countries. The line in each is the predicted relationship between these variables based on the Fisher Hypothesis and assuming a real interest rate of 2%. Specifically, it is the plot of the function:

Interest Rate = Inflation Rate+2%

Although developing countries have much higher inflation rates than industrial ones, a range in all from negative inflation (deflation) to another with inflation above 100%, the Fisher Hypothesis does a remarkable job of explaining nominal interest rates.

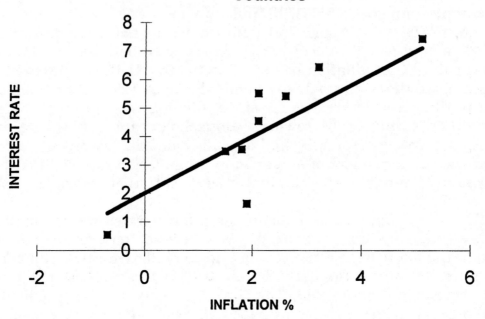

Figure 4.9: The Fisher Relation Across Industrial Countries

Figure 4.10: The Fisher Relation in Developing Countries

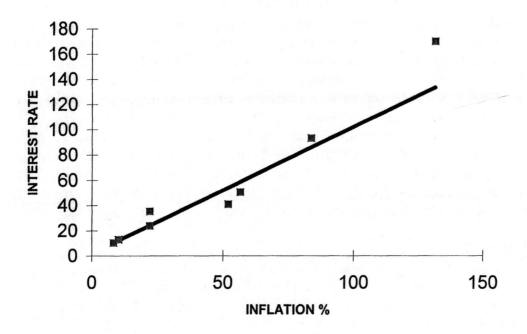

Why doesn't the Fisher equation fit the data exactly? One reason is that the real interest rate is not the same in all countries, it is just less variable than is inflation.

Second, the Fisher Hypothesis is a statement about ex ante real interest rates; the theory discusses agents' expectations of what inflation will be. As in Figure 4.6, we are using past inflation as a proxy for agents' expectations, but it is an imperfect proxy. It also seems likely that it will not be a very good proxy in a country experiencing very rapid and variable inflation, such as Russia which is the highest point in figure 4.10, where economic agents may expect changes to occur due to political developments. Recall that the T bill yield did not track inflation in the U.S. very well in the period between WWII and the Korean War, and that is another situation where recent inflation, reflecting the ending of price controls and fear of new controls, did not capture expectations.

Exercises 4.6

A. You get off the plane in a country you know little about, and you notice that banks are advertising that they will pay 25% per year for savings deposits. Language is no problem, interest rates are universal! What is a reasonable estimate of the local inflation rate? How likely is it that the inflation rate is 5%?

B. Now you make the next leg of your trip and disembark in Zurich, Switzerland. You have read that inflation is unheard of in that country, noted for its sound banks. What range of interest rates do you expect to see advertised there? How likely is it that banks will be offering to pay 25% to savers?

C. What is your relative level of confidence about the two predictions you have just made? Explain any difference.

D. Turkey is a country that has experienced rapid inflation during the 1990s, about 100% per year. What do you suppose is the level of interest rates there, approximately? Now we hope that Turkey can somehow get this inflation under control. If it does so, and we were to check back several years later after inflation had settled down to 5%, what would expect to find had happened to interest rates there?

APPENDIX

Prices from supermarket ads in THE SEATTLE TIMES, Jan. 29, 1948 and comparable prices in 1993.

Item	price in 1948	unit	price in 1993
Roasting chickens	.55	lb	1.39
Bacon	.82	lb	2.99
Beef rib roast	.65	lb	4.99
Swift's Premium ham	.65	lb	3.33
Peanut butter	.53	25 oz.	3.79
Palmolive soap	.15	bath size	.80
Clorox bleach	.27	half gal.	1.29
Libby beef hash	.32	can	1.69
Grapefruit juice	.20	46 oz can	2.59
Wesson oil	.90	qt	2.32
Canned salmon	.47	1 lb. can	3.46
Grapefruit	.07	lb	.79
Oranges	.07	lb	1.69
Lettuce	.10	lb	.67
Avocados	.13	per	.79
Apples, Rome beauty	.08	lb	1.29
Fisher's flour	2.29	25 lb	7.89
Hill's coffee	.50	lb	2.62
Eggs, AA large	.59	dozen	.65
Baby Ruth	.04	bar	.45
Milk, whole	.19	qt	.95
Camels	.16	pack	2.39
Rainier beer	2.89	case (24)	13.98

Subject of personal advice column: "Elderly Men Regret Divorcing First Wife'" by Dorothy Dix.

Index to Chapter 4

Chapter 5

Growth and Recession in the U.S. Economy

Outline
_____

Preview

Index
_____

Preview

In this chapter we will learn why GDP has become one of the most familiar acronyms in the news. In what has become a familiar distinction, we will find that there are both real and nominal measures of GDP. Tracking GDP over time, we see that the economy experiences long periods of growth, interspersed with periods of decline or "recession." Important economic indicators related to the "business cycle" are unemployment, inflation, interest rates, corporate profits, and stock market prices. We will examine the relation of each of these to fluctuations in the economy.

5.1 A Scorecard for the Economy

A few weeks after the end of each calendar quarter the U.S. Department of Commerce announces its estimate of Gross Domestic Product, GDP for short. That evening the national news will include an item like "GDP increased at a rate of 3% in the second quarter." The wide coverage that announcement receives in the media makes GDP as well known an acronym as "NFL." Why is all this attention given to GDP? Because, as the TV news anchor-person says, "GDP is the government's primary indicator for tracking the performance of the US economy." Americans love to keep score and GDP is the closest thing we have to a scorecard for national economic success. It is the broadest possible indicator of economic activity simply because, as we learned in Chapter 2, it is the value of *all* the goods and services produced in the U.S. Since the announced GDP has been adjusted for inflation, 3% in this example reflects a *real* increase in economic activity. When GDP is rising briskly, incumbent politicians smile. But if GDP declines, shock waves reverberate though Washington DC because the electorate will be looking to make changes in the halls of Congress and even the Oval Office.

Does GDP deserve so much attention? While it is the single most important indicator of economic conditions, it is not the only one. The Federal Reserve Board's Index of Industrial Production as well as retail sales, personal income, and several other broad indicators are recorded monthly and therefore much more current than is quarterly GDP. Further, the announced GDP number is necessarily a preliminary statistical estimate, since the economy far too complex for a complete accounting to be done. That estimate is revised in succeeding months, even years later, as more data become available, and those revisions often are large enough to change perceptions about the health of the economy.

We also know that GDP is not the *only* factor in determining our standard of living. The fact that GDP rose last year does not *necessarily* mean that the quality of life improved, or that income was distributed more justly, or that everyone was happier.

But it is also true that most of us would prefer to see GDP growing rapidly rather than slowly, because the capacity of society to provide a better standard of living for all is greater if growth is robust. And a falling GDP is almost certainly a sign that the standard of living is falling. Indeed, a severe decline in economic activity is usually accompanied also by social decay and political instability, as in Russia today.

Nominal GDP

We know that if we want to measure real growth in the economy, we will have to adjust GDP for the effect of inflation. But let's start by taking a look at how GDP measured in current dollars, that is nominal GDP, has grown over time.

Figure 5.1 shows nominal GDP plotted quarterly since 1948. Recall that World War II ended in 1945, so by 1948 the U.S. economy had largely adjusted from a war-time footing to a peace-time one. It is astonishing to see how much nominal GDP has increased, from about $250 billion in 1948 to almost $9,000 billion today! Surely the latter figure would have been unimaginable to people in 1948. Actually, it is even hard for us today to comprehend an economy producing $9,000 billion worth of goods and services in a year. That is $36 billion per work-day! Does it seem possible that in fifty years GDP will be almost 40 times that? It will be if the next half-century is like the last. Notice, too, that nominal GDP almost always goes up, there being only a few brief pauses along the way. Of course nominal GDP has been propelled upward both by growth in output, the quantity of items produced, and by rising prices.

Although GDP is measured for each calendar quarter, it is always expressed at an annual rate. That annual rate is what GDP would total if the economy kept up the pace of that quarter for a full year. For example, the current dollar GDP for the fourth quarter of 1995 is estimated to have been $7,350.6 billion. The actual amount produced during the quarter was one fourth of $7,350.6 billion, but that would be the annual total if the economy kept up the same pace for a full year. It is just like saying "we drove 60 miles per hour during the last quarter hour" when you covered 15 miles in 15 minutes.

GDP is also adjusted for the seasonal variation that occurs regularly and predictably. During the autumn quarter of every year the economy experiences higher levels of production than the winter quarter that follows it. This is partly due to agricultural activity being hectic during the harvest in fall but relatively dormant during the winter. More important quantitatively is the run-up to the holiday season during which a disproportionate amount of retail trade occurs. This seasonal pattern is apparent in unadjusted figures for almost all measures of economic activity. Since we want to know how the economy is performing relative to a normal pattern, this regular, seasonal variation is removed by sophisticated statistical methods. Thus, GDP for the fourth quarter will be adjusted downward relative to the first quarter, normally the slowest. GDP and almost all of the economic indicators announced to the public have been "seasonally adjusted."

We know that part of the phenomenal increase in nominal GDP that we see in Figure 5.1 was due to inflation, and we are ultimately interested in measuring the real growth of the economy. Consequently, we have to come up with a way to measure real GDP.

Figure 5.1: Nominal Gross Domestic Product

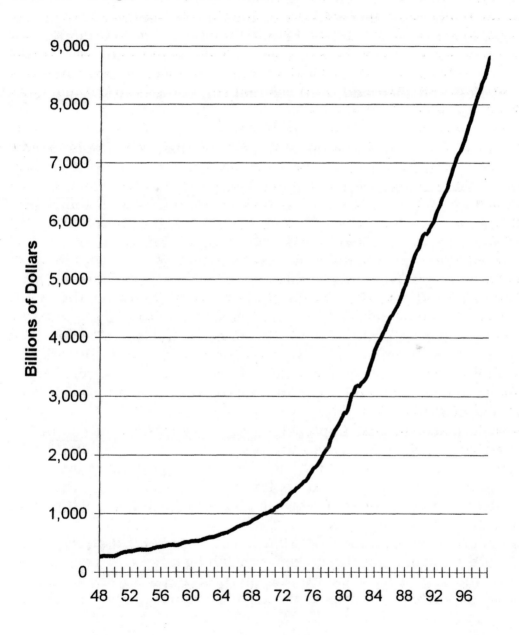

Real GDP

Based on our analysis of adjusting a person's income for inflation in Chapter 4, we might approach the problem of adjusting GDP for inflation by developing a price index for GDP and then divide nominal GDP by that price index to get real GDP. What the national income accountants at the U.S. Department of Commerce, Bureau of Economic Analysis (BEA), actually do is to value the detailed components of GDP individually in constant price, and then add up these real components to get real GDP. They have also recently changed the way in which they base "constant" prices.

The basic idea of calculating real GDP is this. We would like to compare the physical output of the economy between time periods, but prices have also changed. While it would be nice to just be able to add up the physical quantities, it is not clear how you add apples to computers. Instead, we attach values to apples and computers and then add up the dollars. Since we do not want to be fooled by a change in prices into thinking real value has changed, we use constant prices for each good. The traditional approach was always to choose a base period, most recently 1987, and use the prices of that period to value the goods produced in every time period. Thus, the accountants took the number of apples produced and multiplied by the price of apples in 1987, then added that to the number of computers produced times the price of computers in 1987, and so forth across all goods and services. The resulting total was the real GDP of that quarter valued in constant prices, those of 1987.

The basic defect of that approach is clear: the prices of computers have fallen very rapidly *relative* to the prices of other goods like apples. To continue to use 1987 prices is to ignore the fact that computers have become much cheaper, relative to apples, every year. When the quantity of computers changes, we would give it too large a weight relative to a change in the quantity of apples.

This distortion is magnified by what is called substitution bias. That refers to the tendency for the goods with falling prices to be precisely those with the largest increase in quantity produced. Buyers substitute cheaper goods for more expensive ones. Thus, we not only overvalue the computers produced in later years as computers get cheaper, we are overvaluing a rapidly growing number of them. And the distortion gets worse the farther we get in time from 1987. The computer example is not hypothetical; the spectacular fall in their prices and growth in their production has caused the growth of real GDP to be overstated by an estimated half a percent per year in recent years.

The BEA's solution to the problem is essentially to update the base period every year, and then "chain" together the resulting rates of change in real GDP to form a series over time. More concretely, if we wish to compare the real GDP of 1997 with that of 1996, we value the quantities produced in each year using the prices of 1996 and calculate the rate of change. We also can value the output of each year at the prices of 1997 and again calculate the rate of growth. The BEA does it both ways and uses the geometric average as its rate of growth of real GDP from 1996 to 1997. To compute the level of real GDP, we pick a base year, currently 1992, in which real GDP is equal to nominal GDP. Then we apply to that 1992 level the successive rates of change in real GDP until we get to the current quarter. Similarly, we can work backwards to calculate the level of real GDP before 1992. This is called chaining. The resulting series is known as "real GDP in chained 1992 dollars." Fortunately, we as users of these data do not need to understand all the details, only the general principles.

When we plot nominal and real GDP together, the result is the chart shown in Figure 5.2. Of course, real and nominal GDP are the same in 1992 because that is the base year from which real GDP is chained forward and backward in time. It is not surprising that the growth of real GDP is more modest than that of nominal GDP since we have taken out the part of the increase in nominal GDP that was just due to inflation.

While nominal GDP increased almost every quarter since 1960, we notice that there are several periods in the last three decades when real GDP dipped. Most recently, real GDP fell in the fourth quarter of 1990 and continued to decline during the first quarter of 1991. These dips in economic activity are called recessions. and their causes, and possible cures, have been the focus of macroeconomic analysis since the Great Depression of the 1930s.

Figure 5.2: GDP - Nominal and Real

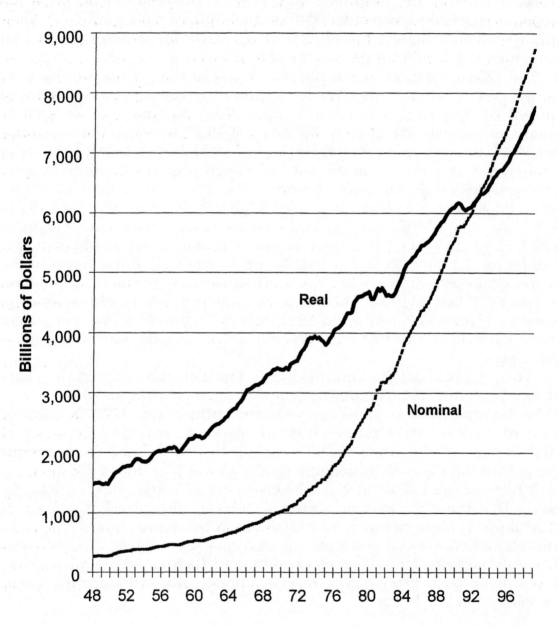

Recession and Expansion

In Figure 5.3 we focus on real GDP by itself to see the recession periods more clearly. As a rule of thumb, *a recession occurs when real GDP declines for two or more consecutive quarters.* The high point before the recession is called the peak and the low point at which Real GDP stops declining and starts to increase is called the trough. Economists date recessions from peak to trough, so the end of a recession does not mean that the economy has recovered and is back to normal, but only that it has stopped contracting. For example, the latest recession began following the peak in July 1990 and ended with the trough in March 1991, marked by down and up arrows, respectively, in Figure 5.3. While the recession ended in March 1991, it was not until about 1995 that the economy had fully recovered.

Each recession is indicated in Figure 5.3 by a downward sloping row of triangles that starts with the first down quarter and continues until the trough. Thus number of triangles is the duration of the recession in calendar quarters, so the length of the diagonal gives a quick visual impression of how severe the recession was. (Note that the triangles mark and event, they have no numerical value.) The lengthiest recessions were in 1948-49 following World War II, in 1973-75 during the energy crisis, and 1981-82 when the Federal Reserve slammed the economy hard in an effort to halt run-away inflation. That last recession came on the heels of a short recession in 1980, and together they resulted in a span of three years during which there was no economic growth.

The intervals between recessions are called expansions, and one of the longest on record began when the economy was at a trough in February 1961 and did not end until the peak of December 1969. The expansion following the 1969-70 recession was rapid but relatively brief; real GDP peaked again in the fourth quarter of 1973. Some expansions are even briefer; the shortest lasting only from July 1980 to the peak in July 1981 that marked the beginning of the very severe recession mentioned above. That one was so short as to be little more than a pause between recessions. The current expansion started at the trough of the last recession, in March 1991 and is setting a record for durability. We will understand some of the reasons why this expansion has been so durable after our study of monetary policy in Chapter 9.

The official declaration and timing of recessions is made by the National Bureau of Economic Research. The "NBER," as it is usually called, is a private organization headquartered in Cambridge, Massachusetts. The NBER has been the arbiter of recession timing since the concept originated, and has been a pioneer in many branches of economic and public policy research. In considering whether a recession has started or ended, the NBER looks not only at real GDP but also at a wide range of other indicators. While real GDP is the most important single indicator, peaks and troughs in real GDP do not necessarily coincide exactly with the NBER's dating of recessions.

Figure 5.3: Peaks and Troughs in Real GDP from the NBER Chronology

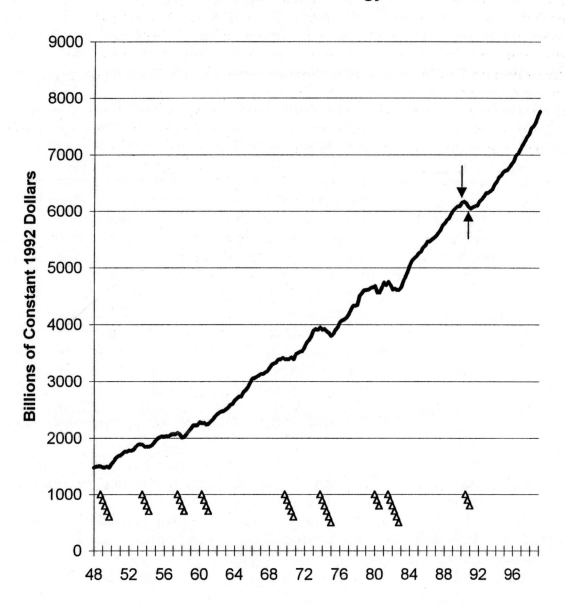

Long Term Growth and Short Term Fluctuations

It is apparent from Figure 5.3 that in spite of recurring recessions the U.S. economy has enjoyed remarkable growth over the past half century. Real GDP is now more than five times as large as it was in 1948 and has doubled just since 1975. This persistent tendency for output and real income to increase over time is called long term economic growth. Indeed, over the past five decades pictured here, the growth rate of real GDP has averaged 3.4% per year. If that rate is maintained, we can expect real GDP to double again by 2020.

Figure 5.4 is a chart of the growth rate of real GDP from quarter to quarter, expressed in *percent at an annual rate*. That is the growth rate which would be realized over four quarters if GDP continued to grow at the rate it did during a particular quarter. It is this annualized growth rate that is announced quarterly in the news, as we mentioned earlier.

The average growth rate of real GDP during the past three decades is shown in the chart as a line at 3.4% in Figure 5.4. Recessions are seen here as intervals of time during which the growth rate is below the zero line for two or more quarters. Notice that there have been a number of instances of zero or negative growth in real GDP for only a single quarter, so they did not qualify as an official recession.

An important fact about real GDP, which is apparent from Figure 5.4, is that its growth rate is highly variable from quarter to quarter. The fact that real GDP may have increased rapidly last quarter clearly does not imply that the economy will continue to expand rapidly next quarter. In other words, there is not much momentum in the economy from quarter to quarter. This "noisiness" in quarter-to-quarter growth should give us a sense of caution about placing great significance on the quarterly announcements of real GDP growth in the news as a reliable indication of the future direction of the economy. Also, it should not be surprising to us that economists have found it very difficult to predict the quarter-to-quarter growth rate in real GDP with any accuracy.

What *is* fairly predictable, however, is that over periods of several years real GDP will grow at a bit over 3% per year on average, in spite of the erratic fluctuations around that average. This is evident in Figure 5.4 where we see that the growth rate has not wandered far from the average

192

for very long. Growth rates in the 1950s fluctuated around 3%, as did growth rates in the 1960s, 1970s, 1980s, and 1980s! What is even more surprising it that estimates of growth rates back to 1870 (not shown here) suggest that there has been no appreciable change in the average over more than a century! The fact that the economy seems to grow no more rapidly today in the era of the microprocessor than it did in the era of steam engines presents a real mystery for economists.

Most students of economic growth have expected technological change to cause the growth rate to accelerate, and certainly the pace of technological change at a microeconomic level seems much more rapid today – technological progress seems to beget even more rapid progress. Typewriters improved slowly until the PC ushered in word processing and the far more rapid gains in information processing we have seen recently. However, we do not yet have credible evidence that the pace of growth has accelerated at a macroeconomic level.

Many sages, mostly non-economists, have long predicted instead that economic growth would slow down over time. The arguments mustered in favor of this gloomy prognosis are mainly that natural resources are limited and will be exhausted in another decade or two, putting an end to the industrial growth era. That view has been heard since the beginning of the industrial revolution. Marxists expected the capitalist system to fail due to what they believed were its internal contradictions. What has actually happened is that growth has continued unabated in the market economies, while Marxist economies have largely disappeared. Natural resources have not become scarce, but relatively cheaper instead. The pessimists failed to see the ability of technology to squeeze more and more output out of the same physical resources, land, labor and capital. Indeed, the areas of greatest growth in the economy today have little to do with natural resources, rather they involve telecommunications and information on the Internet which travel over optical cables made of abundant materials.

How Long Does It Take To Double?

We learned above that at a growth rate of 3.4% per year it would take about 20 years for real GDP to double. Doubling is an increase of 100%, so it may seem surprising that it does not take 100%/3.4% or 29 years to double. The reason that the correct answer is much smaller is compounding; growth each year applies not only to the original amount but also the amounts that have been added since by growth. The same algebra applies to growth of principal invested at interest; you earn interest on the interest over time. A good rule of thumb for computing doubling time is the "Rule of 72" which says that 72 divided by the growth rate in % is *approximately* the number of years it takes to double. Thus, 72/3.4 is 21.4 years, which tells us the economy will double again by 2020, if it maintains its historical average growth rate.

Figure 5.4: Growth Rate of Real GDP
Quarterly at Annualized Rate

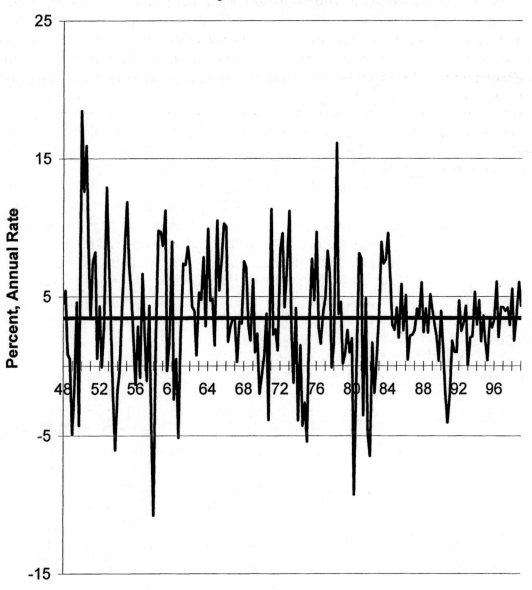

The Implicit Price Deflator for GDP

As discussed above, real GDP is calculated by valuing the quantities produced by the economy at constant prices rather than by first computing a broad price index and using that price index to deflate nominal GDP. But we would still like to be able to see how much of the growth in nominal GDP was just due to inflation. We can easily compute a price index for the whole economy by taking nominal GDP and dividing it by real GDP for each quarter. The resulting index is that which would have produced exactly the real GDP numbers had it been used to deflate nominal GDP. That is why it is called *Implicit* Price Deflator for GDP.

To illustrate, nominal GDP for the fourth quarter of 1995 is estimated to have been $7,350.6 billion and real GDP $6,780.7 in 1992 dollars. Dividing nominal GDP by real GDP we get the ratio 1.084. That is the Implicit Price Deflator for GDP for the fourth quarter of 1995. Indeed, if we deflate (divide) $7,350.6 by the price index number 1.084 we do get the real GDP figure of $6,780.7, even though that is not the way that real GDP number was originally computed. Of course, the "GDP deflator," as it is often called, takes on the value 1.00 or 100% in 1992, the base year for real GDP. The GDP Deflator can be thought of as a price index much like the CPI except that it includes not only prices of consumer goods and services, but also prices of capital goods, items purchased by government, and exports and imports.

Figure 5.5 shows the rise in the GDP Deflator since 1948, expressed as a percent of the 1992 level. Confirming the pattern we saw in the CPI in Chapter 4, prices in the U.S. economy rose relatively slowly in the 1960s, picked up speed dramatically in the 1970s, and then slowed their ascent again in the 1980s. One can see from the chart that this broad measure of the price level has increased almost six-fold since 1948.

As we are well aware by now from our discussions of the CPI in Chapter 4, inflation is not measured precisely because of problems of adjusting for changes in quality, the introduction of new products, and changes in the composition of the market basket. While the BEA has addressed the last problem with its new chaining procedure, the remaining problems carry over to measuring the GDP deflator and are exacerbated by the fact that the BEA is trying to measure price changes of every good and service in the economy.

Biases in measuring the rate of inflation in the GDP deflator will have a corresponding effect on our estimates of growth in real GDP. For example, if we overestimate inflation by 1% because of the difficulty in measuring accurately improvements in quality, then we will correspondingly underestimate the growth rate of real GDP by the same amount.

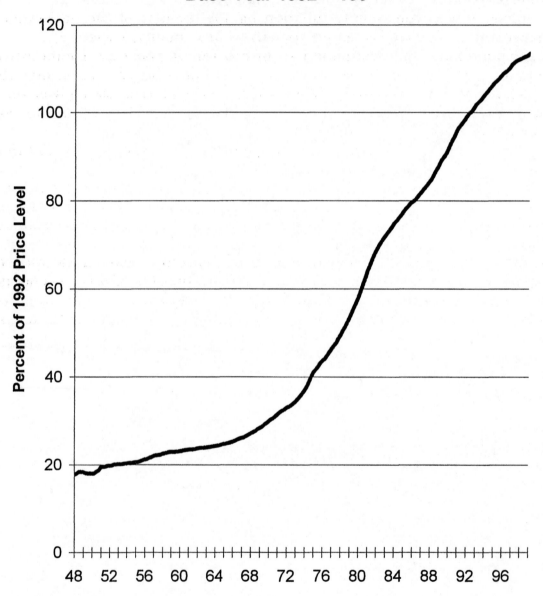

Figure 5.5: The Implicit Price Deflator for GDP
Base Year 1992 = 100

A. Which has grown more, nominal GDP or real GDP? Explain the difference.

B. When was the most recent recession in the U.S.? How severe was it compared to past recessions? Explain how you measure severity.

C. Calculate the average length of recessions and expansions in the U.S. economy since 1960. How long was the shortest recession? the longest? Do you feel that the average length of recession gives us a reliable forecast of how long the next recession will last? Would you conclude the same about expansions?

D. Was the decade of the 1990s one of unusually rapid growth? How was growth in that decade different from past decades?

E. During much of the period after WWII, Japan's real GDP grew at a rate of about 5% per year. How long did it take Japan's economy to double at that rate? Can you give an exact as well as an approximate answer?

F. "The economy finished last year with a rapid 4.8% rate of expansion in real GDP during the fourth quarter giving it enough momentum to almost ensure another year of prosperity." What would be your reaction to that analysis if you heard it on the evening news? Explain.

5.2 The Anatomy of the "Business Cycle"

The recurrence of recession followed by expansion followed by recession, and so on, long ago gave rise to the idea that there is a cycle in economic activity much like the cycles in nature. Recessions and expansions were seen as the ups and downs in a regular "business cycle." As techniques of statistical analysis became more sophisticated and computers allowed economists to test their hypotheses more systematically, they realized that the so-called business cycle does not have a fixed frequency. Instead, the intervals between expansions and recessions are highly variable. Accordingly, most macroeconomists today use the term "business fluctuations" rather than business cycle, although the earlier terminology is still in general use.

While business fluctuations are not mechanically predictable like the phases of the moon, we would still like to know whether there is a tendency for them to occur at known intervals. Does the probability of a new recession increase as the time since the last one increases? Does it make sense to say: "We are about due for another recession"? Do expansions or recessions age? Recent research suggests that recessions are rather like the common cold; the fact that you have not had a cold for a certain number of months does not imply that you are about to get one. That is, intervals do not age. On the other hand, colds do age; when you feel that sore throat coming on, you expect a week of misery followed by recovery in a predictable pattern. Colds, and other illnesses, do age. Similarly, expansions do not age, but recessions do. While the average expansion is about seven years for the U.S. economy, the fact that it has been about nine years since the last recession does not by itself imply that recession is more likely in the year 2000.

Through studying business fluctuations economists have come to recognize regular patterns in key variables in the economy which are useful in understanding the causes and consequences of business cycles. Some variables move in the same direction as output and are referred to as *pro-cyclical*. Other variables move in the opposite direction and are called *counter-cyclical*. In this section we look in turn at several key economic variables, including ones like inflation and interest rates that we have studied, to see how they move with the business cycle.

Much of the rest of the book is concerned with understanding these relationships and the causal mechanisms underlying them.

The Unemployment Rate

Are you unemployed? You are, according to the definition, if you do not have a job but are looking for one. If you have a job and are looking around for a better one, you are not unemployed. People who do not have jobs but are not looking for work are not unemployed; for example retired persons are not unemployed since they do not seek employment. All of the people who are employed or looking for work make up the labor force. The labor force is roughly two thirds of the adult population, and that fraction is called the labor force participation rate.

We are interested in measuring unemployment because we are concerned about individuals who wish to work not finding employment. Unemployment suggests under-utilization of labor resources, a cost to society, and distress to the individual and their family. We would be concerned to see unemployment at an unusually high level, but recognize, for reasons discussed below, that unemployment will never be zero. It is also important to recognize that just because a person or group is not unemployed as defined does not mean that there is no cause for concern. The technical definition misses those "discouraged workers" who have been so disheartened by past attempts to find employment that they have given up. It also misses the roughly one and a half million people who are incarcerated in jail or prison; they are not job hunting for obvious reasons, but their lack of participation in economic and social life is symptomatic of very serious problems. Others are prevented from participating because of chronic health problems.

The unemployment *rate* is the percentage of the labor force that is unemployed. The unemployment rate is estimated monthly by the U.S. Bureau of Labor Statistics (BLS) based on a survey of 60,000 households. People are asked whether they are employed and if not whether they are seeking employment.

Figure 5.6 shows how the unemployment rate has fluctuated over the past half century. The recession marker introduced in Figure 5.3 is shown to indicate periods of decline in the economy. Not surprisingly, unemployment and recession go together. As the production of goods and services declines, employers lay off workers rather than continue to pay wages to people they do not need. When the expansion of the economy resumes, the unemployment rate then declines. The twin recessions of 1980 and 1981-82 were so close together that the unemployment rate barely paused in between them before rising again.

Recession is not the only determinant of the unemployment rate. Demographic factors, such as the age composition of the labor force, are also very important determinants of the unemployment rate. More experienced workers tend to experience unemployment less frequently, so the large number of young workers entering the labor force in the 1970s contributed to a higher over-all level of unemployment during that decade. As those workers gained experience, they tended to produce a lower unemployment rate in the 1980s. That trend is likely to continue to do so in the 1990s. In addition, the number of new workers entering the labor force will be relatively low in the 1990s. Since less experienced workers tend to become unemployed more frequently, this is another demographic factor pointing toward continued moderation in the unemployment rate.

How low does the unemployment rate have to be before we can say that there is full employment? It seems clear that the unemployment rate will never be zero. Even in a robust economy some people will be searching for a new job. Good times have the effect of emboldening people to quit one job and look for a better one, hoping to improve their position. This kind of unemployment that is chosen by the worker is called voluntary unemployment. Some workers seem pre-disposed by health or social problems to have less stable work histories. For all these reasons, economists do not expect that the measured unemployment rate could ever be zero, nor should we want it to be.

Considerable effort has gone into trying to measure a "natural" rate of unemployment based on the demographic composition of the labor force. Estimates of this level of the unemployment rate are currently around 5%. An unemployment rate above 5% suggests that the economy is operating at too slow a rate to make use of the productive workers available to it. That does not mean of course that when the unemployment rate is 5% that everyone who is unemployed is happy about it.

But hold on, hasn't the unemployment rate been well below 5% during 1998 and 1999? It has indeed, and experts are surprised, frustrated, and pleased. They are surprised because the prior estimate of the natural rate of unemployment was evidently too high. They are frustrated because it is not yet clear how they overestimated it. And they are pleased because the robust labor market has succeeded in making job holders of many people previously mired in long-term unemployment. Hopefully we will be able to revise downward our estimate of the natural rate of unemployment based on this experience and not look back on it as a fluke. The next few years will tell.

Figure 5.6: Unemployment Rate %

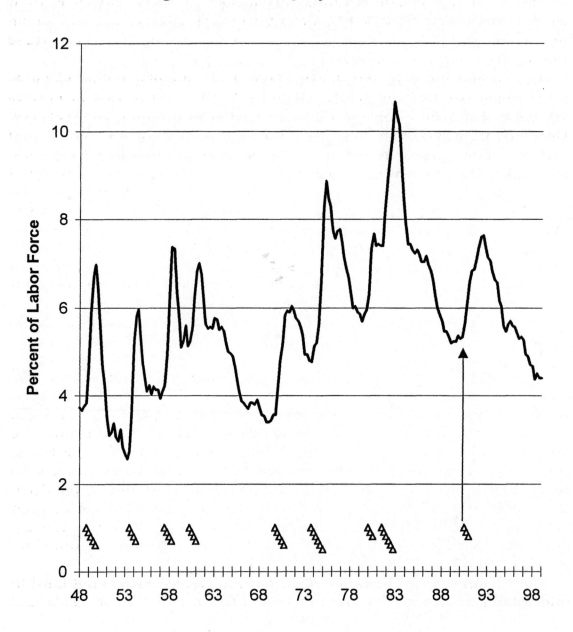

Inflation

It shouldn't surprise us that the rate of inflation declines during recessions and accelerates during expansions. This is pattern is clear when we look at the relation between business fluctuations and inflation in Figure 5.7, where inflation is measured by the annual rate of increase in the Consumer Price Index.

The reason for the pro-cyclical behavior of inflation seems obvious. Expansions are times of strong demand for goods and services, so prices are tending to rise. Recessions are times of weak demand, so prices rise less rapidly or even fall. This is just the familiar law of supply and demand at work. It is important though, to realize that if the business cycle were due primarily to fluctuations in supply, then inflation would be counter-cyclical. For example, the U.S. experienced a sharp reduction in the supply of imported oil in 1974 during the OPEC oil embargo. The resulting rise in energy prices simultaneously discouraged output, due to higher costs of production, and pushed inflation higher. In that case we witnessed a surge in inflation just as the recessions of 1973-75 worsened. The fact that inflation is generally pro-cyclical suggests that business fluctuations are primarily due to shifts in demand.

While inflation is pro-cyclical, it is also clear that inflation almost always lags behind the business cycle. It typically continues to increase for several months after a recession begins and then continues to subside after a recession has ended and the subsequent expansion has gotten underway. Notice that inflation remained higher than it had been for several years as the most recent recession began to unfold in 1990. The business press carried numerous articles at the time expressing surprise that inflation was continuing unabated in spite of a worsening recession, and some asked whether the conventional wisdom that says that inflation slows down in a recession needed to be reconsidered. Such stories are a regular feature of recessions because few people, even among journalists who cover the economy, are fully aware of the lag between the business cycle and inflation. Then, sure enough, inflation subsided on cue in 1991 and fell sharply in 1992.

The reason why inflation slows down during a recession is not hard to understand. Incomes fall during recession so the demand for goods and services decreases. The law of supply and demand tells us that when demand decreases firms will accept a lower price. This is because they are better off selling a smaller quantity at a lower price than nothing at all. Employees find themselves in a similar position during a recession, being willing to take pay cuts in order to get a job or to hold onto one.

What is more difficult for economists to understand, and still not well understood, is why inflation does not respond more quickly to recession. Why doesn't inflation respond immediately to diminished demand? Why doesn't inflation simply stop, instead of only diminishing, when factories and workers are idle?

Figure 5.7: The Rate of Inflation (CPI) and Recessions

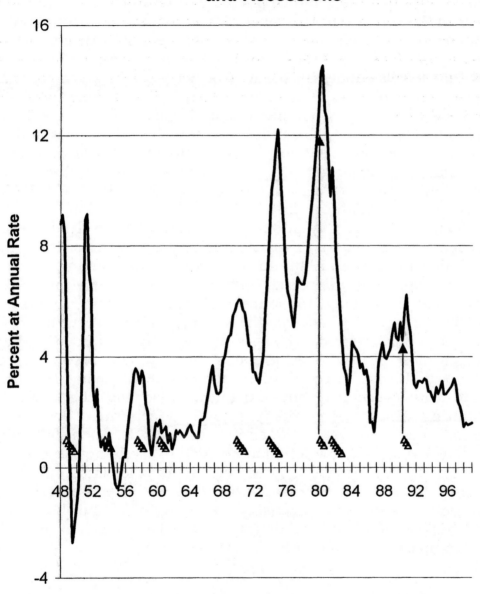

Part of the answer to this mystery certainly lies in the widespread use of contracts that commit parties to abide by a predetermined wage or price. Union contracts, for example, frequently cover a three-year period. Firms incur costs when they change prices. Some of these costs are easy to see, such as the printing new catalogues and menus. Economists refer to these direct costs of changing prices as "menu costs." Other costs are more subtle, involving a firm's unwritten understanding with its customers that it will supply its product or service at a price that the customer can rely on. This is a characteristic of "customer markets" where the good or service is not highly standardized so it is costly for both buyer and seller to shop around. We expect the price of a standard commodity, a bushel of wheat for example, to respond flexibly to a change in demand. In contrast, the price of more individualized items such as your lawyer's hourly fee, will change only after it is clear that the old price is no longer realistic.

Notice in Figure 5.7 that inflation usually continues to decline even after a recession has ended and expansion is under way. (Exception: the jump in inflation in 1951 was due to the Korean War creating the fear that rationing would be imposed, setting off a buying panic by consumers.) That is because the price and wage adjustment process continues for a time. However, as the expansion continues stronger demand starts to push prices and wages in the positive direction again. We see that in most post-WWII expansions this lead to a resurgence of inflation to even higher levels than in the last expansion. The first exception to this pattern is the expansion following the 1981-82 recession during which the economy enjoyed a continued decline in inflation until a mild resurgence the end of that decade. Then, following the 1990-91 recession, we saw inflation subside to levels not seen since the 1960s in spite of a decade-long expansion. By the time you finish reading this book you will understand why all of the expansions before the 1980s were associated with rising inflation, why and how that pattern was broken, and what will determine whether we will experience another resurgence of inflation in the future.

Interest Rates

Interest rates play a critical role in the economy since they are the link between savings and investment, as we discussed in Chapter 3. Figure 5.8 is a chart of the Treasury Bill Rate, which you will recall is the yield on 90 day bills issued by the U.S. Treasury, expressed at an annual percentage rate.

We see from the chart that the Treasury Bill Rate is pro-cyclical, falling during recessions and rising during expansions. Why are interest rates pro-cyclical?

We saw in Chapter 4 that inflation is an important determinant of the level of interest rates. When lenders perceive inflation to be increasing they demand a higher nominal interest rate to compensate them for loss of purchasing power and at the same time borrowers are willing and able to pay a higher nominal interest rate because they are paying back their loans in smaller dollars. This explains the rising level of the Treasury Bill rate in the 1970s as inflation accelerated, and the subsequent decline in the 1980s as inflation subsided. Shorter term movements in interest rates associated with the business cycle are also related to inflation as it responds to recession or expansion. Since inflation is pro-cyclical, the link between inflation and interest rates suggests that interest rates will be pro-cyclical as well.

There are two other reasons why interest rates are pro-cyclical. Both relate to the real component of interest rates. One reason is the pro-cyclical fluctuation in the demand for loans by firms and households. During an expansion, firms go to banks and the bond market seeking capital for investment in plant and equipment. Strong demand means that lenders can charge a higher real rate of interest. Likewise, optimistic households are investing in consumer durables and are willing to pay a higher real rate of interest. The reason other has to do with the operation of monetary policy by the Federal Reserve, which we will discuss in depth in Chapter 9. Briefly, when inflation rises in the later stages of an expansion the "Fed" raises interest rates even further to cool down demand for durable goods such as houses and office building with the objective of slowing down inflation. When this results in recession, as it often has in the past, the Fed then responds in the opposite direction, pushing interest rates down to stimulate the demand for interest rate sensitive goods in order to revive the economy. This sequence of events produces a peak in interest rates prior to a recession followed by a sharp fall in interest rates as the recession continues.

Thus, the forces operating on both the real interest rate and the inflation premium are all pro-cyclical, almost assuring that the nominal interest rates we observe will move in the same direction as economic activity.

Figure 5.8: Yield on Treasury Bills and Recessions

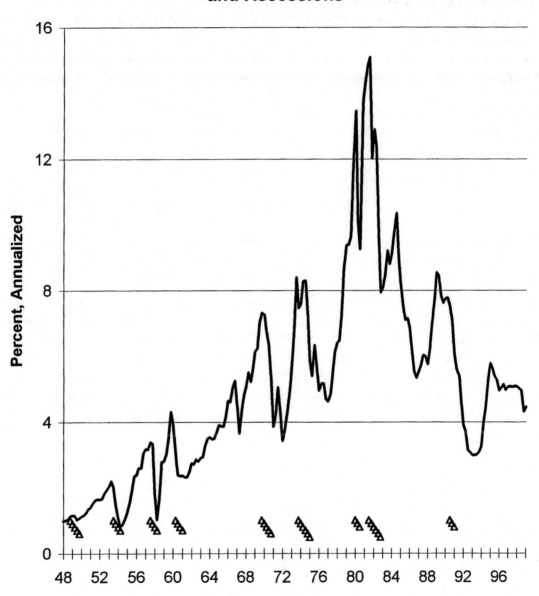

Real Disposable Income

As individuals we experience changes in our own income, the taxes we pay, and the cost of our market basket. Real disposable income per capita summarizes the impact of these factors for the average American. It is widely followed as a barometer of demand for consumer goods by marketing analysts.

Recall that disposable income is personal income less taxes. Deflating by the CPI and then dividing by population, we obtain the average real disposable income of individual Americans, or real disposable income per capita. To make past incomes directly comparable to incomes today, it is then expressed in terms of 1999 dollars. Plotting this measure of our individual purchasing power in Figure 5.9, we see that average disposable income is about $23,000 per year per American. Further, it has tripled in the past 50 years. Note that recessions correspond with dips in disposable income and expansions bring higher disposable income.

Not surprisingly, disposable income is a powerful predictor of elections. Jimmy Carter defeated incumbent President Ford in 1976 and then Ronald Reagan unseated President Carter in 1980. Notice that both of those upset elections coincide with dips in real disposable income. The decline in real disposable income that developed in 1990 and continued into 1991 spelled trouble for President Bush and raised the possibility that a challenger could unseat him. Although disposable income was growing again by 1992, Bill Clinton did just that, under the mantra "It's the economy, stupid!" As incumbent in 1996, Bill Clinton benefited from subsequent growth, and appealed to voters to give him credit for it. The did!

Figure 5.9: Disposable Real Income per Capita in 1999$ and Recessions

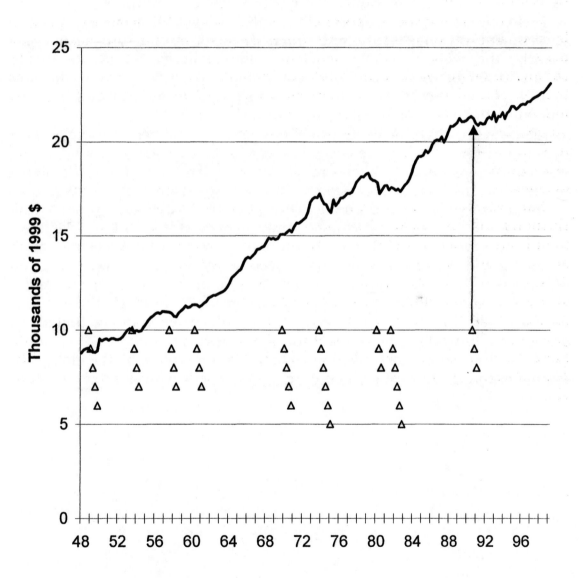

Expenditure Components of GDP

The expenditure components of real GDP; consumption, government purchases, investment, exports and imports, all expressed in real terms; vary considerably in their responsiveness to recession as we see in Figure 5.10. In this figure we go back only to 1972 so to make the fluctuations in the several series plotted more easily seen. Consumption, by far the largest component, and imports are mildly pro-cyclical, while exports and government purchases are not much affected by the business cycle. Clearly, the most cyclically sensitive component by far is investment expenditures on new plant and equipment. That component declines sharply in a recession, often showing weakness before the other components do, then bounces back during expansion.

Imports are directly affected by the business cycle because they reflect demand in the U.S. for foreign goods. When demand for goods is strong, the demand for imports follows along. This explains why the trade deficit tends to shrink during recession and widen again during expansions as demand for imports strengthens. Thus, the trade deficit is pro-cyclical, meaning the trade balance (exports minus imports) is counter-cyclical.

As the economies of the major industrial nations have become more closely linked, business cycles have become more international. Periods of recession in the U.S. are often also periods of recession for our major trading partners. When that happens, declining demand abroad for U.S. goods results in lower US exports. This "coherence" among the major economies mitigates the impact of the business cycle on the trade balance. Another factor affecting exports is the value of the dollar on foreign exchange markets which is related to the business cycle, but that is a story for Chapter 12.

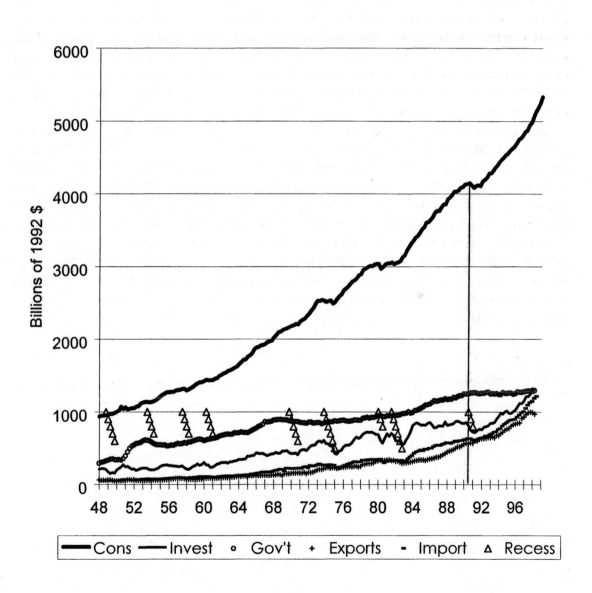

Figure 5.10: Components of Real GDP and Recessions

215

The Investment Accelerator

The strongly pro-cyclical character of investment spending suggests that the demand for capital goods plays an important role in the causation of recessions and expansions. In Chapters 8 and 9 we will be discussing why and how investment spending is a key variable in causing business fluctuations.

In addition to being a cause of business fluctuations, the demand for capital goods is also strongly affected by the business cycle. This is what economists call the investment accelerator. The idea is this: The number of machines that a firm needs, its desired capital stock, depends on its sales volume. As sales grow, the firm buys more machines in order to increase its output. Those new machines are the sales of the capital goods makers. Thus, growing airline travel causes airlines to order more planes to expand their fleets. This keeps Boeing busy building new planes. But when business is slow, firms find that they can get along just fine with the plant and equipment they already have. An airline that finds it is carrying no more passengers this year than it did last year may not need any new airplanes at all. Thus, although the sales of airplane tickets has only leveled off, the number of orders for new airplanes goes into a nose-dive. A slow down in the sales of a final good becomes *accelerated* in its effect on the sales of the capital good used to produce it. Firms specializing in producing capital goods are called "cyclical companies" because their sales are so sensitive to the business cycle.

Exercises 5.2

A. Describe the employment status of: (1) a construction worker who has just been laid off, (2) a construction worker who just quit to move to Oregon and look for work, (3) a retired construction worker, (4) an adult who has never held a job and is not looking for one.

B. How did the aging of the "baby boomers" in the labor force in the 1990s affect the "natural" rate of unemployment? Explain.

C. The tendency of inflation to lag behind the business cycle helps us forecast inflation over the next year or so. In general terms, what is your forecast for inflation for next year; explain your answer.

D. How does the relationship between interest rates and inflation discussed in Chapter 4 help to explain why interest rates vary as they do with the business cycle?

E. News item on the financial page: "Survey of business executives shows greater confidence in strong economics growth next year. Bond prices fall." Explain the connection.

F. During 1990 several articles in prominent business publications suggested that there was something unusual about inflation persisting in the face of an emerging recession. Comment.

G. How do the ups and downs of disposable income during election years seem to correlate with the outcomes of Presidential elections?

H. What are some of the limitations of average real disposable income per capital as a measure of the welfare of a population?

I. A trucking firm requires one truck for every million ton-miles of freight it hauls. Currently it is carrying 100 million ton-miles. How many trucks does it need in its fleet? One truck is scrapped each year. If volume grows by 2% this year, how many trucks will the firm buy? If volume does not grow at all, how many will it buy? What was the percentage change in its sales? The percentage change in its purchases from the truck industry? Which industry is more cyclical: the shipping industry or the truck manufacturing industry?

J. Identify a real company that produces primarily capital goods. Explain why the accelerator principle would lead you to expect the sales of that firm to be "cyclical."

K. Owners of small businesses tend to have incomes that vary more widely from year to year than do many salaried professionals such as teachers and accountants. Explain how the business cycle may be a factor in this difference.

L. Suppose you want to compare the level of disposable income today with what it was 10 years ago, and you would like to make this comparison in the dollars of the current year since those are the dollars we are familiar with. You find that the income data are in nominal dollars and the only cost of living index available is the CPI. How would you do the calculations so as to obtain the comparison you seek?

5.3 The Economy and The Stock Market

The 1990s were been a decade of remarkable prosperity in the U.S. economy and an astounding "bull market" in stocks of a magnitude not seen before in our history. The reasons behind it and whether it will be sustained in the next decade are topics of hot debate and great uncertainty. In this section we will try to put the recent stock market in historical perspective, and try to understand what has happened. We look first at corporate profits. That is the income flow available to stockholders, even if not all or any is immediately paid in cash. As discussed in Chapter 3, when you buy a share of stock you are buying a share of the firms profit flow. How do profits respond to recession and expansion? Do strong profits account for the recent explosion of stock prices?

Corporate Profits

During a recession income falls, and this is felt by households, government, and firms. However, corporate profits are particularly sensitive to recession because many of the costs that a firm has are effectively fixed. As sales decline, overhead expenses such as depreciation, real estate taxes, heating, and many labor costs do not decline. On the other hand, during an expansion when sales rise, these costs do not rise appreciably, so profits increase sharply. That corporate profits are strongly pro-cyclical is clear in Figure 5.11 where corporate profits before tax are plotted in constant dollars. For example, during the twin recessions of the early 1980s, profits fell by about 45% while real GDP fell by only about 3%, illustrating the extraordinary sensitivity of profits to economic activity. On the other hand, when the economy recovers and goes into expansion, corporate profits usually rebound smartly.

While economic growth is usually associated with rising profits, it is also interesting to note that corporate profits showed no appreciable growth during the twenty-year period of the 1970s and 1980s. The reasons for this stagnation are not well understood, but a major factor is undoubtedly the increasing competitiveness of world markets as Europe and Japan recovered from WWII and developing economies entered markets previously dominated by US firms. In response to heightened competition and declining profitability, U.S. industry embarked on widespread downsizing, closing of losing operations, cost-cutting in profitable ones, and exploitation of new computer technologies. The fact that profits did not plunge sharply in the 1990-91 recession and have grown strongly since suggests that these efforts paid off. During the 1990s, the U.S. emerged as the clear leader in major areas of electronics including computers, telecommunications, software, and the Internet.

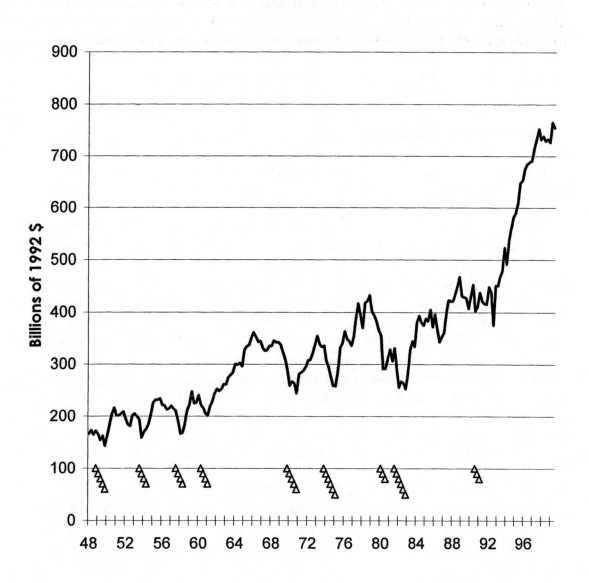

Figure 5.11: Real Corporate Profits Before Tax and Recessions

221

Stock Prices and the Bull Market of the 1990s

Since shareholders in corporations participate in profits through dividend payments, we would expect that the stock market would respond to the business cycle. In Figure 5.12 we plot the Standard and Poor's Composite Index of 500 stocks, both in its usually presented nominal form and in real terms, using the CPI to deflate the nominal "S&P 500." As the name implies, the S&P 500 includes the 500 largest companies ranked by total market value of shares outstanding. It is therefore much broader than the widely quoted Dow Jones 30 Industrials and therefore more representative of the stock market as a whole. The stocks in the S&P 500 are weighted by market value, so a 5% change in the value of Microsoft, the largest company in market value, has a much larger impact arithmetically that a 5% change in one of the small firms represented in the index. That makes it fairly representative of changes in the value of actual diversified portfolios of stocks. The way to think about the real S&P is that it is representative of the purchasing power of a diversified portfolio of stocks over time.

There are two interesting observations to make here. One is the dramatic difference between the real and nominal growth of stock prices since about 1968. There was effectively no real growth in the stock market from the late 1960s through the early 1990s, although in nominal terms stock prices quadrupled. From the high point of late 1968 to the low point of 1982, stocks 60% their value in real purchasing power terms. The 1968 peak was not exceeded again until 1992! Then, in just eight years, the real value of stocks nearly tripled!

Since the market price of a stock is simply what investors are willing to pay for the right to participate in future dividends, the stock market is a barometer of optimism or pessimism. Changes in stock prices reflect changes in investors' expectations about the future. The dramatic decline of stocks in the 1970s gives some indication of the negative impact that unprecedented inflation and severe recession had on Americans' confidence about the future of their economy.

A second important observation that we can make from Figure 5.12 is that the stock market tends to reach a peak or trough well before the economy does. Note the relative timing of the peaks and troughs in the

S&P index relative to the recession marker. Evidently, in the midst of a recession, the stock market starts to see the signs of recovery before it happens and responds accordingly. Similarly, the stock market often reaches a peak before the economy begins to decline into recession. Research shows that the stock market is one of the very best leading indicators of the economy, anticipating both expansions and recessions by several months. How does it do that?

Think of the stock market as a device for processing information brought to it by millions of buyers and sellers. Favorable information causes buyers to bid prices up as they anticipate higher dividends in the future, and unfavorable information pushes prices down as investors revise down their expectations of future dividends. Individuals act on many sources of information: the salesperson who notices a pick up in showroom traffic over the weekend, or the lawyer who notices a lot more calls from clients concerned about bankruptcy, and so forth. The stock market receives all of these inputs in the form of orders to buy or sell shares, so the resulting stock prices reflect all of the information which participants bring to it.

The idea that market prices for stocks and other assets reflect all available information is called the *rational expectations hypothesis* or the *efficient markets hypothesis*. Clearly, optimism about the future of the U.S. economy, and corporate profits in particular, increased spectacularly in the middle of the 1990s. The S&P rose by about one third just in 1995! Market observers relate this optimism to the end of the Cold War, rapid developments in new technologies, the long and non-inflationary expansion of the economy, and the emergence of dynamic new trading partners for the U.S. in developing economies around the world. Indeed, the remaining 1990s were years of extraordinary prosperity.

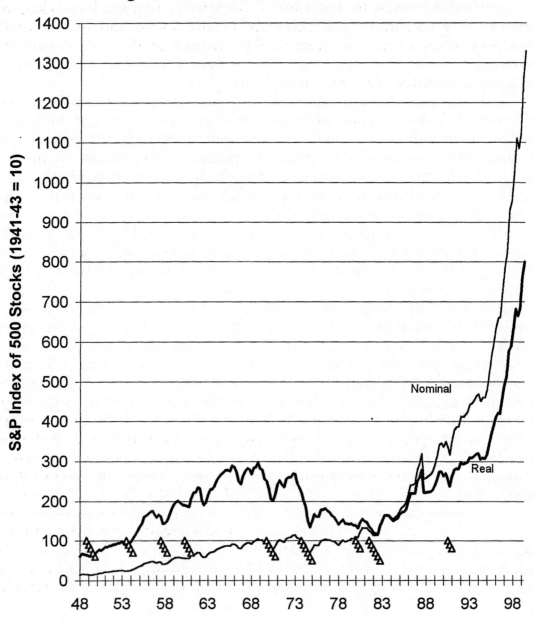

Figure 5.12: Stock Prices, Nominal and Real

Understanding the Bull Market – A Simple Model

We have all just lived through one of the most extraordinary periods of U.S. history, the great bull market of the 1990s when stocks tripled, even when adjusted for inflation. Popular books are now confidently predicting another tripling in the next few years! Whether people will look back on this episode as a reflection of a new age of prosperity or, alternatively, a triumph of optimism over realism, remains to be seen. What we would like to do is understand better what accounts for this extraordinary rise; in particular, are there observed economic "fundamentals" that account for it, or is it the value people put on those fundamentals?

Here is a simple model for thinking about stock prices. Let P stand for the price of stocks and E corporate earnings or profits, both in real terms. GDP will also be real. Remember that any quantity divided by itself is equal to one, so

$$P = P \bullet \frac{E}{E} \bullet \frac{GDP}{GDP}, \text{ then rearranging,}$$

$$P = \frac{P}{E} \bullet \frac{E}{GDP} \bullet GDP$$

This formula says that the price of stocks is the product of three factors. One factor is the ratio of price to earning, known as the *PE ratio*. Recall that when you buy a stock you are buying the stream of earnings it produces, so the PE ratio is how many dollars you pay to get one dollar of earnings per year. The next factor is the ratio of corporate earnings (profits) to GDP. We can think of that as the share of national income that is earned by the owners of corporate capital; it is their share of the GDP pie. The third factor is the size of the pie, GDP in real terms. Now for price P to rise, it has to be that the PE ratio has risen, or that corporations have become more profitable so that their share of GDP has increased, or GDP itself has risen, or some combination of those. The PE ratio is plotted in Figure 5.13 since 1948 and it tells a very interesting story.

Figure 5.13: Price/Earnings Ratio of the S&P 500

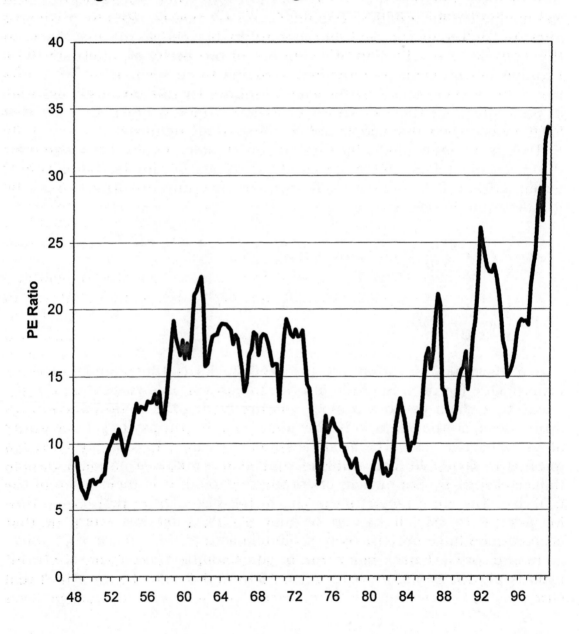

Immediately after WWII investors were willing to pay less than $10 for $1 of corporate earnings. During the 1960s though, they were willing to pay between $15 and $20. Why were they willing to pay so much more? Pessimism was widespread after WWII, many people including economists fearing that the Depression would resume after war spending diminished. Thus, at that time they viewed the earnings stream as a stagnant or possibly diminishing one. By the 1960s Americans were much more confident, so they expected a growing earnings stream from stocks; $1 this year will become $1.10 next year, and so forth. That optimism caused them to be willing to pay far more for earnings than before. That optimism had faded by the 1970s and by 1982 investors were willing to pay less than $10 again for a dollar of earnings. Falling corporate profitability lead them to expect little growth ahead. The last two decades have seen a willingness to pay ever more for earnings until in 1999 it would cost you almost $35 to buy into an earnings stream that is $1 today! Optimism was greater than ever before that growth justified paying a high price to get into the game.

Did corporate profitability fully justify these swings of optimism and pessimism? Figure 5.14 shows that the corporate share of GDP was in fact quite large after WWII, remaining high into the late 1960s. It did deteriorate dramatically in the 1970s, so growing pessimism was based on actual experience. Improvement came only in the 1990s when corporations' share of GDP rose from about 8% to about 10%. Thus while PE ratios tripled, actual corporate profitability improved only about 25%.

Could something other than expectations about earnings growth affect the PE? Certainly, fluctuations in the real rate of interest would affect the valuation of corporate earnings just as it affects the valuation of coupon income in the bond market, low interest rates corresponding to higher valuation. But, as we have seen, real interest rates were quite low in the 1970s and have not been low in the 1990s. Since this does not go in the direction of helping explain the variation in PE, it would seem that swings in optimism are the primary explanation.

Finally, has there been a dramatic change in real GDP, the third factor in the formula? We know from Figure 5.4 that the growth of real GDP has not varied greatly from decade to decade, and has not been unusually high recently. The 1990s are more notable for the stability of the growth rate and that may well give investors a sense of lessened risk that makes them willing to pay more for less risky corporate earnings.

To sum up, the great bull market of the 1990s seems to be mostly due to great optimism about the future rather than being a recognition of higher profits already in the bank. To make the PE ratio of 1999 make sense, investors will have to see rapid growth of corporate earnings in the years ahead, or they will be sorely disappointed!

**Figure 5.14: Corporate Profits
as a Share of GDP**

229

Exercises 5.3

A. Why does Wall Street seem to devote a lot of attention to taking the pulse of the economy and trying to forecast the pace of GDP?

B. The famous economist Paul Samuelson is said to have quipped that the stock market had predicted seven of the last five recessions. How does Figure 5.12 show what he meant?

C. Rework the formula for P in the case of the usual nominal price index we see in the news. Which of the three factors changes?

D. What might you expect to happen to the PE ratio when an innovation of historical magnitude, such as the Internet, comes along? How might it affect the other two factors?

Index

Chapter 6

Money, Banks and The Federal Reserve

Outline

Preview

Preview

Money is one of the essential elements of civilization, as fundamental as the wheel and the written word. It is also one of the most mysterious things we deal with. It is almost magical that a piece of paper can be exchanged for valuable goods. Why is money valuable? What makes money money? Where does it come from? Who makes it? What do banks have to do with money?

In this chapter we will explore these and other questions. Putting money in an historical context, we will see what money has been, and what it is today. Along the way we will see how different forms of money evolved, how banks came about and what role they play in the monetary system, and how the modern central bank has become the ring leader of that system.

6.1 What is Money?

Money is whatever is generally acceptable as payment to the seller of a good or service. If you visited a remote island in the Pacific and noticed that when people traded one person always received shells while the other sometimes received fish and sometimes coconuts or sunglasses, then you would know that shells serve as money in that economy. In a modern economy, money consists of coins, paper currency, and bank deposits that can be disbursed by check since those are what are accepted in payment for goods and services.

Money is so important to the functioning of an economy that economies without money are practically unknown. In situations where money doesn't exist, people invent it. For example, in prisoner-of-war

232

camps in World War II, cigarettes came to be used as money. Why is money so important to every economy?

What Money Does for Us

Think for a minute of the consequences of not having money in the economy. How would your employer, say a computer manufacturer, pay you your wages? You could be paid in the computers that the firm produces, but you can probably only use one computer yourself, you can't eat computers, and your landlord has no use for them. You would have to go out and try to find someone who wants a computer and who also has something that you want, or something that you think you can trade for something you want.

This time-consuming process is called barter, the trading of one good or service for another. There is obviously a huge benefit to society in the elimination of barter by finding one thing that everyone is willing to take in trade for anything. That is why money ranks with the wheel as one of the great inventions of human history. Money serves as the medium of exchange, what you find on one side of every transaction. Money is the oil which lubricates the wheels of trade.

Money performs two other important services in the economy. It provides us with a unit of account, a yardstick, with which economic values can be measured and compared. In a barter economy one might trade three apples for an audio tape and an hour of labor for a compact disk. However, that gives no indication of the cost of a tape compared to a CD unless we know how many apples you can get for an hour of labor. In a monetary economy it is simple to compare the price of an audio tape at $6.95 with that of a CD at $11.95. Since each of us has a sense of what a dollar will buy, a price quoted in dollars conveys information about the costliness of an item very efficiently. For example, you are shopping for your first business suit and the price tag reads $250. You can immediately put the cost of that suit on a scale that allows you to compare it with many other things you would like to buy, and to compare it with your income. If you are offered a salary of $36,000 per year to start, that single number gives you all the information you need, to know the standard of living you will have.

When we say that "you are making $36,000 a year," we are speaking of money as a unit of account. You will probably never actually hold $36,000 at one time if you receive your salary in bimonthly payments of $1,500. Your salary check in the amount of $1,500 is money as the medium of exchange. The amount of money that you hold today is the amount of currency you have plus the balance of your checking account; it is not your income. Money, as the medium of exchange, flows into your bank account as you receive salary payments, and it flows out as you make disbursements.

The amount of money you hold at any one point in time is what economists refer to as a "stock," and can be thought of as being like the amount of water in a storage tank. Income flows into the tank, adding to its level, and expenditures flow out, depleting it. The stock of money you hold at a point in time is money in the sense of medium of exchange, while the rates of the income and expenditure flows are measured in the unit of account. These two uses of money units are clearly closely related, but they are not the same.

Adding to the potential confusion, while money is itself an asset, it is also used as the unit of account for all assets. When we read in a magazine that Bill Gates of Microsoft Corp. is worth $14 billion, it does not mean that he holds $14 billion in the form of money, although one imagines that his money holdings are substantial! What it does mean is that if we add up the market values of his shares of Microsoft and his other assets, including holdings of money, the sum would be $14 billion.

The fact that it is easy to confuse these different meanings of the word "money" certainly contributes to common misunderstandings about the role of money in the economy. For example, we often read or hear statements like "higher consumer spending added money to the economy this spring." In reality, spending transfers money from one wallet to another, but it does not add to the quantity of money in existence, the amount of coins, dollar bills, and checking accounts.

The third very important function of money in the economy is as a store of value, a temporary abode of purchasing power that can be called upon on short notice. For an asset to be a good store of value it must be a liquid asset, one that can be converted into goods or services quickly at low cost and with low risk. A diamond ring is valuable but it is not very liquid because of the large spread between what an individual pays for it at a jewelry store and what one can sell it for, particularly on short notice. Similarly, a house is valuable but not liquid because its sale may take months. Shares in Microsoft Corp. are valuable and can be sold quickly at the market price with payment of only a small commission, but their market value fluctuates from day to day. All stocks and bonds are subject to risk from changes in their market value. A savings account is very liquid because the cost of using it is low and the value does not fluctuate from day to day. A $20 bill in your wallet is even more liquid than a savings account because you don't have to make a trip to the bank to use it to settle a transaction. The fact that money is the medium of exchange means that money is the most liquid of all assets, and that is what makes it ideal as a store of value.

What Makes a Good Money

The earliest kind of money in human history was commodity money which is made of some material that had value in other uses. Arrow heads, cattle, grain, and manufactured metal objects all served as money for primitive people. Early colonists in America used tobacco leaves that they grew and exported to England as a medium of exchange. In Massachusetts, the colonists adopted the monetary system of the native Americans, wampum made by stringing together beads made from shells.

What sorts of commodities would we expect to see used as money? Ones that are:

- **Durable.**

- **Valuable in small sizes and weights.**

- **Divisible.**

- **Easily verified as genuine.**

- **Stable in value.**

From earliest times, copper, silver, and gold were recognized as good materials to make money from. They all possess the characteristics listed above. They are durable because they do not rust, and they are stable in value because their quantity cannot change rapidly. Gold has long been considered the premier commodity money because it is the most valuable of the three metals and its almost uniquely high density make verification very easy; no other metal (outside of a chemistry lab) weighs as much in a given volume. The problem with using simple chunks or bars of metal as money is, of course, that one cannot be sure of the exact volume or content. Thus, coins were invented to make metallic money more readily verifiable.

The Advent of Coins

Since ancient times, governments have stamped metals into standardized disks or other shapes with the value or weight of the coin embossed on it.   This gave some protection against cheating and simplified trading by creating standard denominations.   The first coins are thought to have been minted in the ancient Greek city of Lydia, in what is now Turkey, around 600 BC. These coins were called "staters," from which our word "standard" originates, and were made from a naturally occurring alloy of gold and silver. Traders soon spread these coins throughout the Greek world.   The Romans began to mint coins about 200 BC. They stamped a flattering likeness of their ruler on the face of the coin, a practice which survives to this day.   Coins containing a specific quantity of silver or gold were minted in the U.S. well into this century, with gold coins disappearing from use in the 1930's and silver coins in the 1960's.

The invention of minted coins made it harder for private individuals to cheat on the metallic content of money, although people did always manage to nick off small bits of a coin or rub off some of the metal. The temptation for government, however, to reduce the precious metal content of coins was ever present and during times of war it usually became irresistible. Why not stretch out the government's supply of gold and silver by alloying them with a bit more copper?

For a while, most people could not tell the new, cheaper coins from the old, allowing the sovereign to purchase a few more ships or swords than he could have otherwise. After a while, though, people did catch on to the fact that the new coins contained less precious metal and they would begin to hoard the old coins while trying to pass the less valuable new coins on to others in trade. Based on such episodes, Sir Thomas Gresham (1558) observed that bad money drives good money out of circulation, a principle that has become known as Gresham's Law although it has been a recognized fact since antiquity. Over the several century history of the Roman Empire, the precious metal content of the Roman denarius diminished almost to the vanishing point.

Gresham's Law continues to operate in modern economies including ours. Prior to 1965, U.S. coins contained silver in an amount that was worth somewhat less than the face value of the coin. However, as inflation pushed the market price of silver up along with other commodities in the 1960s, the silver in a coin became worth more than the face value. At that point it cost the U.S. Treasury more than $.25 to make a quarter and it became profitable to melt the coins down and sell the silver. In short, a dime or quarter was worth more dead than alive. To avoid having all coins disappear from circulation, Congress made it illegal to melt coins and silver was replaced in coins by the copper sandwich we have today. Not surprisingly, the old silver coins disappeared from circulation very rapidly as people sifted through their pocket change and set aside the silver coins. No one would settle a transaction with a silver quarter worth, say, $.50 as metal when they could use a new sandwich quarter instead. Today, the pre-1965 silver dimes and quarters still trade as commodities for about three or four times face value, depending on the current price of silver. While it is now legal to melt them down, these coins, as coins always do, serve to provide an easily verified quantity of silver for those who wish to hold it.

Fiat Money

Today, no country uses coins as a medium of exchange that have significant commodity value. The coins in use today are called token coins which have value only because they are legal tender, meaning that the law requires that they be accepted as payment. Paper money is, of course, worth almost nothing as a commodity, but it has value because of the phrase "THIS NOTE IS LEGAL TENDER FOR ALL DEBTS, PUBLIC AND PRIVATE" which is printed next to the picture of a President. Money which has value only because it is legal tender is called fiat money. Each of us accepts fiat money in payment because we know that the next person will accept it from us, and indeed even are required to, by law. Paper money and coins are referred to collectively as currency.

Paper money was in use in China by the time of Marco Polo's visit in the late 1200s, but did not come into use in Europe until the 1600s. Until very recently, paper money was generally a claim on a certain quantity of precious metal held either by a government or by a private bank. As long as people believed that they could redeem their paper money, or notes, for the promised quantity of silver or gold, the notes would be accepted in commerce at their stated value. Governments found that they could print additional notes and use them to pay bills.

The profit that a government makes by manufacturing money is called seigniorage, and it became an important source of revenue. The temptation, of course, was for governments to issue a quantity of notes far in excess of the metal backing them, particularly during times of war. When it became apparent to the public that the notes could no longer be redeemed for metal, the value of the notes would invariably plummet.

In our own history, the early colonies printed their own paper currencies which often lost much of their value when the finances of the colonial government became shaky. During the American Revolution, the Continental Congress issued paper notes called "continentals" which were to be redeemable in a Spanish silver coin called a "dollar." When the costs of the war against King George mounted beyond expectations, as the cost of war always does, the decline in their value gave rise to the expression "not worth a continental." Again, during the Civil War, the printing press became a source of revenue when the U.S. Treasury issued "greenbacks," so called because of the green ink that was used. Greenbacks could not be exchanged for coins and soon declined in value. The last links between paper money and metal in the U.S. were broken when the gold certificates were withdrawn from circulation in 1933 and, finally, when silver certificates were withdrawn in the 1960s. Our paper money today says "FEDERAL RESERVE NOTE" along the top. It is issued by the Federal Reserve, not the U.S. Treasury, and carries no promise of redemption in metal. It is a purely fiat money.

Bank Money and Near Money

When you pay a bill in today's economy you are less likely to use currency than you are to write a check. A check instructs the bank where you have your checking account to pay the stated amount to the person or firm you designate. The balance in your checking account is therefore a kind of money. Unlike currency, your check may not always be acceptable everywhere, but it is more secure from theft than currency. Checking accounts have traditionally been known as demand deposits because funds could be withdrawn on demand as distinguished from savings accounts, sometimes called time deposits, which technically could require a waiting period for withdrawal. A checking account paid no interest, while a savings account did. The depositor could then choose between receiving the liquidity of a checking deposit or the interest income of a time deposit. These distinctions have become blurred in recent years with the emergence of hybrid accounts that pay some interest but also carry check writing privileges. All such checkable deposits serve as money in our economy.

While savings accounts that are not checkable cannot directly be used to pay bills, they are so readily converted into money that they are referred to as near money. Banks today offer a number of types of interest-bearing deposits that are considered near money including Money Market Deposit Accounts and small denomination Certificates of Deposit (or "CDs").

A type of mutual fund called a money market mutual fund functions much like a bank account and is classified as near money. A money market mutual fund invests exclusively in short term securities of low default risk including Treasury bills and commercial paper which is essentially a bill issued by a corporation with a high credit rating. Since these securities mature very quickly the value of the fund is so stable that the value of each share in the money market fund is fixed at $1. All interest income is credited to the shareholders after the expenses of the fund, including a management fee, are paid. What makes money market funds so attractive is that the individual shareholder receives a checkbook and can write checks up to the amount of his or her balance in the fund. The checks are paid by a bank at which the fund maintains a checking account for this purpose.

Let's look now at the amount of currency, checkable deposits, and near money in the U.S. economy. When we add currency in circulation to checkable deposits we have the measure of the quantity of money called M1, and when near money is added to M1 we have M2. Here is what they were in mid 1999, give or take a few billion:

Currency: $480 billion

+ checkable deposits

= M1: $1,100 billion

+ near money

= M2: $4,500 billion

As incredible as it may seem, there is about $2,000 in currency in circulation for every person in the U.S. including children! Since very few of us carries around that much cash, one wonders where it all is. A significant portion is in cash registers in stores rather than in our wallets. Another significant fraction of it circulates in foreign countries as a substitute for less stable local currencies, and in countries that have adopted a dollar-based monetary system it plays a role their monetary system. Argentina is and example. Cash also is used to hide illegal activities since by dealing in cash the parties involved avoiding leaving a record of their transactions in banks. Examples include drug trafficking, political corruption, and tax avoidance. Nobody knows for sure where all the currency is. We do know that the denomination of bills which represents the largest total dollar value is the $100 bill. This fact suggests that much of U.S. currency is used for purposes other than personal daily transactions.

You have probably been wondering how credit cards fit into the constellation of moneys. Even though we often refer to credit cards as "plastic money" they are really a loan to you from the credit card issuer, generally a bank. This loan delays payment until your monthly bill is due at which time money changes hands to settle your account. The credit card issuer earns interest on the loan not from the card holder directly but rather from merchants who accept a small discount on what they collect from the credit card issuer. Of course, if you do not wish to pay the full balance due, the bank will carry the balance as a loan to you and will charge you substantial interest. Credit cards may reduce the need to carry as much currency as one would if they didn't exist, and they surely have reduced the use of travelers' checks, but they are not themselves a form of money.

Exercises 6.1

A. Review the three most important functions that money serves in the economy. How would rapid and erratically variable inflation alter the usefulness of money?

B. The early Massachusetts colonists adopted the native American monetary system called, wampum, which consisted of white and black shell beads. One black shell was worth two white shells. Soon, the colonists discovered that when a white shell was dyed black it was indistinguishable from a naturally black one. What do you suppose happened to the composition of wampum in circulation, and how does this illustrate Gresham's Law?

C. Personal checking accounts are not generally used by households in Japan. Instead, people carry large amounts of currency and even make major purchases with currency. What aspect of Japanese culture and social behavior would you guess may account for this difference?

D. List five assets which are valuable and order them by their liquidity. Explain your ranking.

6.2 How Banks Create Money

Banks are as old as civilization itself. In the ancient world, money changers exchanged coins from abroad for local ones, and also offered deposit and safekeeping of money and valuables for their clients. There were money lenders who charged interest on loans. Roman law contained extensive regulations dealing with banking. Banking fell into disrepute during the Middle Ages when usury, the charging of interest, was condemned by religious authorities. Banking was revived in Italy during the Renaissance; the word "bank" comes from the Italian word "banco" which referred to the bench at which bankers conducted their business.

The most famous of the Italian Renaissance bankers were the Medicis, a family which established their bank in Florence in the late 1300's and accumulated great wealth and power over the next three centuries. They made Florence a center of the arts and learning and produced three Popes and two queens of France. They were also famous for disposing of those who got in their way, poison being the familial weapon of choice.

An important innovation in banking seems to have occurred in England in the 1600's. The story goes something like this:

A Fable

Long ago, a goldsmith opened up shop in a town in Olde England. The goldsmith had a stronger vault for keeping valuables than anyone else in town, so it seemed natural to offer safekeeping services to the townspeople. They soon had deposited gold and silver coins totaling £100 (English pounds) and received receipts or "notes" for that amount in return. The goldsmith found that people only occasionally presented these notes for redemption, most of the time they were content to just hold them. At this point, the goldsmith's reserves, the coins in the vault, were exactly equal to the depositors' claims against those reserves, both £100.

After a while, the goldsmith's notes began to circulate in the community as a kind of money since people realized that the notes could be converted at any time to coins by presenting them for payment at the goldsmith's shop. Soon it occurred to the goldsmith to print up some additional notes that looked just like the original ones and lend them out. The borrower signed a loan contract, say for £10, promising to pay interest, and received from the goldsmith notes which represent a claim on ten pounds. The new notes were spent by the borrower to purchase land, and then circulated in the community along with the notes issued previously. However, now the amount of notes outstanding totals £110, which is £10 more than the amount of the goldsmith's reserves.

Gaining confidence over time, the goldsmith eventually issued a total of £200 of additional notes in return for making loans totaling £200. The goldsmith's balance sheet then looked like this:

The Goldsmith's Balance Sheet			
Assets		Liabilities	
Reserves £100		Notes £300	
Loans £200			
Total £300		Total £300	

The goldsmith had succeeded in creating £200 that did not exist before!

Fractional Reserve Banking

And so was born fractional reserve banking, a system in which the amount of reserves held by the bank is only a fraction of the total amount of the notes or deposits outstanding. Recall that the amount of notes in circulation at first was only £100, but as a result of the goldsmith's lending there was finally a total of £300 in notes circulating in the community. As long as borrowers continued to make payment on their loans, all would be well. If the goldsmith, now banker, had used poor judgment in making loans and they were not repaid, then the liabilities of the bank would exceed its assets and eventually it would be unable to redeem its notes and the bank would fail.

Even if the loan payments were received on schedule, the bank would fail if holders of more than one third of its notes demanded their coin at once. Like modern banks discussed in Chapter 3, this bank holds illiquid assets (loans) while issuing liquid liabilities (notes). A "run" on the bank, perhaps triggered just by rumor of failure, has always been a threat to the life of any fractional reserve bank.

Prior to the establishment of the Federal Reserve in 1913, American banks operated much like our apocryphal goldsmith. The Coinage Act of 1792 established the dollar as the monetary unit for the US and set up the first official mint to manufacture coins. The amount of silver or gold that the coins contained per dollar of face value established both the price of those metals in U.S. dollars and the value of the dollar in terms of those metals. From 1834 to 1933 the price of gold was unchanged at $20.67 per ounce. Except for the greenbacks issued during the Civil War, paper money consisted of notes issued by banks rather than governments. Bank reserves consisted of silver and gold coins, and banks issued notes backed by these reserves.

Wildcat Banking

The most colorful era of American banking was the period of "wildcat" banking from 1836 to 1864 when banks sprung up on the frontier with little more behind them than faith in the future. They took in coin deposits, made loans, and issued their notes to a sometimes trusting and sometimes skeptical public. The notes of hundreds of different banks circulated together, all claiming to be "good as gold." The notes of less trusted banks traded at a discount from face value. If a bank's loans were not repaid, or if it became the victim of a run, the notes could become worth much less than face value, or nothing at all.

The Gold Standard

Although bank notes made the promise to pay in silver or gold dollars, the total amount of notes outstanding always far exceeded the value of the banks' reserves. That, as we have seen, is the magic of fractional reserve banking. Since it was increasingly gold rather than silver that was the most important of the two monetary metals, the system based on a monetary unit that was redeemable in gold became known as the gold standard. While it did not mean that all money was backed by an equivalent amount of gold, as people sometimes mistakenly state, it did have the effect of tying the quantity of money that the banking system could create to a commodity that was in relatively fixed supply.

The gold standard was also an international system in use by the major European countries, most notably Great Britain which was the leading industrial power of the 19th century. The result was that all national currencies were readily convertible into one another since they were all equivalent to a known quantity of gold.

Modern Banks

The U.S. began to move away from the gold standard in the 1860s with the creation of the National Banks, which could issue notes against reserves of U.S. Treasury bonds. Then the Federal Reserve was established in 1913 and granted authority to issue its own notes Gold coins were withdrawn from circulation in 1934 in the midst of the Great Depression. Finally, the U.S. ended the practice of selling gold at a fixed price to other governments in 1971.

Today, the reserves of a bank are not silver and gold coins but rather currency and its own deposits at the Federal Reserve. The principles of fractional reserve banking, however, are essentially unchanged from the days of the goldsmith. A modern bank issues not notes but checking and savings deposits. To each account holder, the balance in their checking account is "money in the bank" available for withdrawal either in currency or by transfer by check to someone else's bank account. In fact, the bank holds only a fraction of the total deposits that it is liable for in the form of reserves; the rest is loaned out and is earning interest.

The balance sheet of a modern bank will have the same form as the goldsmith's, only the details differ.

In its simplest form it looks something like this:

The Modern Bank's Balance Sheet

Assets		Liabilities	
Reserves: currency in vault	$100		
Loans	900	Deposits	$1000
Total Assets	$1,000	Total Liabilities	$1000

This modern bank's depositors have $1,000 "in the bank," but only a tenth of that, $100, remains in the bank's vault in the form of currency as a reserve against withdrawals. A real bank will also have reserves in the form of deposits at its bank, the Federal Reserve, and it can call on these reserves in the form of currency at any time to meet demands for withdrawal by its own depositors. The remaining $900 has been lent out to households and businesses to buy everything from houses to awnings.

The interest earned by lending most of the depositors' money to others is what makes it possible for a bank to provide its depositors with convenient services such as drive-through banking and to make a profit on its investment in those facilities. For simplicity, this illustrative balance sheet omits the value of such facilities that would appear as assets on an actual balance sheet, and it omits the stockholders' equity that would appear along with liabilities as claims on those assets.

Exercises 6.2

A. Imagine our goldsmith decides it is safe to keep on reserve gold equal to only one fourth of the notes issued. What will his balance sheet look like after this change?

B. Explain why the gold standard made it very easy to exchange any of the major currencies for local currency anywhere in the world. Did foreign exchange dealers need to know the latest exchange rate to convert British pounds to US dollars? Why not?

C. Under the gold standard the cost of a market basket of goods changed very little over decades or even centuries. Why did the gold standard make the purchasing power of the dollar very stable?

D. Imagine that the modern bank whose balance sheet appears above decides to keep reserves equal to 20% of its deposit liabilities. What must it do to its loans outstanding to achieve this, assuming its reserves are unchanged. What will happen to the amount of deposits on its books?

6.3 The Federal Reserve System and Central Banks

The Federal Reserve is our central bank, empowered to regulate the quantity of money and the banking system and serve as "lender of last resort" when banks are unable to satisfy demands for withdrawals from their own reserves. It was established in 1913 with the hope that it would end the periodic waves of bank runs and failures which disrupted the economy and brought financial hardship to individuals unlucky enough to be caught holding the notes of defunct banks.

Measured against this objective, the "Fed," as it is called, was not immediately a success, since even greater waves of bank failures occurred in 1920-21 and the greatest of all was in 1929. The latter provided the shock that ushered in the Great Depression that lasted nearly through the following decade.

The History of the Fed

The Federal Reserve was preceded a century earlier by efforts to establish a "national" bank which would serve as banker to the federal government, issue notes of recognized value, and stabilize the private banks by providing credit in times of crisis. The idea of a central bank was always controversial in American politics, being condemned by Thomas Jefferson as a dangerous centralization of power. The First Bank of the United States was established in 1791, but its charter from Congress was allowed to lapse after only twenty years. The Second Bank of the United States was chartered in 1816, largely in response to the disorder following the war of 1812. It incurred the wrath of President Andrew Jackson, again on fear of the centralization of power and his conviction that the Bank would be hostile to the small banks he felt were crucial to the development of the American West. The Second Bank was disowned by the federal government in 1836; continuing as a state bank chartered in Pennsylvania until it failed in 1841. If it weren't for these failures, the Fed would probably have been called "The Bank of the United States," following the model of other central banks like The Bank of England.

While central banking conflicted with the American ideal of decentralized power, the Bank of England was providing an appealing model of a successful central bank. Founded as a private bank in 1694 primarily to handle banking affairs for the government, by the 19th century it had evolved most of the functions that the Fed has today. Its notes were of unquestioned value, making the pound sterling the premier international currency of the 19th century.

Initially, the powers of the Federal Reserve System were vested primarily in twelve "district banks" while the Board of Governors, located in Washington D. C., had little central control. This decentralization was not a coincidence, but rather another manifestation of the traditional American suspicion of centralized power. After the Fed had failed to come to the rescue of the banks in 1929, evidently because of bickering between the New York Federal Reserve Bank and the Board, Congress acted in 1935 to bring the system under the effective control of the Governors. The district banks were relegated to clearing checks between banks and the largely ceremonial function of representing their districts within the Fed, although the presidents of the district banks still retain important voting rights in making policy decisions.

Deposit Insurance

Another response to the runs on the banks in 1929 and during the Depressions years was the establishment of the Federal Deposit Insurance Corporation, or "FDIC." Depositors would no longer have a reason to rush to their bank all at once to try to withdraw their money if they knew that their deposits were insured.

Conceived as a means to stabilize the banking system, it also had the effect of shifting the risk of banking from depositors to the federal government. This left depositors with little incentives to monitor the safety of banks and many economists believe that this created a "moral hazard problem" which played a role in the banking failures of the 1980s. The consequences of moral hazard and the ensuing turmoil in the banking system will be discussed at greater length later on.

Recent Changes in Banking

With the establishment of the Fed came "national banks" which were chartered by the federal government, in contrast to charter by state government, and were required to become "members" of the Federal Reserve system. A national bank was subject to more strict regulation than a state bank, but it had the advantage of being able to borrow directly from the Fed.

Until the early 1980s there was a clear distinction between "commercial banks," which offered checking accounts as well as savings accounts, and "thrifts," which offered only savings accounts. The "savings and loan" was the most familiar type of thrift, and the "savings bank" was another variety. "S&Ls" were originally restricted primarily to residential mortgage lending with the objective of encouraging home ownership. S&Ls could be either federally chartered or state chartered, while savings banks were chartered by the states. Federally chartered S&Ls were regulated by the Federal Home Loan Bank, which operated much like the Federal Reserve, and their deposits were insured by the "FSLIC" which functioned essentially as the FDIC did for banks.

The 1980's were a time of upheaval and change in the structure of our banking system. The catalyst for these radical changes was the disastrous losses suffered by the thrifts in the 1970's as the result of soaring interest rates and inflation. Because the interest payment on a mortgage is fixed for the life of the mortgage, just as the coupon payment on a bond is fixed, rising interest rates decimated the market value of the mortgages owned by the S&Ls.

Meanwhile, the regulatory ceiling on the interest rate that S&Ls were permitted to pay depositors, called Regulation Q, meant that savings were flowing out of the S&Ls and into higher yielding investments such as Treasury bills. This loss of savings deposits is called "dis-intermediation" since it reverses the *intermediation* of savings through the S&Ls. By the end of the 1970s, many S&Ls were insolvent, meaning that the market value of their assets fell short of the their liabilities to depositors and others.

In the hope of restoring the health of the industry, Congress passed the Deregulation and Monetary Control Act of 1980. It gave thrifts the right to engage in many of the activities that were previously reserved for banks, including offering checkable deposits and making personal and business loans. It also raised the limit on deposit insurance from $40,000 to $100,000 per account. The idea was to bolster the confidence of depositors. It also lifted Regulation Q. The latter was a mixed blessing for the thrifts because they were not collecting enough interest on old mortgages to cover the cost of paying depositors a competitive market interest rate. The "control" aspect of the 1980 Act was the extension of the regulatory authority of the Fed to all depository institutions so there ceased to be much distinction between thrifts and commercial banks.

Then the Garn - St. Germain Depository Institutions Act of 1982, named after its legislative authors, erased most remaining distinctions between thrifts and banks. For all practical purposes, we now just have banks.

In the 1980's, desperate and imprudent thrift managements used the guarantee of federal deposit insurance of $100,000 per account to attract deposits from investors who would not otherwise have risked their savings in such shaky enterprises. More aggressive S&Ls advertised nationally to attract more deposits, promising high yields on federally insured Certificates of Deposit. Much of these funds was invested in speculative loans in situations where management had little experience or expertise in the hope of somehow making large enough profits on these new loans to dig their way out of the hole.

Economists refer to this situation as one of moral hazard: S&Ls with no net worth had little to lose by rolling the dice. As one Chicago S&L executive explained to the author, "if we win, great; if we lose, we just mail the keys to the FSLIC." We are all familiar with the disaster which ensued as many of these risky loans went bad, bankrupting hundreds of S&Ls and ultimately the FSLIC itself which had to be folded into the FDIC. So far, the cost to the taxpayers of making good on deposit insurance has come to several hundred billions of dollars.

Commercial banks faced similar strains, and there were many "shotgun weddings" of weak banks with stronger banks during the 1980s, with the Fed and the FDIC acting as insistent parents of the bride and groom. The fact that the assets of banks, commercial and consumer

250

loans, tended to have shorter repayment terms meant that they were better able to adjust to rising interest rates than were the S&Ls. However, deregulation of the S&Ls and the invention of the money market mutual fund, in direct response to the desire of investors to participate in the rising interest rates of the 1970s, meant that competition for the saver's dollar became much more intense. By the 1980s banking had evolved into a dynamic and highly competitive part of the "financial services" industry and many old banks and S&Ls did not survive.

The Fed Today

Partly as a result of this turmoil of the 1970s and 1980s, we now have a monetary system in which authority is highly centralized in the Fed. No doubt Presidents Jefferson and Jackson would turn over in their graves if only they knew! It is important to understand that the Fed is not part of the federal government, rather it is an independent but governmental body. The seven Governors of the Fed are appointed in a process much like that for federal judges; they are nominated by the President and confirmed by the Senate, serving for a term of 14 years. The Chairman is appointed in that capacity for a term of four years and in practice exercises considerable influence over Board decisions. Alan Greenspan is the current Chairman, having succeeded Paul Volcker in 1987.

The most important policy making body of the Fed is the Fed Open Market Committee, or FOMC, which sets the direction of policies aimed at stimulating or restraining the economy. Membership on the FOMC includes all seven of the governors and five of the twelve presidents of the district Federal Reserve banks who serve on a rotating basis. The Fed has traditionally been highly secretive in its deliberations, only releasing only vaguely worded minutes of the FOMC meetings after a gap of several weeks. Under increasing pressure from Congress to become more open, Fed Chairman Greenspan announced changes in Fed policy to the press immediately following FOMC meetings in 1994 for the first time in the Fed's history. Since then the Fed and its famous chairman have found themselves very much in the media spotlight as the importance of the

Fed's role in the economy has become clear to the public. These days, every meeting of the FOMC is anticipated by widespread speculation by news analysts of what its members might be thinking and what it is likely to do. Indeed, the daily gyrations of the stock market are often traced to remarks made by an FOMC member as Wall Street tries to discern their significance as a harbinger of Fed policy moves.

Exercises 6.3

A. Look at the past week's issues of the Wall Street Journal, other newspaper or newsmagazine and jot down the news items pertaining to the Fed. Summarize briefly the issues under discussion. Why do you think so much attention is paid to the Fed and it decisions?

6.4 How the Fed Controls the Supply of Money

The Federal Reserve clearly plays an important role in the economy as the issuer of currency, the regulator of banks, and the lender of last resort to banks in trouble. Its greatest influence over the economy, though, is through the control it has over the quantity of deposits in the banking system and, therefore, the quantity of money. It exercises this control through open market operations in which it adds to or reduces the reserves in the banks by buying or selling US Treasury securities. It is the FOMC that decides what the direction of these operations will be. To understand how the Fed uses open market operations to control the quantity of money we need to think a bit more about fractional reserve banking.

The fraction obtained by dividing the amount of reserves held by a bank by the amount of deposits outstanding is called the reserve ratio. The Fed requires that each bank hold a minimum fraction of reserves, called the required reserve ratio. In addition, a bank may elect to hold excess reserves above the required amount. If a bank finds that reserves fall below the required minimum, it can borrow the needed additional reserves from the Federal Reserve A bank in that situation is said to go to the discount window, referring to a figurative teller's window at the Fed where banks may borrow reserves. The interest rate which the Fed charges on these loans is called the discount rate.

There is little incentive for a bank to hold much excess reserves since, in the event of heavy depositor withdrawals, the Fed stands ready to lend needed reserves to the bank and, in the meantime, reserves do not earn interest for the bank. When a bank finds itself holding excess reserves it can make new loans which earn interest or it may lend excess reserves to other banks who are short of required reserves in the federal funds market. The interest paid on "fed funds" is determined by the supply and demand for reserves among banks and it is called the fed funds rate. Thus, a bank with deficient reserves may borrow at the discount window or in the fed funds market. It can restore its reserves over time by reducing the amount of loans it makes or more quickly by selling loans and marketable securities from its portfolio.

Open Market Operations

Now let's see how the Fed can change the amount of reserves in the banking system through open market operations in which the Fed buys or sells US Treasury securities. If the Fed wishes to increase the amount of reserves in the banking system it need only buy a Treasury bill or bond and pay for it with new money. (Note that the Fed is not part of the U.S. Treasury. That is a department of the administrative branch of the federal government responsible for collecting taxes, making payments for goods and services purchased by the government, funding transfer payments, issuing bills or bonds to cover the budget deficit, and making the coupon and face value payments on those securities.)

To illustrate what we mean by an open market operation, imagine that the Fed bought a U.S. Treasury bond from our friend Jane for $1,000. If you bought that bond from Jane we would have to withdraw $1,000 from our bank. That would simply have the effect of transferring reserves from one bank to another, specifically from your bank to hers, leaving the quantity of reserves in the banking system unchanged. However, when the Fed buys a bond it does so with money that did not exist before.

How can it do that? The Fed simply has the legal authority to issue new money. Suppose that the Fed pays for Jane's bond with 50 new $20 bills. Jane is willing to accept this newly manufactured currency because it is legal tender and identical to all the currency already in circulation. When Jane deposits that $1,000 in currency at her bank, the amount of reserves in her bank and in the banking system will increase by $1,000.

Equivalently, the Fed could write Jane a check which she would deposit at her bank, and which the bank would then deposit in its account at the Fed, which also increases the bank's reserves by $1,000.

What will now be the reserve position of the bank where Jane deposited the $1,000 payment for the bond she sold to the Fed? If the required reserve ratio is .10 then her bank will suddenly have excess reserves of $900 since it only is required to keep $100 of that new deposit on reserve. Suppose it lends that $900 to Joe for home improvements. Joe deposits the $900 in his bank account and then Joe's bank finds itself in a position to increase lending by $810 since it only is required to increase its reserves by $90, or 10% of $900.

Money Multiplication

At each stage of this process, a new deposit gives a bank excess reserves which permits it to make a new loan which, in turn, leads to another new bank deposit. The cumulative effect will be to increase the total amount of deposits in the banking system by much more than the new $1,000 printed by the Fed.

There are two strategies for calculating the total effect of the Fed's open market operation on the quantity of money. The direct strategy is to add up all of the increments as we do in this next table:

The Cumulative Effect of $1,000 of New Reserves When the Required Reserve Ratio is .10

Bank number	receives new deposit of	it keeps .10 of it on reserve	and makes new loans of
#1	$1,000	$100	$900
#2	900	90	810
#3	810	81	729
#4	729	73	656
and so on ..	and so on ..	and so on ..	and so on ..
...	...	...	...
Totals:	$10,000	$1,000	$9,000

The table shows that the first bank, which is Jane's, receives new deposits of $1,000, of which it will keep $100 on reserve and loans out the remainder of $900 to Joe. That $900 is deposited by Joe in the second bank, which must hold $90 of it on reserve but will loan out the remaining $810. At each step, the amounts deposited, kept for reserves, and loaned out is .90 times the amounts at the previous step. That is because the reserve ratio is .10, leaving the fraction (1-.10) or .90 to be passed on to the next bank in the process.

According to the table, when the process is complete, the total amount of new deposits in the banking system will be $10,000, new reserves $1,000, and new loans $9,000. How do we know that these are the total changes that will occur, given that the number of steps in the process is, in principle, infinite? There are at least three ways to see that these totals are correct.

One way is to run the process a very large number of steps on a computer, a spreadsheet is the perfect tool for this kind of experiment, and see empirically that the totals get infinitesimally close to, but do not exceed, the totals in the table.

A more elegant approach is to make use of the result from college algebra that for any fraction, say x, it is true that,

$$(1 + x + x^2 + x^3 + ...) = \frac{1}{(1-x)}$$

which is called the geometric series. Now at each step of the process described in Table 6.1, the amount of the additional deposits, required reserve, and loan is .90 of the amount at the previous stage, so the total effect at the end of the process must be $(1 + .90 + .90^2 + .90^3 + ...)$ times the amount at the first step in the process. Here .90 plays the role of x and the sum of this geometric series is $1/(1-.90)$ or 10. Therefore we can calculate total changes as follows:

New Deposits $= \$1,000 + \$1,000 \cdot .9 + \$1,000 \cdot .90^2 + \$1,000 \cdot .90^3 + ...$
$= \$1,000 \cdot (1 + .90 + .90^2 + .90^3 + ...)$
$= \$1,000 \cdot [1/(1-.90)]$
$= \$1,000 \cdot 10$
$= \$10,000$

and similarly,

New Reserves $= \$100 \cdot (1 + .90 + .90^2 + ..) = \$100 \cdot 10 = \$1,000$

256

and finally,

$$\text{New Loans} = \$900 \cdot (1 + .90 + .90^2 + \ldots) = \$900 \cdot 10 = \$9,000.$$

The third way to see that these must be the correct totals is to notice that expansion of deposits continues until total deposits in banks have increased to the point that the new $1,000 in currency is completely used up as required reserves.

This observation suggests a another strategy for calculating the effect of the Fed's open market operation. With a required reserve ratio of .10, $1,000 is just enough new reserves to support $10,000 of new bank deposits. The difference, $9,000, is then the amount of new loans.

Regardless of which of the three approaches is easiest to understand, we can agree that the general formula for the change in bank deposits in response to a change in reserves is:

$$\text{Change in bank deposits} = \text{Change in reserves} \cdot \frac{1}{\text{Required reserve ratio}}$$

The multiple by which bank deposits change in response to a change in reserves is called the money multiplier. We see from the equation just above that the money multiplier is given by

$$\text{Money multiplier} = \frac{1}{\text{Required reserve ratio}}$$

How the Fed Destroys Money

When the Fed wishes to reduce the quantity of money it simply reverses the process we have described. It sells U.S. Treasury securities, draining reserves from the banks. Finding themselves short of the amount of reserves required at their current level of deposits, banks will reduce the amount of loans outstanding until they can again meet the reserve requirement. When this process is completed, total deposits in the banking system will have decreased by the amount of the decrease in reserves times the deposit multiplier.

For example, if the Fed sells a U.S. Treasury bond from its portfolio to Bill for $1,000, he will withdraw that amount from his bank and pay it to the Fed. The bank where Bill has his account now has $1,000 less in deposit liabilities, so its required reserves have fallen by .10 of that or $100. However, its actual reserves have fallen by $1,000, the amount that Bill withdrew, so it now has $900 less in reserves than it is required to have. Deposits change by -$1,000, required reserves by -$100, so the bank needs to change the amount it has loaned out by -$900 to restore its reserves to the required level. Instead of having excess reserves as it did when the Fed bought a bond the bank now has an equivalent amount of deficient reserves when the Fed sells a bond. Bill's bank can restore its reserves by reducing its loans by $900, which it can accomplish simply by not relending money as it is paid back to the bank by borrowers. Each amount for bank #1 in Table 6.1 now has a minus sign in front of it. Of course, that $900 that bank #1 gets from repaid loans came from the withdrawal of deposits that were in another bank. That is bank #2 which now finds itself with $900 less in deposit liabilities and therefore $90 less in required reserves, but also $810 short in required reserves because it has paid out $900 from its reserves. We can now just put minus signs in front of all the entries for bank #2 Table 6.1.

This process of contraction in deposits, reserves, and loans continues until deposits have fallen by the full amount that would was previously supported by reserves of $1,000, that is $1,000 times the deposit multiplier of 10, or a total of $10,000. Reserves will have fallen by $1,000, of course, and loans by $9,000. Thus, through open market operations the Fed can either increase or decrease the supply or quantity of money in the economy.

The Fed's Policy Instruments

Open market operations are the *most important* policy instrument that the Fed has. Through its control of the money supply the Fed exercises a strong influence on the economy. As we will see in succeeding chapters, too large a money supply will lead to inflation, while too small a money supply will slow the economy down so that people become unemployed and factories idle.

As discussed earlier, open market operations are directed by the FOMC, which meets monthly. The directions of the FOMC are carried out by the New York Federal Reserve Bank, one of the twelve district banks, since it is located in the nation's financial center. The New York Fed buys and sells U.S. Treasury bonds as it seeks to supply or withdraw reserves from the banking system. By 1996 the Fed had acquired Treasury securities worth more than $400 billion through open market operations. There is nothing about Treasury securities that makes them *uniquely* suitable for open market operations, since the Fed could change bank reserves by buying or selling *anything*. However, if open market operations were conducted in wheat, it would disrupt the wheat market and probably distort the allocation of resources to wheat production, harming consumers. (A "wheat standard" has actually been suggested by some as the basis for a sound monetary system; not surprisingly, the advocates are usually from wheat producing states!)

Incidentally, the Fed's income from interest that it collects on its portfolio of Treasury securities is used to fund its operations including the magnificent Roman-style "temple" which houses the Board of Governors on the mall in Washington D. C. and its large staff which includes about 250 Ph.D. economists. (The Fed has been said to be not only the lender of last resort for banks, but also the employer of last resort for economists!) Any profit that is left over is transferred back to the U.S. Treasury. Open market operations are not actually conducted with $20 bills. Rather, the Fed deals with large banks that are dealers in Treasury securities and the Fed then credits or debits the bank's account at the Fed. Since the amount a bank has on deposit at the Fed counts as part of its reserves, this has the same effect on deposit expansion or contraction as would printed money. How can the Fed, in effect, just write checks as it pleases? Because it has the legal authority to do so!

The Fed's *second* policy instrument is to change the discount rate, the interest rate that it charges banks for borrowing reserves. The Fed makes it more or less attractive to banks to borrow reserves by decreasing or increasing the discount rate. In practice, banks do not borrow large amounts of reserves from the Fed because continued use of the discount window will result in a bank being identified as a "problem bank" which then comes under the special scrutiny of the bank examiners. Changes in the discount rate are mainly symbolic, to be interpreted as a signal from the Fed about its intentions. For example, if the Fed announces an increase in the discount rate from 3% to 3.5%, that should be interpreted as confirmation that the Fed is "tightening," intending to make reserves less plentiful and thus reducing the supply of money, or at least to slow its growth.

The fed funds rate, in contrast, is not directly set by the Fed since it is a market rate charged by banks to each other for the loan of reserves. However, the Fed can influence the fed funds rate through its control of the supply of bank reserves, as we will see in Chapter 7. The Fed will often announce a target level for the Fed funds rate, as it did in 1994 when it successively raised the fed funds target in several steps. The Fed will then conduct it open market operations, adding reserves or draining reserves, to achieve that fed funds target. The fed funds rate is also an indication to the Fed and others of the reserve position of the banks; a higher fed funds rate indicates that reserves are scarce and a lower one that reserves are plentiful. The fed funds rate is observed every day, while statistics on the actual amount of reserves is reported only with a delay and even then is subject to technical problems of interpretation.

The *third* policy instrument available to the Fed is changing the required reserve ratio, but this is done very infrequently.

The Fed's use of these three instruments is referred to as monetary policy. In the next three chapters we see how monetary policy affects the level of interest rates in the economy, how interest rates in turn influence purchasing decisions by firms and households, and thereby how monetary policy affects employment, income, and inflation.

Exercises 6.4

A. Suppose that the reserve ratio is .20 and the Fed conducts an open market operation in which it purchases $1 million in Treasury bonds. What will be the impact on the supply of money? on bank reserves? on bank loans?

B. Now consider what would happen in the above scenario if the Fed instead sold $1 million in bonds out of its portfolio.

C. Suppose that Congress passed a law that made gold the only acceptable asset for banks to hold as reserve against deposits. What would this do to the Fed's ability to change the supply of money?

D. Imagine that someone counterfeits one thousand $20 bills that are undetected as fake. Explain what effect the spending of these bills will have on the money supply.

Index

Chapter 7

The Demand for Money

Preview

In the last chapter we saw how the Federal Reserve can change the quantity of money in existence at will. In this chapter we will see how a change in the quantity of money causes interest rates to rise or fall. Since interest rates are a key variable in decisions to buy or invest, the ability to move interest rates gives the Fed a powerful lever to move the economy. That is why it is worth enduring some moderately technical discussion of the demand for money.

We use the familiar supply and demand model of economics to understand how changes in the quantity of money cause interest rates to move. The *supply of money* is the quantity of money, currency and bank deposits, set by the Fed. That is the number of dollars available to be held in wallets and bank accounts. The amount of money that people desire to hold is the *demand for money*. Since every dollar is held voluntarily, the quantity of money supplied by the Fed must be equal to the quantity demanded by money holders. As always, the demand for a good or service depends in part on its price or cost. The cost of holding money is an opportunity cost over time, because the alternative is investing those funds to earn interest. What one gets in return for giving up interest income is the liquidity that money provides. Each of us balances the opportunity cost of holding money with the value of that liquidity.

What happens if the Fed increases the supply of money? An increase in the supply of any good causes its price to fall. It must be the case that when the Fed buys bonds in an open market operation, thereby increasing the supply of money, it causes the "price" or opportunity cost of holding money to fall. Thus, by increasing the supply of money the Fed can push the interest rate down, and by reducing the supply of money it can push interest rates up.

In the next chapter we will see that lower interest rates stimulate investment spending on new plant and equipment by business and spending on durable goods by households because the cost of borrowing has fallen. The result is higher production and higher employment, at least until prices and wages adjust to the increase in demand. If the Fed persists in more rapid expansion of the money supply then inflation will accelerate.

This process operates in reverse when the Fed sells bonds, thereby reducing the money supply. Smaller supply means higher price, in this case higher interest rates. Higher interest rates mean that some investment projects are not undertaken and some houses are not built that would have been otherwise because loans are more costly. Demand for goods in the economy then falls, and with it production and employment. Inflation will decline, but usually not before the economy experiences a recession.

Interest rates, then, are the lever by which the Fed moves the real economy. Interest rates connect the monetary economy of banks and financial markets with the real economy of the production, distribution, and consumption of goods and services. This ability to influence the real economy through interest rates gives the Fed a very important role to play, and it is one which the Fed, as we shall see, has sometimes not played very skillfully.

7.1 What is "the Demand for Money?"

How much money would you like to have? A billion or two? Of course, that is *not* what we mean by your demand for money! What we do mean by your demand for money is this: how much of your wealth do you wish to keep in the form of money, that is, currency and bank deposits?

For example, suppose that the Joneses have $50,000 in financial assets which they divide between investment in bonds and holding money. How are they going to decide how much of their $50,000 to invest in bonds and how much to hold in the form of money, including currency and the balance in their checking account? An investment in bonds pays interest, but currency pays none and the Joneses receive no interest from their bank on their checking account.

Clearly, the opportunity cost of holding money is the rate of interest. If the Joneses keep $1,000, on average, in currency and in their checking account during the year and bonds yield 10%, then it costs the Joneses $100 in foregone interest to hold that $1,000. Why, then, should the Joneses hold any money at all instead of putting all of their wealth into bonds and other assets that will earn a return? For that matter, why does anyone hold any money?

Economists have identified three primary motives for holding money:

- **To settle transactions, since money is the medium of exchange.**

- **As a precautionary store of liquidity, in the event of unexpected need.**

- **To reduce the riskiness of a portfolio of assets by including some money in the portfolio, since the value of money is very stable compared with that of stocks, bonds, or real estate.**

These three motives for holding money are often referred to as the transactions motive, the precautionary motive, and the portfolio motive respectively. Together they provide good reasons for the Joneses to hold some money in their portfolio in spite of the opportunity cost of foregone interest.

Now suppose, hypothetically, that with the interest rate at 20% the Joneses choose to hold $1,000 of their $50,000 in the form of money. What will they do if the interest rate now drops to 5%? With the opportunity cost of holding money reduced, they will very likely choose to increase their money holdings by reducing their bond holdings. After all, it now costs the Jones only 5 cents per year to hold an extra dollar instead of 20 cents, while adding to their holdings of money will give them more of the services that holding money provides. The more currency in your wallet the less frequently you need to stand in line at a cash machine or teller's window. The larger your checking account balance the more readily you can meet unexpected payments, such as buying that suit that is on sale even though your credit card is up to its limit. The larger your cash position, the less worrisome is a fall in the stock market.

As a result of the interest rate falling from 20% to 5% the Joneses might well decide to increase their money holdings, say from $1,000 to

$1,500. They would accomplish that increase in their money holdings by selling bonds worth $500 and keeping the money they would be paid.

The amount of money demanded by the Joneses would change if their income increased. They would demand more money (at a given level of interest rates) primarily because their transactions and precautionary demands would increase at their new higher level of spending. An increase in their wealth would increase their portfolio demand for money. Even a change of jobs could affect their demand for money. Someone who travels a great deal in a sales position will have a greater precautionary demand for money than someone who stays in town.

We see, then, that a households' demand for money depends on the interest rate, their income, and wealth, among perhaps many other variables. Firms are also holders of money, in their cash registers and bank accounts, for essentially the same basic reasons as households. When we add up the demand for money by all households and firms we have the total demand for money in the economy and that demand will be most importantly a function of the interest rate, income, and wealth in the economy.

The demand for any good or service is usually pictured in economics as a function of its price, holding income and other factors constant. In the case of holding money, the "price" is the opportunity cost of holding one dollar for one year, the interest rate. When we plot the quantity of money demanded on the horizontal axis and the interest rate on the vertical axis, just as we would the quantity of oranges demanded and the price of oranges, we will have a demand curve like the one pictured in Figure 7.1.

Note that the quantity of money demanded is higher when the interest rate is lower, just as the quantity of oranges demanded is higher when the price of oranges is lower. As this hypothetical demand for money has been drawn, the demand for money is $600 billion when the interest rate is 5%, but only $150 billion when it is 20%. This inverse relationship between the interest rate and the demand for money just reflects the fact that when the opportunity cost of holding money is low, people will want to hold more of it, and when it is high people will want to hold less of it.

Notice, too, that at very low levels of the interest rate in Figure 7.1, the quantity of money demanded increases dramatically, meaning that people would then want to hold a very great amount of their wealth in the form of money. And why not hold money instead of bonds when the reward to holding bonds is very, very small? After all, money is more liquid than bonds, and bonds are subject to the risk of price fluctuation that we discussed in Chapter 3.

In contrast, even when the interest rate is very, very high, people will still want to hold some money. Even if it costs 30 cents per year to hold a dollar, we will still hold *some* dollars because it is even more costly to revert to barter in making transactions.

What will happen to the demand for money when the income and wealth of households and firms increases? Imagine that over the next decade the economy grows in real terms by 3% per year while the rate of inflation averages 4%, so that nominal income roughly doubles (Remember how to compute doubling time for a given rate of growth?). How will the demand for money change? It is pretty clear that the demand for money will increase, even if there is no change in interest rates. The total sales at the average supermarket will have doubled, reflecting both the larger quantity of goods sold and higher prices. Clearly, then, the transactions demand for money must roughly double.

Further, it is likely that rising wealth will also contribute to higher demand for money holdings through the portfolio motive. Indeed, it seems likely that wealth would also roughly double in nominal terms over a decade in which nominal income had doubled.

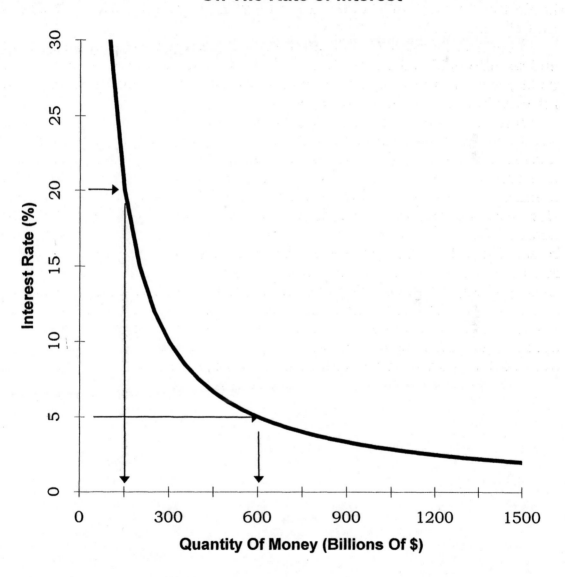

Figure 7.1: The Demand for Money Depends On The Rate of Interest

Overall, the quantity of money demanded at any given interest rate will be much higher a decade later under our assumptions, probably about twice its level a decade earlier. We depict this change in the demand for money by shifting the demand curve to the right. In Figure 7.2, the doubling of nominal incomes and wealth doubles the demand for money at any given interest rate. For example, at an interest rate of 5%, the quantity of money demanded is $1,200 billion at the end of the decade, while it was only $600 billion at the beginning of the decade ago when nominal income and wealth were half as great.

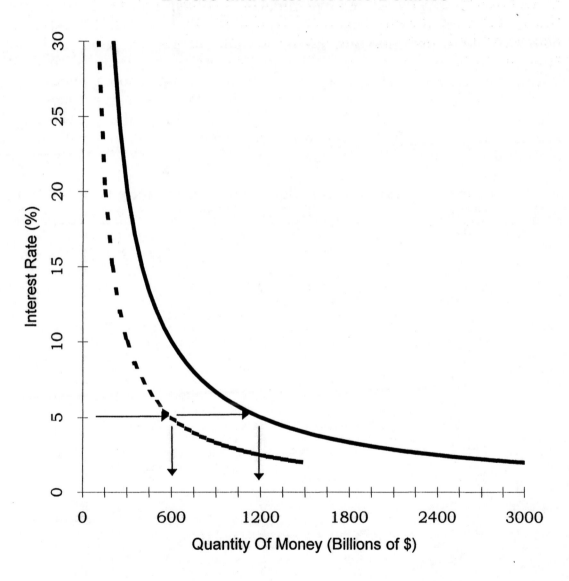

Figure 7.2: The Demand for Money Before and After Income Doubles

Interest Rate (%)

Quantity Of Money (Billions of $)

Exercises 7.1

A. Review the three primary motives for holding money. Indicate how important each one is to your own money holding behavior. How does each motive relate to money being the most liquid of assets?

B. Describe briefly the relative importance of each of the three motives for the following pairs of economic agents: (1) a small business owner as compared to a civil servant, (2) a very old person in poor health as compared with a young adult, (3) a retail store as compared with a law office, (4) a traveling salesperson as compared with a school teacher.

C. Imagine that the demand curve in Figure 7.1 represents the demand for money in the US a year ago. Since then, the economy has grown in real terms by 2% and there has been inflation at a rate of 3%. Sketch the position of the demand curve today relative to its old position a year ago.

D. "The price of a dollar is a dollar!" "No, it is the interest rate!" What is the source of this disagreement? Can both be right? Discuss.

7.2 How the Supply of Money and the Demand for Money Determine the Interest Rate

Just as the price we pay at the store for oranges is the price at which the demand for oranges equals the supply of oranges, the "price" of money is the interest rate at which the demand for money equals the supply of money. Now the supply of money is the quantity of currency and bank deposits which is set by the Fed. Since the supply of money does not vary with the rate of interest, we can depict the supply curve of money simply as a vertical line at the actual quantity of money.

In Figure 7.3 the supply of money is a vertical line at the quantity $300 billion, indicating that in this hypothetical economy the Fed has set the supply of money at $300 billion. The supply of money is fixed at that quantity, and it will remain there until the Fed decides to change it. The quantity of money demanded is equal to the quantity supplied, $300 billion, at an interest rate of 10%. At that interest rate, people are content to hold the quantity of money that is supplied by the Fed. What are the forces that will move the interest rate to 10% in Figure 7.3, and what forces keep it there until the supply or demand curve shifts?

Consider what would happen if, somehow, the interest rate were 9% instead of 10%. At an opportunity cost of only 9% people would want to hold more money than when the opportunity cost is 10%. As we see in Figure 7.3, they would want to hold more money than the Fed has actually supplied. In an attempt to increase their holdings of money to the level they desire, people like the Joneses would sell some of their bonds in order to increase their holdings of money.

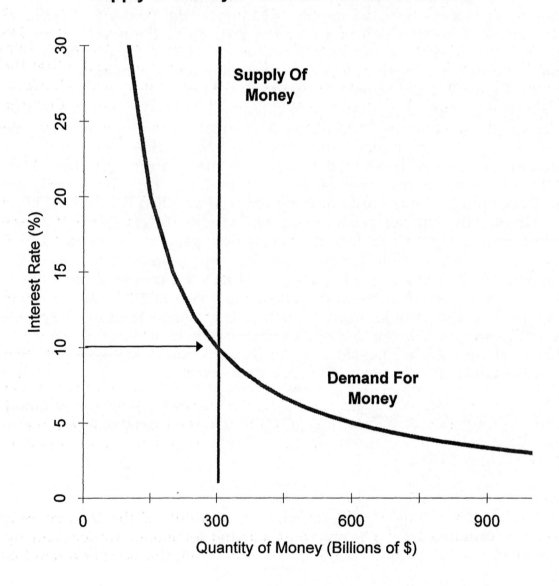

Figure 7.3: Intersection of Demand for Money and Supply of Money Determine the Interest Rate

However, while any one economic agent can increase or decrease the quantity of money that they hold, *all economic agents taken together cannot change the quantity of money that they hold because the quantity of money is fixed.* Currency and bank account balances can move from one agent to another, but only the Fed can change the total amount of money that everybody holds in aggregate. What *can* change is the interest rate. As everybody tried to sell bonds to increase their holding of money, the price of bonds would fall, causing bond yields to rise. Recalling that the interest rate is just the yield on bonds, we see that the interest rate would rise and it would continue to rise until it was back up to 10%. At that point the interest rate would stop rising because then the Joneses and everyone else would be content to hold the quantity of money that exists.

Suppose, on the other hand, the interest rate rose temporarily to 11%. Then the Joneses and others would find the cost of holding money had risen, and they would want to reduce their money balances in order to hold more of their assets in the form of bonds. As the Joneses and others try to purchase bonds, they would bid bond prices up and bond yields down.

Again, keep in mind that the total quantity of money in the economy is not altered by the attempts of individuals to change their own holdings of money. The currency or checking account balance that one person uses to buy a bond only passes into someone else's hands. Therefore, the adjustment process can only be complete when the interest rate has fallen enough so that the Joneses and others are content to hold the existing quantity of money, and that occurs only when the interest rate is 10%. This is why economists refer to the intersection of the demand curve and the supply line as the equilibrium in the money market. In our hypothetical example pictured in Figure 7.3, the equilibrium occurs at an interest rate of 10%.

Two Sides of the Same Coin

Students are sometimes puzzled that we think of the interest rate being determined by the supply and demand for money rather than by the supply and demand for bonds, since, after all, the price of a bond is just a transformation of the interest rate. Indeed, it would be paradoxical if the price of bonds were not in fact determined by the supply and demand for bonds. There is no paradox here because the two markets, for money and for bonds, can be thought of as two sides of the same coin (no pun intended).

Agents make a portfolio decision to divide their financial wealth between money, which offers no reward other than its services, and securities such as bonds and stocks that pay interest and may rise or fall in price. Our analysis is simplified by using bonds to represent all financial assets, and the yield on bonds as the reward for holding financial assets. Agents then decide to divide their wealth between money and bonds in light of the interest rate offered on bonds, and other factors. The interest rate, then, can be thought of as being determined in either the bond market or the money market interchangeably.

A Shift in the Supply of Money

What happens to the interest rate when the Fed increases the supply of money? For example, imagine that the Fed boosts the money supply suddenly from $300 billion to $600 billion. In Figure 7.4 this is indicated by the shift in the vertical supply line to the right. At the old interest rate of 10%, agents wish to hold only $300 billion, not $600 billion. What could induce them to hold the additional money? Certainly an increase in their income or wealth would induce them to hold larger money balances, but it seems evident that these variables do not change very rapidly. What *can* change rapidly enough to clear the money market is the rate of interest. In fact, interest rates do change daily and even hourly in response to Fed actions. How will the interest rate change as a result of our hypothetical doubling of the money supply?

Clearly, the interest rate must fall so that the opportunity cost of holding money is reduced to the point that people want to hold twice as much money. From Figure 7.4 we see that at an interest rate of 5% the quantity of money demanded is equal to the supply, $600 billion. Money is now much cheaper to hold because there is much more of it available.

The mechanism that pushes the interest rate down from 10% to 5% in our example is, again, the efforts of households and firms to adjust their money balances to their desired levels. At the old interest rate of 10%, economic agents find that their money holdings, now $600 billion, are too large. Their ensuing efforts to switch from money into bonds will bid bond prices up and bond yields down until the new equilibrium is reached at the new, lower interest rate. Finally, at an interest rate of 5% the agents in this economy are content to hold the $600 billion supply of money and the money market is again in equilibrium.

This application of the principle supply and demand shows how the Fed uses its control of the money supply to move interest rates up or down. As we shall see in Chapter 8, the ability to move the interest rate up or down gives the Fed a powerful lever with which to move the real economy.

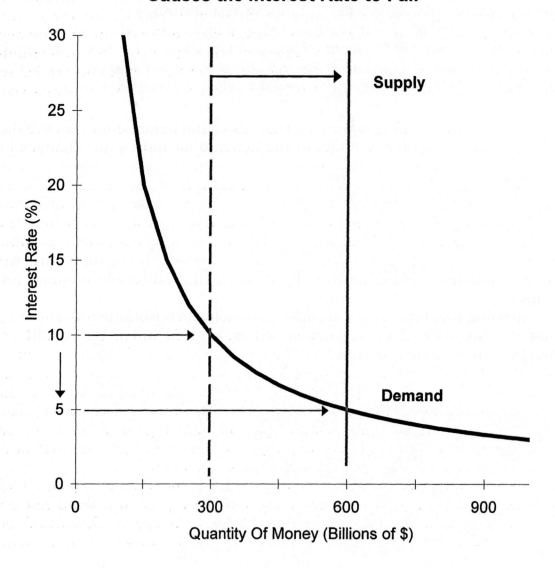

Figure 7.4: An Increase in the Supply of Money Causes the Interest Rate to Fall

Interest Rate (%)

Supply

Demand

Quantity Of Money (Billions of $)

A Shift in the Demand for Money

The interest rate will also change when there is a shift in the demand for money. By a shift in the demand for money we mean a change in the quantity demanded at any given interest rate. We have already surmised that the demand for money depends on nominal income and wealth. It will also be affected by fluctuations in the volume of transactions of assets. Heavy trading on the stock exchanges or rapid turnover in the real estate market, for example, will both increase the quantity of money demanded simply because these transactions are settled in the medium of exchange, money. A great deal of money is used in retail trade, so during the holiday season in December there is always a large increase in the demand for money.

While there are many variables that affect the demand for money, the most important source of shifts in the demand for money are changes in nominal income. One of the key strategies of economic analysis is to simplify, reducing the virtually infinite detail of reality to a small number of key variables which we can reasonably hope to incorporate in an economic model. The test of the model is not whether it is a detailed description of reality, but whether it is useful in explaining the important features of the economy that we seek to understand. In this spirit we choose nominal income as the key variable that shifts the demand for money.

Pursuing this strategy, it seems reasonable, as a working assumption, that the quantity of money demanded at a given interest rate will be roughly proportional to nominal income. This is easiest to see as a consequence of the transactions motive for money holding. If your nominal income doubles you probably will want to keep about twice as much cash on hand since your transactions will be about twice as great in dollars as before. This relation should hold regardless of whether income doubles because of a doubling of the price level, or because of a doubling of real income, or because of increases in both.

For example, if we learn that over time the Jones' income has increased from $25,000 per year to $50,000 per year, we would not be surprised to find that they now have $2,000 in the bank instead of $1,000 (assuming the interest rate is still 10%). In addition, we can think of changes in nominal income as also serving as a "proxy" for other variables, such as wealth and the volume of trading in stocks and real estate, that tend over time to increase in proportion to income. In light of Chapter 2, our measure of nominal income for the economy is, of course, nominal GDP.

A Simple Money Demand Model

This line of reasoning leads us to a simple algebraic model of the demand for money that looks like this:

$$M^d = k(i) \bullet GDP$$

where "M^d" is the quantity of money demanded and "$k(i)$" a coefficient which is a function of the interest rate "i". This simple equation says that the amount of money demanded, at any given interest rate, is proportional to nominal income, as measured by nominal GDP. For example, if GDP increases by 10% then the demand for money increases by 10% as well, at any given interest rate. Graphically, the demand curve shifts to the right by an amount equal to $k(i)$ times the change in GDP.

Since the demand for money varies inversely with the interest rate, the factor of proportionality $k(i)$ must vary inversely with the interest rate. This means that $k(i)$ decreases as the interest rate increases, and this gives the demand curve its downward slope when we graph it.

To see how a change in nominal GDP by itself affects the interest rate, we use Figure 7.5 to show what would happen to the interest rate if there were an increase in nominal GDP with no change in the supply of money. Suppose, hypothetically, that nominal income doubles. (In reality it would take several years for US GNP to double and certainly the supply of money would have grown during that time, but here we are conducting a thought experiment to help us understand how shifts in demand affect the interest rate.) The quantity of money demanded at any given interest rate doubles, because the demand is proportional to nominal GDP.

This is seen in Figure 7.5 as a horizontal shift of the demand curve to the right, so that now the demand is twice what is was before the shift.

We can also see from our simple money demand equation that the demand doubles by using the fact that "new GDP" is just "2 • old GDP" which gives us:

New M^d = k(i) • **new** GDP = k(i) • [**2** • **old** GDP] = **2** • **old** M^d

As we see in Figure 7.5, the new intersection of demand and supply must necessarily occur at a higher interest rate. Before the shift, the demand for money equals the supply of $600 billion at an interest rate of 5%. After the shift, the demand for money at the old interest rate of 5% far exceeds the quantity supplied, which is still $600 billion.

As people seek to increase their holdings of money by selling bonds, the price of bonds falls and the interest rate (the yield on bonds) rises. When the interest rate has risen to 10%, people are content to hold only the previously existing quantity of money in spite or their higher incomes and the higher demand for money that accompanies that higher income.

One of the implications of our money demand model is that if the Fed wishes to keep the interest rate constant, it must increase the supply of money at the same rate as the increase in nominal GDP. For example, suppose that nominal GDP is growing at a rate of 8% per year, consisting of 3% real growth and 5% inflation. To prevent the interest rate from changing, the Fed must keep the money supply growing by 8% per year. If it does this, then both supply and demand are increasing at the same rate so that the equilibrium interest rate is unchanged.

If the money supply were to grow faster than 8% then the supply curve would be shifting to the right faster than the demand curve, and then the intersection of the two would occur at a lower interest rate. Conversely, if the Fed slowed money growth to below 8%, the interest rate would rise. We see, then, that in a dynamic economy in which output and prices are both changing, the effect of the money supply on the interest rate will depend on the *relative* growth rates of money and income.

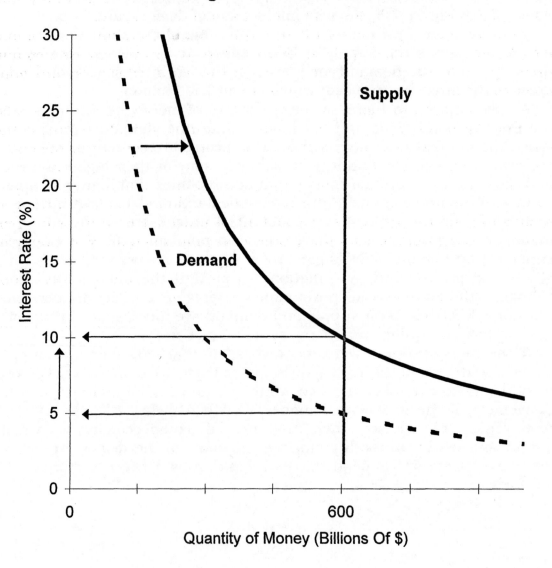

Figure 7.5: Higher Income Shifts the Demand for Money Causing the Interest Rate to Rise

Supply

Demand

Interest Rate (%)

Quantity of Money (Billions Of $)

Exercises 7.2

A. Suppose the Fed announced tomorrow that it is cutting the required reserve ratio for banks. What would be the response of interest rates? of bond prices?

How does your answer change if instead the Fed announced an increase in required reserves? Explain your answer with a supply and demand diagram, being careful to label the axes and curves.

B. Imagine that a recession starts in the fall of 1997 and results in a decline in national income. What prediction does our money demand make about what would be the effect on interest rates? Explain your answer with a supply and demand diagram.

C. If nominal GDP is growing at a rate of 7% per year and the Fed wants to keep the interest rate constant, how fast should it increase the money supply? Explain your answer both algebraically and graphically.

D. Every December retail sales are far greater than at any other time of the year. This heavy volume of transactions results in a large increase in the demand for money which disappears after the holidays are over. What prediction would we make about the seasonal pattern of interest rates if the Fed did not take any action to change the supply of money in December? Explain.

In fact, interest rates are not higher in December than in other months, on average. What inference can we draw about how the Fed manages the money supply?

7.3 *The Demand for Money Really Does Depend on the Interest Rate*

Does the demand for money look anything like the downward sloping, concave curve that we have used in our hypothetical discussions? How can we investigate such a question? The simple model of the demand for money developed in the previous section gives us a framework in which to work. Recall that our model says that the demand for money is given by,

$$M^d = k(i) \cdot GDP$$

while the supply of money is just the actual quantity supplied by the Fed,

$$M^s = M$$

where "M^s" denotes the supply of money and "M" the actual quantity of money. In equilibrium the quantity of money demanded equals the actual quantity supplied, so we have,

$$k(i) \cdot GDP = M$$

and that tells us that $k(i)$ is just,

$$k(i) = M/GDP$$

Now $k(i)$ can be thought of as the quantity of money demanded *per dollar of GDP*. Since in market equilibrium the quantity demanded is always equal to the actual money supply, M, we can observe $k(i)$ at any point in time by dividing the actual quantity of money by GDP. We can then see whether the observed values of $k(i)$ bear the relationship to observed values of "i" that we had hypothesized. In Figures 7.6 and 7.7 we do just that.

Figure 7.6 is an "XY plot," also called a "scatter plot," with the quantity of M1 per dollar of GDP on the X axis and the Treasury Bond yield on the Y axis. Each point corresponds to a paired observation of [M/GDP] and the bond yield during one calendar quarter. For example, in the first quarter of 1994 the bond yield was 6.44% and the ratio of M to GDP was 0.17, so the observation for that quarter corresponds to the black square with coordinates (0.17, 6.44).

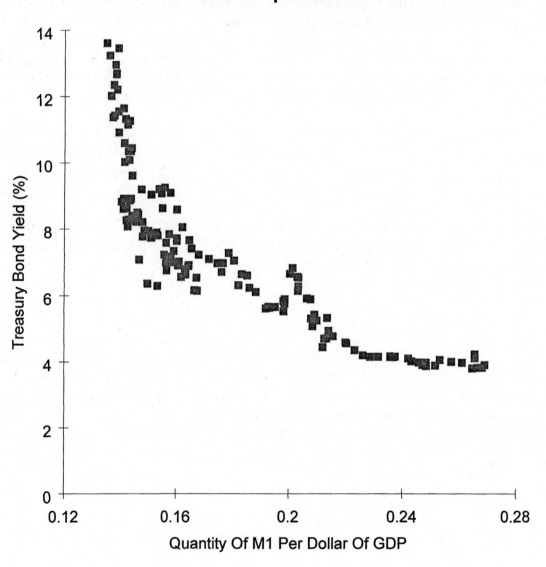

Figure 7.6: Scatter Plot of Yield on T Bonds and M1 per dollar of GDP

Figure 7.7 is a corresponding scatter plot using the yield on US Treasury bills instead of bonds. Why two interest rate and two figures? In theory we speak of "the interest rate" and in reality we observe many interest rates, but the yields on Treasury bills and bonds are two important benchmark interest rates in the economy.

What we see when we look at these figures is that the points do form *a pattern that has the general shape of the demand function that we hypothesized.* It is downward sloping and concave, flattening as it approaches the X axis and steepening as it approaches the Y axis. The points do not, however, lie exactly along a smooth line, rather they appear to be scattered around a curve that has the shape we have described.

Evidently, our model does not describe the demand for money exactly. What might be missing or wrong in the model? We have left out variables besides income and the interest rate that may affect the demand for money, such as the volume of trading on the New York Stock Exchange. It seems unlikely that the effect of income on the demand for money is exactly one of proportionality. More complex models of the demand for money attempt to address these issues, but the simple model is a useful approximation for our purposes.

The relationship between the demand for money per dollar of GDP and the bond yield is smoother and more precise than is the same relationship for the bill yield. Note that there is a good bit of up and down variation, or "noise," in the T bill yield that is not associated with M/GDP. Which interest rate, then, is the "right" one to use? The much more complex models of the demand for money developed and used by the Fed recognize that several interest rates, all representing alternatives to holding wealth in cash, will be involved.

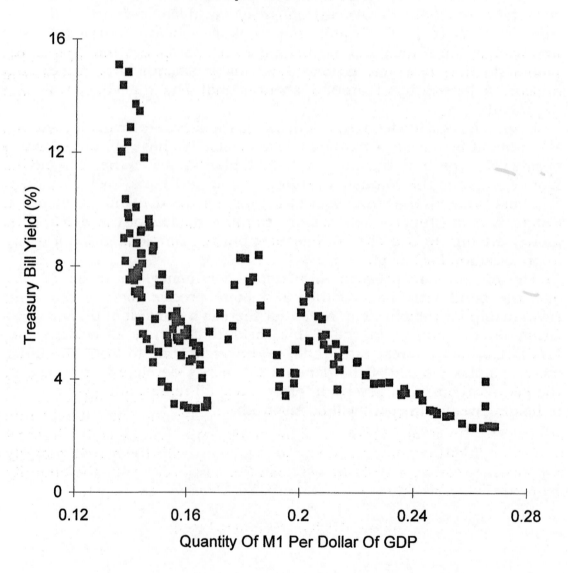

Figure 7.7: Scatter Plot of Yield on T Bills and M1 per Dollar of GDP

The "Velocity" of Money

A useful concept in thinking about the demand for money is the velocity of money which is defined as nominal GDP divided by the quantity of money. Giving velocity the symbol V and using M for the quantity of money we can write the definition of velocity as

$$V = GDP/M$$

This ratio is called the velocity of money because we can think of it as the rate at which dollars circulate through the economy. It is the number of times a dollar gets used per year in the purchase of the goods and services that make up GDP.

In light of what we understand about the relationship between the demand for money and the interest rate, we know that the velocity of money also depends on the interest rate, and it will be higher when the interest rate is higher. The intuition behind this is that at higher levels of the interest rate people will respond to the high cost of holding money by conserving on it. Therefore they will hold less money, M, relative to their incomes, GDP, so the ratio GDP/M will be higher. It may be helpful to think of it this way: when interest rates are higher it pays to run to the bank faster. Following this reasoning, we expect the velocity of money to be higher in Brazil, where interest rates are very high, than in Switzerland, where interest rates are very low. Brazilians go to a lot of trouble to hold as little money as possible; knowing it is expensive to hold money, they convert their pay into goods very quickly. The Swiss, on the other hand, can afford the convenience of larger money balances relative to their incomes because holding Swiss francs costs little.

We can also see the relation between velocity and the interest rate algebraically by using our demand for money equation. Since the interest rate will adjust to equate the demand for money with the actual quantity supplied, we can replace M in the definition of velocity with the quantity demanded which is $k(i) \cdot GDP$. Making this substitution we get,

$$V = GDP/[GDP \cdot k(i)] = 1/k(i)$$

Since k(i) varies *inversely* with the interest rate, i, velocity will vary *directly* with i. If interest rates rises, so will velocity. If interest rates fall, so too will velocity. Of course this is not a precise relationship; it is only as good as our simple model of the demand for money. If we redrew Figures 7.6 and 7.7 with velocity, GDP/M, instead of M/GDP on the X axis, the effect would simply be to turn them upside down.

Exercises 7.3

A. Suppose the interest rate in Japan is 3% and in Russia it is 150%. Which country do you think has a higher quantity of money per dollar of GDP? Which country do you think has a higher velocity of money? Explain your answer in a way that would be understood by someone who hadn't taken economics.

B. From our study of Figures 7.6 and 7.7 we concluded that there are factors besides interest rates and GDP which influence the demand for money. What are some of factors that might influence the demand for money over short periods of time? over long periods of time? Explain briefly how these factors would influence the demand for money per dollar of GDP, increasing it or decreasing it.

C. Imagine that later in the 1990's the Treasury bill yield returns to the levels of the late 1970s. What change would you expect to see in the demand for money per dollar of GDP and in the velocity of money as that change in the level of interest rates takes place? Explain.

D. If credit cards were suddenly declared illegal, what effect would you expect it to have on the demand for money? What would be the effect on interest rates immediately? (Something close to this situation actually occurred in 1980 toward the end of the Carter Administration!)

Chapter 8

How the Fed Moves the Economy

Outline

Preview

In Chapter 2 we learned that GDP is the total value of goods and services produced by the economy in response to demand from the household, business, government, and rest-of-world sectors. If the Fed can cause an increase in the demand for goods from any of these sectors, then it can cause an increase in real GDP, provided firms are willing to produce the additional output. Similarly, if the Fed can dampen demand, then it can reduce real GDP and even cause a recession.

In this chapter we will see how the interest rate becomes the lever with which the Fed moves the demand for goods. We will analyze how a change in the interest rate has its immediate impact on the demand for investment goods (plant and equipment) by the business sector and for durable goods by the household sector. Lower interest rates reduce the cost of buying durable goods such as factories, machines, office buildings, new houses, autos, and major appliances. An increase in the demand for such durables stimulates firms to produce more, thereby boosting real GDP. Conversely, higher interest rates discourage such spending and dampen economic activity. This will lead into our discussion in Chapter 9 of how monetary policy should be conducted by the Fed in light of this ability to affect the real economy.

8.1 The Interest Rate and the Demand for Durable Goods

Imagine that you are running a catering business. As you look at the operations of your business you can see a number of improvements that you could make to reduce costs or increase sales, but they all involve spending money on new equipment or facilities. Having done your MBA you know that the scientific manager makes a list of potential projects, figuring the rate of return on investment or "ROI" for each. Then one ranks the projects by ROI, and usually undertakes those which offer a higher ROI than the cost of capital. But since you haven't really completed an MBA yet, lets find out what all that jargon means with the help of a simple example.

What is the ROI?

Take your two delivery vans for example. They are real junkers and are in the repair shop so much that you could get the same work done with one new reliable van at considerable savings in employee time and repair bills. A new van costs $15,000 and you estimate that during the first year you would save $8,000 in expenses and that the van would have a resale value of $12,000 at the end of the year. Your investment in the van is $15,000, while the value received from your investment after one year would be $8,000 in cost savings plus the $12,000 resale value of the used van.

The ROI for this van is calculated in the same way that we calculate the yield or return on any investment: the amount gained from the investment as a percentage of the original cost:

$$\text{ROI} = \frac{\text{Amount Gained}}{\text{Amount Invested}} = \frac{\text{Cost Savings} + \text{Resale Value} - \text{Cost of Van}}{\text{Cost of Van}}$$

Putting in the numbers for the delivery van we have:

$$\text{ROI} = \frac{\$8,000 + \$12,000 - \$15,000}{\$15,000} = .33 = 33\%$$

a 33% return on investment. You can think of this as being analogous to the yield on a one-year bond, where $15,000 is the price of the bond, $8,000 is the coupon received, and $12,000 is the face value. The yield on a one-year bond is the return on a financial investment, the ROI is the return on an investment in plant and equipment.

If your catering business has liquid assets that it can invest, then you will want to compare the ROI on a new van to the ROI, or yield, on alternative investments, including bonds. If the yield on one year bonds is 10%, then it is clearly to your advantage to buy the van rather than a bond. The interest rate available on bonds is the opportunity cost of buying the van. If the ROI for the van exceeds your opportunity cost, then you surely will buy the van; you are far ahead earning 33% rather than 10%. Of course, the return on a bond is a certainty if held to maturity, while the return on the van is less certain since you may have overestimated or underestimated the resale value of the new van. You will want to keep this distinction in mind when making the decision whether to purchase the van or a bond.

What if you need to borrow to pay for the van? This is the situation that rapidly growing businesses almost always face. If you can borrow the $15,000 from the bank for one year at 15%, you will almost surely go ahead and buy the van. The interest rate the bank charges you on the loan is your cost of capital. Projects with an ROI higher than your cost of capital will be advantageous for you to undertake. In practice, the interest rate your firm can earn as an investor in bonds will generally be less than what a bank will charge you for a loan.

A list of possible investment projects in your catering business with the cost and ROI for each might look like this:

Table 8.1: Potential Investment Projects and Their ROIs

Investment in:	Cost $	ROI
Van	15,000	33%
Freezer	7,500	25%
Pasta machine	2,000	20%
Espresso maker	3,000	15%
Display shelving	12,000	10%
Satellite phone	1,100	5%

With bank loans costing 15%, you will probably buy the first three items because the ROI in each case exceeds your cost of capital. But you might not buy the espresso maker since you expect it to earn you a return that is only just enough to pay for your bank loan. Given the uncertainty of realizing the estimated ROI in practice, it is perhaps prudent to undertake projects only if their ROI exceeds the cost of capital by an amount that compensates you for the risk you are taking that the project will not work out as well as you hoped.

You almost certainly would not buy the last two items which have ROIs that are less than the cost of capital.

What Happens When the Interest Rate Changes?

What would it take to make you change these decisions? Suppose the interest rate charged by the bank on loans jumped to 22%. Then it is very clear that you would drop your plan to buy the pasta machine, and would certainly not buy the espresso maker. On the other hand, if you could get a loan at only 10% then the espresso maker would be on for sure, and maybe the display shelving too.

But why would the bank change the interest rate it charges on loans? Banks can invest their funds in bonds as well as in direct loans to firms or households. Therefore the interest rate on bank loans must be competitive with other interest rates such as yields on bonds issued by the U.S. Treasury or General Motors Corporation, adjusting for risk of default. Of course, your catering business will be required to pay a higher interest rate than the Treasury or GE because the risk that you might default is perceived to be much higher. Because all of these borrowers compete to attract funds from the same lenders, when interest rates rise or fall there is a tendency for all interest rates to move together: bank loan rates, Treasury bond yields, corporate bond yields, home mortgage rates, and so forth.

That is why economists speak of "the" interest rate influencing the demand for capital goods; there are actually many interest rates, but they all move together with the benchmark yield on Treasury bonds. This means that the Fed can affect the rate your business pays for a loan simply by its influence on the supply of money through open market operations.

When the Fed expands the money supply, interest rates fall and more investment projects in businesses like your catering firm become attractive to undertake, so spending on plant and equipment rises. When the Fed contracts the money supply, interest rates rise and many potential investment projects become unattractive, so investment spending falls.

297

The Demand for New Plant and Equipment

Now let's add up the value of all the investment projects that would be undertaken by all the firms in the economy at each level of the interest rate. For example, at an interest rate of 10% the total might be $400 billion, while at 5% a total of, say, $800 billion in investment projects would be undertaken. Plotting these totals with the interest rate (the cost of capital) on the vertical axis and the total dollar value of investment projects on the horizontal axis, we would get a demand curve for investment goods such as we see in Figure 8.1.

Just as the demand for apples is a downward sloping function of the cost of apples, the demand for investment goods is a downward sloping function of the cost of the financial capital used to buy them. At very high levels of the interest rate, there are only a few projects that are worth undertaking. At very low levels of the interest rate there will be many projects that become profitable, and very large projects will become profitable. For example, if the cost of capital were only 1% then it might become profitable to build a land bridge across the Bering Sea between Siberia and Alaska.

According to Figure 8.1, at an interest rate of 10% the demand for investment goods is $400 billion per year, while at 5% the demand is much greater, $800 billion, because the cost of capital to firms is lower. If the Fed cuts the interest rate from 10% to 5% by increasing the money supply, it provides a $400 billion boost to the demand for goods in the economy. If, conversely, the Fed pushes the interest rate up from 5% to 10% by reducing the money supply, then it will reduce the demand for goods in the economy by $400 billion. Of course, these specific amounts are hypothetical, and the actual investment demand curve for the U.S. economy shifts as other economic conditions change. What is important here is the principle that by lowering interest rates the Fed can increase the demand in the economy for capital goods, while by raising interest rates the Fed can diminish the demand for goods.

298

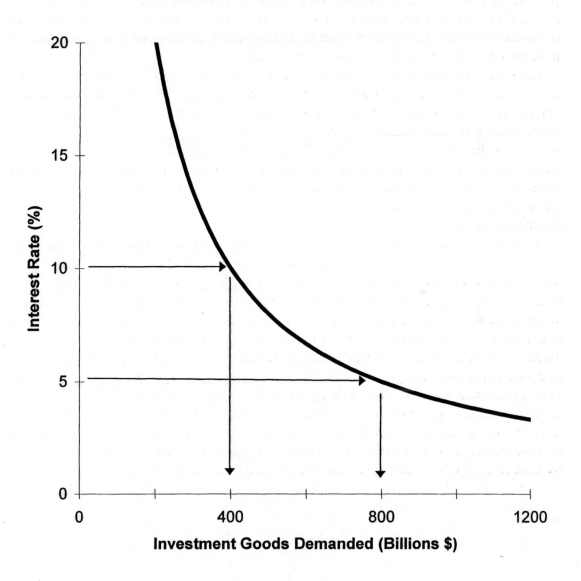

Figure 8.1: The Demand for Investment Goods Depends on the Interest Rate

Household spending on durable goods such as appliances, cars, and housing is also sensitive to interest rates because these are the capital goods of the household. That new refrigerator that uses half as much electricity as the old icebox, makes ice cubes automatically, and is much more reliable has an ROI just as the delivery van does. As consumers, we usually don't go to the trouble of putting a specific dollar value on such benefits to calculate an ROI, but the same factors influence our decisions. Lower interest rates will make more attractive the purchase of refrigerators, homes, autos and other "consumer durables" which are all investments that provide benefits to the household over a period of time.

To sum up, interest rates are the link between the "monetary economy" of banks and financial markets and the "real economy" of production and employment.

The ability to stimulate or dampen the demand for a wide range of goods through its influence on interest rates gives the Fed a very powerful lever to move the economy.

Exercises 8.1

A. By replacing its old personal computers with new powerful workstation computers, an engineering firm estimates it can save 150 hours of an engineer's time per workstation per year. This is because design ideas can be tested with "Cad/Cam" software much more quickly on the faster workstations. Design engineers earn about $40 per hour including fringe benefits. Workstations lose about half their market value in the first year, and cost $10,000 new. What is the ROI to the firm on a new workstation during the first year? If the firm can borrow at 7%, do you think it will buy new workstations? Why? How would your answer change if the interest rate were instead 10%? or 15%?

B. Investment by firms in new computers has surged in the 1990s as the prices have fallen. How would your answers to question A change if the price of the workstation were cut to $8,000? How does this explain the boom in investment in computing equipment in spite of stable and even higher interest rates?

8.2 Aggregate Supply and Aggregate Demand

We have seen now that if the Fed conducts an open market operation to reduce interest rates by increasing the money supply, the effect will be to increase the demand for capital goods. Microeconomics teaches us to expect two things to happen when the demand for a good increases: 1) its price rises, and 2) the higher price induces firms to produce more of it. We will see that these two effects also occur at the macroeconomic level: 1) the price level, as measured by a price index, will rise, and 2) output, measured by real GDP, will rise.

Start at the Micro Level

Let's start by looking at the market for trucks. Figure 8.2 depicts a hypothetical supply curve for trucks, with the price of a truck on the vertical axis and the quantity produced per year on the horizontal axis. A supply curve tells us what price is required to induce the industry to produce a given quantity of the good. The higher the price, the more output is forthcoming from the industry. Why? The marginal (incremental) cost of production rises as the production rate increases because the firm uses its most productive resources first; additional output forces it to use less productive machines and less experienced workers. Because a firm will produce until the marginal cost of producing another unit is just covered by the price it will receive for that unit, a higher price will induce the firm to produce more.

For example, at a price of $12,500 the truck industry produces 600,000 trucks per year, according to the hypothetical supply curve of Figure 8.2, but if the price is $15,000 then the industry will boost production to 800,000 trucks per year. But to induce the industry to boost production to 900,000 requires a very big price increase to $20,000. That is because the marginal cost of production is rising very steeply at higher levels of output. Contributing to these higher cost would be factors such as overtime wages to workers, higher shipping costs to obtain parts from more distant suppliers, a higher rate of wear and tear on machinery, and so forth.

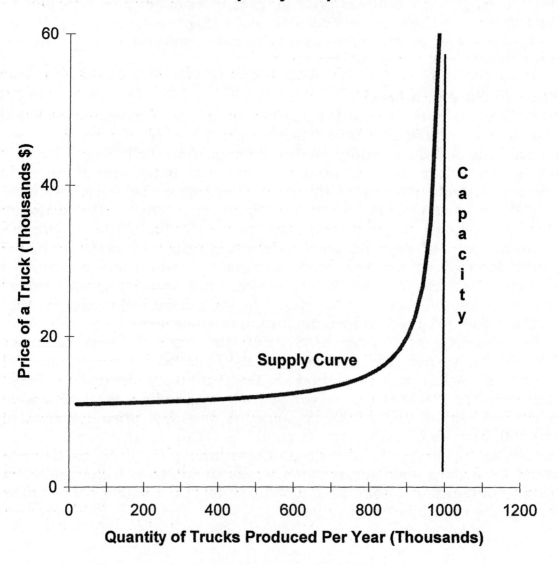

Figure 8.2: The Supply Curve for Trucks and Full Capacity Output

Indeed, there is no price high enough to induce the industry to produce more than about 1,000,000 trucks per year because there are ultimately physical limitations on the ability to produce. Industrial engineers would say that the industry has a capacity of just under a million units. From the perspective of an economist, the important fact is that costs rise very steeply as production rates approach full capacity utilization.

Impact of a Change in the Interest Rate

The impact of a shift in the demand for trucks on the price of trucks and the rate of output of the industry will depend on where demand intersects the supply curve. In Figure 8.3 we have an initial demand curve, the thin line, which intersects the supply curve at point #1.

Recall that the demand curve tells us how many units buyers will purchase at a given price. At lower prices, the quantity demanded is, of course, greater. The position of the demand curve depends on a number of factors that affect demand, including the interest rate. At point #1 in Figure 8.3, the price is such that purchasers are willing to produce exactly the number of trucks that the firms are willing to produce, so the market is in equilibrium at that price.

If the Fed now acts to cut interest rates, then the quantity of trucks demanded at any given price will increase as potential purchasers compare the ROI on a new truck with the lower interest cost. What we will see in the truck market is rightward shift of the demand curve as shown, with the new equilibrium at point #2. As the market moves from point #1 to point #2 there is a large increase in the quantity of trucks produced and little change in price. That is because in this range the firms can boost their production with only a moderate increase in marginal cost.

If the Fed were then to cut interest rates even further, causing another rightward shift of the demand curve, then the market would move from point #2 to point #3 along a portion of the supply curve where prices are rising very steeply. This second shift has therefore resulted mainly in an increase in the price of trucks with little increase in the quantity of trucks produced.

Figure 8.3: The Market for Trucks

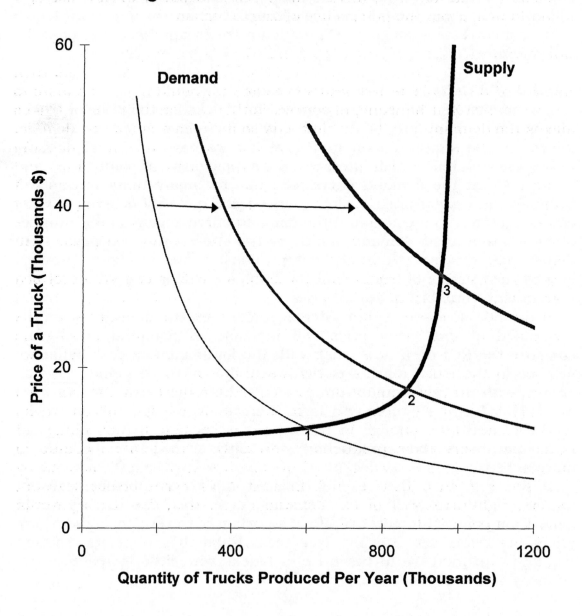

The impact of each rightward shift in demand is divided between the impact on price and the impact on quantity produced. What we have learned from Figure 8.3, then, is that as production approaches full capacity for the industry, further increases in demand will increasingly result in higher prices and less in higher production.

What is the Aggregate Impact on the Macro Economy?

If a change in interest rates affected only the market for trucks then this would be a topic in microeconomics and we would have little more to say about it. What happens, of course, is that a change in interest rates affects the demand for all durable goods so its impact is macroeconomic. We will see that the economy as a whole responds in much the same way to additional demand coming from lower interest rates. If factories and workers are idle then we will see a pickup in production and employment that shows up as in increase in real GDP. But if the economy is already close to full employment with a high level of capacity utilization, then we will see a general rise in prices that is reflected in the CPI and the GDP deflator.

Figure 8.4 shows how these basic relationships can be described graphically as what we call aggregate supply and aggregate demand curves for the whole economy. Instead of the price of a single good on the vertical axis, we have the price level for the economy, measured by the GDP deflator. Instead of the quantity of a good on the horizontal axis, we have the quantity output of the economy, real GDP.

Aggregate supply shows how much real GDP firms in total will produce at a given price level. As in individual markets, there is a full capacity level of output, shown here as a real GDP of $5,000 billion, at which even very large increases in price will result in no additional output. Aggregate demand shows how much real GDP is demanded by buyers at a given price level. It is clear that if lower interest rates shift the demand curves in individual markets rightward, then the aggregate demand curve will also shift rightward.

Figure 8.4: Aggregate Supply and Aggregate Demand

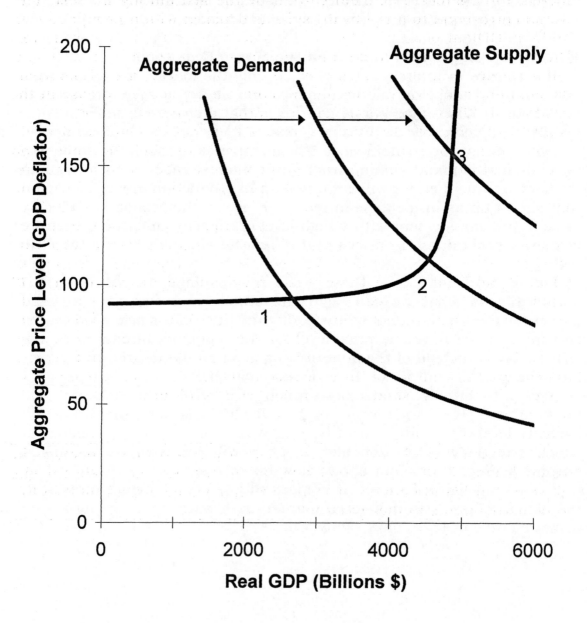

At its initial position depicted by the thin line in Figure 8.4, the intersection of the aggregate demand curve with the aggregate supply curve determines the price level and real GDP are at point #1. An increase in aggregate demand caused by the Fed cutting interest rates would correspond to a rightward shift as depicted with a new price level and real GDP at point #2. This shift results mainly in an increase in real GDP rather than in the price level because the aggregate supply curve is relatively flat over this range. However, a further increase in aggregate demand depicted by the thick line produces a very large increase in the price level with little additional output in the economy at point #3.

As in the case of individual markets, the impact of a shift in demand is divided between the impact on the price level and the impact on output. The closer is the economy to full capacity utilization, the greater will be impact of an increase in aggregate demand on the price level, and the less will be its impact on output.

If the Fed acts to boost aggregate demand in the midst of a recession, when actual output is well below full capacity, then we would expect the economy to respond much as we saw in the move from point #1 to point #2 in Figure 8.4. Real GDP will rise with little increase in the GDP deflator. On several occasions the Fed has taken just such an action to push the economy out of recession. But if the Fed increases aggregate demand when the economy is already operating at close to full capacity, then we would expect the economy to respond as it does here in the move from point #2 to point #3. In that case there would be little increase in real GDP, but there would be a large increase in prices.

Exercises 8.2

A. Referring to Figures 8.3 and 8.4, depict a further increase in demand, both in the truck industry and in the economy. What might cause a shift like this to occur? What will happen as a result of it in the truck industry and in the economy?

8.3 Full Employment, the Natural Rate of Unemployment, and the Natural Rate of Output

Terms like "full" employment, the "natural" rate of unemployment, and the "natural" rate of output help to earn economics the nickname "the dismal science." How can economists talk about the economy being at "full" employment when millions are out of a job? And how callous of them to refer to unemployment as being "natural!" Certainly no politician could ever be elected after saying that the economy is operating at its "natural" rate of output with no promise for greater prosperity after the election! Of course, by now you know that economics is not dismal at all but actually a lot of fun, and that many everyday terms are used in economics to convey a related but more narrowly defined meaning.

The Labor Market

To develop these concepts we look at the labor market when the Fed is boosting aggregate demand. It may seem insensitive to think about a market for workers as if they were just so many trucks, but the supply of labor and demand for labor do depend on the wage rate and, as in any market, they determine the equilibrium price, the wage. In Figure 8.5 we abstract from the fact that there is a wide range of skill levels and wage levels among workers and instead pretend that there is a homogeneous worker who earns a uniform wage. This simplification is adequate for purposes of our macro analysis.

The supply curve in Figure 8.5 shows the wage rate that is required to induce a given number of workers to accept employment. Notice that some workers would accept employment at even very low wages, but that the wage required to induce additional workers to accept jobs rises ever more steeply as the number employed approaches 120 million. At a high enough wage some retired people, homemakers, and students would reenter the labor force, but the total number of adults is ultimately limited. The three demand curves show how a rightward shift in the demand for labor is divided between an increase in the number of workers employed and the wage rate.

From the initial demand curve depicted as a thin line, successive rightward shifts in demand produce less increase in employment and a larger increase in the wage. As employment approaches its hypothetical maximum of 120 million, the equilibrium wage rises very sharply. As in the concept of full capacity utilization for an industry, the concept of full employment in the labor market is not one of absolute physical maximum but rather the range in which the wage would rise very sharply.

When the Fed acts to stimulate the economy by cutting interest rates, the demand curves for durable goods such as trucks shift rightward, consequently aggregate demand in the economy also shifts rightward, and busy firms demand more labor to produce the goods that their customers are demanding. If the economy is in recession when the Fed cuts interest rates, then there is unused capacity in the goods and labor markets and the main effect will be a rise in real GDP with little effect on the price level.

But what if the Fed stimulates the economy when it is already operating close to full capacity and near full employment? From our analysis so far it is clear that there will be little further increase in real GDP or employment, but instead the main effect will be higher prices and wages. But that is not the end of the story. Higher wages and prices will reinforce each other as employers feel the effect of higher wages and households feel the effect of higher prices. The result will be further increases in prices and wages and less of a gain in real GDP and employment, and perhaps none at all.

Figure 8.5: The Labor Market

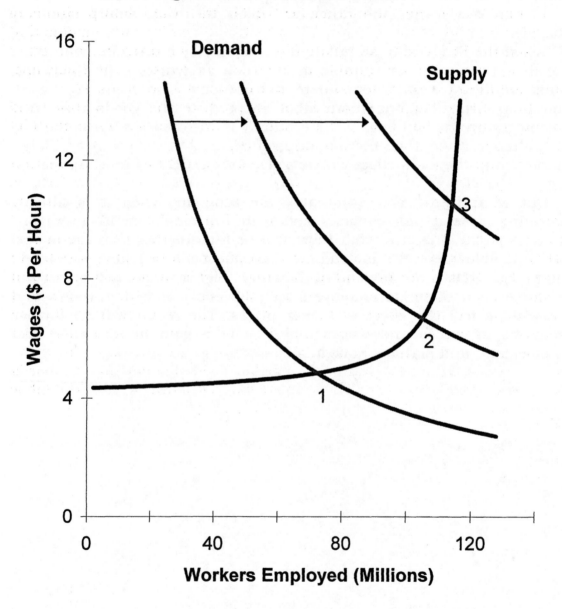

What If the Economy Is Already At Full Employment?

To see how the impact of a monetary stimulus tends to effect only the price level when the economy is already close to full employment, let's trace through the events depicted in Figures 8.6, 8.7 and 8.8.

Figure 8.6 depicts the market for trucks, with the initial positions of the demand and supply curves shown as thin lines. Now we imagine that the Fed cuts interest rates, stimulating the demand for trucks and other durable goods, so the demand curve shifts rightward to the thick line. Equilibrium in the truck market moves from point #1 to point #2.

As we saw before, the effect of this shift is to boost both the price and output of trucks, and since the industry is already close to full capacity output, the effect on the price is substantial.

As we work through Figures 8.7 and 8.8 we will find that this is not the end of the story, however. The supply curve will also shift upward, as shown by the thick line, further boosting the price of trucks and causing the output of trucks to fall back to its initial level.

But why does the supply curve shift upward? Recall that the supply curve represents that price that is required to induce the industry to produce a given level of output. When the costs of production rise, a higher price is required to induce the industry to produce trucks, and this is reflected in a higher supply curve. Production costs rise following the Fed's interest rate cut because lower interest rates are stimulating demand in many markets, thereby pushing up the prices of many goods that truck producers use in making trucks. Booming demand for labor is also pushing up wage rates in the labor market, so the cost of the labor input to the manufacturing process is also rising.

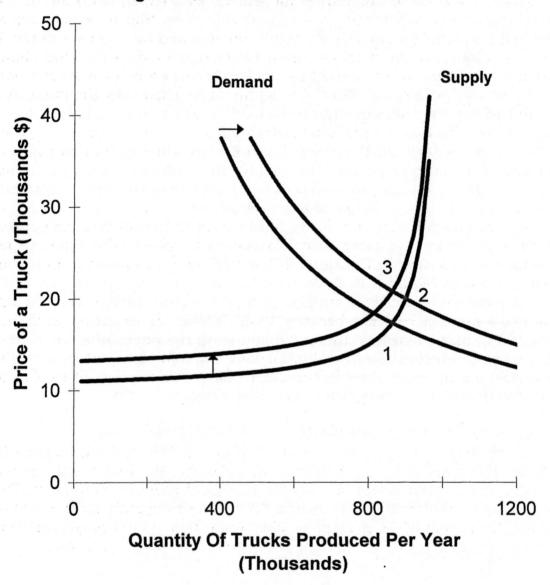

Figure 8.6: The Market for Trucks

The macroeconomic effect of the Fed's interest rate cut is depicted in Figure 8.7, where the initial positions of aggregate supply and demand are shown as thin lines. Aggregate demand shifts rightward as the demand for trucks, airplanes, refrigerators, and thousands of other products is boosted by lower interest rates. The equilibrium in the economy moves from point #1 to point #2, resulting in a substantial increase in the price level in the economy because the economy is already close to full capacity output. Correspondingly, Figure 8.8 shows the initial impact of the Fed's policy change on the labor market where the equilibrium moves from point #1 to point #2, again resulting in a large increase in the price in this market, the wage rate.

Now let's take a look again at the truck market in Figure 8.6. Truck manufacturers find that they are paying higher wage rates, that they are paying higher prices for steel (which is in strong demand from makers of a wide range of products), for machinery, and for energy (also in strong demand from a wide range of booming industries). The marginal cost of producing a truck has increased substantially at every level of output. Therefore, the supply curve for the industry shifts up by the amount that costs rise, resulting in a new equilibrium at point #3 at an even higher price but lower output than at point #2.

At the macroeconomic level, the situation is shown in Figure 8.7 where the aggregate supply curve shifts upward, reflecting the fact that costs are rising not only in the truck industry, but also in practically every industry. From its position at point #2, equilibrium moves in the direction of an even higher price level but a reduction in real GDP, to point #3.

Meanwhile, in the Labor Market

Meanwhile, the supply curve of labor also shifts upward, as seen in Figure 8.8. The wage that workers care about is the real wage, not the nominal wage that is measured by the vertical scale in Figure 8.8. The incentive to work when the wage is $8 per hour depends on the cost of living. If the cost of living rises by 10%, then the nominal wage must rise to $8.80 per hour to provide the same incentive that $8 did before.

313

Figure 8.7: Aggregate Supply and Demand

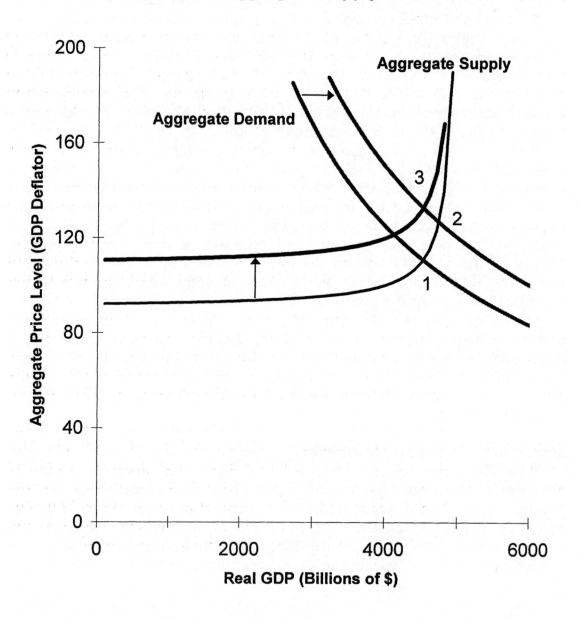

As workers recognize that prices of goods they buy have risen, the supply curve for labor shifts upward since the wage at which they are willing to supply a given quantity of labor will be higher. The effect will be to push wages up even higher and to reduce the quantity of labor that firms wish to employ.

When this process of upward adjustment in supply curves in individual markets, the aggregate economy, and the labor market is complete, the new equilibrium positions will be the points #3 in each of the figures. As the economy moved from point #1 to point #2 and then to point #3, it experienced a boom in output and employment with rising prices and wages, followed by a slump during which output and employment fell back to their original levels, but prices and wages rose even further.

In the end, the Fed's attempt to stimulate an economy that was already close to full capacity output and full employment only resulted in higher prices.

This analysis, which is based on historical behavior of the economy during episodes of excessive monetary stimulus, is that there is a natural rate of output for the economy. Attempts by the Fed to stimulate the economy to operate above the natural rate sets off a process of price and wage increases that, when complete, leaves output back at its natural level following a temporary boom, and prices and wages permanently higher. Long term growth in the natural level of output does occur over time as the labor force grows and productivity increases, and these factors are reflected in the long term growth of real GDP which has averaged about 3% per year.

Since the natural rate of output corresponds to the highest sustainable level of employment in the economy, we say that the economy is then at full employment, even though the measured unemployment rate is higher than zero. The level of the unemployment rate which corresponds to the natural rate of output is called the natural rate of unemployment. The Fed can push the unemployment rate below this level temporarily, but only by setting off a burst of inflation.

Figure 8.8: The Labor Market

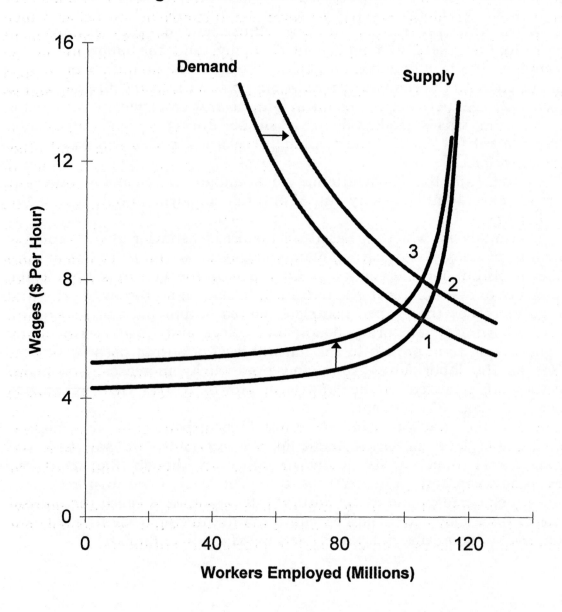

Can We See The Inflation Response in Actual Data?

The response of inflation to the level of unemployment in the U.S. economy is apparent in Figure 8.9. Notice that the rate of inflation tends to accelerate when the unemployment rate dips sharply. But we also see that there is no single trigger level for unemployment below which inflation inevitably jumps upward. For example, when the unemployment rate dipped below 5% in the 1960s, inflation accelerated. But in the 1970s, inflation accelerated when the unemployment rate only dipped below 6%. Most recently, the unemployment rate is well below 5% and so far there is no sign of significant inflation.

This suggests to economists that the natural rate of unemployment is not constant but changes slowly over time as demographics and other factors affect the labor market. Evidently, the natural rate of unemployment was higher in the 1970s than in the 1960s. Recall from our discussion of the unemployment rate in Chapter 5 that the 1970s was a decade during which an unusually large number of young workers, baby boomers, entered the labor force for the first time. Younger workers have higher rates of unemployment, on average, than do older, more experienced workers. As we moved from the 1970s through the 1980s and into the 1990s the ranks of new workers shrank, reflecting the birth-dearth that followed the baby-boom. Meanwhile, by the 1990s the baby boomers had matured into experienced workers with more stable employment. Labor economists estimated that the natural rate of unemployment had fallen to about 5%. So when the unemployment rate fell below that level in 1996 there was renewed concern about the danger of inflation. So far that has been a false alarm, and the unemployment rate is finishing the decade well below 5% without any sign of igniting inflation. This shows just how difficult it is to estimate the natural rate of unemployment in spite of all the data, computers, and statistical analysis we have today.

The decline in the natural rate of unemployment may be ending now, as the echo of the baby boom starts to pour out of the high schools and soon out of colleges to enter the labor force in large numbers.

Figure 8.9: Inflation Accelerates When The Unemployment Rate is Low

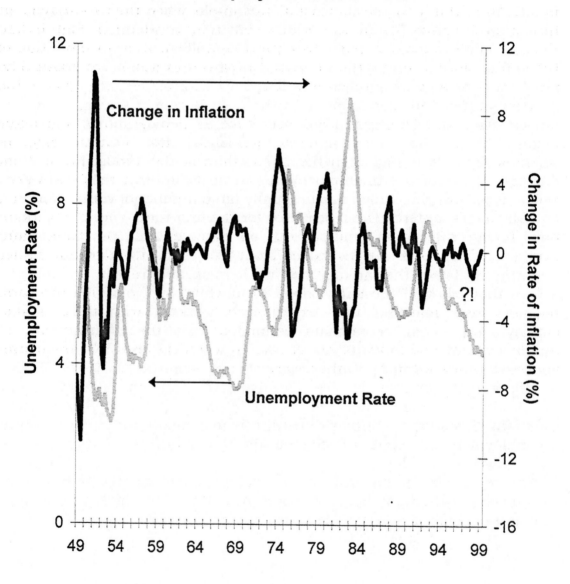

While we have no direct measure of the natural rate of output, the Federal Reserve Board does collect monthly data on the rate of capacity utilization in manufacturing. Firms are asked to compare their rate of output to a hypothetical "full capacity" rate, and the Fed compiles from these responses an index of capacity utilization that is expressed as a percentage. Our analysis suggests that as capacity utilization reaches higher levels, prices will tend to rise faster. Indeed, we see in Figure 8.10 that the Fed's index of capacity utilization does bear a positive relation to the change in inflation. When capacity utilization rises above about 80% inflation generally accelerates. Evidently, 80% corresponds roughly to the natural level of output.

But why isn't the natural level of output at 100% of capacity? Because, what industrial engineers mean by full capacity is the physical capability of their plant if operated without regard to cost control. What we are interested in as economists is the level at which prices and wages accelerate, and that corresponds to about 80% of physical capacity. Notice, too, that there is some lag between a rise in capacity utilization and the ensuing burst of inflation. The process by which wages and prices respond to changes in demand is not instantaneous but rather involves the period of adjustment that we have described.

When prices and wages continue to increase over a period of years, then we say that there is inflation. As you know, inflation has characterized the U.S. economy since 1960. We will discuss the dynamics of inflation in Chapter 9, using our understanding of price level adjustment developed in this chapter.

Figure 8.10: Inflation Accelerates When Capacilty Utilization is High

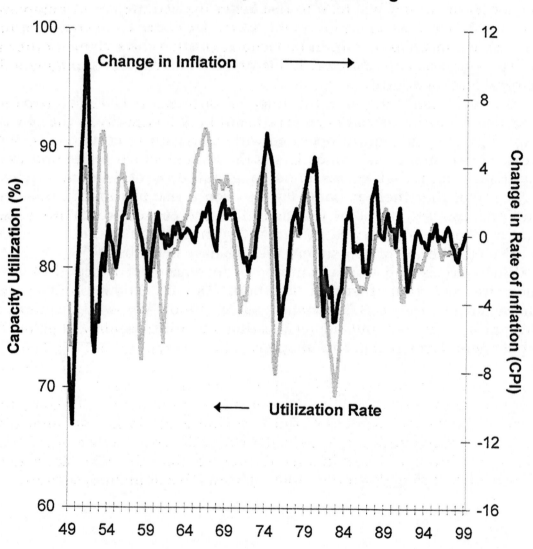

When Inflation Slows Down

We also observe that episodes of accelerating inflation are interspersed with periods of declining inflation, such as the early 1980s and the early 1990s. As we see in Figures 8.9 and 8.10, when unemployment is high or capacity utilization is low, then inflation slows down. At these times the process of adjustment of wages and prices we have described above goes into reverse. When workers are unemployed, employers find that they have plenty of job applicants and so do not need to raise wages as rapidly or at all. When firms have idle capacity they are willing to sell at lower prices than they would otherwise. Consumers find more "Sale" signs in store windows.

We can work through a hypothetical one-time decline in prices and wages by reversing the sequence of shifts in Figures 8.6 through 8.8. Here is how the sequence of events unfolds. First, the Fed boosts interest rates, causing demand curves for durables such as trucks to shift to the left. Output slumps and prices fall. The resulting decline in the demand for labor also causes wages to decline. That is not the end of the story because falling costs of production, including wages, cause supply curves to shift downward.

This downward shift is reinforced when workers recognize that the cost of living has fallen and so are willing to work at lower nominal wages than before. The economy moves, then, from an initial position at point #3 to the unnumbered intersection of the thin demand curve and the thick supply curve, and finally to point #1. During this transition the economy has experienced a temporary slump in output and employment, but returns to the natural levels of these variables with the only permanent effect being a fall in the price level and wages.

In actual practice, inflation has already been underway for some time when the Fed boosts interest rates, so the effect is not an immediate decline in prices and wages but rather a decline in the rate of inflation. But it is through this adjustment process that the Fed slows down inflation by slowing down the economy with a boost in interest rates.

Exercises 8.3

A. Discuss how the following changes in the economy would affect the natural rate of unemployment: 1) a large influx of untrained workers into the labor force, 2) the aging of the baby boom generation, 3) improved vocational training, 4) improved health standards.

B. Concern about renewed inflation was heightened in 1988 and 1989 before the recession of 1990-91 got under way. What factors in the economy might have lead to this concern? What happened as a result of the 1990-91 recession that dampened fears of inflation? Why had those fears returned by 1993?

C. In what way have the late 1990s have been a surprising time for macro-economists. What explanations have been put forward to account for the puzzling behavior seen in Figure 8.9?

8.4 The Quantity of Money Determines the Price Level

Our analysis and study of the data suggest that if the economy is at full employment when the Fed pushes interest rates down, the end result will only be an increase in the level of prices and wages. In that case there will be no permanent effect on real GDP or employment after the adjustment process is complete. Now we will argue that the resulting percentage increase in the price level is approximately equal to the percentage increase in the money supply, less the long-term growth rate of real GDP over the period of adjustment. How can we possibly know this?

It is implied by our model of the demand for money which says that the quantity of money demanded is proportional to nominal income at a given rate of interest. Consider this simple thought experiment:

Suppose that the economy starts the year with real GDP at its natural level. At the beginning of the year the actual supply of money was equal to demand so we start with the relationship

Supply	=	Demand
M	=	k(i) • P • Q

where P stands for the price level as measured by the GDP price deflator, Q is real GDP, k(i) is a function of the interest rate I, and the symbol "•" means multiply.

The price deflator times real GDP is of course just nominal GDP, so this is the same money demand model we studied in Chapter 7. Let's use the symbols M, P, Q, and i to mean here the particular values of those variables at the beginning of the year. Suppose now that the Fed increases M by 10% at the beginning of the year to 1.1•M. Further, it takes this imaginary economy a year to adjust to the effects of a money supply change and return to its natural level. This means that real GDP will be 1.03•Q a year later, because the long-term growth rate of the economy is 3% per year. We cannot be sure what will happen to the interest rate, but let's assume for the time being that it will still be "i" a year later.

So far we have that one year later the quantity of money supplied by the Fed is 1.1•M, real GDP has grown to 1.03•Q, and i is unchanged. The only unknown variable is the price level P. This new price level can be expressed as X•P, where "X" is the unknown factor we want to solve for. Setting the supply of money equal to demand one year later, we have

Supply   =   Demand

1.1 • M   =   (X•P) • (1.03•Q) •k(i)

How much of an increase in P is required to equate the increased money supply with demand? Divide both sides of the equation by M, using the fact that M = P•Q•k(i). This leaves

1.1 = X•1.03

so the factor X is about 1.07, since X = 1.1/1.03 = 1.07, approximately.

In words, the equation tells us that a 10% increase in the supply of money leads to a 7% increase in the price level. That is because 7%, along with the normal 3% growth in real GDP, just enough to cause 10% more money to be demanded in the economy. Thus, the balance between money demand and money supply has been restored at the natural rate of output.

The shifts in the money supply and demand curves that correspond to these two equations are illustrated in Figure 8.11. The initial quantity of money supplied by the Fed is set at $600 billion, indicated by the thin line. The initial demand for money is the thin curve which intersects the supply line at point #1 where the interest rate is 5%. When the Fed increases the supply of money by 10% to $660 billion, indicated by the thick line, the new intersection with the demand curve is at point #2 where the interest rate is only 4.5%. This rate is low enough that people are willing to hold 10% more money.

That drop in the interest rate sets in motion the process we studied in Section 8.3: higher investment spending, greater aggregate demand, greater demand for labor, and then higher prices and wages causing an upward shift in aggregate supply.

As prices and wages continue to rise, the demand for money curve shifts rightward because the quantity of money demanded at any given interest rate increases in proportion to the price level. When the amount of that rightward shift has reached 10%, then the demand and supply curves intersect again at the original level of the interest rate which is labeled point #3. An increase of 7% in prices, combined with an increase of 3% in real GDP over the one-year adjustment period, is enough to do it.

Now that the interest rate is back at its original level of 5%, the adjustment process is complete. The interest rate will stay at 5% until something else happens that shifts either the supply of money or the demand for money. But, how do we know that?

Recall that the economy moved initially because an increase in the money supply had reduced the interest rate, stimulating demand for consumer and business durable goods, resulting in increased aggregate demand at the original price level. This lead to a temporary rapid increase in real GDP and the price level was rising. The process of adjustment to the new and higher price level was complete when real GDP had fallen back to its natural level because then there is no further upward pressure on prices and wages.

At the new higher price level, the demand for money is equal to the new higher supply at the old level of interest rates. With interest rates back at their old level, the demand for durable goods is also back to its original level. That is why real GDP is also back at its natural rate. Of course, the natural rate of GDP has continued to grow at its usual 3% per year during this adjustment.

In the end, the change in the money supply has only determined the level of prices.

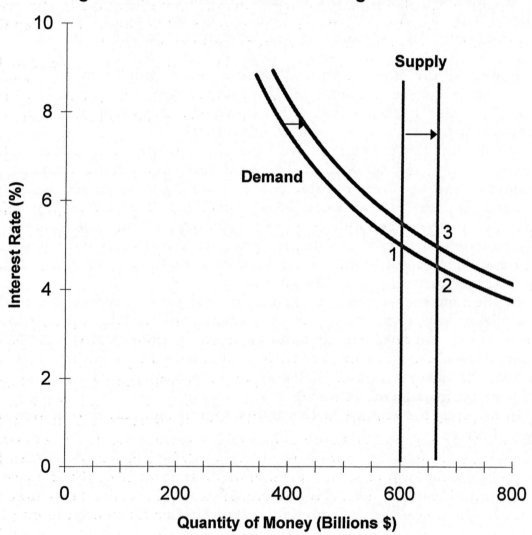

Figure 8.11: The Transition to a Higher Price Level

326

The Quantity Theory of Money

The idea that the price level is determined by the quantity of money is called the quantity theory of money. It is a very old idea in economics, having been clearly articulated by the English economist and philosopher David Hume in his essay "On Money" published in 1734. Hume observed that the large quantity of gold brought to Europe from the New World by the Spanish had been followed by a proportionate increase in the price level. In Hume's day, money was based on a gold standard. But does the quantity theory of money still work in our economy today?

The quantity theory says that the change in the price level can be predicted from the change in the quantity of money if we adjust for long term real growth in real GDP. From 1960 to 1999 the quantity of M1 increased by a factor of 7.9 while real GDP increased by only a factor of 3.5. The quantity theory of money clearly implies that there should have been a large increase in the level of prices. Certainly there has been considerable inflation in the U.S. economy during those forty years, but how close does the quantity theory of money come to predicting the right amount? It predicts that the GDP deflator price index should have increased by a factor of $7.9/3.5 = 2.3$ over the same period, more than doubling. In fact, we experienced even more inflation than that. The price level actually increased by a factor of 4.9. So the theory explains about half of the increase in the price level over this period, and the actual increase was even more than predicted.

What is the explanation for this difference? First, we have the fact that interest rates are higher than they were in 1960. Recall that $k(i)$ is the demand for money per dollar of nominal GDP as a function of the interest cost of holding money. Higher interest rates mean that holding money is more expensive $k(i)$ is smaller as people economize on their holding of money. The ratio of M1 to GDP did decline from .27 in 1960 to .12 in 1999, while the Treasury bond yield rose from 4% in 1960 to over 6% in 1999. Now look again at the equation "$M = k(i) \circ P \circ Q$." With M and Q given, and $k(i)$ lower than it was in 1960, it must be that P is even higher than it would have been if interest rates had remained constant.

A second part of the explanation is that $k(i)$ has fallen even more due to changes in how we use money that make it easier for people to economize on the use of cash. The proliferation of ATMs and credit cards are the most visible examples, but electronic transer of funds has also had a major impact in reducing the amount of M1 that we need to do business.

The margin of error in the quantity theory of money can be traced, then, to its simplifying assumption that k(i) remains constant. The quantity theory of money can be thought of as an approximation that explains the direction and rough magnitude of the change in the price level over long periods of time. Experience over many historical periods and many countries has demonstrated its usefulness. What is the lesson?

The quantity theory of money implies that when a country increases its money supply faster than the long term growth rate of real GDP, it will almost surely experience inflation. And the change in the price level will be approximately the difference between the growth of money and the growth of real GDP.

Exercises 8.4

A. Suppose that in 1997 the unemployment rate in the U.S. is 4.9% and the yield on T bills is 4%. A new Fed Chairperson urges the FOMC to order open market operations that will result in an immediate 20% increase in the quantity of M1. By doing this, the new Chair hopes to push the unemployment rate down to near zero. At the time you are working as assistant to the president of manufacturing firm, and she asks you to prepare a forecast for the economy taking account of the Fed's new monetary policy. Use the analytical framework of this chapter to sketch a forecast of interest rates, the price index, and real GDP. Use graphs to illustrate the sequence of events.

B. Imagine that you have been appointed Chair of the Federal Reserve, and you would like to conduct monetary policy in way that will keep interest rates at their present levels without a large increase or decrease. Assume that unemployment is at 5%, inflation is at 2%, and the Treasury bill yield is 4%. What should be the rate of change in the supply of money per year in order to accomplish your objective?

C. During 1993, Russia experienced rapid inflation while her central bank printed new money at a furious pace. The head of Russia's central bank was quoted in the press as claiming that there was no connection between inflation and the fact that the central bank was printing money rapidly. Use the framework of money demand and the natural rate of output to explain why there is most likely a strong connection between these two phenomena.

D. Using the data given above, what can you say about how the velocity of M1 has changed since 1960? Is that change consistent with what has happened to variables that affect velocity?

Index

Chapter 9

Monetary Policy, Inflation, & Business Cycles

Outline

Preview

In Chapter 8 we analyzed the response of the economy to an increase in the supply of money. Briefly, the interest rate initially falls since people are willing to hold a greater quantity of money only if it is cheaper to do so. The lower cost of borrowing then stimulates the demand for durable goods, including new plant and equipment and consumer durables. As firms respond to increased demand, output and employment rise and the unemployment rate falls. But prices also rise in response to the increased demand for goods and wages rise in response to strong demand for labor. Rising labor costs further reinforce the upward adjustment in the price level. As the price level rises, the demand for money increases, pushing the interest rate back up. With the cost of borrowing rising, the demand for goods subsides and real GDP moves back toward its "natural" level.

This adjustment process is complete when the price level has risen by just enough so that the demand for money equals the increased supply of money at the original rate of interest. The price level will rise by the same percentage as did the supply of money, after subtracting 3% per year for normal growth in real GDP.

In this chapter we want to analyze how the economy will respond to a *continuing* increase in the supply of money, and to changes in that rate of increase in the supply of money.

For example, suppose that it is the policy of the Fed to increase the supply of money at a rate of 5% per year, year after year. What will be the rate of inflation? To the rate of interest? To the level of unemployment? If the Fed alters its monetary policy so that the growth rate of the money supply jumps to 10%, how will real GDP, unemployment, inflation, and interest rates be affected? What will happen then if the Fed reverses itself and cuts the growth rate of money from 10% back to 5%?

In fact, the history of monetary policy in the U.S. is one of widely fluctuating money growth rates as the Fed, under pressure from Congress and the White House, has lurched back and forth between fighting unemployment and fighting inflation. What have been the consequences of uneven monetary policy for the U.S. economy? How should the Fed conduct monetary policy? What grade should we give the Fed on its performance in recent years?

9.1 How the Growth Rate of Money Determines the Rate of Inflation and the Interest Rate

To answer questions like these about rates of change we need a dynamic version of the demand for money model which was introduced in Chapter 7 and used in Chapter 8. We will then be able to use the model to link together rates of change in the money supply, the price level, the interest rate, and real GDP. Recall that setting the supply of money equal to the demand we had the simple equation:

$$\underline{\text{Supply}} \quad = \quad \underline{\text{Demand}}$$
$$M \quad = \quad k(i) \cdot P \cdot Q$$

Reviewing briefly, this equation says that the supply of money set by the Fed, M, is equal to the demand for money, and that the demand for money is proportional to the price level, P, times real GDP, Q. That factor of proportionality, called $k(i)$, can be interpreted as the amount of money demanded per dollar of income because the equation can be rearranged as $k(i) = M/(P \cdot Q)$ and $(P \cdot Q)$ is just nominal GDP. Further, $k(i)$ varies inversely with the interest rate, i, since people wish to hold less money when the opportunity cost of holding money (instead of bonds) is high. In Chapter 7 we saw that this very simple model provided a reasonable approximation to the actual relationship that we observe in the U.S. economy between the ratio of nominal GDP to M1 and the interest rate.

Putting the Money Demand Model Into Motion

Now we convert this equation into a relationship between the rates of change in these variables by using the familiar algebraic fact that the percent change in the product of two variables is approximately the sum of the percentage changes in each. Recall that if $Y = X \cdot Z$, then the percent change in Y is approximately the percent change in X plus the percent change in Z, and the approximation is better for small changes. The model therefore implies that the percentage change in money is approximately equal to the percentage change in k(i), plus the percentage change in the price level, plus the percentage change in real GDP, which we can express in equation form as

$$M\% = k(i)\% + Q\% + P\%$$

where "%" means the percentage annual rate of change in the variable it follows, and "_" means "approximately equal to." The degree of error in the approximation is small enough that we can ignore it for our purposes, since rates of change are relatively small in the US economy. Consequently, we replace "approximately equal" with "equal" and write our model as:

$$M\% = k(i)\% + Q\% + P\%$$

What does this equation tell us about the inflation rate if the Fed continues to increase the money supply at a rate of 10% over a long period of time, say several years? Since we want to predict P%, let's put it on the left hand side of the equal sign and all the other variables on the right, so we have:

$$P\% = M\% - k(i)\% - Q\%$$

This result says that the inflation rate will be equal to the rate of change of money, minus the rate of change of k(i), minus the growth rate of real GDP. Notice that the growth rate of real GDP, Q%, is subtracted from the growth rate of money to get the rate of inflation. Evidently, real growth in the economy exerts a negative influence on inflation. This makes sense because the growth of real GDP is a source of growth in the demand for money, since the physical volume of transactions that need to be settled with money is growing. That growth uses up Q% of the M% growth in money, leaving the remaining (M%-Q%) to fuel to inflation.

To calculate the value of P% using this equation we need to have values for the rate of change k(i)% and Q%. Taking Q% first, we recall that the growth rate of real GDP is limited over any long period of time to the long term growth rate of the full employment or natural level of GDP which is about 3% per year. Thus, the rate of inflation over a period of several years will be approximately

$$P\% = M\% - k(i)\% - 3\%.$$

Now what can we assume about the value of k(i)%, the rate of change of the demand for money per dollar of income, over a long period? Since in our simple model k(i) depends only on the interest rate, this is equivalent to asking: What we can assume about the behavior of the interest rate over a long period? Let's conjecture that if the money supply is growing at a constant rate, then the interest rate will find a level at which it will be stable, so that the function k(i) of the interest rate will also be stable. (If a variable does not change, then a function of that variable does not change.) This means that we can set k(i)% at zero in our equation for P%. Whether this conjecture is reasonable will become apparent when we finish our solution to the model.

For our example of a continuing 10% growth rate of money, then, the equation predicts that the inflation rate P% will be:

$$P\% = 10\% - 0\% - 3\% = 7\%.$$

Does this equation make sense from what we understand about the demand for money? It says that inflation at a rate of 7% will be the result of a policy by the Fed of increasing the supply of money at a rate of 10% per year over a long period. The rate of growth in the demand for money (7% due to inflation plus 3% due to long term growth in real GDP) just balances the 10% growth in the supply of money. Therefore, since money demand and money supply remain in balance in this scenario, there is no pressure on the interest rate to move either up or down. Thus, the amount of money demanded per dollar of income remains constant. Now it is clear that our conjecture that we could set $k(i)$% at zero is consistent with the solution to the model which it implied. This is a good example of a general strategy for solving models in economics and other fields: use your intuition to conjecture some key features of the solution and then use them to obtain the complete solution, finally showing that the resulting solution is internally consistent.

What Will the Interest Rate Be?

What stable value of the interest rate is consistent with an inflation rate of 7%? If the economy is to be operating at its natural level of employment, with real GDP growing at is long term rate of 3%, then the real rate of interest must be at its long run average level. If the real rate of interest were lower than that, then the economy would be booming and employment and real GDP would be above their natural levels, causing, in turn, a further increase in inflation. If the real rate of interest were above its long run average level, then the economy would be in a recession, with high unemployment and falling inflation. The economy being at its natural level of employment requires that the real rate of interest also be at its "natural" level, where the demand for durable goods is consistent with normal long run growth in real GDP, not unusually high nor unusually low. We therefore take the long run average of the real rate of interest as our measure of its natural level.

Recall that in Chapter 4 we saw that the real rate of interest for Treasury bills, the nominal interest rate minus the CPI inflation rate, has averaged about 2%. Also, the nominal interest rate, i, is related to inflation and the real rate, r, by the definition:

$$i = P\% + r$$

This means that we can expect that over a long period of time that i will be approximately P% + 2%, thus

$$i = P\% + 2\%.$$

In our example, where the inflation rate is 7%, we would expect the T bill yield therefore to be about 9%.

What we have now is the full solution to our model of inflation for a situation in which the money supply grows at a constant rate of 10% per year. The rate of inflation will be about 7% and the rate of interest about 9%. Since the growth rates of all the variables turn out to be constant, this type of situation is called a steady state.

A Simple Lesson About Inflation

The rule of thumb about the steady state that emerges is this:

To the extent that the rate of growth of the money supply exceeds the long term growth rate of real GDP, it will eventually result in inflation at a rate approximately equal to the difference in those two growth rates. Further, the nominal rate of interest will reflect the rate of inflation, tending to be approximately the rate of inflation plus a relatively stable real rate of interest.

How useful is this conclusion for understanding economies in the real world? After all, we never really see a central bank increasing the money supply at a constant rate indefinitely. Haven't we just gone through a thought experiment that is unrelated to real experience? No, not really.

First, we need to understand the properties of the steady state before we can make sense of the more realistic question that we tackle in the next section: what happens when the Fed boosts the money supply growth rate from, say, 5% to 10%?

Second, the properties of the steady state are very useful for comparing economies where there is a large difference between the average money growth rates in the two economies. In that case, the steady state solution provides a useful benchmark for how their inflation rates and interest rates are likely to compare. For example, in Switzerland the growth rate of money has averaged only slightly more than the long term growth rate of real GDP. You can be confident that the inflation rate there is only a percent or two, and interest rates are only a bit more, perhaps 3% or 4%. But if you visit Russia, where the central bank helps to finance government spending by printing money, you will find that the inflation rate is very high, with interest rates at similarly stratospheric levels. An implication of our understanding of the steady state is this. If Russia were politically able to stop printing of money (requiring effective tax collection), then it would enjoy low inflation and low interest rates like Switzerland or like any country that maintains a slow growth rate of money over long periods.

Exercises 9.1

A. Give a forecast of inflation and the Treasury bill yield in the case that the Fed keeps the money supply growing at a steady rate of 4%.

B. Country X has a persistent inflation rate averaging about 25% per year while country Y has little inflation. What would you expect to find if you compared the rates of growth of the money supply in the two countries? interest rates? the demand for money per dollar of income? the velocity of money?

9.2 The Transition to a Higher Rate of Inflation

Imagine that the money supply has been growing for several years at a rate of 5% per year. What do we expect the rate of inflation and the interest rate to be? The analysis of the steady state developed in the previous section tells us. To find the rate of inflation we take the growth rate of the money supply, in this case 5%, and subtract 3% for long term growth in real GDP, implying that the rate of inflation is 2%. The equation is:

$$P\% = M\% - k(i)\% - 3\% = 5\% - 0\% - 3\% = 2\%$$

Recall that in steady state the interest rate, i, does not change, and that is why the rate of change of k(i) is set to zero.

To calculate the level of the interest rate in this steady state we again make use of the fact that the real interest rate has been relatively stable at about 2%. Combining the 2% inflation rate with a real interest rate of 2%, we have a nominal interest rate of about 4%. The equation in this case is

$$i = P\% + r = 2\% + 2\% = 4\%$$

Comparing this steady state for 5% money growth with the one that we worked out above for 10% money growth, we see that the rate of inflation is lower by 5% and the nominal interest rate is also lower by 5%. A lower money growth rate translates directly into lower inflation, which, in turn, is reflected in the lower level of nominal interest rates.

A Paradox

Suppose that now the Fed comes under political pressure from Congress and the White House to speed up the growth of the economy, perhaps because of approaching elections that look unfavorable to the party in office. As it has all too often in the past, the Fed responds to this pressure by boosting the growth rate of the money supply, in this case from the 5% rate prevailing in the past to 10% per year. Further, it keeps increasing the money supply at a 10% rate indefinitely. How will the economy respond?

We know from our analysis in Chapter 8 what will happen *initially*: With the supply of money now growing more rapidly than the demand, the cost of holding money, the rate of interest, will fall. That decline in interest rates will stimulate demand for durable goods, so booming production and employment will follow. Then, inflation will accelerate as firms raise their prices and pay higher wages to compete for workers.

We also know from our analysis in the previous section how the economy will look *after* this adjustment process is complete and the economy is back in steady state with the money supply growing at 10%: Real GDP will grow at its long term growth rate of 3% while the rate of inflation will be about 7%, since that is the amount by which a 10% growth rate for the money supply exceeds the 3% long term growth rate of real GDP. Further, the nominal interest rate will be approximately 9% since the real rate of interest is relatively stable at about 2%, and the nominal interest rate is the real rate plus the rate of inflation.

We conclude, then, that in moving from a growth rate of 5% in money supply to a growth rate of 10% in money, the rate of inflation will rise from 2% to 7% and the nominal interest rate will rise from 4% to 9%.

If you are not slightly confused at this point you have not been paying close attention! In the previous chapter we reasoned that if the Fed increases the money supply, interest rates will *fall*. Here we conclude that if the Fed keeps on increasing the money supply, interest rates will *rise*. How can it be that more rapid expansion in the money supply can both decrease and increase interest rates? This conundrum is known as the paradox of monetary economics. The resolution of the paradox is, of course, in the timing. When the Fed starts increasing the money supply more rapidly interest rates fall, but if the Fed persists in increasing the money supply then the interest rate will bounce back and finally end up higher by the amount that inflation has increased.

Inflation and ROIs

But why doesn't the higher rate of interest, 9% in our example above, discourage the purchase of durable goods and send the economy crashing into a recession? Because economic agents understand that inflation will alter the ROI on prospective investment projects.

Consider the example of the ROI on a new rental house that costs $100,000 and produces $5,000 in net income the first year. If we expect the market value of the house to increase with inflation, then when the rate of inflation is 2% the market value of the house after one year will be $102,000 so the ROI will be

$$\text{ROI} = \frac{102 + 5 - 100}{100} = .07$$

for the first year. If the rate charged on loans to home owners is less than 7%, then the house will probably be built. Now what happens when people realize that the rate of inflation is likely to be 7% over the next year? The same house will have a market value at the end of the year of about $107,000 so the ROI is now

$$\text{ROI} = \frac{107 + 5 - 100}{100} = .12$$

Now, if the rate charged on loans to home-owners is less than 12%, then the house will probably be built.

What has happened is that as inflation increased from 2% to 7% the additional capital gain of $5,000 on the market value of the house is enough to pay for an additional 5% in interest cost.

People making all sorts of purchasing decisions for durable goods are comparing the nominal interest rate with what they *expect* the rate of inflation to be, the difference being the real interest cost of making the purchase. Once people understand that the price level is rising steadily at 7% per year, they do not regard a nominal interest rate of 9% as being any more costly than a 4% nominal interest rate was when inflation was only 2% per year.

341

We can summarize the state of the economy at any point in time by writing down the values of the key variables M%, k(i)%, P%, and Q% along with the unemployment rate, denoted U, to show how close the economy is to full employment. Since labor economists estimate that the natural rate of unemployment is currently about 5%, we will use that value to indicate that the economy is at full employment, producing its natural rate of output as measured by real GDP. We will also note the level of the nominal interest rate, i. We will call the initial steady state, when M% was only 5%, "Steady State Lo," and it is described as:

	M%	=	k(i)%	+	P%	+	Q%	with	U	and	i
Steady State Lo	5%	=	0%	+	2%	+	3%		5%		4%

Similarly, the second steady state, after the economy has adjusted fully to a money growth rate of 10%, is called "Steady State Hi" and is described as:

	M%	=	k(i)%	+	P%	+	Q%	with	U	and	i
Steady State Hi	10%	=	0%	+	7%	+	3%		5%		9%

Note that M% is always equal to k(i)% plus P% plus Q%, because that relationship is required by our money demand model. Also note that the unemployment rate, U, is 5% in both cases. That is because each describes a steady state in which the economy has adjusted to its natural level of unemployment. Finally, although the interest rate, i, differs between the two steady states because the rate of inflation differs, k(i)% is zero in both steady states because the interest rate is stable when the economy is in steady state.

But what happens to these variables as the economy adjusts from Steady State Lo to Steady State Hi? How does the economy get from here to there? Our money demand model tells us that at any point in time the key variables must satisfy the equation M% = k(i)% + Q% + P%. That means that when one of the variables changes there must be a change in one or more of the other variables that keeps the equation true.

The Liquidity Phase

Consider what happens initially when the Fed boosts the growth rate of the money supply from 5% to 10%. Will it be k(i)%, or Q%, or P% that changes first? As in Chapter 8, the initial effect of a change in the money supply will be felt in the interest rate, followed by real GDP, and finally by prices and wages. With the supply of money initially rising faster than the demand for money, the interest rate begins to fall, allowing the demand for money per dollar of income, k(i), to rise. In reality, interest rates move daily, and even hourly, in response to open market operations by the Fed. It is this fall in the interest rate that will lead, over time, to a change in real GDP and then a change in the price level.

Since this initial decline in the interest rate is due to an excess of liquidity, economists call this first phase in the adjustment process the "Liquidity Phase." It begins immediately when the Fed boosts money growth and continues until other variables in the model begin to change. Taking a snapshot at the point when the Fed changes its policy we will find that the economy looks something like this:

Phase	M%	=	k(i)%	+	P%	+	Q%	U	i
Steady State Lo	5%	=	0%	+	2%	+	3%	5%	4%
Liquidity	**10%**	**=**	**5%**	**+**	**2%**	**+**	**3%**	**5%**	**4-%**

Note that the higher M% is exactly balanced by a higher k(i)%, so the equation still holds. That means that, initially, all of the additional money supply growth is absorbed by correspondingly more rapid growth in the demand for money per dollar of income. This is made possible by a falling interest rate. Since this is a snapshot taken just as the growth rates change, the interest rate has not fallen much yet, as indicated by "4-%." The unemployment rate U is still at its initial value and natural level of 5%.

The Boom Phase

Now let's think about how this economy might look several months later. The interest rate has continued to fall and it is down to, say, 3%. Since inflation has not increased much yet, the real interest rate is very low, and this has ignited a boom in the demand for durable goods. Again, the real cost of a loan to purchase any durable good is the nominal interest rate minus what the lender expects the rate of inflation to be. At this point in the adjustment process, inflation is still only 2%, so the real cost of borrowing has fallen by the amount of the decline in the nominal interest rate. With demand for durable goods strong, real GDP is growing rapidly, say at an annual rate of 7% instead of its usual 3%.

The booming economy is boosting the demand for money, so the nominal interest rate is no longer falling. With the interest rate at a low point but not falling further, k(i)% is now zero. Reflecting stronger growth in production and employment, the unemployment rate is down to a low 4%.

Adding this "Boom Phase" to the table we have now:

Phase	M%	=	k(i)%	+	P%	+	Q%	U	i
Steady State Lo	5%	=	0%	+	2%	+	3%	5%	4%
Liquidity	10%	=	5%	+	2%	+	3%	5%	4-%
Boom	**10%**	**=**	**0%**	**+**	**3%**	**+**	**7%**	**4%**	**3%**

At this point the incumbent President looks to be a shoe-in for re-election. Employment and incomes are booming, inflation is not a problem (yet), and interest rates are low. What could make the electorate happier?

The Friedman Inflation Surge

During the next year or so, however, the booming economy generates a surge of inflation. Wages rise in response to the strong demand for labor and rising costs of production, which in turn, push prices up even more rapidly. Further, employees begin to realize that wage gains are being offset by more rapid inflation, so employers find that they need to offer even more rapidly rising wages to attract workers. This interaction of "demand-pull" and "wage-push" results in a dramatic rise in the inflation rate. The combination of rapidly rising prices and rising output puts strong upward pressure on the nominal interest rate because the demand for money is now growing very fast. A higher nominal interest rate means that the demand for money per dollar of income, k(i), must be falling, meaning that k(i)% is now negative. However, a rising interest rate does not kill off the boom because people's expectations are adjusting to the higher inflation rate so they still perceive the real rate of interest to be relatively low.

During this "Inflation Surge Phase" the key variables in the economy will look something like they do in the new line in the table:

Phase	M%	=	k(i)%	+	P%	+	Q%	U	i
Steady State Lo	5%	=	0%	+	2%	+	3%	5%	4%
Liquidity	10%	=	5%	+	2%	+	3%	5%	4-%
Boom	10%	=	0%	+	3%	+	7%	4%	3%
Inflation Surge	**10%**	**=**	**-10%**	**+**	**15%**	**+**	**5%**	**3.5%**	**6%**

Notice that the rate of inflation is now even faster than the rate of increase of the money supply, and much faster than it will finally be in Steady State Hi. How can the inflation rate exceed the growth rate of money? It can because as the nominal interest rate rises, the demand for money per dollar of income is falling. As people try to economize on their holdings of money they provide the fuel for an added burst of inflation. In the table, 10% from M% combines with another 10% from k(i)% giving a total of 20% to be divided between P% and Q%. Given that Q% is ultimately limited to 3% over the long run, there must be a period in which P% is very high, and that is the inflation surge.

Another way to see the necessity of the inflation surge is to go back to our basic equation: $M = k(i) \cdot P \cdot Q$. In the course of the adjustment to a higher rate of inflation, the increase in the level of the money supply that occurs must be divided between k(i), P, and Q. Since real GDP returns to its natural level by the end, Q can have increased by only 3% per year. Meanwhile, k(i) will have decreased, because higher inflation brings higher interest rates so people will want to hold less money per dollar of income. The price level then must absorb not only the amount of increase in M that exceeds the natural growth in Q, but it must also increase an additional amount to offset the fall in k(i). This temporary extra kicker to the inflation rate is often called the Friedman surge after Nobel Prize winning economist Milton Friedman who discovered it.

Stagflation

Although the *growth rate* of real GDP has cooled down somewhat by the time we are in the Inflation Surge phase, the *level* of real GDP is still well above its natural level. Correspondingly, the unemployment rate is well below its natural rate. The upward pressure on prices will continue until these variables are back at their natural values. That means that the growth rate of real GDP must slow sufficiently so that the natural level of real GDP, growing at its 3% rate, can catch up. As real GDP stagnates, the unemployment rate will move back up towards its natural rate of 5%. The U.S. economy was in just this situation at the end of the 1970s and the term stagflation was coined to describe it.

This "Stagflation Phase" of the adjustment process is depicted in the last line of the table:

Phase	M%	=	k(i)%	+	P%	+	Q%	U	i
Steady State Lo	5%	=	0%	+	2%	+	3%	5%	4%
Liquidity	10%	=	5%	+	2%	+	3%	5%	4-%
Boom	10%	=	0%	+	3%	+	7%	4%	3%
Inflation Surge	10%	=	-10%	+	15%	+	5%	3.5%	6%
Stagflation	**10%**	**=**	**-1%**	**+**	**11%**	**+**	**0%**	**4.5%**	**8%**

The stagflation phase is a time of rapid inflation, no growth, and rising unemployment. It is at times like this that incumbent politicians are in real trouble at the polls. Indeed, Jimmy Carter went down to defeat in 1980 in large part because of the stagflation that followed the inflationary boom of the late 1970s.

The High Inflation Steady State

Finally, the economy reaches its new steady state in which real GDP again grows at 3%, the demand for money is stable, inflation settles down to a rate of 7% which reflects money supply growth of 10%. Everybody understands that they should expect inflation to continue at 7%, so with the nominal interest rate at 9% the real interest rate is again at its natural level of 2%. Unions and employers build the expectation of 7% inflation into their wage agreements, and long term contracts of all sorts are written to allow for inflation at that rate.

The whole process of adjustment will have taken perhaps five years. The line depicting "Steady State Hi" completes the table:

Phase	M%	=	k(i)%	+	P%	+	Q%	U	i
Steady State Lo	5%	=	0%	+	2%	+	3%	5%	4%
Liquidity	10%	=	5%	+	2%	+	3%	5%	4-%
Boom	10%	=	0%	+	3%	+	7%	4%	3%
Inflation Surge	10%	=	-10%	+	15%	+	5%	3.5%	6%
Stagflation	10%	=	-1%	+	11%	+	0%	4.5%	8%
Steady State Hi	**10%**	**=**	**0%**	**+**	**7%**	**+**	**3%**	**5%**	**9%**

Steady State Hi is not as unpleasant as the Stagflation phase because the economy is growing again and inflation has moderated. But in real life we rarely see this steady state fully realized because political pressures will cause the Fed to change its policies before the steady state is reached. In 1979 President Carter appointed Paul Volcker to the Chairmanship of the Federal Reserve Board with a strong mandate to control inflation. Volcker quickly shifted monetary policy towards control of money supply growth to bring inflation under control. By 1981, President Reagan had replaced Carter as President and the economy was heading into a recession caused by the Fed's efforts to slow inflation. Well aware of Carter's mistake in letting inflation get out of control, President Clinton was content in 1994 to let the Fed take action to head off inflation early. Indeed, in 1996 Clinton was able to take credit for a robust, low inflation economy.

The Great Inflation Speed-Up

Let's see now how this framework can help us understand the actual speed-up of inflation that occurred during the late 1970s. Recall from Chapter 4 that it was during these years that inflation, measured by the CPI, went from about 6% to over 14%.

Figure 9.1 shows that the growth rate of M1 picked up in 1976 and accelerated sharply in 1977. Why did the Fed undertake such a stimulative monetary policy? It was in response to the very severe recession of 1974-75 and the Fed over-reacted by pushing M% up to about 8%. As we would expect, interest rates fell initially in reaction to more rapid money supply growth. However, as the Liquidity phase gave way to the Boom phase, interest rates reversed direction and headed upward, reaching higher levels by 1978.

The response of the key real variables, the growth rate of real GDP and the unemployment rate, are shown in Figure 9.2. Responding to low real interest rates, the growth rate of real GDP exceeded its long term average of 3% for three years (1976 through 1978) and the unemployment rate declined as the economy moved through the Boom phase and into the Inflation Surge phase. However, by late 1979 the wind had gone out of its sails: real GDP growth fell sharply and the unemployment rate started moving back up (recall that the unemployment rate was higher in the 1970s for demographic reasons, so 6% was then a relatively low rate). By 1980, the economy was in the Stagflation phase and President Carter's chances for reelection were dim indeed.

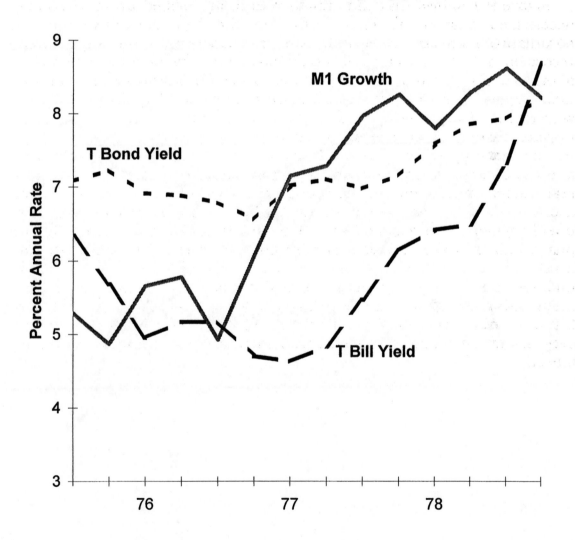

Figure 9.1: Interest Rates Fell Initially, Then Bounced Back Strongly

Figure 9.2: The Economy Boomed Until 1979
Then Growth Stagnated and Unemployment Rose

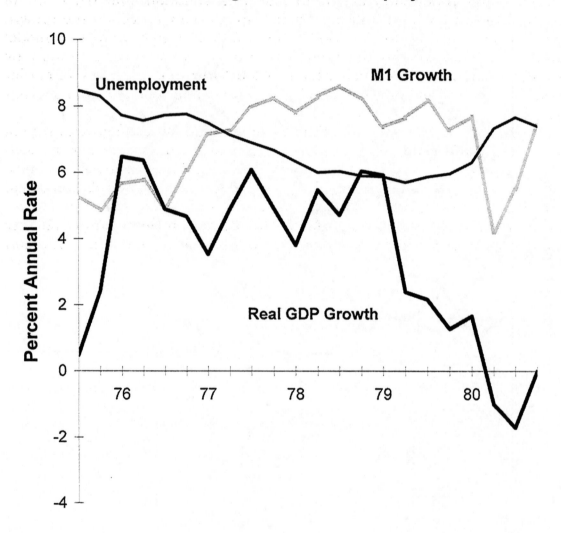

Figure 9.3 traces the inflation rates registered by the GDP price deflator and the CPI during this period. During 1976, inflation rates were declining, showing the lingering effects of the 1974-75 recession. By 1978, though, the economy was entering its Inflation Surge phase and in 1979 the CPI inflation rate skyrocketed to unheard-of "double digit" levels. Many Americans began to fear that inflation was truly out of control. Note that both inflation rates substantially exceeded the growth rate of M1 during this period, the inflation surge that the model predicted. Even though the growth rate of M1 was starting to slow by 1980, inflation was still responding to the "easy money" policy of earlier years and the economy suffered through the Stagflation phase that doomed Jimmy Carter's presidency.

Our model further predicts that if the Fed had kept the growth rate of M1 at around the 7% rate of 1979, the economy would have experienced continued slow growth with subsiding inflation until it reached a new steady state with real GDP growing again and much lower inflation rates. Not content to let us economists see the results of that experiment, on October 6, 1979 the Fed under its new Chairman Paul Volcker announced a program to slow money supply growth and bring inflation under control.

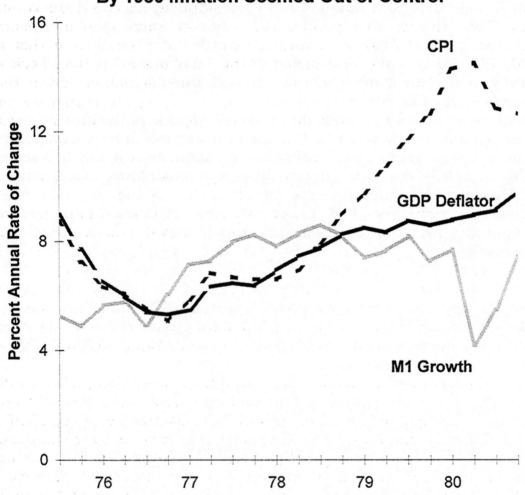

Figure 9.3: The Friedman Surge
By 1980 Inflation Seemed Out of Control

How Rapid is the Transition to High Inflation?

Why did the inflation speed-up of the 1976-to-1980 period take as long as it did? Why didn't it happen over two years or one year or one month instead of five years? Indeed, why don't prices and wages adjust every day to the levels implied by the amount of money supplied by the Fed, leaving the economy to perk along at its natural rate?

Economists think that the speed of adjustment depends importantly on how rapidly people's expectations adjust to the new monetary policy. The expectations of workers and employers have received particular attention from economists who have thought about this issue, back at least to David Hume writing in the 18th century. If workers are slower than employers to realize that inflation is speeding up, then they will happily supply more labor in response to higher nominal wages, mistaking higher nominal wages for higher real wages. Employers, realizing more quickly than workers that prices are rising faster, will be happy to employ more workers at lower real wages during the boom phase of the adjustment.

In time, workers realize that they are falling behind in real wages, and the resulting catch up of the nominal wage brings the real wage back to its natural level as the economy returns to its natural level. If everyone understood exactly what the Fed was doing, and agreed on the implications, wouldn't they simply agree to adjust wages and prices immediately? In that case, monetary policy would have no effect on real variables, employment and output, but would just determine the price level. In that case, the quantity theory of money would hold in the short run as well as in the long run.

In addition to the adjustment of expectations taking time, it is also the case that wages are often set in advance by contract between unions and employers and cannot be changed until the contract expires, often a period of three years. Also, there are many arrangements by which prices are established by contract for a period in the future. An example are rental contracts. Even where there is no formal contract, there are costs to changing prices frequently, such as printing catalogs and menus. Also, firms may fear that their relationships with customers will be damaged by unexpected price increases. All of these factors tend to slow the adjustment of prices to changes in Fed policy. Abraham Lincoln is reputed to have said

"You can fool all of the people some of the time, and you can fool some of the people all of the time, but you can't fool all of the people all of the time!"

Some historians dispute whether Lincoln actually said this, but it is still a classic aphorism!

Americans learned from the experience of the 1970s and will no doubt be faster to adjust to inflation if it arises again. More contracts now include automatic inflation adjustment clauses, and people are much more familiar now with the distinction between nominal and real wages and between nominal and real interest rates. The bond market today reacts very quickly to any hint of inflation with a drop in bond prices and a consequent rise in long term interest rates. This sensitivity suggests that any future money-fueled boom would be limited by a rapid rise in interest rates. Some have argued that these "bond vigilantes" make a repetition of the 1970s less likely and, indeed, less attractive to a central bank tempted to over-stimulate the economy.

Exercises 9.2

A. Explain briefly why the growth rate of the money supply and the interest rate seem to move in opposite directions over short periods of time, but together over longer periods.

B. Suppose that the President appoints Fed officials who feel that fighting inflation is no longer important but rather that the Fed should strive to stimulate employment. Describe a policy that the Fed might follow and sketch the likely sequence of events over the following several years.

C. In every major industrial country the central bank is a separate institution from the elected government. Why do you think that societies which differ in many other respects, have all chosen to grant considerable independence to their central banks?

9.3 Putting on the Brakes:
The Transition to Slower Inflation

As we discussed above, on October 6, 1979 the Fed, under its new Chairman Paul Volcker, announced a program to slow money supply growth and thereby slow down the inflation that was then raging out of control. What should we expect to happen when the Fed slows down the growth rate of the money supply to slow down inflation? Putting the adjustment process of the previous section into reverse, we will observe a sequence of phases that looks something like this:

Phase	M%	=	k(i)%	+	P%	+	Q%	U	i
Steady State Hi	10%	=	0%	+	7%	+	3%	5%	9%
Illiquidity	5%	=	-5%	+	7%	+	3%	5%	9+
Recession	5%	=	0%	+	7%	+	(-2)%	6%	12%
Disinflation	5%	=	7%	+	0%	+	(-2)%	7%	6%
Slow Recovery	5%	=	1%	+	0%	+	4%	6%	5%
Steady State Lo	5%	=	0%	+	2%	+	3%	5%	4%

In the "Illiqidity Phase" the Fed has just slashed the growth rate of the money supply from 10% to 5%. Inflation and real GDP do not respond immediately, but the interest rate starts to rise in order to balance the growing demand for money with a slower growing supply of money. The Fed has made liquidity a scarcer commodity, and the rising interest rate, the opportunity cost of liquidity, reflects that scarcity.

As nominal and real interest rates rise, the demand for durable goods and therefore aggregate demand begin to fall. The economy slides into the "Recession Phase" but inflation, to everybody's dismay, continues unabated. Interest rates are at a very high level but cease their climb, so the demand for money per dollar of income, k(i), stops falling. Unemployment starts to move upward. There is a hue and cry for the Fed to cut interest rates to stimulate the economy, and the press declares the Fed's effort to curb inflation a failure.

In the "Disinflation Phase" inflation finally yields to the downward pressure on prices and wages caused by excess inventories of unsold goods, idle production lines, and millions of workers looking for jobs. The slowdown in inflation is made more dramatic by a reversal of the Friedman surge. Slower growth in GDP means that the demand for money is no longer growing as rapidly and the interest rate begins to fall. It must fall by 5% before we reach Steady State Lo. Since the demand for money *per dollar of income* is rising as the cost of holding money falls, k(i)% must be positive and that term must be offset in our equation with an even lower P% or Q% or both. During this phase, the inflation rate will subside below the level it will have in Steady State Lo, just the reverse of the Inflation Surge phenomenon we saw in the previous section.

A Non-Inflationary Recovery

Since the economy is now operating at below full employment and its natural level of real GDP, it will have to grow faster than 3% to get back there. But it can't grow very fast because M% is only 5%, k(i)% continues to be positive as the interest rate continues to decline, and inflation does not readily take on a negative value. Deflation, negative inflation, is limited by the fact that the nominal interest rate cannot be negative (since cash always offers at least a zero interest rate) and the real interest rate must remain low if the economy is to continue growing. Thus, a non-inflationary recovery is, of necessity, a slow recovery, so we call this the "Slow Recovery Phase." The Fed has come under frequent attack on Capitol Hill over the slowness of the recovery from the 1990-91 recession, but the recovery was non-inflationary and has lasted through the decade. The durability of that recovery was in no small part due to the fact that the Fed resisted the temptation to push the recovery ahead too fast. By taking a steady-as-you-go approach, we avoided a repetition of the boom-recession cycle that over-stimulus inevitably leads to.

If we are patient enough, the economy will finally reach Steady State Lo, with normal growth again in real GDP and the unemployment rate back at its natural level.

The War Against Inflation

This stylized sequence of phases describes pretty well what happened in the early 1980s. The inflation rate was brought back down, but at the cost of the recession of 1981-82 which was one of the most severe in decades.

In Figure 9.4 we see that as the Fed slowed the growth rate of M1 in 1979 and through 1980, interest rates shot up. This reflected illiquidity, the scarcity of liquidity making money very costly. At the time, Fed Chairman Paul Volcker warned that it was time to "batten down the hatches" in preparation for the storm that was to come.

As we see in Figure 9.5, there was a brief recession in 1980 and then Volcker's storm hit the economy with full force in 1981-82 when it experienced the worst recession in decades. These twin recessions meant that real GDP did not grow for a four year period. Growth resumed in 1983 with a brief bounce, but the recovery proceeded at a relatively slow pace, the unemployment rate not getting back down to 6% until 1987.

Inflation yielded to the downward pressure of a recession only after a year or more, and we see this clearly in Figure 9.6. The inflation rate was still rising at the end of 1980, and the press proclaimed that the medicine was not working. Disinflation finally became evident in 1982 when the inflation rate collapsed. The severity of the decline, keeping in mind that M1% had fallen only a couple of percentage points, is explained by the inflation surge going into reverse. Falling interest rates caused the demand for money per dollar of income to rise, thereby absorbing some of the growth in money and leaving less to fuel inflation.

Figure 9.4: When the Fed Put on the Brakes
Interest Rates Soared

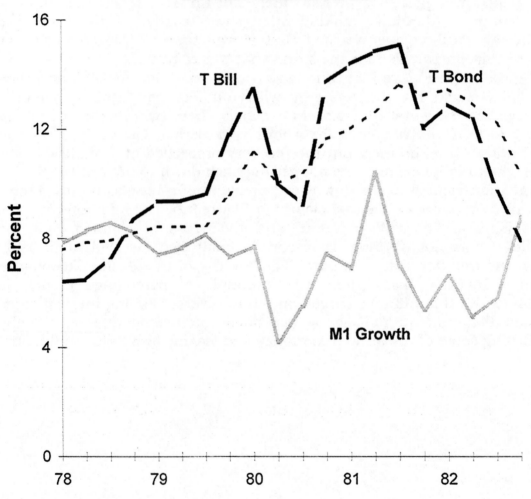

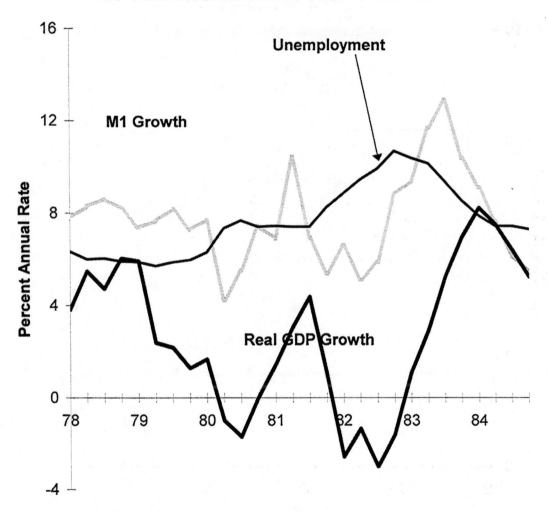

Figure 9.5: Tight Monetary Policy Produced The Twin Recessions of 1980 & 1981-82

Unemployment

M1 Growth

Real GDP Growth

Percent Annual Rate

16

12

8

4

0

-4

78   79   80   81   82   83   84

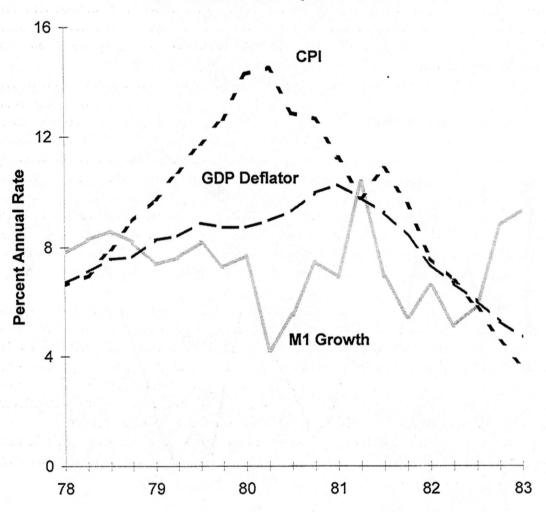

Figure 9.6: The Friedman Surge Reversed And Inflation Collapsed in 1981-82

CPI

GDP Deflator

M1 Growth

The Painful Costs of Stopping Inflation

The painfulness of the disinflation of the 1980s brings home the high cost of stopping an inflation once it is under way. The twin recessions cost many people their jobs or businesses. The stock market was so low by the summer of 1982 that one major business weekly proclaimed "The Death of Equities," equities being another word for stocks. Gloom and doom were so pervasive that the two leading Wall Street seers of the day were dubbed "Dr. Gloom and Mr. Doom" by the press for their steady outpourings of dismal prognostications, most of which proved all too correct for a time.

Why wasn't the disinflation process quicker and less disruptive to the real economy? Why couldn't people just agree that the inflation was over, set new wage and price levels accordingly, and get on about their business without holding a recession? Again, economists tend to focus on expectations in their explanations of the real effects of monetary policy. Even though Volcker made very clear statements about what the new monetary policy would be, the Fed had made many earlier promises to get tough on inflation and not delivered on them. Many assumed the Fed would reflate the economy at the first sign of recession, as it had too many times in the past. If people had believed that the Fed would carry out its policy, which it actually did, no doubt they would have adjusted more rapidly with less damage to the economy.

I recall one business executive boasting in 1981 at having just signed a new labor contract that called for a 12% wage increase every year for the next three years. When I suggested that perhaps inflation might be diminishing, the executive responded that inflation was a permanent feature of the U.S. economy and could only get worse! That decision and many others like it were costly for those who made them and, together, raised the cost to society of bringing inflation back under control.

It took a decade for the Fed to re-establish the credibility that it had squandered in the 1970s, and the Fed is still struggling to maintain that credibility on inflation today.

Exercises 9.3

A. Give your forecast for the U.S. economy for the next four years under the assumption that the Fed sticks to a target growth rate of about 4% for M1.

B. Imagine a situation in which the yield on Treasury bills has been about 8% in recent years and you, as Chair of the Federal Reserve Board, are determined to see it fall to 5%. Outline a strategy for achieving this goal, and explain how it illustrates the paradox of monetary economics.

C. What were the consequences of the 1980 and 1981-82 recession for your family? How long did it take the family to recover economically? Did it have any permanent effect on the family, such as having to move to another city or divorce?

9.4 The Evolution of U.S. Monetary Policy

Today, monetary policy is seen to play a key role in the health of the US economy, having a direct impact on interest rates, employment, and inflation. The media give prominent coverage to the statements and speeches by Federal Reserve officials because everyone knows that the Fed can send interest rates tumbling or zooming as it attempts to keep the economy on the path to non-inflationary growth. Wall Street reacts almost daily to any sign that worsening inflation might cause the Fed to tighten, or that a weaker economy might convince the Fed to ease. This acknowledgment of the importance of monetary policy is relatively recent and arose largely from the failures of monetary policy rather than its successes.

From the end of World War II until the 1970s, the role of the Fed was thought to be to keep interest rates low so as to foster the capital investment that is the engine of long term economic growth. Following the deflation that occurred during the Great Depression in the 1930s and the stringent price controls of World War II, inflation was not seen as a potential problem for the US economy. The relatively low rate of inflation that did occur during those years was usually attributed to "cost-push" resulting from firms passing on higher wages won by powerful labor unions and from the supposedly monopolistic structure of important industries such as steel and autos. Occasionally it was necessary for the Fed to "take away the punch bowl," as one former Fed Chairman put it, when the economy showed signs of inflationary over-heating. The field of macroeconomics was dominated by concerns that the economy might again stumble into a depression, and it was felt that government spending would be the most potent remedy if that happened. There was relatively little interest in the economics profession in monetary policy, indeed the prevailing sentiment was that "money doesn't matter."

Interest in monetary policy and a new appreciation of its power to cause both inflation and recession were reawakened in the second half of the 1960s as inflation rates crept up to levels that began to cause serious concern. When the Fed tightened monetary policy in 1966, there were two conflicting opinions among economists as to its probable effect. One said that it would have little impact on the economy which would continue to expand in response to higher spending for the Vietnam War. The contrary view was that it would result in a dip in the economy and slower inflation. The "mini recession" of 1968 seemed to bolster the "money matters" camp in the profession, and monetary policy began to be seen as an important area of research and public debate.

How the Fed's Role Changed

The debate intensified as the 1970s saw waves of worsening inflation interspersed by severe recessions. To what extent was monetary policy responsible for worsening inflation? Could it cure inflation?

The debate over monetary policy came to a head at the end of the 1970s when President Carter appointed Paul Volcker to the Chairmanship of the Fed with a clear mandate to bring inflation under control even at the cost of severe recession. Few economists at that point doubted that inept Fed policy was at least partly to blame for the stagflation that plagued the economy, or that the cure for inflation had to involve a change in Fed policy. Since that time, the goal of Fed policy has been to push inflation down to very low levels and maintain it there. By the early 1990s it even became possible to talk of "price stability," or zero inflation, as being within reach.

When we look at a chart of the growth rate of M1 along with the yields on Treasury bills and Treasury bonds over the past four decades, as in Figure 9.7, we see a break in the pattern after 1980. Before that date, the growth rate of M1 fluctuated around a rising trend. Over short periods, faster money growth meant lower interest rates as the Fed sought to give the economy a boost. When attention shifted to fighting inflation, slower money growth pushed interest rates upward. Over the whole period from 1961 to 1980, though, both the money growth rate and interest rates trended upward. Clearly, the Fed had failed in its mandate to keep interest rates low, not by creating money too slowly but by creating it too fast over a long period of time. In our study of the dynamic interaction of money supply growth, inflation, and interest rates we learned that money supply growth and interest rates are negatively related over short periods, but positively related over long periods. Given time, inflation adjusts to money supply growth and interest rates, in turn, to respond to inflation. It is those dynamics that we see in Figure 9.7. By 1979, it was clear that this vicious circle of higher interest rates and higher inflation had to be broken.

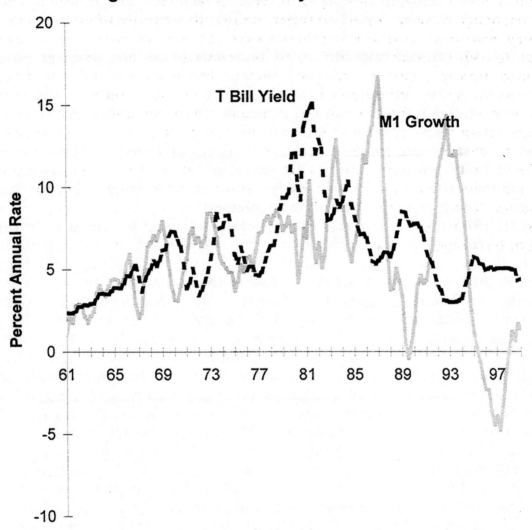

Figure 9.7: The Monetary Roller Coaster

Should the Fed Target Interest Rates or Money Growth?

When the Federal Reserve announced Chairman Volcker's new monetary policy in 1979 the emphasis was to be on controlling the supply of money rather than on controlling interest rates. The Fed thereby acknowledged the critical role of money and the fact that previous policy aimed at achieving interest rate targets had failed. In the succeeding four years, the Fed did reduce the growth rate of M1, although its growth rate continued to fluctuate widely, often creating doubts in the minds of economists and the public about the Fed's dedication to its announced targets. During this period, the Fed maintained that it did not have any specific target for interest rates, and that interest rates could fall only as the result of successful control of inflation over several years. Indeed, after reaching unheard of level in the early years of the new policy, interest rates did retreat, reaching levels not seen since the 1960s by the early 1990s. It is sobering to realize that it took a decade to undo the effects of inflation!

After 1984 the Fed reduced its emphasis on targeting the growth rate of M1 which has fluctuated widely since then, surging to new heights in 1986, dropping to zero in 1989, soaring again in 1992, and plummeting in 1994. Although there is no clear upward trend that suggests a new era of inflation ahead, the extreme variation of these fluctuations has been the source of renewed concern about monetary policy in the 1990s. Why the large variations and what does the Fed hope to accomplish by them?

To answer these questions, we need to think about alternative strategies for conducting monetary policy. A simple strategy would be to just add new reserves to the banking system at a steady pace designed to keep M1 increasing at a rate consistent with zero inflation. Such a money growth rule has long been advocated by the monetarist school of thought in macroeconomics. The argument in favor of a money growth rule is basically that it is the only way of ensuring price stability over a long period. The Fed has shown that it is unable to "fine tune" the economy, having caused several recessions while failing to control inflation.

The argument against the monetarist position is that an enlightened Fed can do better than blindly follow a fixed rule. For example, suppose that there is an increase in the demand for money due to heavy trading volume on Wall Street. Shouldn't the Fed accommodate such an increase in transactions demand by increasing M1 faster? If it doesn't, the Fed would be allowing an unnecessary shortage of transactions balances to occur which would push up interest rates and cause a slow down in the economy.

In addition, the economy is subject to real shocks, changes in productivity that alter the natural level of output. For example, suppose that the development of micro computers causes the natural growth rate of the economy to accelerate from 3% per year to 4%. Shouldn't the Fed accommodate this more rapid growth by increasing money growth by 1%? On the other hand, if world oil prices jump due to conflict in the Middle East, the resulting fall in our natural level of real GDP would seem to call for reduced money growth; otherwise inflation would accelerate.

Rules vs. Discretion

These are the arguments on the two sides of the "rules versus discretion" debate on the conduct of monetary policy. It is clear from the wide fluctuations of M1 growth in recent years that the discretion philosophy has prevailed at the Fed. Chairman Greenspan is certainly someone who believes not only that money matters but that the Fed can use its influence to improve the performance of the economy. With concerns about inflation on the rise in the late 1980s, Greenspan moved to put on the brakes. The resulting recession of 1990-91 convinced him to ease monetary policy sharply in 1992 when M1 growth zoomed and interest rates plummeted. Renewed inflation concerns in 1993 brought another tightening of monetary policy in 1994 with rising interest rates and lower M1 growth into 1995. Has the performance of the economy been better as a result than it would have under a monetary policy rule? Can the Fed continue its good record with a less skilled driver than Greenspan at the wheel? These are questions that will continue to be debated for decades to come.

Assuming that we are to have a discretionary monetary policy, should the Fed be aiming to achieve a certain level of money supply growth, or should it aim for a certain level of interest rates? When the Fed reduced its emphasis on stabilizing the growth rate of money in 1984 it also shifted back towards interest rates as its target variable. The key policy question from this perspective is this: Should interest rates be higher or lower now, given our objective of non-inflationary growth?

For example, in 1994, the Fed felt that interest rates were too low since the economy was expanding at a brisk rate with unemployment and capacity utilization at levels that raise concerns about upward pressure on inflation. The Fed then embarked on a series of tightening moves aimed at pushing interest rates up. It announced its intentions to the public in terms of its target for the federal funds rate. That is the interest rate charged by banks to each other for the over night loan of bank reserves. It is the shortest term of interest rates and it is the most directly affected by the Fed's open market operations. As the Fed reduces its purchase of Treasury securities, banks immediately find reserves more scarce and therefore the interest cost of obtaining reserves is bid up in the "fed funds" market.

People sometimes get the impression that the Fed sets the fed funds rate directly as it does the discount rate (the rate at which banks may borrow reserves from the Fed). Rather, the fed funds rate is the Fed's barometer of the tightness or ease of monetary policy. The trick is to set the fed funds target rate so as to achieve the impact on the interest rates that affect borrowers that will, in turn, have the desired effect on aggregate demand and, ultimately, inflation. Not a simple calculation!

The potential pitfall in the interest rate target approach to monetary policy is that you will repeat the mistakes of the 1970s, never raising interest rates quite enough to bring inflation under control. It is easy to do that because the Fed only affects the nominal interest rate, and an increase in the nominal interest rate will not dampen aggregate demand unless it is also an increase in the real interest rate. Successively higher nominal interest rates failed to curb aggregate demand in the 1970s because expected inflation was rising even faster, keeping the real interest rate low. Interest rate targets also make the Fed's job more difficult politically because high interest rates are always unpopular.

We Have Been on a Money Growth Roller Coaster

Continuing our perspective on monetary policy over the past four decades, Figure 9.8 charts the growth rate of M1 along with two key real variables, the growth rate of real GDP and the unemployment rate. As we would expect, sharp drops in M1 growth are often followed by drops in real GDP growth and a rise in unemployment, while faster M1 growth is followed by a pick up in real GDP growth and lower unemployment. Equally important is the fact that there is evidently no correlation over longer periods between money growth on the one hand and these two real variables on the other. *Evidently, monetary policy can affect the real economy over short periods, but over longer periods the real economy returns to its normal state.*

If anything, the real growth rate of the economy was lower and unemployment higher during the years when money growth was at its most rapid. Some economists argue that high inflation rates damage the efficiency of the economy because they make the price system less meaningful to economic agents and because people expend real resources avoiding the costs that inflation imposes on holding money and through the taxation of nominal income.

Finally, in Figure 9.9 we see the growth rate of M1 along with the inflation rate as measured by both the GDP deflator and the CPI since 1961. While the effect of changes in M1 growth on real GDP was seen to be fairly quick in the previous figure, we see here that inflation responds to changes in money growth with a lag of about two years. It is easy to see why economists became concerned again in 1986 that the Fed had allowed money growth to become excessive. Indeed, inflation bubbled up in 1988 and the Fed responded by stopping M1 in its tracks. Following the jump in M1 growth during 1992, inflation again became a concern in 1994 and the Fed again stepped on its monetary brakes.

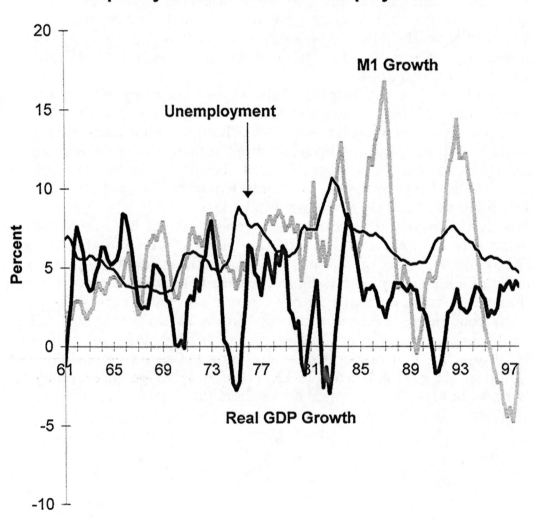

Figure 9.8: Rapid M1 Growth Produces Only Temporary Gains in GDP and Employment

M1 Growth

Unemployment

Percent

Real GDP Growth

Figure 9.9: Erratic Money Growth is Reason for Concerns About Long-Term Stability

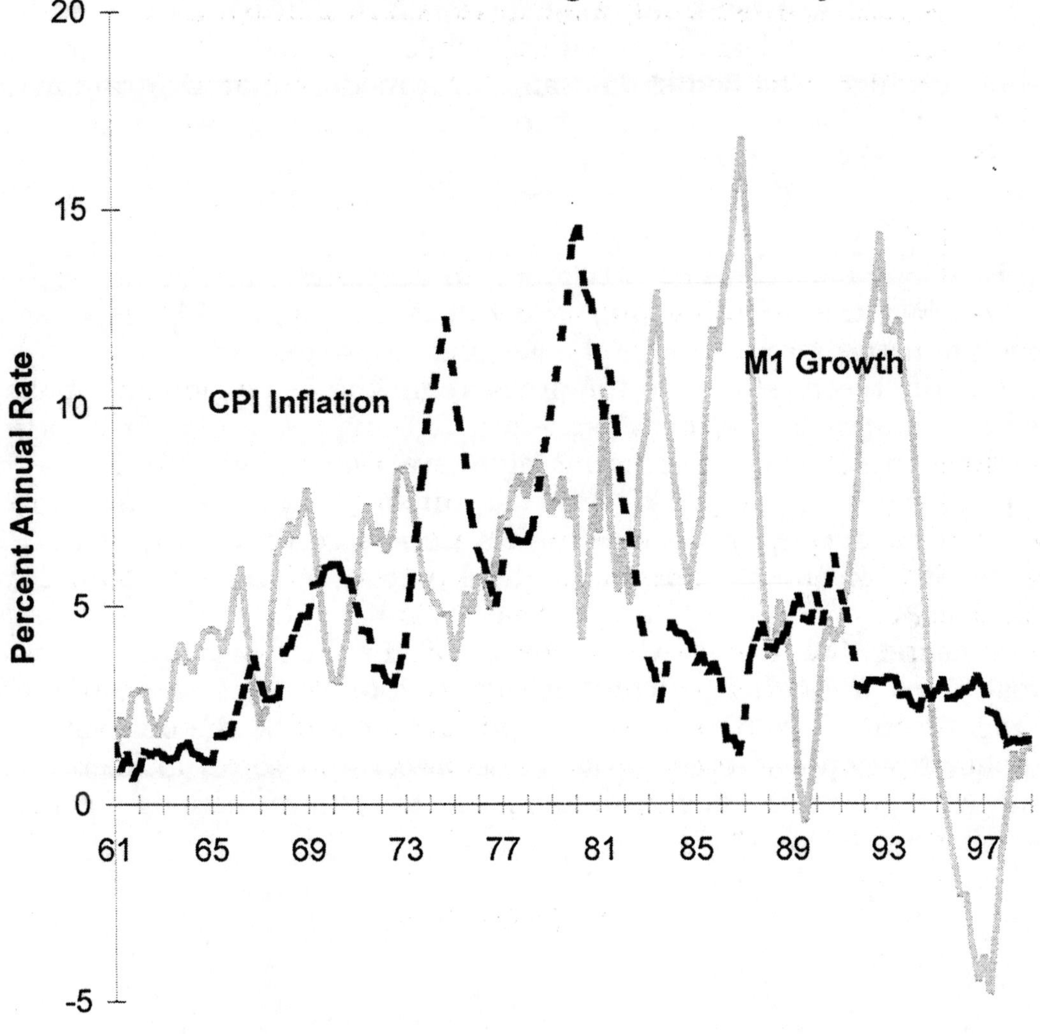

CPI Inflation

M1 Growth

Percent Annual Rate

20

15

10

5

0

-5

61   65   69   73   77   81   85   89   93   97

In summary, it is hard to escape the conclusion that the Fed took the economy on a roller coaster ride which resulted in successive waves of inflation that culminated in the crisis of 1979-80. Meanwhile, booms and recessions alternated as the Fed attempted to successively stimulate economic growth and then tame the ensuing inflation. One can only hope that the Fed has learned from this experience that attempts to stimulate the economy easily lead to inflation, while the costs of undoing the inflation are high. The Fed should aim for a moderate growth rate in the money supply that is consistent with the long run growth rate of the economy and low inflation.

Exercises 9.4

A. How long does it seem to take for an acceleration in money growth to show up in the inflation rate? How does this lag in the response of inflation to money growth make the Fed's job more difficult?

B. Identify recent stories in the press about the Fed's monetary policy. Does the emphasis seem to be on fighting inflation or fighting unemployment? Is the Fed announcing a target for the growth rate of the money supply or a target for interest rates? What are the current targets? Has the Fed been meeting its targets recently, and if not, in what way is it off track? How do political pressures seem to be affecting Fed policies?

C. Imagine that a new Chairperson of the Fed sets out to lower interest rates from their current levels, say to cut the rate on home mortgages from 9% to 6%. What do you predict will be the outcome of a Fed policy that cuts interest rates immediately and seeks to keep them down? What would the Fed have to do now to achieve the long term goal of lower mortgage rates?

9.5 The "Phillips Curve" and How It Disappeared

In 1958 a New Zealand economist named A. W. Phillips pointed out that the unemployment rate and the rate of change in wages had been negatively correlated in the UK. During the next decade the idea that this represented a fixed trade-off between unemployment and inflation took hold in the economics profession and soon became known as the "Phillips curve." Phillips' observation was reinforced by the experience of the 1960s which started with unemployment high and inflation low and ended with unemployment low and inflation high.

The quarterly observations on these two variables are plotted in Figure 9.10 and indeed they trace out a neat curve. If this were a stable relationship it would imply that a country can have low unemployment or low inflation, but not both. Some economists jumped to the conclusion that a little inflation was good for economic growth. Indeed, third world countries were counseled to use inflation to stimulate rapid development. From the perspective of our present understanding of the dynamics of inflation and unemployment we would now say that there is only a temporary trade-off between unemployment and inflation during the transition from a lower inflation rate to a higher one.

A temporary trade-off of lower unemployment for higher inflation is indeed what we saw when we studied how the economy adjusts to a new steady state. Further, our study of the transition from a higher inflation rate to a lower one leads us to expect that the unemployment rate will rise before the inflation rate finally subsides. We see in Figure 9.11 that when the Fed moved to slow inflation at the end of the 1960s the result was rebounding unemployment associated with the recession of 1969-70. As the Fed struggled successively to reduce unemployment and then reduce inflation during the 1970s it created the rising spiral that we see in this chart. By 1980 the unemployment rate was no lower than it had been two decades earlier, but inflation was in double digits. The real economy had returned to its natural rate of employment, only inflation had changed.

Figure 9.10: The Phillips Curve in the 1960s
A Choice Between Inflation and Unemployment?

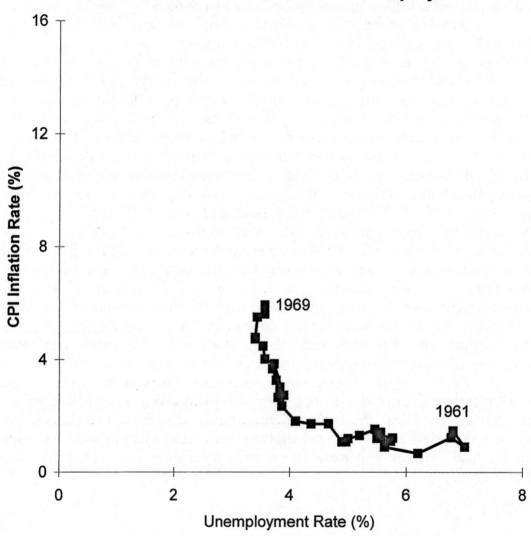

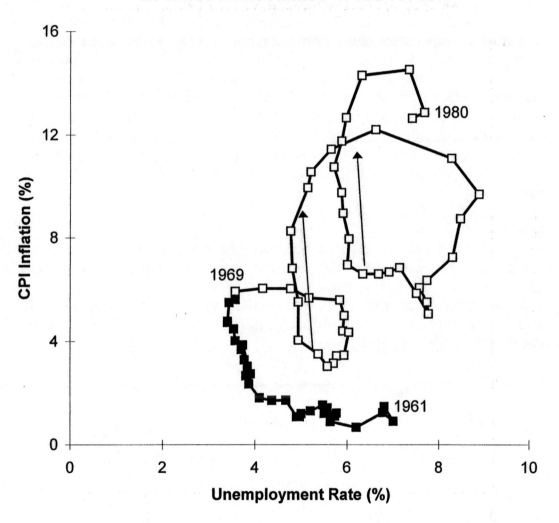

Figure 9.11: The Phillips "Curve" Becomes a Spiral as Inflation Escalates in the 1970s

When the Fed finally brought the inflation spiral under control in the 1980s we experienced the reversal seen in Figure 9.12. Unemployment surged during the 1980-82 double dip recession and then inflation subsided dramatically over the next few years. By 1987 the unemployment rate and the inflation rate were again almost exactly where they had started in 1961!

The lesson that economists learned from seeing the Phillips curve turn into a spiral was that monetary policy cannot by itself reduce the unemployment rate permanently, rather it can only reduce it temporarily at the cost of higher inflation and, ultimately, recession when the inflation is extinguished. Today most economists accept the idea of a natural rate of unemployment, which may not be an ideal rate but represents a tendency toward equilibrium in the economy. Better and more education, investment in technology, and expanded opportunities are the only sources of improvement in the standard of living over the long run.

Exercises 9.5

A. Judging from our experience with the Phillips "curve," what would be a reasonable estimate of the natural rate of unemployment in the U.S. economy?

B. Suppose that the Fed begins this year to increase the money supply at a rate of 10%. Sketch the path that the Phillips curve might take over the next several years.

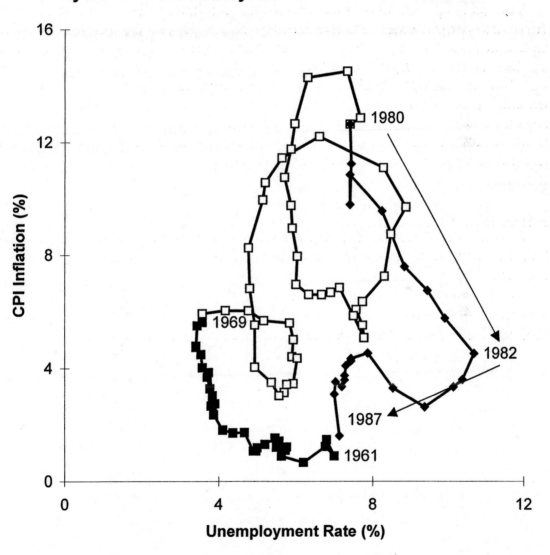

Figure 9.12: The Phillips Curve Becomes a Circle By 1987 the Economy Was Back Where It Started!

Index

Chapter 10

Fiscal Policy: Government Spending and Taxation

Outline

Preview

Government at all levels - federal, state, and local - collects taxes, pays the costs of providing services, makes transfer payments, and borrows when its expenditures exceed its tax revenues. In a course on macroeconomics we focus on the federal government because its actions most directly affect the entire national economy. Acts of Congress and the actions of the Executive Branch which determine what taxes are collected, what expenditures are undertaken, and how any gap between expenditures and tax revenues is to be financed are referred to as fiscal policy.

The most troubling fact about fiscal policy in recent decades has been a large and persistent deficit in the federal budget. The most surprising fact about fiscal policy in recent years has been the sudden and unexpected disappearance of that deficit! To many Americans, the chronic deficit was a very disturbing development that for some seemed to point to an inability to get government spending under control. To others, it was symptomatic of an unwillingness of Americans to face up to the real costs of government. It is important that we, as citizens, try to understand how this deficit came about, how it has suddenly shrunk, and what is likely to happen in coming decades. If we return to deficit budgets, what might be the long run consequences of a continuing deficit of recent proportions?

The federal deficit was a major political issue in the 1992 presidential campaign, with Congress and President Bush each blaming each other for not reducing it. Candidate Clinton, whose defeat of incumbent President Bush was in part due to voters' concern about the deficit, made enactment of his package of tax increases and spending cuts a top legislative priority during his first year as President. In 1996 incumbent President Clinton was able to claim substantial credit for the narrowing of the deficit when he ran for successfully for re-election.

10.1 What Happened to the Federal Budget Deficit?

During most of the period since WWII the U.S. government has had a large and persistent budget deficit. The arithmetic of deficits is simple. The federal government has spent more, about $290 billion more in 1992 alone, than it was collecting from taxpayers. The question "What can be done to reduce the deficit?" never had an easy answer: Congress would have to reduce spending, or increase taxes, or some of both.

The hard part was deciding which spending programs were to shrink and whose taxes were to be increased. We were all in favor of reducing the deficit, but few of us are eager to see programs we benefit from curtailed or the taxes we pay increased. There was no shortage of blame to be passed around, but there was an acute shortage of politically acceptable solutions to the deficit problem. By the mid-1990s most observers concluded that the deficit problem was simply intractable.

Then came one of the biggest surprises of recent history. Somehow, the deficit suddenly disappeared. For 1999 the federal government actually has a surplus, about $100 billion! How did that happen, when no massive spending cuts were mandated by Congress and no major new taxes enacted? Before we see the answer, a few basic facts about federal spending and taxation.

Spending by the federal government includes two major categories: purchases of goods and services and transfer payments. Goods and services include durable items that represent an investment by government in plant and equipment, such as new military aircraft and Post Office buildings. Also included are items that are consumed quickly such as jet fuel and the services of the National Park rangers that guide your hike (or rescue you if you went on your own). Both types of goods and services are the part of the output of the economy that is used by the federal government.

The other category of federal expenditures are payments to individuals and firms that are entitled to receive them under laws enacted by Congress. These are called transfer payments or entitlements. They are not payment in return for goods or services, but rather a transfer of purchasing power from taxpayers to entitled groups. Transfer payments include Social Security, Medicare, welfare, unemployment benefits, and food stamps. In addition, the federal government makes grants-in-aid to state and local governments that help fund specific programs. Medicaid, which pays medical expenses of low income households, is administered by the states but is jointly funded by the states and the federal government.

Together, both kinds of expenditure by the federal government are called outlays. In principle, Congress has distinguished between on-budget outlays and off-budget outlays, the latter being primarily Social Security. This distinction was intended to isolate the Social Security system from political wrangling over the budget, but has been largely ignored. When deficit or surplus numbers are mentioned by politicians or the press, they are almost always for the combined budget, and the current surplus is due to the large surplus in the Social Security fund, that is, off-budget. If we look at on-budget items, see still a deficit, but a smaller one nevertheless.

The federal government collects taxes from households, primarily through the personal income tax, and from firms, primarily through the tax on corporate profits. Social Security and Medicare are financed by separate "payroll" taxes that are a percentage of wages and salaries and are paid by both employees and employers. There is also excise tax on the sale of certain items such as tires, customs duty on imports, and the estate tax on inheritances. The total of all federal revenues from these sources is called total receipts.

The magnitude of the federal budget is simply staggering. Outlays and receipts each now exceed $1.8 trillion per year, about $7,000 per American.

Putting the Federal Budget in Historical Perspective

A challenge of presenting historical data is to do it in a way that has some consistent meaning over time. Expressing items like federal expenditures as a percent of the GDP in the same year is one way that we have used before in this book. In Figure 10.1 we plot federal outlays and receipts expressed as a percent of GDP to get an idea of their magnitude relative to the size of the economy, and trends in their relative size over time. The period covered starts in 1950, after the large distortions due to WWII had disappeared (at the height of the war effort, military spending approached 40% of GDP!). The data are annual for fiscal years which currently end in September rather than in December. The source of the data is the Economic Report of the President 1999. These annual reports are a rich source of historical statistics and commentary on current developments, and can be purchased through book-sellers.

As you look at Figure 10.1, note that there is little apparent trend in receipts: they have averaged about 18 percent of GDP since 1950. In contrast, expenditures have grown faster than the economy until recently, and they have been above 20% of GDP for much of the post-WWII period. The deficit, the gap between outlays and receipts, emerged during the 1970s, and expanding in the 1980s, as outlays soared, growing much faster than the economy, while receipts remained a fairly stable fraction of GDP. There was a small decline in receipts following President Reagan's tax cut of the early 1980s, but it was quickly followed by tax law changes that raised payroll taxes and closed many tax "loopholes." Although the 1980s are frequently portrayed as a period of spending cuts by the Reagan administration, we see that it was actually a decade during which federal expenditures took a quantum leap upward, opening up the wide gap between expenditures and receipts that we see here.

Figure 10.1: Federal Outlays and Receipts as a Percent of GDP

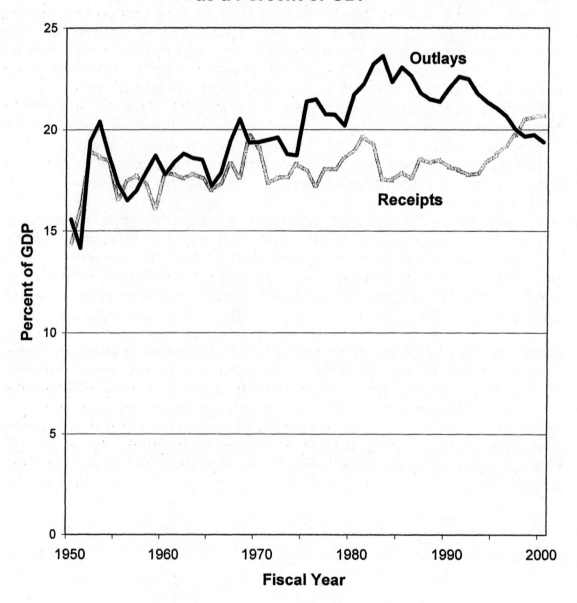

During the Clinton years, expenditures declined relative to GDP. Meanwhile, taxes rose more rapidly than GDP, partially because of higher income tax rates enacted at President Clinton's instigation. The net effect was shrinkage of the deficit until now, at least for the time being, it has given way to a budget surplus. It is already apparent that how to spend that surplus, or whether to turn it into tax cuts, will be a major subject of debate in the next Presidential campaign. However, as we will discuss further, demographic forces will tend to push the budget back in the direction of deficits as we move into the next century.

Changes in the magnitude of federal deficit are even more apparent in Figure 10.2 where the budget balance, positive for a surplus, negative for a deficit, is expressed as a percent of GDP.

Notice that during the 1960s the federal budget was more often in deficit than in surplus, but the magnitude of the deficit was only about 2 percent of GDP. A large deficit occurred briefly in the mid-1970s but that was associated with the very severe recession of 1974-75. It was after 1980 that a large deficit became stubbornly persistent. Finally, we see the dramatic swing to surplus at the end of the 1990s.

Notice too that the budget balance slumps into deficit, or deeper deficit, when the economy slumps into recession. Evidently the budget balance is pro-cyclical. Why?

During a recession, tax revenues shrink more rapidly than does GDP. The decline in personal income tax receipts is accentuated by progressive tax rates which rise with a household's income. As the incomes of many households decline during a recession, the percent of that income that they pay in federal income tax also declines. Thus, receipts from the income tax become a smaller percentage of a smallerGDP. The negative impact of recession on tax receipts is also accentuated by corporate profits being strongly pro-cyclical, as we saw in Chapter 5. This pro-cyclical behavior of tax revenues as a fraction of GDP is apparent in Figure 10.1.

Figure 10.2: Federal Budget Balance

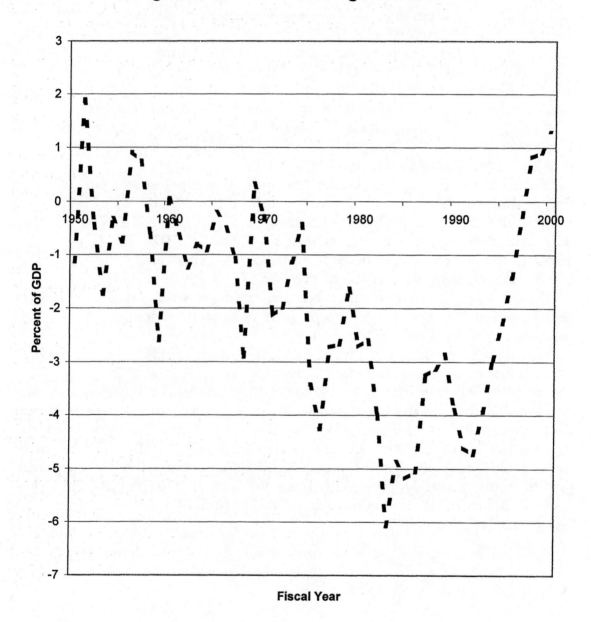

On the expenditure side, the unemployment associated with a recession puts greater demands on federal programs that provide income security, so expenditure tend to rise as GDP falls. The tendency of expenditures to rise as a percentage of GDP is also apparent in Figure 10.1.

When the economy recovers from a recession, these forces are reversed. During the ensuing expansion, personal income tax revenues are a rising percentage of rising incomes due to progressive tax rates, and corporations are paying income tax on rapidly rising profits. On the outlay side, unemployment benefit payments decrease.

The combined effect of the pro-cyclical behavior of tax revenues and the counter cyclical behavior of expenditures is to make the budget balance strongly pro-cyclical or, equivalently, the deficit strongly counter-cyclical. Consequently, much of the short-term variation in the budget deficit is related to fluctuations in the economy. Recall that the 1974-75 recession was a particularly severe recession. As the economy recovered, the deficit shrank rapidly and the budget balance was approaching zero in 1979. Then the twin recessions of 1980 and 1981-82 got underway and sent it plunging once again.

What was new in American experience in the 1980s was that the deficit did not disappear when the economy recovered. Even in the boom years of 1988 and 1989 the deficit remained stubbornly at 3 percent of GDP. When the recession of 1990-91 got underway, the usual cyclical factors caused the deficit to widen once more.

What we learn from Figure 10.1 is that the shrinkage of the deficit during the Clinton years was due *both* to declining outlays *and* to rising receipts, as fractions of GDP. Higher tax rates enacted in President Clinton's deficit reduction plan have increased federal tax receipts. But the big surge in receipts has come at the end of the 1990s as the strong economy and spectacular performance of the stock market have swelled the Treasury's coffers with additional tax revenue. On the outlays side, defense expenditures have shrunk, even in nominal dollar terms, with the end of the cold war. We will look at the factors behind both outlays and receipts in more detail shortly.

What is in store for the deficit as we look ahead? Many economists who are experts on the federal budget expect that the largest cuts in defense spending are behind us, while spending on entitlement programs is likely to continue to grow rapidly as the baby boom generation approaches retirement age after about 2010. We will return to these longer-term trends and their potential consequences later in the chapter.

The National Debt

When the federal government spends more that it receives in taxes it is obliged to borrow the difference. It does this by selling U.S. Treasury bills, notes, and bonds to households, financial intermediaries, corporations, and foreigners. The Federal Reserve also is a buyer of federal securities through its open market operations. The accumulated value of outstanding U.S. Treasury securities is referred to as the federal debt or more often in the media as the national debt. Some of the debt is held in Social Security and other government trust funds; the remainder is held by the public. We will focus on this latter amount.

The national debt is about $3.7 trillion, a huge number by any standard, amounting to about $15,000 for every American! To put this number in perspective and help identify trends we again use the device of expressing it as a percent of GDP. That is what is charted in Figure 10.3.

The data are annual, back to 1940 to show the impact of WWII. Of course, the federal government incurred very large deficits to finance the massive war effort. The long post-war decline in the federal debt ended, as we see here, in 1975. After that watershed year, the federal debt began to grow faster than the economy, due to the widening and increasingly chronic budget deficit. From a post-war low of 24% of GDP in 1975, the federal debt had soared to nearly 50% of GDP by 1996.

Figure 10.3: Federal Debt (Held by Public) as a Percent of GDP

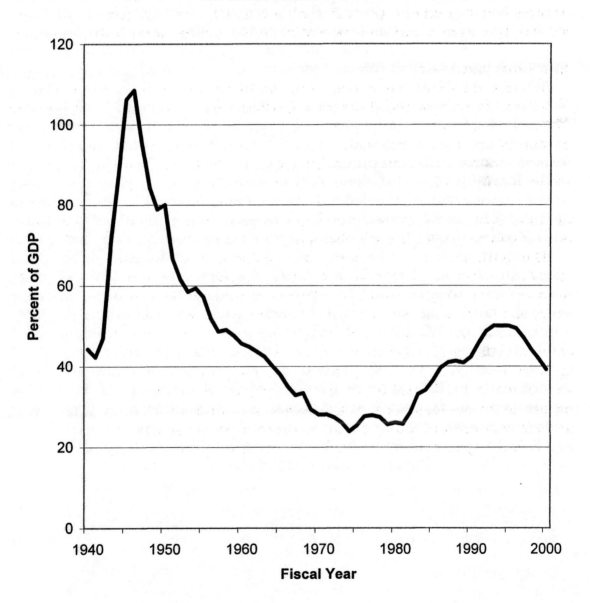

What are the consequences of this huge debt? Whom do we owe it to? Is it just "money that we owe to ourselves" or is it "money borrowed from future generations?" How are we going to pay it back? When, if ever, are we going to pay it back? What will happen if foreign owners of U.S. Treasury securities decide that they want their money? These are some of the toughest questions facing America today and ones on which economists and others often disagree. We will come back to these questions again later in the chapter.

Finally, we should say a few words about state and local governments. Because the federal budget is national news but state and local budgets are only local news, we tend to be unaware of just how large these governments are in aggregate. In 1996 total expenditures by state and local governments were approaching $1 trillion, about two thirds the size of the federal budget and about 13% of GDP.

As in the case of the federal government, transfer payments are a growing component of state and local budgets, currently about one third, with Medicaid being the primary force in that growth. Unlike the federal government, though, state and local budgets are in surplus, about $100 billion in total for 1996! This reflects the fact that most of our state constitutions require that the operating budget be balanced, allowing only for borrowing for capital projects such as bridges. Also, local governments cannot count on being able to sell bonds as readily as does the U.S. Treasury, nor does the Federal Reserve buy their bonds.

Significantly, over $200 billion of the receipts of state and local governments in 1996 were in the form of grants-in-aid from the federal government. Such grants are increasingly questioned at a time when state budgets are in better shape than the federal budget.

Government at all levels now collects a total of about $3 trillion per year in taxes of all kinds, about a third of GDP.

Exercises 10.1

A. One hears that "Reagan cut taxes" or "Clinton raised taxes." In the American system of government, what is the process by which federal taxes are changed, and what is actually the role of the President.

B. Give a concrete example of an action that could be taken that would reduce the federal deficit. Which groups in society do you think would be in favor of your proposal? which opposed? What are the chances that your proposal could actually become law?

C. How large are federal expenditures today, expressed as a percentage of GDP? How large are government expenditures at all levels together? Do you expect these to rise or fall over the next decade? Explain briefly.

D. If a major recession were to occur in 1998, what would be your forecast of the direction of the budget balance? the deficit? Explain why you would be confident in your prediction or why not.

E. If every American were to devote 10% of their disposable income to reducing the national debt, how long would it take to pay that debt off, assuming we incurred no further budget deficits.

F. Does the government of the state you live in run up a large debt? What restrains your state legislature from acting like the U.S. Congress in this regard? Contrast the situation of American states with that of Canadian provinces.

10.2 Growth in the Role of the Federal Government

Certainly one of the most dramatic and far reaching developments in American society in this century has been the growth in size and influence of the federal government.

One way to see this growth is in the collection of taxes. At the dawn of the twentieth century, there was no income tax. Both the Union and the Confederacy had enacted an income tax during the Civil War (1860s), but the tax was unpopular and was dropped after the war. The need for tax revenues was modest in peace-time because there was little that the federal government did beyond national defense. Modern entitlement programs did not exist; Social Security was not adopted until the 1930s and Medicare not until the 1960s.

The Income Tax

An income tax passed Congress in 1894, but was declared unconstitutional by the Supreme Court. The door to an income tax was finally opened by the 16th Amendment to the Constitution in 1913, and President Wilson signed the income tax into law that year. Wisconsin, however, had beaten the federal government to the punch, adopting the first state income tax in 1911.

President Wilson's income tax was 1% on incomes above $20,000, a very substantial income in those days, and the percentage went as high as 6% for the very wealthy. Only a few years later, the financial burden of fighting World War I lead to a sharp increase in tax rates, as high as 65% on the highest incomes. After falling again between the wars, the federal income tax rate soared again in World War II, the rate on the highest incomes reaching a peak of 91%. These very high marginal tax rates did not end with the war and were reduced in steps, beginning with President Kennedy's tax cuts in the early 1960s.

Today, the income tax rate is 15% on the taxable income of a married couple up to about $39,000 and rises to 39.6% on taxable income above $250,000. Keep in mind that "taxable income" reflects various deductions and exemptions, including interest on home mortgages and charitable contributions.

Figure 10.4 shows the fraction of tax returns at various income levels and how much of tax revenue they account for, based on Internal Revenue Service data. While most returns show taxable income of less that $50,000, we see that the bulk of the income tax is paid by the relatively small fraction of taxpayers with incomes above $50,000. One of the important tax changes during the Reagan administration was the virtual elimination of the income tax for very low incomes. For low-income households, the primary tax burden is Social Security and Medicare as well as state and local taxes.

Contrary to popular impression, the average income tax rate does rise as income rises, reaching about 25% for the highest income group. Figure 10.4 shows that people reporting an income over $1 million pay 10% of the entire income tax. Clearly, we all owe Michael Jordan and Bill Gates a heartfelt "thank you." Although they are less than 1/10 % of all returns there were about 60,000 of them!

While it is fun to think about the problems of the very rich, it is important to notice that the middle class carries most of the burden of the income tax. Indeed, the income tax could not otherwise generate over $900 billion revenue per year. Returns below $20,000 add up to only about 16% of total household income, while those above $500,000 add up to only 9%. The bulk of income is earned by households in middle range, and those are the people who carry the burden of the income tax.

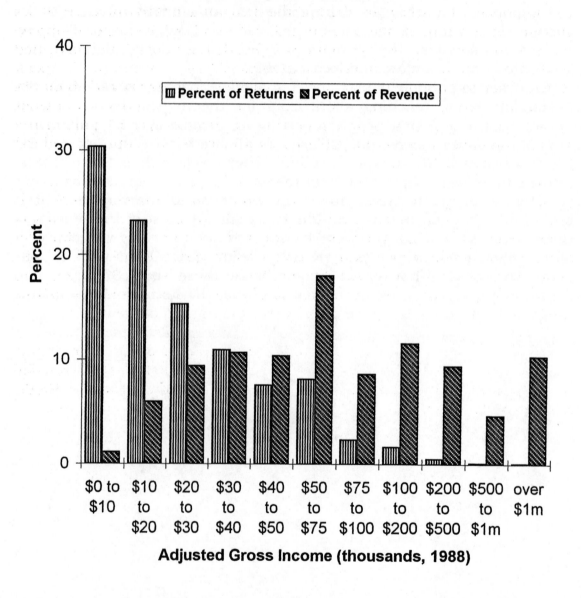

Figure 10.4: Percent of Tax Returns and Revenue by Income Level

Percent of Returns   Percent of Revenue

Percent

Adjusted Gross Income (thousands, 1988)

Trends in Federal Spending

Let's now look at the major programs within the federal budget to see where it has grown and what has enabled outlays to shrink as a fraction of GDP in recent years.

Figure 10.5 shows total outlays and the part due to defense since 1940. Notice that the war effort consumed almost 40% of GDP at its maximum, and represented the bulk of all federal outlays. After dropping sharply and temporarily at the end of WWII, defense spending has drifted downward from a Korean War peak of 14% of GDP, a Vietnam War peak of 9%, a Reagan build-up peak of 6%, to a post Cold War low of about 3% today. The trend has been for defense to be a decreasing portion of what the federal government spends money on, and a decreasing part of the whole economy. But what is the other 17% or so of GDP that the federal government spends?

Entitlements are the growing part of the federal budget, and the major entitlement programs are shown in Figure 10.6. Notice that Social Security was not significant until after 1950. That was because so few people had qualified for retirement until then, and benefits were initially very modest. Medicare dates only from 1966. Income security, including welfare programs such as Aid to Families of Dependent Children, has grown, but is eclipsed by the newer entitlements that are not linked to income level.

The growth we see in these programs reflects the emergence of the federal government as the guarantor of minimum levels of income and health services, sometimes referred to as the "safety net." Transfer payments overall have grown from being about 5% of GDP in the 1960s to about 10% today.

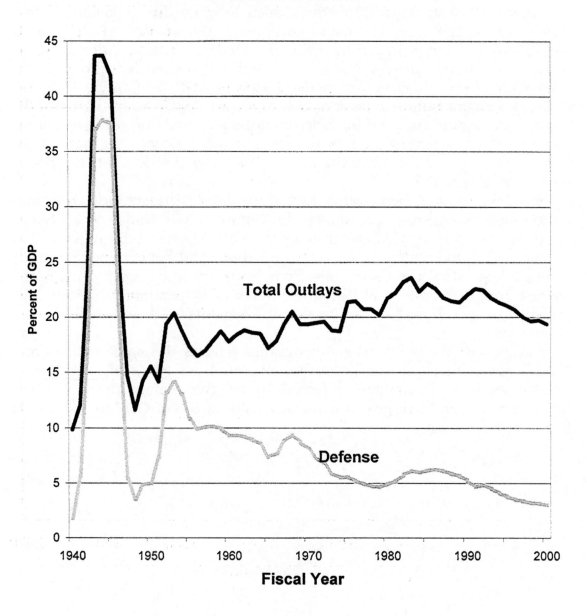

**Figure 10.5: Federal Outlays:
Total and Defense**

Total Outlays

Defense

Percent of GDP

Fiscal Year

396

Figure 10.6: Federal Entitlements

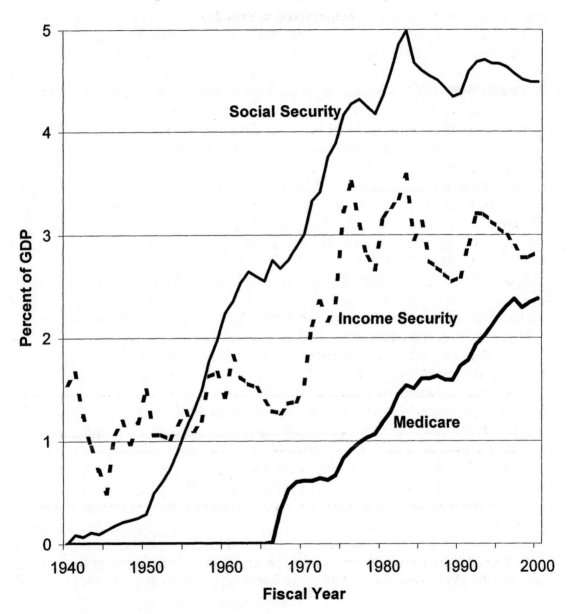

The Social Security System

Social Security, which accounts for most of the growth in transfer payments, dates back to 1935 when it was conceived as a retirement program funded by a tax on payrolls. Initially the tax rate was only 1 percent and applied to only the first $3,000 of wages. In accordance with the concept of a retirement plan, people did not qualify to receive social security benefits until they had paid into the plan and reached retirement age.

Thus in the early years of social security very few individuals were receiving benefits while a very large number were paying the payroll tax. This enabled the system to pay out to early beneficiaries far more in benefits than they had paid in Social Security taxes prior to retirement.

The first individual to receive benefits under Social Security was Mary Fuller who retired in 1940 after having paid an accumulated total of $22 in Social Security taxes. Her first monthly check was for slightly more than $22. Over more than three decades of retirement her benefits totaled more than $20,000!

As time went on, Congress saw fit to broaden Social Security benefits and loosen the connection between an individual's eligibility for benefits and the Social Security taxes they had paid. By the 1980's the Social Security system was dispersing about 36 million checks each month to not only retired participants in the system but also to elderly who had not paid into the system, to disabled workers and their dependents, and to deceased workers' widows and widowers. Social Security is not a retirement plan which puts away the savings of workers for their use in retirement. Rather, it is a "pay-as-you-go" system that transfers funds collected by payroll taxes from those working to its beneficiaries.

Some observers have likened the social security system to a "Ponzi scheme," named after a Boston confidence man of the 1920s. Charles Ponzi promised to pay investors far more than the market rate of interest and assured them that they could withdraw their principal plus interest at any time. Initially the scheme appeared to be enormously profitable for those who invested their money with Ponzi. The amount of money entrusted to Ponzi grew rapidly, and few chose to withdraw their money.

In reality, he had not discovered a new way to earn more than the market rate of interest.

Of course, Ponzi was able to make the scheme work only as long as the amount of money received from new investors exceeded the amount being paid out to old investors. Eventually the scheme collapsed when too many investors tried to cash in. Some analysts fear that the Social Security system will suffer the same fate.

As the Social Security system enters the twenty-first century, the large baby boom generation born between the mid-1940s and the mid-1960s will reach retirement age and will be expecting to receive the same level of retirement benefits that the smaller generations before it enjoyed. Meanwhile, the age groups paying taxes will be smaller because of the "birth dearth" after 1965. How the Social Security system can remain financially and politically viable under those circumstances remains a very open question. It seems very probably that, like Ponzi's investors, later participants in the Social Security system will not reap the benefits that they envisioned when they entered it.

Medicare

Medicare was enacted in the mid-1960s as part of President Johnson's Great Society Program. It provides medical insurance coverage for the elderly. The growth in Medicare benefits has been breathtaking, exceeding the original projections of its proponents by a factor of ten (even after taking inflation into account). The factors contributing to this explosion are several.

First of all, there is the "law of demand" which says that the demand for any good or service varies inversely with price. When Medicare reduced the price of medical services *to the patient*, much more service was demanded. At the same time, health care providers have an economic incentive to perform more procedures and raise their prices at the expense of Medicare. In response, Medicare has begun an aggressive program of cost containment, but other forces are at work to keep expenditures growing.

Because of advances in medical technology people are living longer as new and ever more expensive procedures have become available to prolong life. One of the striking developments in modern American medicine is the great concentration of medical care resources on the terminally ill. It is estimated that about one third of all of the medical expenditures in the US are incurred by the elderly during the last year of life.

Clearly, modern technology poses not only economic challenges but also grave ethical ones. Until antibiotics and modern surgery appeared in the 1930s, physicians could do little to alter the course of disease or injury. People either died or got better on their own. Expending economic resources had little effect. All the king's horses and all the king's men couldn't put Humpty-Dumpty back together again.

Today, Humpty may possibly be put back together again, and those are the greatest accomplishments of modern medicine. However, in other situations, Humpty can only be kept alive, perhaps indefinitely, and a substantial fraction of the king's budget will be required. Should every effort be made to prolong life regardless of the quality of that life? If not, who will decide when to withhold further effort? Physicians take an oath to preserve life, and the Judeo-Christian ethic does not recognize an alternative. The ethical dilemma posed by modern medicine is not one that our ancestors faced, but is one we will have to come to terms with.

We have seen that federal government expenditures have shifted during the last five decades away from national defense, and towards transfer payments. Now we take a look at how spending on three other major federal budget items has shifted over this period. Figure 10.7 tracks spending on international affairs, health, and interest on the federal debt.

Notice that we spent a lot on international affairs immediately following WWII, partly for rebuilding and partly to counter what was perceived a major threat by the then-formidable Soviet Union. However, foreign aid programs have shrunk dramatically in relative size to the point where they are hardly significant.

Figure 10.7: Other Major Federal Outlays

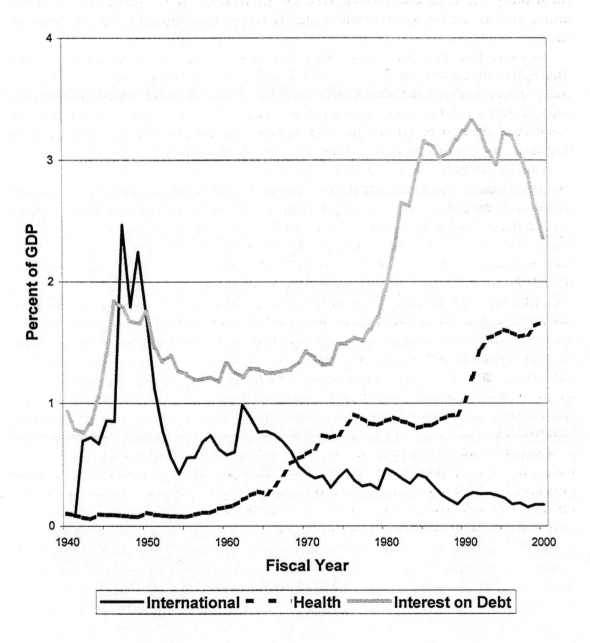

Not surprisingly, health is a major area of growth. This is not Medicare or Medicaid, but rather all the other federally supported programs such as National Institutes of Health. It seems likely that an aging population and exciting opportunities in biotechnology will drive further growth in the health area.

Exercises 10.2

A. Characterize briefly how the role of the federal government has changed in the twentieth century.

B. What are the demographic trends in America that will have a dramatic effect on the finances of the Social Security system in the coming decades?

C. Suggest three options for keeping the Social Security system financially viable, and evaluate the political chances of their being adopted by Congress.

10.3 Long Term Consequences of Budget Deficits

Although the federal budget is in the black at present, demographic trends suggest that spending on entitlements will grow rapidly in the decades ahead. It seems unlikely that we will avoid future deficits, and we all wonder what will be the long-term consequences will be for ourselves and for our country. The U.S. is not unique; several other major industrialized nations have an even larger national debt relative to their GDP. However, history offers little guidance for our situation. Large deficits in the past have usually been due to wars, after which government spending shrank back to normal. This is what we have seen happen after WWII. But the forces driving the growth in transfer payments show no signs of diminishing. Where, then, do we go from here?

Recall from Chapter 2 that we have been financing our large federal deficit in significant part by borrowing from the Rest-of-the-World. If foreigners should become less interested in buying U.S. assets than they have been, then there must either be greater savings by U.S. households and business, or reduced investment in new capital goods. If the latter happens, then the growth of the economy will slow since more and newer tools of production are an important source of increased productivity.

Some observers fear that the growing burden of the national debt may ultimately lead to its monetization, meaning that the government would cover the deficit not by borrowing but by printing more money. This would require either the cooperation of the Fed or its abolishment by Congress as an independent body. The resulting inflation would remove the burden of the debt by eroding the real value of bonds, but at the cost of monetary, economic, and perhaps social chaos.

Economists A. Auerbach, J. Gakhale, and L. Kotlikoff have estimated the percentage of income that would have to be paid in taxes by future generations if government at all levels is to make good on all the promises it has made to those already alive. This "intergenerational accounting" makes use of government projections of population and economic growth. Their findings, reported in the *Budget of the U. S. Government, Analytical Perspective, 1995*, are that future generations would have to surrender 93% of their income in taxes to finance all the programs now in place! It hardly seems likely that our children will be willing to make such a severe sacrifice. Many of us will probably have to settle for much less in benefits than current law now provides, and will also be paying higher taxes than we do now.

Exercises 10.3

A. Suppose that the Fed agreed to buy all newly issued U.S. bonds directly from the Treasury using newly printed money. What do you think would happen 1) the rate of inflation, 2) the rate of interest, 3) the value of the US dollar in terms of Swiss francs, 4) the growth rate of real GDP?

Index

Chapter 11

Keynesian Fiscal Policy and the Multipliers

Outline

Preview

Very few individuals have had the impact that John Maynard Keynes has had on how we view the world around us. Just as Isaac Newton's laws of motion have become common knowledge and hardly anyone doubts Sigmund Freud's basic idea that we have a subconscious, Keynes' framework of macroeconomic analysis pervade our thinking without our knowing it. Most fundamentally, Keynes saw GDP as being determined in the short run by aggregate demand, a concept we have already encountered. Recession or depression was due to demand falling short of the productive capacity of the economy, and the remedy was to stimulate demand. That is the viewpoint of almost all macroeconomic analysis today, and is certainly reflected in this book. We have already discussed the role of the Fed in nudging aggregate demand in the right direction by pushing interest rates up or down. Keynes' emphasis was on the potential for government spending and taxation to influence aggregate demand. By boosting spending, for example, Congress could add to aggregate demand and thus pull the economy out of a recession. This chapter presents the basic model that was developed to explain how that kind of discretionary fiscal policy would work. We will see that the model has an algebraic simplicity that is highly appealing and leads to some surprising implications. One is that changes in government spending or taxation are multiplied in their effect on the economy. The key element in this multiplier effect is how consumers respond to changes in their incomes. While some of Keynes' followers may have been too optimistic in seeing fiscal policy as a panacea, the legacy of Keynes' ideas is very much with us today.

11.1 Lord Keynes and the Great Depression

When the economies of the world were mired in the deep and prolonged recession of the 1930s known as the Great Depression, British economist John Maynard Keynes, later Lord Keynes, declared that governments should increase spending and cut taxes to boost their economies. This was considered heretical since the prevailing view at that time was that a market economy would recover on its own, automatically, without government action. Keynes, in contrast, argued that an economy could languish indefinitely with high unemployment if aggregate demand is inadequate.

Keynes contended that monetary policy was powerless to boost the economy out of a depression because it depended on reducing interest rates, and in a depression interest rates were already close to zero. Increased government spending, on the other hand, would not only boost demand directly but would also set off a chain reaction of increased demand from workers and suppliers whose incomes had been increased by the government's expenditure. Similarly, a tax cut would put more disposable income in the wallets of consumers, and that too would boost demand. Keynes contended, then, that the appropriate fiscal policy during periods of high unemployment was to run a budget deficit. These ideas flew in the face of the conventional wisdom that budget deficits were always bad.

The governments of Britain and the U.S. did not embrace the policies advocated by Keynes and instead continued to try to balance their budgets until the outbreak of World War II. His ideas had an enormous impact, however, on the field of macroeconomics after the war and, to some extent, on actual fiscal policy. Keynesian fiscal policy, the management of government spending and taxation with the objective of maintaining full employment, became the centerpiece of macroeconomics both in academic research and in the public debate over national policy. The Employment Act of 1946 committed the federal government in the U.S. to use fiscal policy "to promote maximum employment, production, and purchasing power." Indeed, a course in macroeconomics until quite recently was typically devoted almost entirely to the ideas of Keynes.

U.S. Experience with Fiscal Policy

At the high tide of belief in Keynesian fiscal policy in the 1960s, some macroeconomists claimed that we had acquired the ability to "fine tune" the economy, keeping it humming along at full employment. The 1970s and 1980s, however, saw a renewal of interest in the role of money in economic fluctuations and a decline in the perception of fiscal policy as an important tool of macroeconomic policy among both economists and the public. Why did this drastic reassessment of fiscal policy occur?

Certainly one factor is simply that Congress has proved to be too slow-moving to take significant action on spending or taxation in the short time frame of recent recessions. The most notable achievement of Keynesian fiscal policy was the tax cut enacted under President Kennedy to combat the recession of 1959-60. Even then, the cut came after the economy was already showing signs of recovery. Since that time, Congress seems to have become more prone to deadlock, so the idea of Congress acting promptly to execute counter-cyclical fiscal policy has become less credible. The Reagan tax cut of 1981 was motivated not by the idea that it would stimulate demand, but by the idea that lower taxes would enhance incentives to work and invest.

Further, the emergence of a chronic deficit of alarming proportions during the last decade, and political pressures to contain it, have made it practically impossible for Congress to conduct discretionary fiscal policy. Note the lack of enthusiasm from a skeptical electorate for Presidential candidate Bob Dole's proposed 15% tax cut, even though Dole claimed that spending cuts would offset the revenue loss. Any proposed act of Congress that had the *intention* of increasing the deficit would surely be met with a firestorm of opposition. Indeed, the recent recession of 1990-91 was notable for the almost complete absence of any inclination in Congress towards fiscal action to combat it. President Clinton's tax increase of 1993 was not an attempt to slow down the economy by taking disposable income away from consumers, but rather it was proposed as a measure to reduce the deficit and, hopefully, free some savings for productive investment.

Another factor in the reduced emphasis on discretionary fiscal policy has been the reexamination of the causes of the Great Depression. Historical research pioneered by Milton Friedman and Anna Schwartz has convinced many economists that the Depression was mainly the result of inept monetary policy in both Britain and the U.S. rather than the inability of monetary policy to influence the economy. Many economists had expected a resumption of the Great Depression when World War II ended, but instead the U.S. economy experienced an era of spectacular growth. To the surprise of almost everyone, the most aggravating problem of the post-war economy has been inflation, while recessions have been relatively brief and mild.

Reappraisal of the Fed's role in the Great Depression and the emergence of inflation as a serious problem in the post war economy have caused attention to become focused on monetary policy. In retrospect, the Great Depression is seen largely as a failure of an inexperienced Federal Reserve, founded only 16 years before the Crash of 1929, to do its job of providing liquidity to the banking system. Instead the Fed stood by while thousands of banks failed. Money is the oil that lubricates the wheels of commerce and when the oil leaks out the machine creaks to a halt.

Further, there has been a general disillusionment since President Kennedy's day in the efficacy of *discretionary* policy of any kind, whether fiscal or monetary. For reasons discussed above, Congress seems unlikely to take discretionary fiscal action. As discussed in Chapter 9, the record of the Fed does not inspire great confidence in its ability to fine-tune the economy either. Instead, many economists now feel that the Fed's attempts to conduct counter-cyclical monetary policy have often aggravated business cycles and inflation rather than controlling them. The emphasis now is on maintaining a stable and predictable monetary environment in which the actors in the economy can make their decisions. Economists recognize that the economy will nevertheless experience business fluctuations and to some extent these are normal and even healthy.

The Legacy of Keynes

What, then, is the legacy of Keynes and his analysis of fiscal policy? The concept of aggregate demand which has proved so useful in understanding the macroeconomy comes out of Keynes' analysis. It is also surely true that if the economy were again to experience a depression, there would be broad agreement that under those circumstances aggressive fiscal stimulus.is warranted.

Another legacy of Keynes is our understanding of how the income tax system provides the economy with an automatic stabilizer. Here is how it works. During a recession, tax revenues shrink, as we saw in Figure

10.1, both because incomes are shrinking and because taxpayers are moving down the progressive tax rate schedule. These two factors effectively provide an automatic tax cut that puts some of those lost income dollars back in the pockets of households, cushioning the fall in their disposable incomes.

It seems clear that households will not cut back as sharply on consumption spending as they would if their tax burden remained unchanged. Indeed, Figures 10.1 and 10.2 show that falling tax revenue is generally sufficient to produce a federal budget deficit during a recession, thereby carrying out Keynes' prescription for fighting recession, but doing so automatically!

Exercises 11.1

A. Contrast the motivations behind the tax changes of the Kennedy, Reagan, and Clinton administrations.

B. What was the concept of "fine-tuning" and seems to be the status of this idea today?

C. Compare the automatic stabilizing effect of a progressive income tax, one that taxes higher incomes at a higher rate than low incomes, with a "flat tax" system that would tax all income at one rate.

11.2 Government Spending and Tax Multipliers

The followers of Keynes believed that fiscal policy can be a powerful lever to move the economy because the effect of an increase in spending or a cut in taxes would be multiplied by stimulating additional demand for consumption goods by households.

Imagine that in the midst of a recession Congress appropriates $100 million for new highway bridge construction. Idle workers and machines will be put to work on bridge construction, resulting in an increase in GDP of $100 million over the period of construction. In addition, construction workers and firm owners will find that their incomes have risen by $100 million. (Recall from Chapter 2 that GDP always represents both spending on one hand and income on the other.) These people will spend at least part of that $100 million on additional consumer goods and services, but they will also save some of the additional income. This sets off a chain reaction in which additional spending boosts the income of sellers of goods and services who, in turn, spend more on other goods and services.

Similarly, if Congress enacted a tax cut, households would find themselves with additional disposable income. Their inclination to spend a portion of that additional income would set off a chain reaction of spending, increased incomes, and more spending.

The key element in this process is that households respond to having additional disposable income by spending at least a part of it on additional consumption. The fraction of an additional dollar of disposable income that is spent on additional consumption is called the marginal propensity to consume. The term "marginal" is used in economics to mean the response to an incremental change, so it is being used in the sense of "at the edge" rather than "unimportant."

The Marginal Propensity to Consume and the Multiplier

Let's build a simple model to see how the marginal propensity to consume determines the impact of a change in government spending on GDP. We begin with a hypothetical $1 increase in government purchases of goods and services in an economy which consists of households having identical marginal propensity to consume which we will abbreviate mpc. To simplify the model, households in our model provide goods or services directly to the government, so we can imagine that the government pays the $1 to one household, say household #1. Now household #1 will spend the fraction equal to its mpc of that additional income to purchase consumption goods, and for simplicity we suppose that the purchase is made directly from household #2. Seeing its disposable income rise by $1 times mpc, household #2 will purchase additional consumer goods worth mpc times that amount, say from household #3. We see that the additional consumption spending at each step of this chain reaction is mpc times the amount at the prior step.

We summarize this process in a table that shows the incremental spending by each household, abbreviated HH, at each step:

The Impact of Government Spending on GDP (in Dollars)

The gov't purchases	1	$ which is income to
HH #1 which spends	mpc • 1	$ which is income to
HH #2 which spends	mpc • mpc • 1	$ which is income to
HH #3 which spends	mpc • mpc • mpc • 1	$ which is income to
HH #4 which spends	$mpc^4 • 1$	$ which is income to
.. and so on ..	.. and so on ..	.. and so on ..
Adding all these up :	$1 + mpc + mpc^2 + etc.$	dollars
which just equals	1/(1-mpc)	dollars in total.

This table depicts a chain reaction of spending which continues on indefinitely as it produces ever smaller increments to GDP. To add up all the increments we used the fact that for any fraction such as mpc:

$$(1 + mpc + mpc^2 + ...) = \frac{1}{(1 - mpc)}$$

The quantity 1/(1-mpc) is called the government spending multiplier.

It is clear from this algebraic result, and from our intuition, that the larger is the mpc the larger will be the impact of additional government spending on GDP. For example, if the mpc is .5 then the impact of each additional dollar of government spending on GDP is,

$$\frac{1}{(1 - mpc)} = \frac{1}{(1 - .5)} = 2$$

while if the mpc is .9 the impact on GDP is,

412

$$\frac{1}{(1 - \text{mpc})} = \frac{1}{(1-.9)} = 10$$

or $10 of GDP for every dollar of increased government spending! Clearly, the marginal propensity to consume is a crucial parameter in this analysis, and we will discuss what is known about the value of the mpc in the next section.

How About a Tax Cut?

Congress can also provide stimulus to the economy during a recession by cutting taxes. A tax cut or rebate of $1 would set off a chain reaction of increased household income and consumption spending as in the table above, but it would not include the initial $1 of government spending. The total impact of a $1 cut in taxes would therefore be equal to (mpc + mpc^2 + mpc^3 + ...) which is the same as the spending multiplier excepts that it lacks the first term "1+".

Keeping in mind that a tax cut is a negative change in taxes, we have the result that the tax cut multiplier equals minus the spending multiplier less one, or [1/(1-mpc)]-1. It is easy to remember that the tax cut multiplier is always exactly one less than the government spending multiplier. The tax cut multiplier may also be written as [mpc/(1-mpc)] which is equivalent. Because the tax cut multiplier is always smaller than the spending multiplier, tax cuts are regarded as less potent in boosting the economy during a recession than are spending increases.

Finally, what will happen if Congress increases spending by $1 billion, but pays for it with a tax *increase*. Since the new tax exactly offsets the effect of the added expenditure on disposable income, there is no multiplier effect. You can verify that if you subtract the tax multiplier from the spending multiplier that the result is exactly 1 regardless of the value of the mpc. This balanced budget multiplier is always equal to one.

Exercises 11.2

A. Consider an economy in which the typical household tends to spend about three quarters of each additional dollar of income it receives: (1) what is the mpc in this economy? (2) what is value of the government spending multiplier? (3) the tax cut multiplier? (4) why do they differ?

B. Suppose that you want to do something to boost the economy out of recession. How could you conduct a personal fiscal policy aimed at this objective? Are both spending and "tax" policies possible? If so, what would the multipliers be?

11.3 How Large Are the Multipliers?

The government spending and tax cut multipliers depend on the marginal propensity to consume, the fraction of each additional dollar of disposable income that households will spend on consumption. If the mpc is large then the multipliers are large, but if the mpc is zero, then government spending will have no multiplier effect on the economy and a tax cut will have no effect at all. The key parameter is the mpc and the key question is: how large is the mpc?

How Large Is the MPC?

Let's start this investigation by looking at the fraction of disposable income that households spend on consumption. In 1996 the total disposable income of U.S. households was about $5,550 billion, out of which they spent about $5,300 billion on consumption and saved about $250 billion. Thus the fraction of income consumed was .96. Does that mean that the mpc is .96? It does only if consumers would spend 96¢ out of an *additional* $1 of income.

What we do know is that consumers spend an *average* of 96¢ out all of their dollars of income. This fraction is called the average propensity to consume, abbreviated apc. While the apc can be measured very easily, it does not help us much in figuring out the value of the mpc. Here is how to see that.

The relationship between the income of a household and its consumption expenditures is called the consumption function. The simplest example of a consumption function is the linear relation,

$$C = a + b \bullet Y$$

where "C" denotes consumption expenditures, "Y" denotes disposable income, and where "a" and "b" are the intercept and slope respectively. Now, how much more will this household spend if its income increases by one dollar? The answer is that a one dollar increase in Y results in an increase in C of $b, so b is clearly the mpc. If you are not convinced, see what the difference is in C if Y is $10,001 instead of $10,000.

We have then,

$$mpc = b$$

The parameter "a" can be interpreted as the level of consumption when income is zero since it is the intercept in the consumption function.

The apc is the fraction of income that is consumed or C/Y which is

$$apc = \frac{C}{Y} = \frac{a + b \cdot Y}{Y} = \frac{a}{Y} + b$$

We see from this expression that the apc depends on both parameters of the consumption function, a and b. We can readily compute the apc, but we cannot solve this *one* equation for the *two* unknown parameters, a and b. Consequently, we cannot deduce the value of the mpc, or b, just from the apc. That's too bad, since apc is something we can easily observe.

For example, the apc of .96 for U.S. households in 1996 when Y was $5,550 billion could equally well have been the result of an mpc of .96 and an "a" of zero, or an mpc, or "b," of zero and a value of $5,300 billion for "a." At one extreme, the implied value of the government spending multiplier is 25 and at the other it is 1! In the language of econometrics, the methodology of making inferences from economic data, the mpc is just not "identified" from knowledge of the apc alone.

The Solution to an Important Puzzle

The solution to this puzzle was discovered in the late 1950s by Milton Friedman and by the team of Franco Modigliani and Richard Brumberg.

Friedman called his solution the permanent income theory of consumption and Modigliani/Brumberg called theirs the life-cycle theory of consumption. While the two theories differ in exposition and detail, the basic idea behind both theories is that consumption expenditures depend mainly on the household's perception of its income over a long time horizon into the future rather than on just its disposable income today. This is because people seek to smooth their consumption over time since a steady level of consumption is preferred to feast followed by famine.

For example, imagine that one friend of yours won $10,000 in the lottery while another friend won $10,000 per year for the next twenty years. The incomes of both have increased by $10,000 this year. Now you are asked to guess how the consumption spending of each will change *this year*. The permanent or life-time income of the first friend has changed little as a result of the lottery since investing the $10,000 would produce an income stream of only a few hundred dollars per year. However, the income of the second is increased by $10,000 per year over a long horizon into the future.

If these lottery winners are typical consumers, they will plan their expenditures with their average future income level in mind. Consequently, we would expect the first to spend only a small part of the lottery prize and save the rest. In contrast, we would expect the second friend to spend a large fraction or nearly all of the $10,000 because that is permanent income. Keep in mind that the purchase of a durable good such as a new refrigerator is mostly savings, the amount consumed only being the amount that the durable depreciates.

The implication of this theory is that the mpc out of a change in income depends on whether it is perceived to be a change in permanent income or whether it is regarded as just transitory income. The mpc for permanent income should be high, actually the same as the apc. However, the mpc for transitory income should be very low, because most people will want to smooth out their consumption over time. Statistical studies based on the response of consumption to income changes over time and across households support these predictions.

With the distinction between permanent and transitory income in mind, let's consider again the likely impact of a government spending increase or a tax cut. Taking a tax cut first, if the tax cut is perceived to be temporary, the resulting increase in disposable income will be seen by households as transitory, so the mpc will be small. One reason that a tax cut might be seen as transitory, is if people anticipate that their taxes will have to be raised in the future to pay for the additional government debt that has been incurred as a result of the tax cut. If they fully anticipate the need to pay those future taxes, the tax cut may have no effect at all on their consumption spending since it leaves permanent income unchanged.

In the case of a spending increase that is not accompanied by higher taxes, households may well see it as a temporary increase in their income. And, again, if they expect that the resulting deficit will have to be made up sometime in the future by higher taxes, they have even more reason to restrain their spending.

To sum up, the mpc out of transitory income changes is small. This suggests that the multipliers for fiscal policy are much smaller than would be the case if the *marginal* propensity to consume were as large as the *average* propensity to consume.

A. If the mpc were equal to the apc for the US, what would be the value of the government spending multiplier? the tax cut multiplier?

B. A family has the consumption function C = $4,000 + 0.5•Y. 1) What is the mpc? 2) the value of consumption at an income of zero? 3) the apc at an income level of $10,000?

C. Suppose that the Anderson household spends .9 of what it perceives to be its permanent income. In 1993 the Andersons anticipated that their household income would average $30,000 per year. However, in 1994 their actual income increased to $40,000 which caused them to revise their estimate of their average income in the future upward by $1,000. What was the Andersons' 1) permanent income in 1993, 2) consumption in 1993, 3) permanent income in 1994, 4) consumption in 1994. Write down the consumption function for the Andersons as of 1994, relating actual consumption to actual income.

11.4 The Keynesian Expenditure Model

From the perspective of Keynes, in an effort to understand the Depression, GDP is reasonably thought of as being determined by aggregate demand. When the unemployment rate is 20%, there is plenty of aggregate supply, so it seems reasonable to assume that firms will supply as much as is demanded. To put it another way, GDP in that situation is determined not by limitations on the supply of goods and services but rather by the limited demand for them.

The components of aggregate demand are consumption, investment, government purchases, and net exports. Let's denote aggregate demand by AD. Thus we have,

$$AD = C + I + G + X$$

where X stands for net exports. In the Keynesian model, aggregate supply, denoted AS, is just equal to the actual value of GDP that we observe. Thus:

$$AS = GDP$$

Setting aggregate supply equal to aggregate demand, we have,

$$GDP = C + I + G + X$$

This equation should look familiar; it is the accounting identity for GDP that we studied in Chapter 2. But in the context of the Keynesian model, it is also a statement about *how GDP is determined*. It says that GDP is determined by the sum of demand from the four sectors of the economy. Economists sometimes characterize the Keynesian model by saying that in it GDP is "demand determined."

The consumption function that we discussed in the previous section says that the consumption component of aggregate demand can, in turn, be expressed as a function of disposable income which we called Y. Let's write disposable income as,

$$Y = GDP - T$$

where we can think of T as taxes net of transfer payments. In the simplest version of the Keynesian model presented here, we treat T as a lump sum amount, not as a function of GDP. A more sophisticated model would allow T to be a function of GDP, so that we could study the effect of a change in the tax rate.

The consumption function is then,

$$C = a + b \cdot Y = a + b \cdot (GDP - T)$$

Substituting for C in the expression for GDP we get

$$GDP = a + b \cdot (GDP - T) + I + G + X$$

which we can solve for GDP. The result is,

$$GDP = \frac{1}{(1-b)} \cdot [a + I + G + X] - \frac{b}{(1-b)} \cdot T$$

This equation tells us how the level of GDP will change in response to a change in any of the autonomous components of spending, those that do not depend on GDP, at least according to the assumptions of this model. We can see that a one dollar change in either a, I, G, or X will result in a change of 1/(1-b) dollars in GDP. Of course, this is just the spending multiplier again, but we see that it applies not just to government spending but also to any increase in spending by any sector. The tax cut multiplier is still b/(1-b), keeping in mind that a tax cut is a negative increase in T.

How Does it Work? An Example.

The Keynesian expenditure model is illustrated by a hypothetical example in Figure 11.1. It is assumed that consumption function is given by,

$$C = 2 + 0.5 \bullet Y$$

so consumption demand is $2 trillion (the "a" parameter) plus 0.5 (the mpc or "b" parameter) times disposable income. In words, the household sector will consume half of its income plus $2 trillion. To calculate Y from GDP we need to know T.

Let's assume that the government sector collects taxes of $1 trillion and that taxes do not depend on the level of GDP. Consumption demand is given then by

$$C = 2 + 0.5 \bullet (GDP-1)$$
$$= 1.5 + 0.5 \bullet GDP$$

This is gray line in Figure 11.1. Notice that if GDP were zero, households would still want to consume $1.5 trillion. At a level of GDP of $3 trillion, households would consume all of GDP, and at levels of GDP above $3 trillion consumption demand is less than GDP.

To obtain aggregate demand, we now add $1 trillion in investment demand by firms for capital goods, $1.1 trillion in demand for goods and services by the government sector, and a net $-.1 trillion in demand from the ROW. The latter reflects a trade deficit of $100 billion. Adding these to consumption demand we get the thick black line in Figure 11.1. Now we assume that aggregate supply is just the amount of GDP, so it is the thin line that goes through the origin and has a slope of one. Aggregate demand and supply intersect at a GDP of $7 trillion, and that is the same value one obtains by plugging our assumed values for the variables into the equation above for GDP.

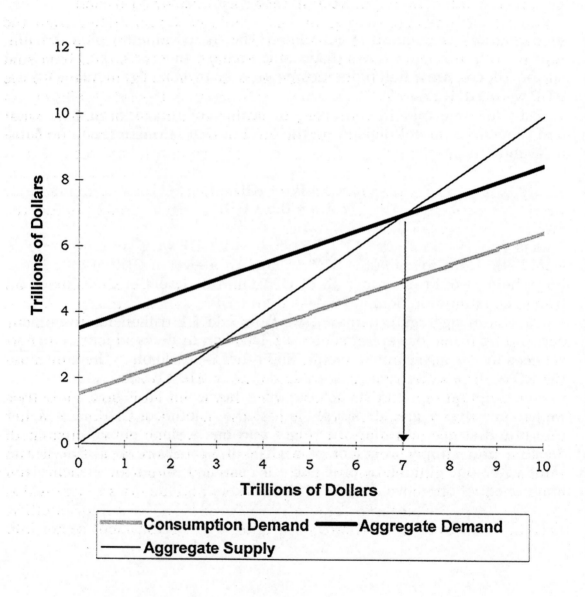

Figure 11.1: The Keynesian Expenditure Model

What Happens If Government Spending Jumps $0.5 Trillion?

We know that the multiplier in this model is 2, since that is 1/(1-0.5). That implies that GDP will rise by $1 trillion. This can also be seen graphically in Figure 11.2 where the aggregate demand line is shifted up by $0.5 trillion. The new aggregate demand line intersects the aggregate supply line at $8 trillion, indicating that GDP rises by $1 trillion.

Note that the same change in GDP would occur no matter what the source of the jump in aggregate demand; it could come from investment, net exports, or even consumption if the parameter "a" shifts. It is said that the economy boomed in 1955 because the public fell in love with the wrap-around windshield that was introduced that year! Similarly, an investment boom based on a new invention or just on optimism, what Keynes called the "animal spirits" of entrepreneurs, would have the same multiplier effect on GDP as does a boost in demand from government. A surge in the demand for our exports, due perhaps to a boom in Europe, would also have the same multiplier effect on our economy. Demand for computer and telecommunications related products is helping to fuel the strong growth of the late 1990s.

Are There Limits?

Taken literally, this model seems to imply that we can achieve an unlimited level of income simply by legislating more government spending! That seems just too good to be true, but what is the catch? The catch, of course, is the assumption that the economy will produce as much as is demanded, that supply is "infinitely elastic." Keep in mind that Keynes was analyzing a depression, not normal times.

We discussed in Chapter 8 what happens when individual industries and the economy approach full capacity: higher output requires higher prices and wages and output above a certain level cannot be sustained. More purchases by government would result in a crowding out of private purchases in an economy that is already producing near full employment. There are just so many workers and factories to be divided among alternative uses, and more of one use requires less of another. Recall that in Chapter 2 when we introduced the government sector into an economy operating at full employment, it meant that less was produced for consumption and less for capital investment.

The problem faced by most of the industrialized world today is not a lack of aggregate demand but rather it is on the aggregate supply side of the economy: rapidly aging populations and radical changes in the kinds of skills that are needed in an environment of new technologies of production and information. The countries of the former Soviet Union are faced with an unprecedented transformation of their economies from highly wasteful production of mainly military goods for their formerly communist government to the competitive production of goods that someone will actually want to buy. These are very different challenges from those facing the industrialized economies of the 1930s.

Exercises 11.4

A. Referring to the hypothetical example portrayed in Figure 11.1, what is the value mpc? the apc when GDP is $7 trillion? the government deficit?

B. Suppose that instead of an increase in G of $0.5 trillion there was a tax cut of that amount in the hypothetical economy portrayed in Figure 11.1. What is the value of the tax cut multiplier in this model? How would the consumption function and aggregate demand lines in Figure 11.1 shift in response to the tax cut? Show algebraically and using the figure, how GDP would be affected by the tax cut. Why is the impact of a tax cut different than the effect of a spending increase of the same amount?

C. At a time when the unemployment rate is 4.2% Congress enacts a $100 billion program of increased spending on road construction without a corresponding tax increase. You are asked to comment on the effect of this program on real GDP. How much of an increase in real GDP would you expect? What effect would you expect the program to have on the breakdown in the division of real GDP between consumption, investment, government purchases, and net exports?

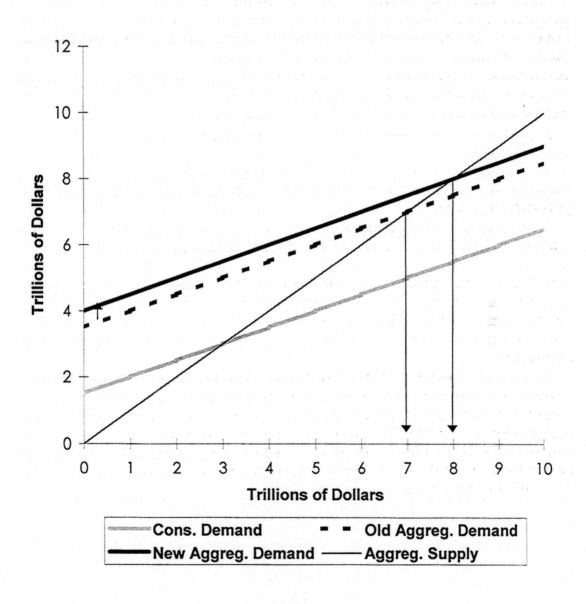

Figure 11.2: The Effect of an Increase in Government Purchases

Index

Chapter 12

The International Economy

Outline

Preview

Imagine that you could stand at the border between the U.S. and Canada and observe the transactions that take place across it. Natural gas flows southward through pipelines to utilities in the U.S. Personal computers made in California are trucked northward to be sold in Canadian stores. Tourists from each country head for destinations in the other. Some transactions take place over the telephone, without the movement of any physical goods. For example, a mutual fund in Chicago buys 1,000 shares of a mining company traded on the Toronto Stock Exchange, or a Canadian real estate developer gives the go-ahead to construct a new shopping mall in Atlanta.

In each of these transactions, a payment is made to a party in the other country and that payment must be converted to the currency of the other country. The Canadian supplier of natural gas pays wages, taxes, and dividends in Canadian dollars. When it receives payment from a customer in the U.S., it takes those U.S. dollars to its bank and exchanges them for Canadian dollars so that it can pay its bills.

In this chapter we will learn how the rate of exchange is determined and what might cause it to change. We will also find out what is meant by the balance of payments between countries. The U.S. has a very large trade deficit, and we will discuss why that is the case and whether it is cause for concern. Finally, we will explore what motivates countries to trade with one another in the first place.

12.1 Exchange Rates

The cost of one currency in terms of another is called the exchange rate. What makes an exchange rate different from most prices is that it is "two-sided."

The U.S./Canada exchange rate is expressed both in Canadian dollars per U.S. dollar, and as U.S. dollars per Canadian dollar. If you went to your bank in the U.S. to buy Canadian dollars for a trip in October 1999, it was offering to sell you Canadian dollars for about US$0.68 each. If, instead, you waited to exchange dollars until you arrived in Canada, you would have found that the bank there was offering to buy your U.S.

dollars for about C$1.47. These two prices, US$0.68 and C$1.47 are equivalent prices since the first states that

$$C\$1 = US\$0.68.$$

Dividing both sides of this equations by .68 we solve for the price of a US$:

$$US\$ = C\$1/.68 = C\$1.47$$

The exchange rate is expressed interchangeably as the price of a Canadian dollar in U.S. dollars, or the price of a U.S. dollar in Canadian dollar. Notice that the one is just the reciprocal (recall that 1/x is the reciprocal of x) of the other.

Determined by Supply and Demand

The exchange rate is like any other price in that it is determined by the forces of supply and demand. What is novel and sometimes confusing in the case of the foreign exchange market is that instead of the price of a good like compact disks being quoted in dollars, we have the prices of two kinds of dollars being quoted in terms of each other. It is equally correct to think of the U.S dollar as the good being traded with its price quoted in Canadian dollars, or the Canadian dollar as the good being traded with its price quoted in U.S. dollars. It is important, though, to remember which side of the market you are looking at or it is easy to become very confused as any experienced traveler abroad can attest.

Because of the two-sided nature of the foreign exchange market, a shift in the demand for one currency is equivalent to a shift in the supply of the other. For example, if we think of the Canadian dollar as the good traded, then a U.S. utility buying Canadian dollars to pay for more Canadian gas this winter is increasing the *demand* for Canadian dollars in the foreign exchange market. That will tend to push up the price of Canadian dollars in terms of U.S. dollars. We could equally well have thought of this as a situation in which the U.S. dollar is the goods being traded, so the U.S. utility is increasing the *supply* of U.S. dollars in the foreign exchange market. That pushes down the value of the U.S. dollar in terms of Canadian dollars, but the effect on the exchange rate is the same whichever way we think of it.

Similarly, the Canadian retailer increasing its purchasing of U.S. personal computers for sale in Canada will need to sell Canadian dollars for US dollars in order to pay the manufacturer in California. That transaction increases the supply of Canadian dollars in the foreign exchange market and therefore tends to push down the price of Canadian dollars in terms of U.S. dollars. But we could have thought of that transaction as one that increases the demand for U.S. dollars, thereby pushing up the value of the U.S. dollar in terms of the Canadian dollar. Again, we reach the same conclusion about the transaction affects the relative values of the two currencies. It is changes such as these in the demand and supply of the two currencies that causes the exchange rate to change.

Exercises 12.1

A. If the exchange rate between the U.S. and Japan is quoted in the newspaper at 125 Japanese yen to the US dollar, how many dollars will one yen buy? What is the price, then, of a yen in dollars?

B. Locate the Foreign Exchange table on the business page of your newspaper. What is the quote for British pounds? What is the value of a U.S. dollar in terms of British pounds?

C. Suppose that there is an unusually mild winter that reduces the demand for natural gas in the U.S. How does this affect supply and demand in the foreign exchange market? What will be the effect of the mild winter on the price of U.S. dollars in Canadian dollars? on the price of Canadian dollars in U.S. dollars?

12.2 The Balance of Payments

A remarkable fact about the international transactions between residents of any country and the Rest-Of-the-World (ROW) is that the total of all payments made to the ROW will equal, or balance, the total of all payments received from the ROW! Let's see why this must be so.

Consider the simplified case of a world consisting of two countries, say the US and Canada. We will imagine that all foreign exchange transactions between U.S. and Canada are handled by one firm, so that we can see the quantities of currencies traded. Further, imagine that this dealer is on the US side of the boarder. It holds an inventory of Canadian dollars, standing ready to buy more C$ or sell C$ from its inventory. The exchange rate is posted by the dealer for all to see, and it is free to change that posted rate as it sees fit. Canadians making payments to the US come to the dealer and sell their dollars for US dollars. These transactions cause the dealer's inventory of Canadian dollars to increase.

Meanwhile, Americans making payments to Canadians go to the same dealer to buy Canadian dollars, causing the dealer's inventory of Canadian dollars to shrink. The dealer wishes to hold only enough Canadian dollars in inventory to accommodate its customers, since they serve no other purpose for the dealer. The dealer's inventory of Canadian dollars will remain stable as long as it is buying about the same quantity of them as it is selling. The dealer makes a profit by charging a small commission on each transaction.

How Do the Payments Get Balanced?

Now suppose that a warm winter causes the demand for Canadian gas, and therefore for Canadian dollars, to plummet. The dealer suddenly finds that its inventory of Canadian dollars is growing rapidly. What should the dealer do? The appropriate response is to reduce the quoted price for Canadian dollars to encourage their purchase and discourage their sale. This makes it less expensive for Americans to buy goods and services in Canada and more expensive for Canadians to buy in the U.S. The dealer will continue to reduce the price of Canadian dollars until its inventory of Canadian dollars is again stable, the sale of Canadian dollars again balanced by purchases. At this new equilibrium in the foreign exchange market, the sales of Canadian dollars is just balanced by purchases.

We can see from this simple example that the total of all payments to the U.S. from Canada is equal to, or balances, the total of all the payments from Canada to the U.S. The balance is maintained because an imbalance means that the dealer's inventory of foreign exchange either increases or decreases and the exchange rate is then adjusted until the balance is restored.

In the real world there are transactions among many countries through many dealers, but still the total payments received from each country by the ROW balances the total of payments made by each country to the ROW. The basic mechanism is the same as in our simple example: the currency of each country is useful to foreigners only to make payments in that country. Non-Canadians have no desire to accumulate Canadian dollars beyond the inventory held by foreign exchange dealers. Each Canadian dollar that goes abroad finds its way back home. The only way this can happen is if payments to Canada by non-Canadians balances payments made by Canadians to non-Canadians.

What Kinds of International Payments Are There?

The balance of payments for the U.S. is broken down into its various components in the table on the facing page.

The payments which the U.S. receives from the ROW are listed in the first column. These include receipts for merchandise exported, interest and dividends from US-owned assets abroad, payment for services sold to the ROW, and transfers from the ROW. Interest and dividends can be thought of as payment for the exports of services of factors of production. Services in international trade are often called "invisibles" because they are not seen crossing the border. These include insurance and other financial services; and tourism. Transfers are gifts from the foreigners to Americans. Together, these receipts make up the current account.

432

The U.S. Balance of Payments

Receipts from ROW	Payments to ROW	Balance
Current Account		
Merchandise Exports	− Merchandise Imports	= Merchandise Trade Balance
Income on US Assets Abroad	Income on Foreign Investment	
Services Exports	Services Imports	
Transfers	Transfers	
Exports of Goods and Services	− Imports of Goods and Services	= Balance on Current Account
Capital Account		
Change in Foreign Assets in US	Change in US Assets Abroad	
Change in Foreign Official Assets	Change in US Official Assets	
Exports of Capital	− Imports of Capital	= Balance on Capital Account
Total Receipts from the ROW	− Total Payments to the ROW	= Balance of Payments (= zero)

The capital account includes private purchases by foreigners of U.S. assets, such as the purchase of 10,000 shares of Blue Skies Airlines by a pension fund in Paris. It also includes purchases of U.S. assets by foreign governments, such as the sale of $1 billion of U.S. Treasury bills to the German central bank (the Bundesbank). Receipts on capital account can be thought of as payments received for the export of capital assets.

The total of current account receipts is called "exports of goods and services" and the total of capital account receipts is called "exports of capital." Together, they make up the total of all U.S. receipts from the ROW.

Similarly, the second column lists all payments made by the U.S. to the ROW in the same categories. The sum of "imports of goods and services" plus "imports of capital" is the total of payments received by the US from the ROW.

The third column shows the balance between receipts and payments. The difference between merchandise exports and merchandise imports is called the merchandise trade balance The merchandise trade balance has been negative for the U.S. during the past decade and is one of those discouraging sounding statistics often reported in the press.

The difference between exports and imports of goods and services is called the balance on current account which has also been negative. The difference between exports of capital and imports of capital is the balance on capital account.

Finally the balance of payments is, equivalently, the sum of the balances on current and capital account or the difference between total receipts and total payments. In either case it is equal to zero!

Rest-of-World Savings, the Flip Side of the Trade Deficit

In Chapter 2 we saw how the trade deficit of the U.S. has helped to finance the federal budget deficit that emerged during the past decade since it is a source of savings for the U.S. economy. The balance of payments gives us another perspective on this important relationship.

The balance of payments table tells us that

Balance on Current Account + Balance on Capital Account
= Balance of Payments.

But since the balance of payments must equal zero, we have,

The Balance on Current Account = - The Balance on Capital Account

Note that this says the balance on current account is the *negative* of the balance on capital account. Now, each of these is, in turn, the difference between exports and imports, so we have,

{Exports of G&S - Imports of G&S}=- {Exports of Capital- Imports of Capital}

which we can rearrange as,

Net Exports of Goods and Services = - Net Exports of Capital

Finally, since the trade deficit is the negative of Net Exports of Goods and Services, we have

Trade Deficit = Net Export of Capital.

which says that a deficit in the net export of goods and services must be accompanied by a surplus in the net export of capital assets. It is guaranteed since total international payments must balance. The U.S. has been exchanging U.S. Treasury bonds, ownership of film studios in Hollywood, and other capital assets for foreign-made cars and imported crude oil. It is the trade deficit that gives the Rest-of-the-World the U.S. dollars to purchase those capital assets, and the ROW sector has been a major source of savings as we saw in Chapter 2.

Exercises 12.2

A. Suppose that investors around the world decide in 2002 that Russia's economy is one that offers many attractive investment opportunities. What effect would you expect this development to have on Russia's exchange rate? balance of trade? balance on current account? balance on capital account? balance of payments?

12.3 Why Do Exchange Rates Fluctuate?

Exchange rates are a staple of the news media these days: "the dollar rose against major currencies in heavy trading," "the Euro hit a new low today," "the British pound rebounded in New York," and "the dollar falls below 100 yen," are typical evening news items. Why do exchange rates fluctuate? Does a country gain an advantage by having a "strong" currency as opposed to a "weak" one? Can governments control exchange rates? Should they control them? Can we anticipate how monetary and fiscal policies will affect foreign exchange rates? These are increasingly important questions as our economy becomes more international and Americans often find themselves involved in international transactions.

The currency of Germany is the Deutsche Mark, abbreviated DM. It is a very "strong" currency, meaning that its value has risen relative to other major currencies, including the U.S. dollar. Let's see if we can understand some of the factors underlying the changing relationship between the DM and the U.S. dollar, the two most important currencies in the world today.

The exchange rate between DM and US$ over the last three decades is plotted in Figure 12.1. It is expressed as the value of the US$ in terms of DM, or, in other words, the number of DM that one US$ could buy. Three features of the chart are worth noting. First, there was almost no fluctuation in the exchange rate until 1969, when the dollar dropped sharply. Second, by the early 1990s, the U.S. dollar was worth less than half as many DM as it was in the 1960s. Third, the continuing decline of the dollar was interrupted by a surge in its value in the mid-1980s.

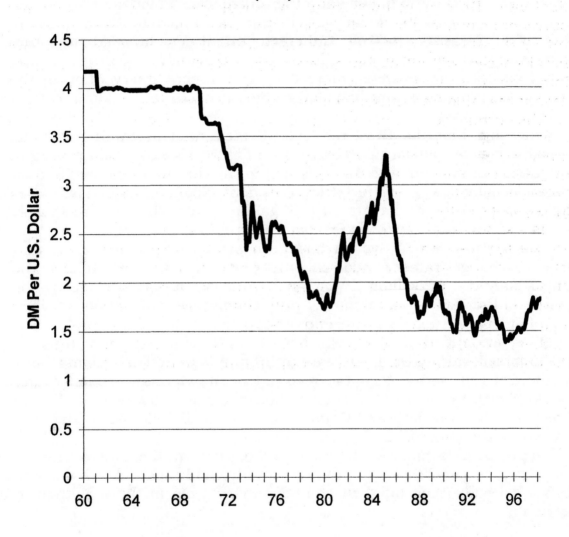

Figure 12.1: The Exchange Rate Between German Marks (DM) and U.S. Dollars

Bretton Woods

The exchange rate did not fluctuate before 1969 because it was fixed under a system agreed upon in 1944 by the major industrial nations at a meeting in Bretton Woods, New Hampshire. The Bretton Woods System made the U.S. dollar the benchmark currency and it established rates of exchange between the dollar and other currencies which were to remain fixed. The value of the dollar was, in turn, anchored by the promise of the U.S. Treasury to sell unlimited quantities of gold to other governments (but not to individuals) upon demand, at $35 per ounce. Fixed exchange rates were enforced by government intervention in the foreign exchange markets whenever the rates started to deviate from agreed upon levels.

One sign that the Bretton Woods System was in trouble was the "revaluation" of the DM in 1969, seen in Figure 12.1 as a sharp drop in the US$. The problem was that inflation in the U.S. had rendered $35 an unrealistically low price for gold. President Nixon ordered gold sales halted in 1971 to avoid a run on U.S. gold reserves. The US$ fell sharply again and the Bretton Woods System was in ruins.

The Bretton Woods System had been established in the belief that fixed exchange rates would encourage world trade by taking the uncertainly out of dealing in foreign currencies. It was undone by the failure of the U.S. to maintain the purchasing power of the dollar when its inflation rate sped up at the end of the 1960s.

It is evident that the US$ had been overvalued, and the DM undervalued, during the later years of Bretton Woods. The growing value of the DM reflected in part the recovery of the German economy after World War II. But why did the dollar then continue to fall against the DM over the next two decades? Could relatively rapid inflation in the U.S. have been the major factor?

Figure 12.2 compares the rate of inflation in the two countries, measured by the CPI of each. Neither country had much inflation before 1966, but since then inflation has been more rapid in the U.S. than in Germany.

Figure 12.2: Inflation Rates In Germany and the U.S.

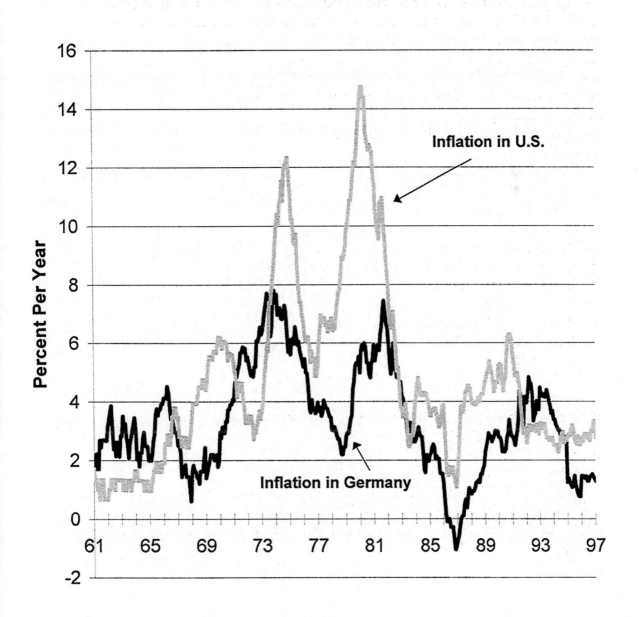

Since inflation diminishes the purchasing power of a currency, it is intuitive that more rapid inflation in the U.S. would diminish the purchasing power of the US$ in terms of DM. Now we will find out if that is the whole explanation, or just a partial explanation for the strength of the DM.

The Law of One Price and Purchasing Power Parity

The law of one price states that a good should sell for the same price everywhere, allowing for transportation costs. For example, a hamburger should sell for about the same price in Chicago as in Hamburg, Germany. If hamburgers sell for less in Chicago than in Hamburg, entrepreneurs will ship frozen beef, catsup, and wheat flour from Chicago to Hamburg and reap the price difference as a profit. This will cause the price of a hamburger in Hamburg to fall and the price in Chicago to rise until finally a hamburger sells for the same price in both cities.

Exploiting a difference in price for the same good in different locations is called arbitrage. When price differences occur, arbitrage will tend to eliminate them, enforcing the law of one price. If a hamburger sells for $1.50 in Chicago, it should sell for the DM equivalent in Hamburg, which is $1.50 times the exchange rate expressed as DM per US$, which we will denote by "DM/$." Thus, at an exchange rate of two DM per dollar, a Hamburger (a resident of Hamburg) should be paying about DM3.00 for a hamburger.

In practice, transportation costs, differences in taxes, and the fact that some goods cannot be transported means that the law of one price does not hold exactly. For example, the land that the hamburger store occupies may be much more expensive to rent in Hamburg than in Chicago, so the difference in land rental cost will be reflected in a higher price for hamburgers in Hamburg.

Similarly, the difference between the cost of an apartment in Tokyo and in St. Louis is not readily arbitraged since we cannot ship land from Missouri, where it is plentiful, to Tokyo, where it is very scarce. However, world travelers can attest that the law of one price holds remarkably well for hamburgers.

If the law of one price held exactly for all goods, then the cost of a given consumer's market basket should be the same in the U.S. as it is in Germany. Thus, if we took the cost of the basket of goods priced in the U.S. and converted that dollar cost to the equivalent number of DM at the exchange rate, the result should be the same as the actual cost of the same market basket purchased in Germany. If that were true, then we would have the equality:

Cost of Basket in U.S. • *Exchange rate in DM/$*

=

Cost of Basket in Germany

Suppose that the weekly supermarket purchases of a family in Chicago are $250 at a time when the exchange rate is 4 DM/$. Under the law of one price, the cost of the same goods in Germany would be

$$\$250 \bullet 4 \text{ DM/\$} = \text{DM1,000.}$$

Now, suppose that the U.S. experiences a doubling of the price level over the next decade so the same weekly purchases then cost $500 in the U.S. while in Germany the cost is still DM1,000. What must happen to the exchange rate to keep the costs of the two market baskets equal? Clearly, the dollar will have to fall to 2 DM per US$, and then we will have the equality,

$$\$500 \bullet 2 \text{ DM/\$} = \text{DM 1,000.}$$

If the exchange rate adjusts to equate the costs of equivalent market baskets across countries, then there is said to be purchasing power parity, often abbreviated PPP. If PPP held *exactly*, then differences in inflation rates would account for *all* of the movement in exchange rates.

The Real Exchange Rate

To what extent do the differing inflation rates in the U.S. and Germany actually account for the decline and fluctuation of the DM/$ exchange rate that we saw in Figure 12.1? We answer this question by adjusting the DM/$ exchange rate for the differing rates of inflation in the U.S. and Germany and see how much variation is left. The inflation-adjusted exchange rate is called the real exchange rate and we can think of the unadjusted exchange rate as the nominal exchange rate. We use the CPIs of the two countries, denoted CPI^{US} and CPI^G, in the formula,

$$\textit{Real DM/\$ Exchange Rate}$$
$$=$$
$$\textit{Nominal DM/\$ Exchange Rate} \cdot (CPI^{US}/CPI^G).$$

Suppose again that the cost of living in the U.S. doubles but that in Germany stays the same. As we saw above, PPP implies that the *doubling of the CPI^{US}* should be accompanied by a *halving of the DM/$* exchange rate. If that happens, the *real* DM/$ exchange rate will be unchanged as we see here:

$$\textbf{\textit{New}} \textit{ Real DM/\$} = \textbf{\textit{New}} \textit{ DM/\$} \cdot \textbf{\textit{(New}} \textit{ CPI}^{US}/CPI^G$$

$$= ((\textbf{\textit{1/2}}) \cdot \textbf{\textit{Old}} \textit{ DM/\$}) \cdot (\textbf{\textit{2}} \cdot \textbf{\textit{Old}} \textit{ CPI}^{US}/CPI^G)$$

$$= (\textbf{\textit{Old}} \textit{ DM/\$}) \cdot (\textbf{\textit{Old}} \textit{ CPI}^{US}/CPI^G)$$

$$= \textbf{\textit{Old}} \textit{ Real DM/\$}$$

This example illustrates the following general result: if PPP holds exactly, then the real exchange rate remains constant through time. Any variation in the real exchange rate reflects a departure from PPP and therefore reflects the influence on the exchange rate of factors other than differing inflation rates.

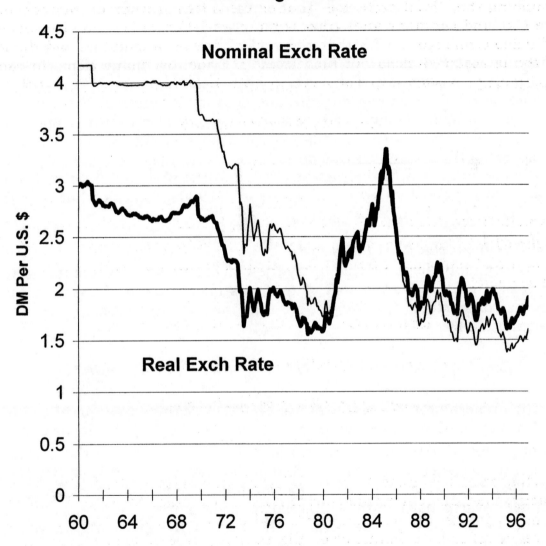

Figure 12.3: Nominal and Real DM/$ Exchange Rates

Figure 12.3 plots the real and nominal DM/$ exchange rates. The two CPIs share the same base period, 1982-84, in which they are both equal to 100 by definition. Like the CPI, the real exchange rate is a relative rather than absolute measure that is anchored to its nominal counterpart in the base period. That explains why the real exchange rate and nominal exchange rates come together in 1983.

We see in Figure 12.3 that the real exchange rate is not constant, implying that PPP does not hold *exactly*. Evidently, many items in the CPI market basket are more like apartments than hamburgers; they cannot be readily transported from one country to another. But we also see that the real exchange rate has moved much less than the nominal rate, implying that differing inflation rates do account for much of the weakness of the dollar over this period.

We are still left with the puzzling surge in the real value of the dollar relative to the DM that occurred in the mid 1980s. That is what we will try to explain in the next section.

Insights from the Real DM/$ Rate

To help us understand and apply the real exchange rate, it is useful to think of it as the relative cost of the consumer's market basket in the U.S. as compared to Germany. Note that the real exchange rate can be rearranged as,

$$Real\ DM/\$ = DM/\$ \cdot (CPI^{US}/CPI^{G}) = [CPI^{US}] / [CPI^{G}/(DM/\$)]$$

The numerator in the last expression, CPI^{US}, can be thought of as the cost of the market basket when purchased in the U.S. in dollars. The denominator, $CPI^{G}/(DM/\$)$, can be thought of as the cost of the market basket in Germany in terms of U.S. dollars that have been converted to DM. Therefore, when the real DM/$ rate falls, it means that goods have become less expensive in the U.S. relative to Germany.

Now we see why the low level of the *real* DM/$ rate in recent years has lead many economists to believe that the U.S. is more competitive with Germany in world markets. Potential customers in Brazil or Singapore will find that goods are cheaper to buy in the U.S. than in

Germany, and indeed U.S.-made cars have made rapid inroads in both U.S. and foreign markets at the expense of German car-makers. Recognizing this shift in costs, BMW built a plant in South Carolina and Mercedes Benz is producing its new SUV in Alabama. In fact, the parent company of Mercedes, Daimler Benz bought the Chrysler Corp. in 1999.

With another simple rearrangement of the formula for the real exchange rate, we can show that the real DM/$ rate is also equivalent to the *relative* purchasing power of the US$ in Germany compared to its purchasing power in the U.S. We can write:

$$Real\ DM/\$ = DM/\$ \cdot (CPI^{US}/CPI^{G}) = [(DM/\$)/CPI^{G}] / [1/CPI^{US}]$$
$$=$$
Purchasing power of US$ in Germany/Purchasing power of US$ in U.S.

To see why this makes sense, recall from Chapter 4 that $1/CPI^{US}$ is the purchasing power of the dollar in the U.S, and the higher the CPI, the less will one dollar buy. Now let's convert that dollar into DMs at the exchange rate and see what the purchasing power of that dollar is in Germany. That will be $(DM/\$)/CPI^{G}$. The ratio of the latter to the former gives us the relative purchasing power of the U.S. dollar in Germany as opposed to its purchasing power in the U.S.

Thus, the decline in the real DM/$ exchange rate that we have seen since 1985 means that the U.S. dollar has lost purchasing power in Germany even more rapidly than it has in the U.S. This is consistent with the observation that German cars and other consumer goods have become much less competitive in the U.S. market since 1985, with the sales of some formerly strong sellers, such as Porsche cars, falling to a fraction of their 1980s level.

Exercises 12.3

A. An American family that had visited Germany in 1984 returned in 1988. They were surprised at how the cost of a vacation in Germany relative to the U.S. had changed in those eight years. Were they pleasantly or unpleasantly surprised? How does the change in the real exchange rate over that period give you a basis for answering the question?

B. In what direction have real exchange rates for the U.S. dollar moved against major currencies? How do you think that is likely to show up in patterns of tourism internationally? Does your observation of the nationality of tourists here and abroad support that prediction?

12.4 Why Do Real Exchange Rates Fluctuate?

The value of the U.S. dollar rose sharply in the period 1981-1985 against all major currencies, the DM/$ rate doubling in real as well as nominal terms. What could explain such dramatic changes?

Let's think about why foreigners buy U.S. dollars. They buy U.S. dollars in order to buy U.S. goods and also in order to buy U.S. assets. It seems clear that dollars were not in demand by foreigners buying U.S. goods in the mid 1980's since that was a time of rapidly widening US trade deficits. Looking back at Figure 5.10 we see that U.S. exports were stagnating while imports were soaring during that period.

Could dollars have been in demand by foreigners wanting to buy U.S. assets? Recall that the real rate of interest on U.S. Treasury bills, plotted in Figure 4.5, jumped in 1981 and remained very high. In Chapter 4 we attributed that increase in real interest rates to the burgeoning federal budget deficit. The U.S. Treasury was obliged to pay higher real interest rates on its bonds and bills to induce people to buy more of them. Foreigners were attracted by these higher real interest rates too, and purchased large quantities of U.S. dollars to buy U.S. Treasury securities.

As this increased demand for U.S. dollars pushed up the real exchange rate, U.S. goods became relatively expensive on world markets. Foreign goods, on the other hand, were relatively cheap for Americans to buy with their more valuable dollars. The effect of the high real exchange rate in the mid 1980s was therefore a decline in U.S. exports and a rise in imports to the US. This is how the trade deficit was caused by the federal budget deficit, and it is the real exchange rate that links those twin deficits together.

Let's check if we can see the relationship between the real interest rate and the real exchange rate in the data. Since investors are constantly *comparing* real rates of interest across countries, it is the *difference* between real rates in the U.S. and Germany that is important. Figure 12.4 plots the real DM/$ exchange rate along with the difference between ex ante real short term interest rates in the two countries.

Notice that during the Bretton Woods System of fixed exchange rates, there is little relation between the two variables, but that a closer relationship emerges in the 1970s, as governments abandoned their attempts to fix exchange rates. An unusually large spread between U.S. and German real interest rates did emerge in the early 1980s and that coincided with the sharp rise in the dollar. As the spread between real interest rates then declined, the U.S. dollar declined too.

The early 1990s were a period when real interest rates were relatively high in Germany. That reflected efforts by the Bundesbank, the German central bank, to stop inflation that developed after reunification caused a temporary increase in Germany's money supply. Notice that the resulting negative differential between U.S. and German real interest rates is associated with a further decline in the U.S. dollar against the DM as we would expect.

The recent behavior of the DM/$ is not fully explained by real short term interest rates. The dollar was weak in 1993-94 in spite of a shift in the real interest rate spread in its favor. The dollar strengthened in 1996, but has not been as buoyant as we would expect on the basis of the real interest rate differential alone.

Figure 12.4: The Real DM/$ Exchange Rate and U.S. & Germany Real Interest Rate Spread

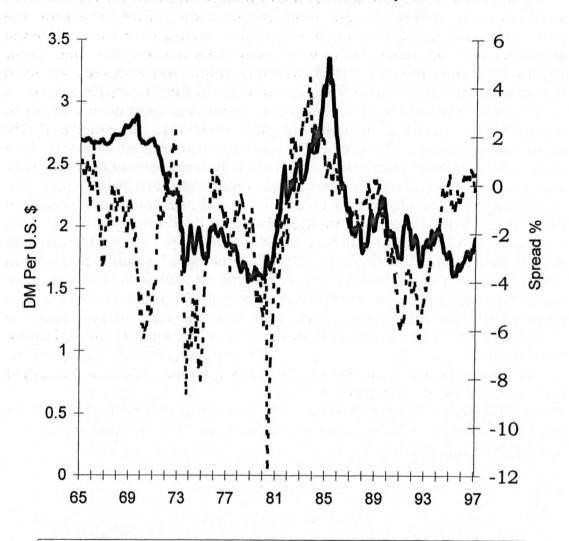

Should Countries "Defend" Their Currency?

The fact that real interest rates affect exchange rates means that monetary and fiscal policies are important factors in the foreign exchange markets. Sometimes policies are adopted with the specific intent of influencing the exchange rate.

In the early 1990s exchange rates among European currencies were fixed in preparation for adoption of a single currency within the European Community. When the German Bundesbank raised interest rates sharply in 1992, putting upward pressure on the DM, other European countries were obliged to followed suit to maintain their fixed exchange rate with the DM. At one point, the Bank of Sweden raised its overnight rate to 500% to "defend" the Krona! Britain and Italy chose to devalue their currencies rather than push interest rates higher and risk serious damage to their economies. Indeed, Sweden became mired in a protracted recession. The move towards a common European currency did not get back on track until 1999 when the Euro was launched.

This episode illustrates the principle that it is impossible to have simultaneously 1) free international movement of capital, 2) fixed exchange rates, and 3) independent monetary policy. The European countries had 1) and 2) until the Bundesbank's actions made them acutely aware that they had lost the third. Given the choice, they abandoned 2) to regain 3). The U.S. today has 1) and 3), but at the cost of having to let the market determine the exchange rate. Under the Bretton Woods System, many countries found that they had to impose controls on the movement of capital to preserve an independent monetary policy. No wonder this mutually exclusive trio is often called the "unholy trinity" of monetary policy.

Exercises 12.4

A. During 1992 the Bundesbank pursued a vigorous anti-inflation policy which raised the level of real interest rates in Germany. At the same time the US Federal Reserve was pursuing a policy of trying to stimulate the US economy as it struggled to recover from recession. Explain how the Fed's policy influenced the differential between the real interest rates of the two countries and, consequently, the real exchange rate.

B. The major continental countries of Europe have joined in a currency union and all agreed to adopt the Euro as their common currency. What are some of the potential advantages of their doing so? What do individual countries give up in terms of policy flexibility by doing so?

12.5 International Trade

Trade between groups of peoples, whether tribes or nations, is as old as the human race. Archeologists have found stone tools in pre-historic sites made of materials quarried many hundreds of miles distant. Why has trade been such an enduring feature of human activity? Should we today encourage trade and welcome its growth, or does it threaten our well-being?

Nations trade for the same reason that we don't all make our own shoes: specialization makes possible a much higher standard of living. To see why trade makes the traders better off, recall Robinson Crusoe and Friday on their island and imagine that they live on fish and coconuts. They can each spend some time gathering coconuts and some time fishing, or they can each specialize in one of the two activities and meet at the end of the day to trade fish for coconuts. Would they find it advantageous to specialize, and if so, which should each specialize in?

If Crusoe is a superb fisherman and a lousy tree climber while Friday is the opposite, then it is easy to see that Crusoe should stick to fishing and Friday to coconut gathering. That way they would each make best use of their absolute advantage in each activity. What is perhaps surprising is that the benefits of specialization and trade are still there if

Friday is much better at both activities! According to the principle of comparative advantage, each should specialize in the activity in which he has the *lowest opportunity cost*.

To see how comparative advantage works, imagine that Friday can catch four fish per day or gather eight coconuts per day. Evidently, it takes him twice as long to catch a fish as it does to harvest a coconut. Friday can mix his activities so that he can also produce three fish and two coconuts, or two fish and four coconuts, or one fish and six coconuts. Notice that Friday's opportunity cost of producing one fish is two coconuts, since to produce one more fish his output of coconuts drops by two. Similarly, his opportunity cost of producing one coconut is half a fish.

The production possibilities open to Friday are portrayed in Figure 12.5 as the gray line.

Crusoe is an Englishman educated at Oxford University where he received the equivalent of our MBA, so he has almost no practical skills. He can catch only three fish per day if that is all he does or instead can gather three coconuts. His production possibilities are illustrated by the dashed line in Figure 12.5.

We see that Crusoe's opportunity cost of producing one fish is one coconut, since to produce one more fish he must sacrifice the production of one coconut. Similarly, his opportunity cost of producing one coconut is one fish.

The Principle of Comparative Advantage

The principle of comparative advantage says that each agent in the economy should specialize in the activity in which they have the lowest opportunity cost. This means that Crusoe should specialize in fishing because his opportunity cost is only one coconut while Friday's is two, and Friday should specialize in gathering coconuts because his opportunity cost only half a fish while Crusoe's is one fish.

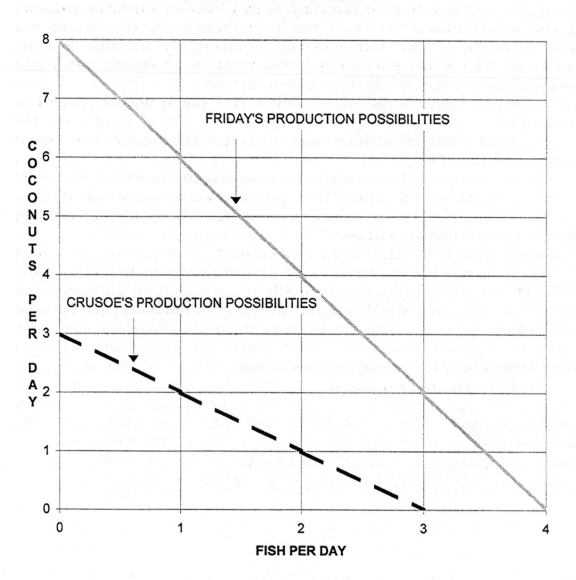

Figure 12.5: Without Trade, Crusoe's and Friday's Choices Are Limited To Their Own Production Possibilities

FRIDAY'S PRODUCTION POSSIBILITIES

CRUSOE'S PRODUCTION POSSIBILITIES

COCONUTS PER DAY

FISH PER DAY

They will need to agree on a price for fish in terms of coconuts, or vice versa, at which Crusoe will trade his fish for Friday's coconuts at the end of the day. That price must be higher than one coconut per fish, or else Crusoe would be better off producing coconuts for himself. The price must be lower than two coconuts per fish, or else Friday would be better off producing his own fish. The price must be between their opportunity costs for both to find trade attractive, say 1.5 coconuts per fish. At that price, Friday can then get a fish by giving up only 1.5 coconuts in trade instead of 2 by catching it himself. Crusoe can get 1.5 coconuts for a fish in trade instead of only 1 by gathering it himself.

That situation is illustrated in Figure 12.6 where the dark gray line shows Friday's trading opportunities ranging from keeping all the coconuts he produces to trading away all but two of them. At every point corresponding to trade, Friday has more of both fish and coconuts to consume. Similarly, Crusoe's trading opportunities are the solid black line, and trade also allows him to increase his consumption of both goods. Both people are made better off by specializing and then trading; these are the gains from trade.

As simple as it seems, the principle of comparative advantage is one of the most powerful ideas in economics. It was first articulated by the English economist David Ricardo in 1817 and is still the primary basis for the advocacy of free trade between nations. There is perhaps no position that enjoys broader support among economists than that international trade should be free and open. Why not spread the gains from trade as widely as possible? Economists since Ricardo have found the case for free trade compelling.

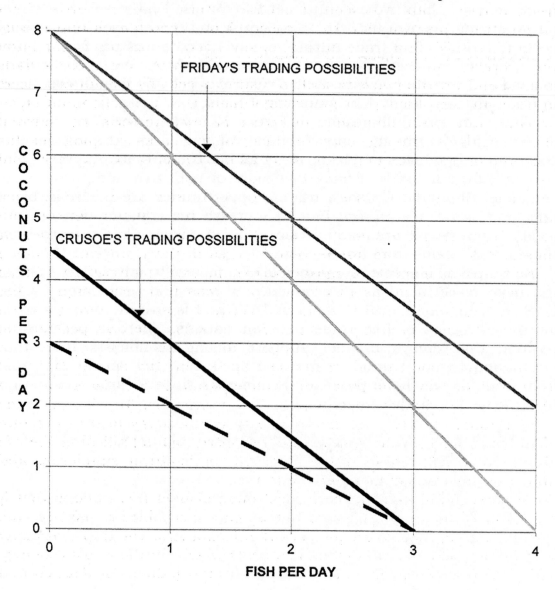

Figure 12.6: Trading Enlarges The Consumption Possibilities For Both Crusoe and Friday

FRIDAY'S TRADING POSSIBILITIES

CRUSOE'S TRADING POSSIBILITIES

COCONUTS PER DAY

FISH PER DAY

Trade Policy in the Real World

In reality, governments put many obstacles in the way of free international trade, such as tariffs, import quotas on certain goods, and licensing requirements. Economists have usually argued against these trade barriers, but they persist. Why? Tariffs are a source of tax revenue that is relatively easy to collect. More important is that special interest groups lobby governments against allowing imports that harm their private interests. Agricultural lobbies have been particularly successful in getting government to restrict access by foreign producers in order to keep their prices artificially high. U.S. restrictions on sugar imports and the Japanese prohibition on rice imports are current examples. While the domestic producer of the protected good benefits from protection, the consumer is harmed by having to pay more and society is denied the gains from trade.

Arguments against free trade have also been based on national security considerations and the idea that a country can develop new industries only if it protects them from foreign competition during their "infancy." However, the spectacular success of the European Common Market, which eliminated most barriers to free trade within Europe following World War II, has provided a model for negotiating other agreements. These have included GATT (the General Agreement on Tariffs and Trade) and NAFTA (North American Free Trade Agreement) to reduce barriers and encourage freer trade. The latter has lead to explosive growth in trade across the boarders of Canada, the U.S. and Mexico, as well as significant strains as patterns of specialization change in response to new competition and opportunities. The World Trade Organization, or WTO, has major new talks underway to try to resolve points of conflict involving intellectual property rights (critical in the age of computer software and the Internet), agricultural standards, and numerous environmental and labor issues.

Perhaps the argument heard most often against free trade is that it costs American jobs. When we import cars assembled in Mexico, the argument goes, it costs the jobs of US auto-workers. The trap that many fall into here is failing to distinguish between jobs in the whole economy and particular jobs. The emergence of an auto industry in Mexico and the import of some of those autos into the U.S. reduces the demand for workers in the U.S. auto industry. However, the sale of Mexican-made cars in the U.S. puts US dollars into Mexican hands. Those dollars are not used in Mexico; they will be spent in the U.S. The displacement of auto workers by auto imports is easy to see; jobs created by new demand from Mexico as a result of the Mexican auto industry are not so easily seen.

This is not to say that changing patterns of trade do not impose high costs on individuals and firms that have invested in specialized technologies and skills and find their value reduced by new competition. But when the dollars come back home they also create new opportunities for U.S. industry and workers.

Exercises 12.5

A. Identify several issues of trade policy that are currently being debated in Congress and in the press and summarize the positions and arguments on the two sides.

B. What are some of the issues being debated by the WTO? What are some of the issues being raised by critics of the WTO? Discuss.

Index

Course Materials on the Internet

Answers to the exercises, review questions, lecture notes, and errata can be accessed through the web page at:

http://www.econ.washington.edu/user/cnelson/STUDENT.html

Instructors interested in obtaining the author's testbank and lecture slides should contact him by e-mail at cnelson@u.washington.edu, fax at (206) 685-7477, or mail at

Dept. of Economics
Box 353330
University of Washington
Seattle, WA, 98195.

About The Author

Charles R. Nelson is the Ford and Louisa Van Voorhis Professor of Political Economy in the Department of Economics at the University of Washington in Seattle. He teaches macroeconomics and econometrics. Among his main research interests are the problem of disentangling the trend and cyclical components of GDP, and its implications for the analysis of business cycles. Other areas of interest are the term structure of interest rates, inflation dynamics, instrumental variables in econometrics, and the predictability of stock market returns.

In addition to papers in professional journals, Prof. Nelson is the author of *The Investor's Guide to Economic Indicators* and co-author of *State Space Models with Regime Switching* (with Chang-Jin Kim). He is a trustee of the Stein Roe Mutual Funds of Chicago, and serves on the editorial board of *The Journal of Money, Credit and Banking*.

He has been a Visiting Scholar at the Bank of Japan and a consultant to the Board of Governors of the Federal Reserve System.